REGULATORY REFORM
What Actually Happened

REGULATORY REFORM
What Actually Happened

EDITORS

Leonard W. Weiss
University of Wisconsin, Madison

Michael W. Klass
*Glassman-Oliver
Economic Consultants, Inc.*

Little, Brown and Company
Boston   Toronto

Library of Congress Cataloging-in-Publication Data
Main entry under title:

Regulatory reform.

　　Includes bibliographies and index.
　　Contents: Introduction / Leonard W. Weiss — Rail
and trucking deregulation / Thomas Gale Moore — The
changing airline industry / Daniel P. Kaplan — [etc.]
　　1. Trade regulation — United States.　2. Industry and
state — United States.　I. Weiss, Leonard W.　II. Klass,
Michael W.
KF1600.R44　1986　　　342.73′066　　　85-23796
ISBN 0-316-92898-4　　　347.30266

Copyright © 1986 by Leonard W. Weiss and Michael W. Klass

All rights reserved. No part of this book may be reproduced
in any form or by any electronic or mechanical means including
information storage and retrieval systems without permission
in writing from the publisher, except by a reviewer who may
quote brief passages in a review.

Library of Congress Catalog Card No. 85-23796

ISBN 0-316-92898-4

9 8 7 6 5 4 3 2 1

DON

Published simultaneously in Canada
by Little, Brown & Company (Canada) Limited

Printed in the United States of America

Acknowledgments

Table, p. 175: From *Bank Expansion Quarterly,* XXXIII, no. 2 (1983),
71. Reprinted by permission of Golembe Associates, Inc. *Tables,
pp. 286–287, 288, 289:* From T. H. Tietenberg, *Emissions Trading:
An Exercise in Reforming Pollution Policy* (Washington, D.C.: Resources
for the Future, 1985), pp. 10, 42–43, 46. Reprinted by permission
of the publisher, Resources for the Future © 1985.

Preface

This book is a second generation descendant of work we did in 1976 and 1977 for the Senate Governmental Affairs Committee. At that time Senator Kennedy had held important hearings on airline deregulation, and some railroad reform legislation had been passed. Still, in those years regulatory reform was basically a theory. It is not just a theory any longer.

Our charter from Senator Ribicoff had been to assemble experts in major regulatory areas and to direct their writing of case studies of the reasons for, consequences of, and alternatives to conventional regulation. We did that, and as we sadly reported in the preface to our previous book for Little, Brown, not much else resulted from our work. What did result was that book — a work that we believed added something important to the few publications available on regulatory reform. What that book contributed and what this book also contributes are relatively current pieces accessible to nonspecialists (not just economists). These pieces are all written by experts in particular regulatory areas. Unlike "textbooks" in the area, we did not attempt to present or impose a single view of the proper role of regulation or of its effects. In 1980 (and for this book) we simply asked our authors to be accurate, to be as current as they could, and to use good economics. We also asked them to make their papers challenging and interesting to students, professors, and others in the field. We feel that our authors met this challenge then, and the present authors have done at least as well.

In this book both the authors and the areas covered are somewhat different from the first. Regulatory change has been faster and more extensive than we had expected — at least in some areas — and we have changed the book accordingly. In 1980 Hans Stoll's excellent paper documented the freeing of commissions on the New York Stock Exchange. That revolution is over, and just as Hans predicted, there have been no dire consequences. Thus, there was no real need for Hans to update that piece. Banking and telephone regulation, on the other hand, are in complete flux, so we have added papers in these areas. In order to include the many new changes taking place in regulation we had to leave out an updated version of Leonard Weiss' paper on state utilities. Otherwise, we cover many of the same areas we did in 1980.

We have some new authors and many new issues. Not only are airlines deregulated, but the Civil Aeronautics Board was abolished this year. Its flag and seal now reside in the Smithsonian's National Air and Space Museum. In 1980 our airline paper was by Theodore Keeler, a leading academic expert; Daniel Kaplan, who wrote the current airline paper, was chief economist at the CAB during some of the most active deregulation. Thomas Moore, who writes in this book on freight regulation, was probably the first economist strongly to support trucking deregulation. Our paper on natural gas addresses the same basic regulatory framework as in 1980 but focuses on complicated and unexpected problems that partial deregulation may have caused. Finally, in 1980, reform at EPA and OSHA were theoretical possibilities, and our authors mainly criticized and suggested. Now, Thomas Tietenberg can describe the use of marketlike incentive mechanisms, however incomplete, that have been implemented by EPA. While there have not been the same kinds of basic reforms at OSHA, Kip Viscusi can describe substantial evolution and redirection as well as potential for change.

As before, we think this book is ideal to use in courses on regulation, industrial organization, government and business, or public control of business. Leonard Weiss has used the earlier book successfully in a principles course at the University of Wisconsin at Madison. The papers here are as current as the publishing process allows. We hope that they will help to inform readers and to keep alive the reform movement of recent years.

Michael W. Klass
Leonard W. Weiss

Contents

Introduction:
The Regulatory Reform Movement / *1*

Leonard W. Weiss

The Scope of Regulation / *2*   The Case for Regulatory Reform / *3*
Regulatory Reform in Practice / *9*   The Rest of the Book / *13*

Case 1
Rail and Trucking Deregulation / *14*

Thomas Gale Moore

Introduction / *14*   Effects of Regulation / *17*   Partial
Transportation Deregulation / *22*   Conclusion / *36*   Notes / *37*

Case 2
The Changing Airline Industry / *40*

Daniel P. Kaplan

Introduction / *40*   A Brief History of Airline Regulation / *41*   The
Airline Deregulation Act and an Overview of Its Effects / *47*   The
Growth of Hub-and-Spoke Route Networks / *51*   The New
Entrants and the Trend to Lower Costs / *55*   Pricing Policies in the
Deregulated Industry / *61*   The Competitive Environment / *64*
Subsidizing Service to Small Communities / *66*   Airport Access: A
Continuing Regulatory Issue / *68*   Conclusion / *70*   Notes / *72*
Bibliography / *75*

Case 3
The Rise and Fall and Rise of Cable Television Regulation / 78
Bruce M. Owen and Paul D. Gottlieb

Introduction / 78   History of Cable Regulation / 81   Cable Regulation at Full Flood / 85   Distant Signals and Copyright Liability / 88   Why Was Cable Deregulated? / 90   Cable Television Since the 1980 Deregulation / 92   The Cable Communications Policy Act of 1984 / 99   Prospects for Future Deregulation / 103   Bibliography / 104

Case 4
Petroleum Regulation and Public Policy / 105
R. Glenn Hubbard and Robert J. Weiner

Introduction and Background / 105   Public Intervention in the Oil Industry: Background / 111   Economic Analysis of Government Intervention / 115   Energy Policy after Price Deregulation / 127   Conclusion / 132   Notes / 133   Bibliography / 135

Case 5
Natural Gas: The Regulatory Transition / 137
Ronald R. Braeutigam and R. Glenn Hubbard

Introduction / 137   The Regulation of Natural Gas / 139   Consequences of Regulation / 142   Wellhead Market Structure / 150   The NGPA: Provisions and Consequences / 151   Regulation and Contracting in Natural Gas Markets / 155   Conclusion / 164   Notes / 165   Bibliography / 167

Case 6
The Partial Deregulation of Banks and Other Depository Institutions / 169
Lawrence J. White

Introduction / 169   The History of Regulation / 171   Regulation as of the 1970s and Its Consequences / 181   Deregulation and Its Consequences / 194   Conclusion / 199   Notes / 202   Bibliography / 205

Case 7
The Regulatory Change in Telecommunications: The Dissolution of AT&T / 210
Gerald W. Brock

Introduction / *210*   Equipment Competition and Regulatory Changes / *213*   Long-Distance Competition / *218*   The Antitrust Suit / *226*   Regulatory Problems after Divestiture / *229*   Conclusion / *232*   Notes / *233*

Case 8
Reforming OSHA Regulation of Workplace Risks / 234
W. Kip Viscusi

Introduction / *234*   How Markets Can Promote Safety / *236*   Inadequacies in the Market / *243*   OSHA's Regulatory Approach / *246*   The Reform of OSHA Standards / *249*   OSHA's Enforcement Strategy / *253*   The Impact of OSHA Enforcement on Worker Safety / *259*   Agenda for Policy Reform / *263*   Notes / *265*

Case 9
Uncommon Sense: The Program to Reform Pollution Control Policy / 269
T. H. Tietenberg

Introduction / *269*   The Traditional Regulatory Response / *273*   The Nature of the Reform / *280*   The Evolution of the Reform Program / *285*   An Appraisal / *297*   Notes / *301*

Index / *305*

REGULATORY REFORM
What Actually Happened

Introduction: The Regulatory Reform Movement

Leonard W. Weiss
University of Wisconsin, Madison

This book has as its topic a remarkable series of events that occurred in the United States during the 1970s, peaking in 1978–1980. The subject, of course, was regulation. The change came to be known as the "regulatory reform" movement, and there were many participants: businessmen who found themselves pestered with a flood of reports to file, businessmen who felt that regulations were raising their costs of production or weakening their competitive positions, economists who thought that regulation often reduced competition and increased costs, and political scientists and lawyers who thought that the regulatory agencies were often captured by those they were meant to regulate.

Three successive presidents — Nixon, Ford, and Carter — took active roles in the regulatory reform movement, each sending numerous proposed bills on the topic to Congress. Reagan also supported it, and, while his appointees have generally followed the path of regulatory reform as they administered their agencies, most of the big changes had already been made when he reached office. The Reagan administration did push through two major pieces of regulatory reform in banking and telecommunications.

Now, five or more years later, how have the new rules affected us? The proponents of regulatory reform had painted glowing pictures of increased efficiency, lower prices, and greater consumer choice. And the opponents had predicted disaster. Who was right? And what unexpected side effects occurred? That is the topic of this book.

THE SCOPE OF REGULATION

Table 1 (see pp. 4-6) lists the major regulatory agencies and their dates of establishment, jurisdictions, and 1980 and 1985 budgets. They are broken into two groups. The first comprises those agencies devoted to "economic regulation." These almost always controlled entry into the regulated field, and commonly controlled both prices and service. The second category includes those agencies devoted to "environmental, safety, and health regulation" — what is often referred to as the "new regulation" (though some of it goes back to 1906) because it grew rapidly in the 1960s and 1970s. One can see by their budgets that the new regulation involved a much greater administrative effort than the traditional economic regulation. The EPA alone spent as much on administration in 1985 as *all* the federal economic regulatory agencies put together. There is some logic to this. Economic regulation deals with small segments of the economy, such as railroads and trucks, but the EPA regulates all industries.

Since the general price level rose by about 28 percent from 1980 to 1985, increased expenditures for agencies like the FCC, the FERC, the FMC, and several of the environmental, safety, and health agencies were needed just to maintain similar programs to those they had in 1980. By these standards, several of the economic regulatory agencies were cut substantially. The ICC's budget was half what it had been, and the CAB's budget was one-sixth as much. Actually, the small amount for the CAB is because it went out of business completely on December 31, 1984, a rare event in the case of long-established government agencies. Although oil prices were deregulated the day after Reagan was inaugurated, the process had already been under way for ten months: Carter had been deregulating a certain proportion of oil each month since the previous March to avoid a large jump in inflation, and the entire program would have been over on the first of October 1981 if he had been reelected.

The environmental, safety, and health agencies' programs were still largely intact, however, even after five years of regulatory reform and a President and Congress desperately seeking to cut the budget in any areas other than defense and social security. Even the much criticized EPA and OSHA remained as they had been, and the cost of these agencies to the business firms that they regulate continues to exceed their appropriations in the budget.

The large budgets of the banking agencies stand out sharply. One reason for their healthy appearance is that these agencies need not go to the OMB or Congress for funds. The Comptroller of the Currency is financed by assessments on national banks. The Federal Reserve earns about $13 billion interest a year on its $150 billion of federal securities. It meets its expenses and returns the rest to the Treasury.

The two insurance corporations collect insurance premiums from banks and savings and loan associations, cover their expenses, and put the rest into their insurance funds. The Federal Home Loan Bank Board assesses anyone it can get its hands on, receives a transfer from FSLIC, and even borrows on the open market, but it does not need to go to the OMB or Congress either.

Table 1 shows that regulation cost the government $2,890 million in 1980 and $3,280 million in 1985. That growth is all inflation. In 1985 dollars the 1980 regulatory budget would be $3,699 million, or 113 percent of the actual 1985 budget. The real cost of regulation to the federal government fell by about 11 percent, mainly in the economic regulation sector. The current dollar cost of such regulation fell from $787 to $650 million, and the real cost of economic regulation to the federal government fell from $969 million 1985 dollars to $650 million, or 33 percent. The new regulation stayed about the same — $2,133 million in 1980 dollars and $2,730 1985 dollars to $2,632 million in 1985. The total cost of federal regulation is several times these figures because of expenses incurred by business in response to regulation.

The lesson to be gleaned from this part of Table 1 is that to minimize pain as a public servant, join an agency with an earmarked source of funds.

THE CASE FOR REGULATORY REFORM

While there were many different participants in the regulatory reform movement, economists played especially important roles. They did most of the critical studies that led to it, they were the sources of many of the particular proposals for change, and several became regulators, even chairmen, of the agencies to be reformed.

The first course in public utilities came with the first modern public utility commission — both in Wisconsin in 1907. Like the Wisconsin Public Service Commission, the course was widely copied and became a standard part of many university offerings in the 1920s and 1930s. Most of the literature produced in the field was aimed at better regulation; it especially criticized judicial restrictions on the regulators. Few scholars in the field seriously contemplated deregulation of any of the conventionally regulated industries. The major exception was in the area of trucking. Within a year of the legislation assigning responsibility for interstate motor carriers to the ICC, economists were publicly criticizing the move for its clearly anticompetitive effects in an inherently competitive industry.

Table 1. The Major Regulatory Agencies, Their Jurisdictions, and Their 1980 and 1985 Budgets

Agency	Date Established	Jurisdiction	1980	1985
Economic Regulation				
Interstate Commerce Commission (ICC)	1887	Interstate railroads (1887) Interstate trucks (1935) Interstate water carriers (1940) Interstate telephone (1910–1934) Interstate oil pipelines (1906–1977)	80.0	49.0
Federal Communications Commission (FCC)	1934	Interstate telephone (1934)[b] Broadcasting (1934)[c] Cable television (1968)	77.2	95.4
Federal Power Commission (FPC) and Federal Energy Regulatory Commission (FERC)	1935 1977	Interstate wholesale electricity (1935) Interstate natural gas pipelines (1938) Field price of natural gas sold in interstate commerce (1954) Oil pipelines (1977) Intrastate gas and gas pipelines (1978)	72.3	97.1
Civil Aeronautics Board (CAB)	1938	Interstate airlines (1938)[d]	29.7	5.6
Federal Maritime Commission (FMC)	1936	Ocean shipping (1936)[e]	11.7	12.3
Federal Energy Administration (FEA) Changed to Economic Regulatory Administration (ERA)	1973 1977	Petroleum prices and allocations (1973)	155.4	—
Comptroller of the Currency	1864	National banks (1864)	No report in 1980; 129.8 in 1982	179.4

Table 1. The Major Regulatory Agencies, Their Jurisdictions, and Their 1980 and 1985 Budgets — cont'd

Agency	Date Established	Jurisdiction	1980	1985
Federal Reserve Board (The Fed)	1913	Member banks (1913)	12.7[f]	17.3[f]
Federal Deposit Insurance Corporation (FDIC)	1933	Insured banks (1933)	130.7[g]	142.8[g]
Federal Home Loan Bank Board	1933	Federally chartered savings and loan associations (1933)	34.5[g]	25.8[g]
Federal Savings and Loan Insurance Corporation (FSLIC)	1934	Insured savings and loan associations (1934)	21.9[g]	26.4[g]

Environmental, Safety, and Health Regulation

Agency	Date Established	Jurisdiction	1980	1985
Food and Drug Administration (FDA)	1906	Safety of food, drugs (1906), and cosmetics (1938), effectiveness of drugs (1962)	324.2	409.7
Animal and Plant Health Inspection Service	1907	Meat and poultry packing plants (1907)	258.6	242.0
Federal Trade Commission (FTC)	1914	False and misleading advertising (mainly after 1938)	31.0[h]	31.9[h]
Securities and Exchange Commission (SEC)	1934	Public security issues and security exchanges (1934) Public utility holding companies (1935)	72.9	106.4
Federal Aviation Administration (FAA)	1958	Airline safety[j] (flight standards program only	227.9	264.4
Atomic Energy Commission (AEC)	1947	Licensing of nuclear power plants (1947)	368.2	448.2
Nuclear Regulatory Commission (NRC)	1975			

Continued

Table 1. The Major Regulatory Agencies, Their Jurisdictions, and Their 1980 and 1985 Budgets — cont'd

Agency	Date Established	Jurisdiction	1980	1985
National Highway Traffic Safety Administration (NHTSA, pronounced Neetsa)	1970	Automobile safety (1970), automobile fuel economy (1975)	58.9	58.5
Environmental Protection Agency (EPA)	1963– 1972[k]	Air, water, and noise pollution[j]	420.0	661.7
Occupational Safety and Health Administration (OSHA)	1971	Industrial safety and health (1971)	187.2	220.8
Mine Enforcement Safety Administration (MESA)	1973	Safety and health in mining, especially coal mines (1973)	144.1	152.0
Mine Safety and Health Administration	1978			
Consumer Product Safety Commission	1972	Safety of consumer products (1972)	40.2	36.0

1980 and 1985 Budgets (Millions of Dollars)[a]

Sources: The Budget of the United States, 1981, 1986, and telephone calls to FTC and FAA.
  [a] Excludes subsidies, research, and training programs.
  [b] Regulated by the ICC from 1910.
  [c] Regulated by Federal Radio Commission from 1927.
  [d] Partially regulated by the ICC and the Post Office from 1934.
  [e] Partially regulated from 1916.
  [f] Regulation only.
  [g] Administration costs.
  [h] Consumer protection, excludes antitrust.
  [i] Various environmental laws were enforced by several agencies from 1963–1972 combined into EPA 1972.
  [j] Regulated by CAB, 1938–1958.
  [k] Excludes grants.

Most of the economic criticism of regulation, however, developed after World War II. Criticism of the anticompetitive characteristics of ICC regulation of surface transportation was widespread in the postwar period. The critics claimed that the main effects of ICC regulation were to prevent price competition among carriers, to shift freight to high-cost carriers, to impose high costs on the railroads by resisting abandonment of uneconomical branch lines, and to discourage cost-saving innovations. Defenders of surface transportation regulation warned that the railroads would drop their passenger service, which they did, of course, except in cases where there were heavy subsidies. They foresaw large-scale bankruptcy among railroads and certain types of trucking firms, and predicted that many small communities would lose truck service. The regulated firms (especially truckers) and the unions they dealt with (especially the Teamsters) were ardent defenders of regulation. By the late 1970s most American economists had concluded that ICC regulation was oriented toward protection of the carriers and, far from reducing costs to shippers, it almost certainly increased their costs by perhaps billions of dollars a year.

Airline regulation was studied by a number of economists starting in the late 1950s. The picture that had emerged by the mid-1970s was one of many limitations on competition among the airlines imposed by the CAB. Over the years, from the establishment of the CAB in 1938 up to 1978, the agency never permitted another trunk airline to enter, although demand had increased by several thousand percent. It systematically prohibited fare competition among the airlines. Airlines on competitive routes tried to win customers by offering more flights. As a result, these airlines commonly had far more seats than customers. Airlines that flew only within individual states (California and Texas) were exempt from CAB regulation. It turned out that they offered lower fares, better service, and less excess capacity.

Defenders of regulation predicted that deregulation would result in ruinous fare wars and the bankruptcy of all but a few carriers. During the shakeout desperate airlines would skimp on maintenance, causing air accidents to soar. Quality of service was supposed to deteriorate. We would have fewer departures and smaller seats. Small cities such as Grand Rapids would lose service. This example was common while Gerald Ford, who came from Grand Rapids, was president. When only a few airlines were left, air fares were going to rise. Among the most ardent defenders of regulation were many of the airlines plus the unions they dealt with, such as the Airline Pilots Association.

The FCC regulation of broadcasting, especially cable TV, was widely criticized. Economists have argued that by assigning too small a band to VHF (very high frequency) TV and by emphasizing localism in allocating frequencies, the agency left room for only three viable commercial networks. Moreover, they argue that by restricting importation of distant signals by cable companies, the FCC slowed the spread of cable in larger markets and, again, left viewers with a great deal less choice than they might have had otherwise.

On the other hand, defenders of the FCC maintained that we had more channels than most countries. (While this may be true in relation to Europe, Japan has four commercial channels and two public networks.) If the FCC had followed a policy of allowing stronger signals, fewer cities would have had local stations. With respect to cable, the defenders of regulation argued that more cable channels would divert viewers from local broadcasters and drive many of them off the air. Many of the defenders of regulation were broadcasters, and elected politicians find it difficult to argue with broadcasters who write so much of the news.

With respect to natural gas, many economists claimed that by limiting price increases on old gas (gas developed and committed to interstate commerce before a specified date), the FPC and the FERC after it have maintained retail gas prices far below marginal costs and given the consumers inadequate incentive to conserve. Moreover, even the prices of new gas (gas not previously committed to interstate commerce) were kept below equilibrium levels, though the prices of new gas in successive periods were raised regularly. In view of the costs of other fuels during the 1970s, this policy offered little incentive to explore and provided strong incentives to withhold newly discovered gas in anticipation of higher prices later.

The American oil price controls after 1973 and especially after 1975 were criticized for similar reasons. Again, oil was priced in several tiers with much of it kept below world prices. These various prices were converted into oil-product prices by means of an extremely complicated procedure that lent itself to errors and fraud. Retail prices were below world levels, thereby encouraging high levels of consumption. Newly developed domestic oil yielded producers less than imported oil was bringing. Many economists felt that government price policies were encouraging the country's rapid shift to imported oil.

While oil and gas companies generally agreed with the reformers on these issues, there were still many who disagreed — including some economists. The enormously high world energy prices were unquestionably monopoly prices set by an international cartel. Why should domestic oil and gas producers get rich at our expense just because Saudi Arabia was also getting rich at our expense? Don't monopoly prices distort consumer decisions? Why not keep those prices as low as possible? Why should we produce more oil and gas at home? The policy of energy self-sufficiency that we often heard about sounded suspiciously like "drain America first."

The answer to this last point of view became clear in 1984. High oil prices had induced oil companies to look for oil elsewhere. And the same high prices had also induced consumers to conserve — small cars and increased insulation — even thermopane glass in Texas! The result was an oil glut: by 1985 prices were down by a quarter — from thirteen times the 1972 level to ten times the 1972 level.

Despite increasing concern about the costly and anticompetitive effects of regulation, we increased the scope of regulation greatly during the 1970s. Most of this increase occurred in environmental, safety, and health regulation areas (though our tortuous oil regulation began in 1973 as well). In this book the EPA and OSHA represent such areas of increasing regulation. The new agencies, especially EPA and OSHA, are widely criticized for imposing costly rules that bring about few if any benefits. Running EPA is very expensive in itself, but the costs to industries and municipalities of complying with EPA orders have been estimated to be billions of dollars per year. OSHA has a smaller budget, but its impact on industrial costs is not small, and benefits have been hard to identify. It seems unlikely that agencies such as EPA and OSHA will go away soon, but many economists feel that those agencies' procedures and rules could be greatly improved.

REGULATORY REFORM IN PRACTICE

Regulation became a hot topic among economists after World War II, and in the late 1970s their criticisms began to have an effect.

One of the first changes took place on the stock market. After careful study both Congress and the SEC took steps to prevent the exchanges from fixing brokerage fees. The SEC ordered an end to the practice as of May 1, 1975. There were substantial changes in fees and some change in the structure and practices of the brokerage industry, but the disaster that the industry predicted did not occur.

The next major change came in the airline industry. In 1975 Senator Kennedy held extensive hearings on the CAB, publicizing the many criticisms that had been aimed at it. Early in the 96th Congress (January 1977) a bill was introduced that would generally deregulate airlines over a period of several years. Most of the airlines opposed it vigorously.

At the same time, however, two well-known economists were appointed to the CAB — A. E. Kahn (as Chairman) and E. E. Bailey. Under Kahn's leadership the airlines were given much more freedom in pricing and much easier access to routes they had not previously served. The results were spectacular. Fares for tourists fell drastically (though fares for business travel did not). The planes filled up, and airline profits soared. By the time the Cannon-Kennedy bill came to a vote in the autumn of 1978 there was little opposition, and the bill passed by a large majority.

In the case of cable TV, regulatory reform came entirely from the inside. In July 1980 the FCC issued an order eliminating most of its regulation of cable TV, although aspects of the industry are still regulated at the state or local levels.

The toughest nut to crack was surface freight transportation. Regulatory reform came harder there because the carriers were less likely to improve their profitability the way the airlines seemed to do. However, on January 1, 1980, a well-known economist and regulatory reformer named D. Gaskins became Chairman of the ICC, and a second economist, M. Alexis, became one of its six members. By mid-1980 it seemed certain that major reform would come from inside the Commission. Apparently the trucking industry became convinced that it would receive better treatment from Congress than from the ICC; in any event, a new trucking bill sailed through Congress and became law in June 1980. The legislation did not end truck regulation, but it left individual truckers with much more freedom in pricing, made entry much easier, and eliminated a number of costly restrictions the ICC had imposed.

The regulation of gas and oil were two of the leading issues before the 95th Congress (1977–1978) and, in the case of oil, of the 96th Congress (1979–1980) as well. The gas legislation in 1978 resulted in the transfer of regulatory responsibility from the FPC to the FERC, regulation of intrastate as well as interstate gas production by the FERC, and complete deregulation of *new* gas as of 1985.

The Carter administration proposed that oil prices be allowed to rise to levels that reflected world oil prices to encourage conservation but that taxes be imposed on oil that had been selling at less than world levels to eliminate the "windfall profit" that would otherwise accrue. From 1976 to 1980 Congress and the President wrangled about taxes on oil producers. In April 1980 Congress finally passed a set of "windfall profits taxes" designed to capture for the government some, but not all, of the gains from higher crude oil prices. President Carter then began deregulating domestic oil at a rate of so much per month such that deregulation would be complete on October 1, 1981. The reason for the gradual approach was to minimize the effect on inflation. The huge rise in crude oil prices imposed by OPEC in 1979 had resulted in our worst peace-time inflation, and the administration was trying to deregulate without adding to that disaster. One of President Reagan's first acts after inauguration was to remove all remaining controls on oil prices. The price of oil hardly changed.

Banking was one area where regulatory reform was far from complete when Reagan became president. Banks had been regulated from the start of the republic, mainly to prevent bank failures. After the collapse of thousands of banks in 1929-1933, Congress, the President, and the many bank regulators were convinced that the problem had been "excessive competition." So banks were prohibited from paying interest on checking deposits, and a ceiling was put on interest rates for savings deposits. "Over-banking" was supposed to be part of the problem, so the regulators made it almost impossible to get new bank charters in most communities for many years. The bank failures did end. They were rare events after 1933. Many economists were convinced that the low bank failure rate resulted more from federal deposit insurance than restrictions on competition. In the postwar years restrictions on bank competition were gradually lifted, and bank failures returned. Failures increased from four a year in the 1950s to six a year in the 1960s to eight a year in the 1970s to ten a year in 1979-1981 to forty-two in 1982 and forty-eight in 1983. These failures were not restricted to small, local banks; some very large banks were also in danger. Continental Illinois of Chicago and Seattle First National in Washington needed rescuing. The process of regulatory reform is still under way. Not everyone is in favor of it.

Competition in the telephone industry seemed obviously inefficient to the ordinary subscriber. Imagine running two sets of telephone lines down each street, and he'd have to subscribe to both companies to reach all his friends. Not many economists have advocated that, but important parts of the business could be competitive. Outsiders could sell telephone equipment to subscribers and, for that matter, to the Bell companies themselves. From the 1960s on, as long distance shifted from coaxial cable to microwave transmission, even long distance became a possible area for competition. Some firms with large communication needs along routes such as pipelines or railroads found it worthwhile to build their own microwave systems.

But the huge, all-embracing Bell system remained. Bell owned Western Electric, by far the largest telephone equipment producer in the world. It consistently refused to permit "foreign attachments" to its system, until the FCC ordered it to do so. The FCC could do nothing about the Bell system's own purchases. Bell companies also consistently refused to interconnect with independent long-distance firms, until the FCC ordered them to do that too. As long as the local service business was owned by the same firm as the equipment supplier and the long-distance service, prospects for competition remained poor.

The Justice Department instituted an antitrust suit in 1975. Then in 1982 the AT&T management changed its mind and agreed to a dissolution with the case still undecided. Starting on January 1, 1983, what had been the largest privately owned firm in the world was subdivided into seven regional companies offering local service on a regulated monopoly basis and the new "AT&T," which sold telephone equipment, computers, and long-distance service on an unregulated basis.

What was gained? In view of the company's willingness to be dissolved, it seems unlikely that the parts will earn less profits than the old AT&T would have. But competition has changed long-distance rates and the variety and prices of telephone equipment in the market.

The "new regulation" by such agencies as the EPA and OSHA concerning the environment, safety, and health was clearly not likely to go the way of airline regulation. Few scholars advocated deregulation in these fields, but many proposed that in evaluating new regulations more weight be given to costs.

Even here, however, there was some movement toward more economic regulation. The EPA had adopted a policy whereby firms in areas with high pollution levels (such as Los Angeles) can install new plant and equipment that might create more pollution if they produce greater reductions elsewhere within the area. For instance, a firm planning to build an oil terminal can do so if it can find ways to reduce pollution from laundries and street paving by more than the new pollution the terminal will cause. This means that polluters clean up where it is easiest to do so, a result that is economically preferable to the situation where EPA orders a particular type of cleanup in an industry regardless of how costly it is or how readily available cheaper alternative cleanup possibilities might be.

There has been some movement at OSHA, too. The agency has deemphasized its pettifogging, accident-oriented equipment standards (for instance, elaborate rules that specify the material and design specifications for ladders), where workers' compensation already covered those injured and, for large firms, imposed insurance charges that reflected their accident experience. OSHA has shifted emphasis to serious accident records, regardless of equipment specifications, and to industrial diseases where workers' compensation generally does not apply. For instance, byssinosis is a disease that affects a quarter of the workers in cotton (but not synthetic) textile mills, leaving them wheezing for the rest of their lives. We have known about the origins of this disease since the beginning of the industrial revolution about 170 years ago, but nothing much was done about it until OSHA became involved.

Under Ford, Carter, and Reagan regulatory agencies answerable to the president, such as EPA and OSHA, have been required to estimate the costs and benefits of new orders before issuing them. For instance, OSHA estimated that its new cotton dust standard would cost about $200,000 per case of byssinosis prevented. The question becomes whether it is worth that much to prevent a disease similar to asthma (somewhat incapacitating, but seldom involving early death) for a quarter of the workers in cotton textile mills. OSHA did in fact adopt the cotton dust standard.

There are other types of safety and health regulations that will not be covered in this book, and they deserve some comment. The National Highway Traffic Safety Administration's early rules on automobile safety apparently did reduce auto deaths significantly, going by the lower death rates in accidents involving car models built after its orders were in force. A major factor here was probably the requirement of seat belts as standard equipment.

The Consumer Product Safety Commission claims responsibility for a greatly reduced rate of child overdoses on drugs owing to those infernal new drug bottle tops. The Food and Drug Administration has certainly saved lives and prevented tragic personal disabilities by keeping thalidomide off the American market. On the other hand, its requirement since 1962 that new drugs be effective as well as safe has been accompanied by a sharp drop in the number of "new chemical entities" (wholly new drugs) introduced each year. To some extent the decline may simply mean that many of the new drugs introduced earlier were ineffective, but it probably also partially results from the greater risk and delay in introducing new drugs under the new rules.

THE REST OF THE BOOK

Altogether, something very important happened in regulation in the late 1970s and early 1980s. Now five or more years have passed since most of the changes were instituted. What has happened as a consequence of the changes? Were the advocates' hopes realized? What about the opponents' warnings? And what were some of the unexpected side effects? The purpose of this book is to shed some light on these questions.

In the first case study Tom Moore reviews the effects of regulatory reform of the ICC's regulation of trucks and trains. The second case study is Dan Kaplan's analysis of deregulation of airlines, and the third an analysis of cable TV deregulation and its effect by Bruce Owen and Paul Gottlieb. In the fourth case study Glenn Hubbard and Robert Weiner review the effects of deregulation in oil, while Ron Brauetigam and Glen Hubbard report on the lessening regulation in the natural gas industries in the fifth case study. Larry White analyzes regulatory reform in banking in the sixth one, while Jerry Brock reports on the regulation of telecommuncniations and especially the dissolution of AT&T in the seventh. The eighth case study is Kip Viscusi's report on OSHA. Finally, Tom Teitenburg tells us about EPA and environmental controls in the ninth case study.

CASE 1

Rail and Trucking Deregulation

Thomas Gale Moore
Hoover Institution, Stanford University, and Council of Economic Advisers

INTRODUCTION

While the first railroads were built before the Civil War, the major expansion began at the end of that conflict. Because of a strong national need to tie the United States together after the war, the federal government provided large subsidies to the nascent railroad industry. To promote development, state and local governments competed among themselves to attract passage of railroads through their communities. Given a $1.3 billion incentive in state and federal subsidies[1] and an overabundance of optimism, the network that was built was undoubtedly excessive — the miles of track ballooned by 50 percent between 1870 and 1876.[2]

During the 1870s and 1880s competition among railroads was so keen that many markets were served by a multitude of competitors. For example, by 1880 twenty different railroads were operating between St. Louis and Atlanta.[3] In such a competitive situation the railroads had difficulty charging profitable rates. As a result, they attempted to restrict price cutting through pools and other cartel-type activities. Most pooling and cartel arrangements failed within a short period. For instance, in the St. Louis–Atlanta market eight pools were established by 1879, all quickly failing except for one.

The general failure of these self-policing methods led the railroads to search for other alternatives to stabilize rates and increase profitability. By the mid-1880s a few leaders of the railroad industry began to recognize that government intervention might be necessary if the railroads were to increase their profitability. For example, John P. Green, Vice President of the Pennsylvania Railroad, testified before a congressional committee that

Introduction

a large majority of the railroads in the United States would be delighted if a railroad commission or any other power could make rates . . . with such a guarantee, they would be very glad to come under the direct supervision of the National Government.[4]

Legislation forbidding rebates and price discrimination was also proposed by numerous shippers, who claimed that competitors sometimes were charged lower rates than they were forced to pay. At the same time the National Grange agitated for regulation as farmers grew increasingly discontent with the railroads. Growers often felt exploited, since those served by only one line frequently had to pay significantly higher shipping charges than those served by several. Higher rates often were charged for shipments to and from small communities than for shipments to and from major hubs involving greater distances.

The traditional justification for the establishment of regulation of transportation has been that railroads in the nineteenth century were subject to extensive economies of scale, implying that they were natural monopolies. When they exploited their monopoly position and set rates greatly in excess of costs, they attracted competitors. Competition then became cutthroat and unstable, with prices declining and losses inflicted on most participants.

From a variety of evidence, economists studying this industry have concluded that after a certain point there are no substantial economies of scale.[5] In particular, studies of railroads in the nineteenth century have concluded that for medium-sized railroads, lower costs were not functions of larger size.[6] Moreover, had there been substantial economies of scale, there also should have been a substantial merger movement.

In certain small-shipment, short-haul markets, railroads are, and probably always were, natural monopolies. Nevertheless, for many markets and for most traffic, railroads do not and did not have a natural monopoly. The advent of railroad regulation would seem to originate from various interest groups who were seeking benefits, rather than from economies of scale.

With broad support from the railroads, agricultural interests, and some shippers and merchants, the Interstate Commerce Act was passed early in 1887. The initial act simply established a commission, required that all charges be reasonable and just, prohibited unreasonable or unjust rates, prohibited discrimination between shippers and barred rebates, prohibited geographic discrimination (a benefit to New York merchants), prohibited a higher price for a short haul than for a long haul, required publication of rates, and prohibited pooling of freight or earnings.

The original act soon failed in its mission to eliminate rebating and price cutting. Further legislation followed, and by 1920 Congress actually specified that one objective of the legislation was to ensure adequate profits. One provision of the act specified that "the Commission shall . . . adjust such rates so that the carriers . . . will . . . earn . . . a fair return. . . ."[7]

During the 1920s rail carriers as a whole failed to earn what the commission specified as a fair return. Part of the difficulty came from the development of competition in the form of trucks and buses. Initially, motor carriers competed only for short-haul traffic; as a consequence, the railroads reacted by attempting to secure state regulation of motor carriers. Virtually all state regulation of trucks and buses was initiated between 1914 and 1931 by railroad interests, usually supported by state regulatory commissions. For instance, in California trucking regulation came only after the railroads took the state regulatory commission to court to force extension of regulation to motor carriers.

In 1925 two Supreme Court decisions eliminated the authority of states to control any interstate trucking or busing.[8] This effectively eliminated most state control of entry or rates, since by operating across state lines motor carriers were exempt from regulation. Naturally railroads, state regulatory commissions, and the Interstate Commerce Commission (ICC) began to campaign for federal regulation.

Efforts to extend federal government control to motor carriers failed until the mid-1930s. Pressure for regulation came from the ICC, railroads, and state regulatory commissions. Opposing federal legislation were shippers, most freight motor carriers, and vehicle manufacturers. Joseph Eastman, the federal coordinator of transportation (a position established by the Emergency Railroad Transportation Act of 1933) and an ICC member, claimed that many rail lines were being forced into bankruptcy due to "cutthroat" competition.

After the Supreme Court ruled unconstitutional the National Recovery Act, which had been used by the industry to stabilize prices, the American Trucking Associations in 1935 ceased their opposition to federal regulation. The resultant Motor Carrier Act of 1935 remained virtually unchanged until the 1980 Motor Carrier Act.

Essentially this 1935 Act required all existing motor carriers to document their previous service. Based on this, the ICC issued "grandfather" operating licenses. Of some 89,000 grandfather applications, the ICC granted less than a third and these with considerable limitations.[9] New and existing carriers who wished to extend their authority found the Commission hostile. Only if no other carrier had authority to offer the proposed service did the Commission consider a request for a new license.

Rates were also strictly controlled. All rates had to be filed with the Commission thirty days before they became effective. If the proposed tariffs were protested by another carrier, a railroad, another trucker, or a regulated water carrier, the Commission normally suspended the rates pending an investigation of their legality. If the proposed charges did not cover the full cost of transportation as estimated by the ICC, the proposal was rejected. After 1948, with the passage of the Reed-Bulwinkle Act, carriers were exempted from the antitrust laws when they agreed on rates in rate bureaus.

In summary, railroads were regulated partly to help stabilize their cartel pricing and partly because they often had monopolies on short-haul traffic. Truckers were regulated because they provided competition for short-haul traffic, thus eliminating the one area where railroads had a significant monopoly. With the advent of motor carriers, any effort to regulate railroads disappeared, except for blatant attempts to profit specific industries.

EFFECTS OF REGULATION

The deregulation movement for trucking was born the moment that the Motor Carrier Act of 1935 was passed.[10] Economists began to criticize the idea of regulating such an inherently competitive industry. In the past fifty years scholars and government agencies have conducted numerous studies of the effects of regulation on transportation. For example, the Department of Agriculture examined unregulated agricultural trucking and found that it was more efficient and considerably cheaper than regulated trucking.[11] In a study done for a Brookings Institution Conference this author found that the costs imposed on the economy by ICC regulation of surface freight transportation were somewhere between $3.8 and $8.9 billion in 1968 dollars.[12] In 1985 dollars this amounts to between $12 and $27 billion.

Another study revealed that the benefits of trucking regulation accrued to the owners of the trucking firms and to organize labor.[13] While shippers were overcharged by about 25 percent for motor carriage, both the owners of the operating rights and the members of the Teamsters Union received about three-quarters of this amount in the form of extra income. Trucker owners earned an extra $1.5 to $2 billion in 1972 dollars, the equivalent of $3.8 to $5.1 billion in 1985 dollars. Teamster members at the time earned on average about 50 percent more than in a competitive market, for a total of between $1 and $1.3 billion, or the 1985 equivalent of from $2.6 to $3.3 billion. These numbers explain why the Teamsters and the American Trucking Association have been so outspoken against deregulation.

In most other industrial countries of the world regulation of motor carriers stemmed from common forces: regulation was imposed to protect the market position of railroads. Some countries, such as Australia and Great Britain, have abandoned trucking regulation to the benefit of shippers and no harm to the long-run sustainability of the industry.[14]

President John Kennedy, in 1962, was the first president to send a transportation message to Congress recommending a reduction in regulation of surface freight transportation.[15] The proposed congressional bill went even further than the administration's recommendations. The Johnson administration, unenthusiastic about the bill, contended it deregulated too much by eliminating all controls over agricultural shipments by rail as well as by truck.

The next major effort at reducing motor carrier controls was a 1971 Department of Transportation proposal. The White House decided not to introduce the bill because of opposition from the Teamsters Union, one of the few unions sympathetic to the Republican cause.

Penn Central's bankruptcy in 1972 shifted interest to the railroads. While the problems of Penn Central were deeper than regulatory issues, Congress did pass, in 1976, the Railroad Revitalization and Regulatory Reform Act, called the 4-R Act. This Act provided for a "zone of reasonableness" within which rates could not be challenged solely on the grounds of reasonableness. Rates could be considered too high only if the carrier had "market dominance," the definition of which was left to the ICC. Unfortunately, ICC's interpretaton of "market dominance" significantly limited railroad flexibility, rendering the 4-R Act almost useless. This Act, however, is a landmark, representing the first legislation reducing regulation of any transportation sector in the history of the United States.

In November of 1975 President Gerald Ford called for legislation to reduce trucking regulation. Although President Ford's bill received no support in Congress, the earlier appointment to the ICC of Daniel O'Neal by President Nixon and the appointments of Betty Jo Christian, Robert Corber, and Charles L. Clapp by Ford signaled a change in philosophy at the ICC. By the end of Ford's term these commissioners were speaking out for a more competitive policy at the ICC, a position rarely articulated in the previous eight decades of transportation regulation.

The first actual deregulatory action was a new ICC rule, issued in June of 1975, that prohibited rate bureaus for both trucking firms and rails from protesting independent rate filings by members. On December 30, 1976, in another significant move the Commission approved (though with a strong dissent from the traditional regulators) a major expansion of the commercial zones (zones within which trucking is exempt from federal regulation) around major cities, thus effectively deregulating a large new area.

Shortly after taking office, President Jimmy Carter appointed Daniel O'Neal Chairman of the ICC. Working cautiously and with only a small majority, O'Neal moved toward deregulation. Initially, he appointed a task force to examine ways of easing entry. Their report, which brought protests from the regulated truckers and teamsters, recommended thirty-nine changes that would ease entry and permit carriers to serve new routes. Complaints by the industry, corroborated by the data in Table 4, show that the Commission was approving an increasing proportion of applications for new authority. For example, a spokesman for the American Trucking Association said that "we are seriously alarmed by the phenomenal rate of entry (93 percent) for applicants desiring only to handle truckload volume of general freight-type commodities."[16]

In October 1977 Senator Edward Kennedy, Chairman of the Antitrust and Monopoly Subcommittee of the Senate Judiciary Committee, opened hearings on how rates are set in the trucking industry. These hearings spelled out the cost of regulation to shippers and consumers. Conservative groups, such as the American Conservative Union, as well as liberal groups, such as the Consumer Federation of America, testified in favor of less regulation.[17] John Shenefield, Assistant Attorney General of the Justice Department's antitrust division, testified in favor of substantial deregulation. The White House increasingly supported measures to curb government control, although Brock Adams, Carter's Secretary of Transportation, remained opposed to the idea.

In late 1978 the Commission ruled that companies wishing to haul for themselves could apply for interstate trucking authority to haul for others as well. The commission also in effect deregulated all shipments under federal contracts. Further, it reversed a forty-year-old policy and authorized private carriers to engage in regulated for-hire operations.

At the end of 1978 Chairman O'Neal proposed that the ICC grant a license for truckload carriage to any applicant that meets the fit standard. He further recommended that rate controls be relaxed substantially, with a zone of reasonableness within which the Commission would not suspend.

The White House was also planning a major deregulation effort. Success of the airline deregulation bill earlier in 1978 provided momentum for those seeking to deregulate surface transportation. During 1978 the Department of Transportation drew up plans for deregulation of motor carriers and some further reduction of regulation for railroads. The 4-R Act was accomplishing little. The Department of Transportation claimed that the ICC had minimized the effect of the new law. "The ICC still constrains the railroads' freedom of action," according to the report.[18]

Unlike the trucking industry, the nation's railroads supported deregulation. They were disappointed with the conservative action of the commission in implementing the 4-R Act. The President of the Association of American Railroads claimed that unless the ICC reduced its controls, the industry would end up "dead in the water."[19] They wanted greater freedom to set prices on their own and the ability to drop money-losing routes.

In March 1979 President Carter sent a bill to Congress that would largely deregulate the industry over a five-year period. At the end of the period railroads would be free to set their rates without constraint; the bill also would make it easier for railroads to abandon unprofitable service.

Early in 1979 the Commission abolished the restriction that contract motor carriers could haul for no more than eight shippers. Airport zones, which are exempt from regulation, were expanded. The Commission announced that it would consider rates as a factor in granting operating rights to truckers.

In May 1979 the ICC chairman's task force on reforming motor carrier regulation proposed new relaxed entry standards in twelve market segments, including bulk transport, the building materials industry, and the movement of household goods. The task force report recommended that entry requirements be confined to meeting a fitness test and that "master certificates" be issued to authorize a wide area to be served and wide range of commodities carried. Rates would also be allowed to fluctuate within a zone of reasonableness. In all, they recommended abolishing control over about one-fourth of the tonnage and one-third of the revenue moved by trucking.[20]

A trend-setting act passed in November 1978 gave the railroads a new freedom by ruling that it was no longer illegal for railroads to operate under long-term contracts with shippers. In May 1979 the Commission followed by acting for the first time on the basis of a provision in the 4-R Act that exempted from regulation rail movements of fresh fruits and vegetables. Thus the ICC began to take seriously the idea of reducing regulation of railroads as well as trucking.

On June 21, 1979, President Carter and Senator Kennedy proposed a joint legislative package that would significantly deregulate the motor carrier industry. During the spring and summer of 1979 Congress held hearings on the rail bill and the Carter-Kennedy bill.

During that summer the President also appointed three new commissioners: Thomas Trantum, Darius Gaskins, Jr., and Marcus Alexis (Gaskins and Alexis were economists and Trantum was a security specialist). These three brought a pro-competitive viewpoint that greatly strengthened the deregulation majority on the Commission.

Early in October 1979 the Commission acted on the "master certificates" proposal and issued a notice of intent to open rule-making for each of the specialized fields of transportation, with the exception of household goods. The Commission announced plans to institute rule-making, with the last proceeding to start before January 1980.

Also in October the Commission adopted a policy of easing entry into both the bus and trucking areas. It announced discontinuation of a forty-three-year-old test requiring an applicant for bus or truck operating rights to prove that the new service could not be performed as well by carriers already licensed. New applications that demonstrate they will meet a "public need or demand" would be considered favorably. The ICC would no longer reject applications on the grounds that incumbent carriers would lose business.

By this time the trucking industry and Congress were seething. The Commission, apparently ignoring the law and over forty years of precedent, was totally deregulating the industry. Senator Howard Cannon, Chairman of the Senate Commerce Committee, speaking at an ICC-sponsored meeting, warned that Congress "was mad as hell."[21] He told the Commission that they should proceed cautiously with deregulation. He promised that if the Commission delayed further deregulation, he would get a bill out of Congress on trucking regulation by June 1, 1980.

During 1979 and the first half of 1980 trucking industry spokesmen and Teamster representatives became increasingly vocal in opposition to ICC's policies and to any further reduction in regulation. At first they attempted to promote legislation that would roll back the actions of the ICC in freeing entry.

On the other side, the National Association of Manufacturers was spearheading the effort to deregulate the industry. Major shippers, such as Union Carbide Corporation, Lever Bros. Company, Nabisco Inc., CPC International Inc., Whirlpool Corporation, and Kraft Inc., appeared in support of less regulation of entry and less government control in general.[22] Together with representatives of small shippers, they urged passage of the Senate bill that Senator Cannon was sponsoring, although some deregulators felt it did not go far enough.

Although exceeding Senator Howard's June 1 deadline, Congress passed the Motor Carrier Act in June. It became law July 1, 1980, and the Commission acted swiftly to implement it.

As mentioned above, railroad deregulation had the support of the rail industry but, of course, not of all shippers. Labor continued to oppose deregulation of any industry. But the financial problems of the nation's railroads put strong pressure on Congress to act. The choices were nationalization, subsidization, or deregulation. Nationalization of passenger rail transportation and Conrail resulted in large and growing subsidies. Conrail, for example, lost $1.4 billion in its first four-and-one-half years.[23] The only way to stop the financial drain was to permit the railroads to price as they wished and to ease the roadblocks to eliminating money-losing routes.

Moreover, the ICC was deregulating the railroad industry as well as motor carriers. The Commission, taking a permissive stand on rate flexibility, proposed permitting substantial rate change without the need for regulatory consideration. Thus some shippers and congressmen believed that legislation was preferable to letting ICC deregulate on its own. However, because of controversy concerning the implications of the deregulation on coal rail rates, rail legislation, officially known as the Staggers Act, did not pass Congress until the fall of 1980.

PARTIAL TRANSPORTATION DEREGULATION

When transportation deregulation finally became a reality, it produced enormous benefits for consumers and shippers: trucking rates fell and the nation's railroads offered new services. Passenger and freight transportation were once among the most heavily regulated industries in the United States. Now that federal economic regulation for surface transportation was reduced significantly the benefits appeared swiftly.

Railroad Regulatory Reform

The Staggers Rail Act provides the railroads with new pricing freedom. ICC jurisdiction is limited to those rates where railroads exercise "market dominance." Moreover, the definition of market dominance is more limited than under the 4-R Act of 1976. Hence, nearly two-thirds of railroad rates are free from maximum-rate regulation. Since any rate equal to or exceeding variable cost cannot be considered unreasonable, railroads now have much more freedom to reduce rates as well.

This act also extends Interstate Commerce Commission authority, originally granted in the 4-R Act, to grant exemptions from regulation for particular traffic. Starting in 1979 with fresh fruits and vegetables, the Commission has used this power to exempt from regulation a growing list of products. Railroads responded by reducing prices when demand was low and equipment available and increasing rates during periods when demand was high and rail cars in short supply. Railroads offered low backhaul rates to fill up trailers, containers, and freight cars that previously had returned empty.

The exemption of fresh fruits and vegetables has been successful, permitting a number of western railroads, such as Santa Fe, Burlington Northern, Southern Pacific, and Union Pacific, to increase their business significantly. The railroad share of the market for perishables increased from 11 percent to almost 15 percent within one year.[24] As shown in Table 1, after the 1979 exemption for fresh fruits and vegetables, the railroads were able to more than double the carloads carried, while shipments of grain grew only modestly, if at all. The ability of railroads to negotiate long-term contracts starting at the end of 1978 is reflected in the strong growth of the coal business.

In March of 1981 the ICC deregulated most aspects of "piggyback" traffic (TOFC). This has led to lower rates and more traffic. Even though 1981 was a recession year for the transportation industry, intermodal traffic actually increased compared to the previous year. Motor carrier traffic declined about 15.5 percent during 1981 compared to the previous year.[25] Moreover, TOFC traffic increased about 10 percent from 1981 to 1982, even though 1982 was a very poor year economically and total intercity ton-miles moved by all modes was down about 9 percent.[26] Such traffic has continued to grow. Some railroads, however, do not view this as a blessing, arguing

Table 1. Index of Rail Carloadings of Various Types of Traffic (1978 = 100)

Traffic	1969	1975	1978	1979	1980	1981	1982	1983	1984
Fruit	632	274	100	104	136	196	232	260	—
Vegetables	538	284	100	92	140	203	232	192	—
Coal	116	106	100	119	129	130	127	118	134
Grain	96	100	100	107	117	101	94	103	106
TOFC[a]	84	71	100	101	90	95	105	127	146

Source: *Freight Commodity Statistics* (1970–1982), American Railway Association.
[a] Trailer on flat car.

that lower piggyback rates simply have diverted boxcar traffic to this lower priced service.

More recently, the railroads asked the Commission to exempt coal exports from regulation with the objective to raise rates. Nevertheless, the railroads are constrained from exploiting any monopoly position by foreign competition for coal and by competition for export coal from different regions.

Early in March 1983, after more than a year without a decision, the Commission voted to remove export coal from rate regulation by a three-to-two margin. Upon appeal by coal companies, the U.S. Court of Appeals for the District of Columbia, in September 1984, struck down the exemption from regulation of coal for export.

Also in March 1983, by the same vote, the Commission exempted from regulation commodities carried in boxcars. Rates for the movement and storage of empty cars also were exempted from federal control under this ruling. However, under pressure from Congress, the Commission postponed boxcar deregulation until January 1, 1984. Car-hire and car-service rule changes for boxcars owned by the smallest category of railroads, class III carriers, however, were not deregulated until July 1, 1984. In June 1984 the D.C. Circuit Court partially overturned the exemption and threw out the Commission's ruling as it pertained to joint rates on boxcar traffic. Both the coal and boxcar cases are currently before the Supreme Court.

The Staggers Act set a new precedent by authorizing railroads to enter into contracts with shippers. At the end of 1983 some 13,000 contracts had been filed with the Commission, covering practically every commodity.[27] These contracts now account for over one-quarter of the revenue of major railroads. Most shippers have received reduced rates under contracts. Railroads had used contracts to attract traffic from other modes. Bulk products such as chemicals and minerals account for about one-quarter of all contracts.

Emphasizing the railroad industry's positive appraisal of the effects of the Staggers Act, Richard Briggs, Executive Vice-President of the Association of American Railroads, credited deregulation, at least in part, for helping the railroads survive the 1981–1982 recession. He said:

Who would have thought the railroad industry could have withstood two years of severely depressed traffic levels without at least a few companies going under and without major government bailouts? . . . Because of deregulation . . . I am much more confident about the future of the railroad industry than at any time in the past 10 years.[28]

Briggs was right; the loosening of regulatory constraints on the railroads has been beneficial. Table 2 gives some data on the earnings,

Table 2. Railroad Industry Performance in Recent Years

	1969	1975	1978	1979	1980	1981	1982	1983
Net operating income (millions)[a]	1,724	629	632	1,111	1,566	1,444	742	1,781
Revenue ton-miles (billions)	768	754	858	914	919	910	798	828
Employees (class 1 rails) (thousands)	578	488	472	483	459	436	379	322
Miles of class 1 railroad lines owned (thousands)	197	192	176	170	165	162	159	na
Average hourly earnings[a]	9.98	11.46	12.47	12.26	11.96	11.82	12.26	12.87
Average annual earnings (100 of dollars)[a]	244	274	304	300	288	283	291	311
Revenue per ton-mile[a]	3.55	3.66	3.49	3.46	3.34	3.37	3.21	3.02

Source: Railroad Facts (1983 edition), Association of American Railroads.
[a]All monetary figures are in 1982 dollars.

traffic, labor costs, rates, and productivity of the rail industry in recent years.

As can be seen from this table, since regulatory constraints were first loosened in 1979, profits for the industry are up sharply. Even in 1982, a poor year for transportation and for the railroads, the profits were greater than in 1975, which was also a recession period. In 1983, as the economy grew out of the recession, profits reached record levels. From the pre-deregulation year of 1978, profits more than doubled by 1981 and nearly tripled by 1983. In part this was because the new competitive environment permitted or forced the industry to reduce labor costs. The number of employees was cut 32 percent from 1978 to 1983. While the number of workers was reduced, which continues a long-term trend, average hourly earnings simply leveled off after 1978 — as did annual compensation, which grew at less than half of one percent over the five-year period. However, this reduction in compensation cannot be attributed to deregulation, as railroad workers actually gained slightly while real weekly earnings fell for the economy as a whole over the same period.

Revenue per ton-mile, a proxy for rates — albeit a poor one, declined about 13 percent from 1978 and even more from 1975. The 7.5 percent fall in revenue per ton-mile up to 1982 is consistent with the shipper data, discussed below, showing that a group of major shippers surveyed reported that the rates they paid fell in real terms some 9 percent from 1978.

While rates apparently have declined for most shippers, coal companies, some utilities, and a few others claim that the railroads have been able to raise their rates to "captive" shippers. They have been advocating a major change in the Staggers Act to force the ICC to control rates. At this time the Reagan administration is resisting any changes in the legislation.

Trucking Regulation Reform

The Motor Carrier Act of 1980 substantially relaxed controls on trucking. Its most significant provision shifts the burden of proof from the applicant to the protestor. Formerly *the applicant* had to show that any requested new authority was "required by the present or future public convenience and necessity"; now *the protestor* must show that it is "inconsistent with the public convenience and necessity." Furthermore, only those motor carriers that have authority to offer the proposed service are permitted to file protests, and a diversion of revenue from existing carriers is not to be construed *in itself* as inconsistent with the public convenience and necessity. The act also requires that the Commission provide procedures permitting carriers to reduce limitations on their operating authority, such as gateway requirements, narrow property definitions, rigid territorial constraints, restrictions on return hauls, and restraints on service to intermediate points.

Actually, deregulation of the motor carrier industry began considerably earlier than the 1980 act. As described, some loosening of regulation can be traced back to 1975, although major reform began in 1979.

Studies of the Impact. Virtually all the major studies of reduced regulation have concluded that in the short period since trucking was partially deregulated, rates have decreased, service has improved, and shippers are pleased with the results. Service to small communities has improved and complaints by shippers have declined. Improved service and lower rates by for-hire carriers may indicate that private carriage has declined.[29]

In one of the first systematic studies of the impact of the 1980 act, Harbridge House, Inc., surveyed 2,200 manufacturers.[30] Seventy-seven percent of the shippers surveyed favored deregulation of trucking and 63 percent favored deregulation of rail. Sixty-five percent reported lower trucking rates and 23 percent claimed to be enjoying lower rail charges since deregulation.[31] Shippers reported that carriers were much more willing to negotiate rates and services than prior to deregulation.

An ICC report found that the number of new firms increased but that the distribution of sizes was not affected.[32] The ICC reported that the number of entry applications rose from 6,746 in fiscal 1976 to 22,235 in fiscal 1980; and in the first six months of fiscal 1981 another 14,096 were acted on.[33] The percent fully or partly granted rose from about 70 percent in fiscal 1976 to 97 percent in fiscal 1980, and 96 percent in the first half of 1981. The number of grants to new carriers quadrupled from 468 in all of 1976 to 1,101 for the first six months of 1981, with some 8 percent of all grants in 1981 going to new firms.

In the first three months of 1981, under the Motor Carrier Act provision permitting firms to remove existing restrictions on operating licenses, the ICC processed 1,349 applications and granted virtually 100 percent in some form. About 92 percent of these applications requested broader territorial authority and 86 percent included a request for broader commodity descriptions. In 1980 the number of independent rate filings outside the rate bureaus was the highest in any year for which the ICC had data.[34] A sample from two bureaus showed that the vast majority of independent announcements involved rate decreases. Between 34 and 44 percent involved less-than-truckload (LTL) rates. Furthermore, this report indicates that trucking profits have not suffered from deregulation. The return on equity, which had been only 8.8 percent in the recession year of 1975, was 12.5 percent in 1979 and 14.3 percent in 1980.

A Federal Trade Commission staff paper submitted to the Motor Carrier Rate Making Study Commission in 1982 found that the Motor Carrier Act (MCA) of 1980 produced none of the disastrous results that the industry had forecast.[35] The paper concluded:

> During the first year following passage of the MCA, a substantial number of firms were permitted to enter the trucking industry and existing carriers took advantage of increased freedom to expand the scope of their operations. Competition among an increasing number of carriers has created downward pressure on rates and forced firms to increase productivity, e.g., by seeking removal of restrictions on operating certificates and by seeking concessions from labor. Lower rates and costs will insure that society gets more out of each dollar spent on trucking service. Increased competition also means that the monopoly profits made possible by protective regulation are being squeezed out of the system.

In response to a congressional mandate the ICC released a study of the impact of the MCA on small community service.[36] The Commission concluded that

> regulatory reform has caused no dramatic changes in small community rates or service, changes that did occur were generally favorable . . . improvement in service was reported much more often than service deterioration. Complaints about trucking service in small communities have decreased significantly since passage of the MCA . . . rates to and from small communities have increased less rapidly than rates to or from larger cities.

In a study of truckers and shippers in the Twin Cities area of Minnesota, transportation professor Donald Harper of the University of Minnesota's School of Management found that the number of motor carriers operating in the area had increased since 1977.[37] His survey found that regular-route, LTL carriers complained that other LTL carriers had expanded into their territory, but truckload (TL) carriers had experienced significant competition from new firms. Apparently the cost of setting up terminals and building a business from scratch inhibited entry into the LTL business, but entry into truckload carriage was easy.[38] Many carriers were satisfied with the liberal rate-regulation policy of the ICC. Harper quotes one carrier: "Most changes made to date in all areas have been needed and are good and will benefit the shipping public and motor carriers alike."[39]

As might be expected, a large number of shippers were satisfied with liberalized entry control. For almost all shippers the number of carriers competing for their traffic had increased.[40] Only 45 percent of the shippers, however, were satisfied with ICC rate policy.[41] Large shippers were more satisfied than smaller ones. More than one-half thought that rates had been too high. On the other hand, they reported more rate flexibility than before 1977. Some complained of discrimination or too frequent rate changes. Many shippers reported that quality of service had improved. Size of the shipper did not affect the quality of service reported.[42] In summary, with the exception of two firms, the shippers studied expressed satisfaction with the reduction in regulation. Harper reported:

> The benefits accruing to shippers from reform were more freedom to work with carriers, more competition in the industry, more carriers available to choose from, lower rates, and more flexibility. A traffic manager employed by a large manufacturer of printed material said, "I was against deregulation but have since changed my mind. Competition is good for all companies."[43]

The General Accounting Office (GAO) has testified to Congress that the Motor Carrier Act generally has had a favorable effect.[44] It reported that the ICC found, in October 1983, that since 1980, rates charged by LTT carriers had fallen; in many cases they were down 10 to 20 percent and some shippers had reported declines of as much as 40 percent. The GAO reviewed a number of reports on the impact of the act. They asserted to Congress:

> The reports we reviewed generally found that trucking deregulation has not adversely affected service to small communities and small shippers. These studies indicate little change in quality or availability of truck service since passage of the act. . . . Most shippers reported that rates have risen only as fast as the overall price level has increased, or have declined slightly. . . .
>
> In conclusion, we believe the Motor Carrier Act of 1980 . . . has increased competition in the trucking industry . . . create[d] pressures on firms to operate efficiently and [kept] prices of truck transportation lower.[45]

Additional Data.[46] Probably the best indicator of the loosening of regulatory reins is the value of operating licenses. When regulation was very strict, certificates of public convenience and necessity sold for thousands and sometimes millions of dollars.[47] Table 3 shows what has happened to the value of these certificates over the last eight years. Even though there appears to have been a drop in the value of certificates in 1978, not until 1979 was there any indication that de-

Table 3. Purchases of Operating Authority

| | | Average Value | |
Year	Number in June	Common Carriers Only[a]	Number in Sample
1975	43	$398	20
1976	23	579	17
1977	15	531	28
1978	36	370	25
1979	13	55	24
1980	3	171	4
1981	3[b]	13	1
1982	0	15	2

Sources: *Traffic World* (various dates), and motor carrier finance cases from the files in the Docket Room, ICC.
[a]Thousands of 1982 dollars.
[b]For the period February through June.

regulation was beginning to have a major effect. Starting in 1979 the number of purchased authorities during the month of June declined sharply; but even more significant, the value of the authorities fell by more than 80 percent, from over $350,000 per transaction in the previous few years to about $55,000. In 1980 there were only three transactions in all of June and only four in the sample. Therefore the figure of $171,000 has little significance. By 1981 and 1982 the value was negligible for the few purchases of operating rights that took place.

As can be seen from Table 4, entry into the motor carrier industry progressively has become easier. The number of applications for new authority from existing carriers, as well as the number from new carriers, has ballooned since 1975. Moreover, the percentage of such applications approved by the Commission rose greatly up through 1981. The result can be seen in the last column, which shows a gradual rise in the number of licensed property carriers up through 1979 and then a sharp escalation as the number jumps by over 1,000 the next year, then by 4,000 and another 3,500 up to 1982. These increases in number of licensed carriers are reflected in the sharp decline in the value of licenses in 1979.

As mentioned above, not only has the number of new carriers increased but a large number of existing carriers have been granted additional authority. Consequently, these figures on licensed carriers

Table 4. Entry and Number of Property Carriers

Year	Authority Applications from Carriers - Existing	Authority Applications from Carriers - New	Percentage Granted - Existing	Percentage Granted - New	Number of Carriers
1975	2,822	276	55	61	16,005
1976	6,406	586	61	62	16,462
1977	8,622	558	65	72	16,606
1978	12,983	703	69	78	16,874
1979	20,687	974	69	80	17,083
1980	18,788	1,490	73	86	18,129
1981	19,135	4,576	88	85	22,270
1982	9,150	4,925	84	55	25,722

Sources: Interstate Commerce Commission, special preparation, and *Annual Report to Congress* (various years).

fail to indicate the degree to which competition has increased over this period.

Table 5 gives an index of freight rates paid by shippers over the period 1975–1982. These data come from two surveys of shippers by the author in early 1983. Overall usable responses represented seventy-one large to very large shippers.

The firms surveyed were asked to provide an index of the freight rate paid for TL, LTL, and rail shipments over the period 1975–1982. They were also queried on their view of service quality after the Motor Carrier Act of 1980.

Table 5 shows an average of rate changes over the 1975–1982 period, adjusted by the CPI for inflation. As the reader can see, prices have fallen significantly. Real rates for truckload shipments have declined steadily since 1976, while rates for LTL movements have fallen since 1977. These indexes suggest that even the modest deregulation of 1976 and 1977 had some effect. Part of the decrease in trucking rates is attributable to the economic recession of 1979 and again in 1981. As would be expected from greater entry into the truckload business than into LTLs, real rates for TLs have decreased more dramatically than LTLs.

In comparison, rail rates did not start to decline until 1979 and have fallen less than trucking rates. This could be expected as railroads, which had supported deregulation, were interested, at least in part, in the ability to raise rather than lower rates. Nevertheless, in many cases, such as following deregulation of fresh fruits and vegetables, railroads did reduce charges.

Table 5 also presents an example of motor carrier rates filed with the ICC for the 1975–1982 period. These rates are general commodity rates for Denver to Los Angeles for class 100. Whether they are typical cannot be ascertained, but they indicate that rates did begin to fall after 1977 but then turned up in 1980 or 1981. A greater decline in TL rates over LTL rates is also reflected in these data. However, the rates filed with the ICC show no net decline over the period 1977–1982, which is puzzling given the sharp fall in rates actually paid by shippers.

Table 5 also shows that since 1977 labor costs have fallen sharply — about 14 percent for all workers and 21 percent for drivers and helpers paid on an hourly basis. Data for 1983, not shown, indicate that earnings continued to fall. For example, on the basis of 1975 equals 100, the index for drivers and helpers reached ninety-nine and eighty-seven on a mileage and hourly basis. Drivers and helpers make up the core of the Teamster members in trucking. Thus the Teamsters' opposition to deregulation was justified: deregulation lowered their earnings sharply.

Table 5. Indexes of Real Freight Rates and Average Compensation

Sample Size	1975	1976	1977	1978	1979	1980	1981	1982
Rates Paid by Shippers								
TL 35	100	100	100	99	95	88	81	75
LTL 30	100	103	105	104	101	98	91	89
Rail 23	100	102	96	102	101	100	90	93
LA-Denver Posted Rates (Class 100)								
TL	100	102	101	na	93	90	89	102
LTL	100	105	107	na	103	103	110	117
Average Compensation								
All employees	100	94	103	96	94	93	87	89
Drivers and helpers								
Mileage basis	100	117	124	109	105	105	106	100
Hourly basis	100	88	114	92	92	92	92	90

Sources: Author's survey as described in text; ICC Rate Filings; ICC *Annual Reports;* and ICC *Transport Statistics in the United States.*

Table 6 shows the average revenue per ton-mile received by class I and II regulated motor carriers, which for the period 1977–1981 indicates a decline of about 10 percent — less than the decrease in rates paid by the survey companies but much more than the official class rates. Apparently, independent and special commodity rates became more important and undercut the class structure of rates. The tremendous increase in independent filings reported in the 1981 ICC study of the trucking industry supports this interpretation.[48]

The decline in rates after 1977 cannot be explained simply by the recessions that have occurred since 1979. Not only did the rates paid by the sample of shippers fall after 1977, but so did the average revenue per ton-mile, well before the recessions of 1979–1980 and 1981–1982. Moreover, in the earlier 1973–1975 recession, which was as deep as the 1980–1982 economic downturn, ICC data on average revenue per ton-mile for class I intercity common carriers showed an increase of 25 percent in real terms during the recession period.[49]

Further evidence on the impact of deregulation on the financial position of the industry is shown in Table 6. In the two years prior to 1979 the return on transportation investment for the trucking indus-

Table 6. Financial Data on Major Trucking Firms

Year	Number of Firms in Group	Return on Transportation Investment (%)	Payroll to Revenue (%)	Revenue Per Ton-Mile[a] (¢)	Industry Bankruptcies
1973	1144	25.7	na	na	na
1074	972	25.5	na	na	231
1975	803	19.5	43.4	21.5	240
1976	748	19.7	43.2	22.0	276
1977	963	22.8	41.7	21.7	193
1978	857	24.0	41.7	20.1	162
1979	721	14.5	40.2	19.7	186
1980	704	15.1	39.4	19.9	382
1981	704	11.1	38.7	19.4	610

Sources: G. Barry Kohler, *Financial Analysis of the Motor Carrier Industry* (1978), Bank of America and American Trucking Associations, and Patricia Lisciandro, *Financial Analysis of the Motor Carrier Industry*, (1982), Chase Manhattan Bank and American Trucking Associations. Bankruptcies are from Dun & Bradstreet's *Business Failure Record* (January 28, 1983), and reflect failures in the whole industry, regulated, unregulated, and local carriers.

[a]1982 dollars.

try was over 50 percent higher than in subsequent years. Earnings in 1979 and 1980, however, were comparable to earnings in other sectors of the economy. Moreover, profits in 1975, a recession year, were considerably higher than 1980, a recession year, or even 1981 in which a modest recovery was witnessed. Earlier profits reflected the protected and monopoly position of major carriers. These data also show that the industry managed to reduce its labor costs as a percent of revenue.

Table 6 also shows that deregulation has taken a toll on trucking firms. Bankruptcies increased greatly in 1980 and 1981 compared to earlier years. Part of the rise in bankruptcies is a result of the severe recessions that the economy has suffered in the last few years; nevertheless, the 1973–1975 recession is comparable in terms of decline in manufacturing production,[50] and bankruptcies were much fewer. While the number of licensed trucking firms has increased about 60 percent, their growth cannot explain the much larger rise in bankruptcies — about 154 percent through 1981. In comparison, business failures in the economy as a whole were 47 percent higher in 1981 than in 1975,[51] a much smaller rise. No doubt, regulation protected many inefficient carriers which, when faced with competition, simply folded.

In the paper presented at the 1972 Brookings Conference this author argued that deregulation would probably lower trucking rates by about 20 percent.[52] Table 5 shows that truckload rates fell about 25 percent from 1977 to 1982, and LTL rates declined about 12 percent. These declines, which certainly are in the range predicted, occurred during a period of time when fuel costs more than doubled for the industry.

While the data do not allow us to determine clearly how much of the fall in rates is attributable to the recession of 1981–1982 and how much to deregulation, it is obvious that the recession has played a role. Perhaps rates would have remained high despite deregulation, but given that trucking firms and railroads had the freedom to reduce rates, a recession was destined to bring about a fall. This is appropriate. In a competitive market a decrease in demand will normally cause a drop in prices. It is certainly indicative that in the earlier recession of 1973–1975 rates did not fall.

The decline in TL rates of about 16 percent since 1976 does not mean that rates will stay that low or might not fall even further. The impact of deregulation has only begun, so further rate reductions are possible. On the other hand, as prosperity returns and traffic grows, transportation companies will be in a better position to charge higher tariffs.

The 1979–1982 recessions were costly for transportation, and for trucking in particular. The total intercity ton-miles moved in the

United States declined by 13.2 percent from the peak years of 1979 through 1982; in comparison, the decline to 1975 from its previous peak was only 6.9 percent. For federally regulated motor carriers, however, the fall was 16.2 percent for the latest recession and only 9.5 percent for the earlier one.[53]

The Motor Carrier Act apparently has not hurt motor carrier share of the market. In 1975 carriers had 44.1 percent of the market and in 1982, 44.6 percent. On the other hand, the railroads appear to have benefited from the Staggers Act. Their share of the market increased from 33.2 percent in 1975 to 36.4 percent in 1982. While the regulated trucking industry was carrying less in 1980 than in 1979, the railroads actually increased the ton-miles they hauled in 1980 over 1979. No doubt their superior performance was partly the result of the sharp increase in fuel prices, which play a bigger role in trucking costs than in rail, but the deregulation of fruit and vegetables and of piggyback must have been significant also.

Clearly, deregulation has reduced rates in trucking, but has it also reduced services? The American Trucking Associations claimed, prior to deregulation, that without regulation service quality would decline, service to small communities would be hurt, and the industry would become dominated by large firms. The ICC report on service to small communities, referred to above, shows that some parts of the country have benefited from deregulation.[54] Another ICC report found no appreciable change in the size distribution of firms.[55]

Table 7 presents the results of a survey on service quality. In terms of seven major quality dimensions, service has either improved

Table 7. Quality of Service after Motor Carrier Act of 1980

	Sample Size	Percent Improved	Percent Unchanged	Percent Worse
Quality of trucks	71	24	68	8
Promptness of service	70	47	46	7
Availability of service	71	73	17	10
Reliability	71	37	52	11
Adjustment of claims	71	18	63	19
Need for supervision	70	14	69	17
Willingness to serve off-line points	71	34	42	24
Overall	495	35	51	14

Source: Author's survey of major shippers. Data include multiple responses by firms; when different divisions of the same firm responded, they were treated as separate responses.

or stayed the same since the Motor Carrier Act of 1980. Only for "Adjustment of Claims" and "Need for Supervision" does the number of respondents who conclude that service declined barely exceed the number who believe it improved. Overall, about 35 percent of the responses indicate an improvement in quality, 51 percent reported unchanged, and only 14 percent thought it worse.

The improvement in quality of service is reflected in a decline in number of complaints. In 1975 and 1976 the ICC reported processing 340 and 390 motor carrier complaint cases.[56] In 1977 complaints dropped to sixty, then sixty-four the next year. In 1980 and 1981 only twenty-three and forty such complaint cases came before the Commission.

CONCLUSION

Deregulation of railroads and motor carriers has been of significant benefit to shippers and consumers. Government studies and studies by independent scholars conclude that rates have declined and service quality has either improved or remained the same. The results of deregulation are in line with what proponents of change had predicted prior to decontrol.

A growing body of data documents the benefits for the motor carrier industry. Rates have declined; service quality has improved. Monopoly profits have been eliminated and the value of operating rights has fallen to negligible levels. The return on investment in the industry is comparable to the return in other sectors of the economy. Labor costs have been reduced, mainly through substitution of nonunion labor for union labor. Facing competition of nonunion firms, the Teamsters Union has become much more reasonable in its demands. So far none of the problems that the industry predicted, except a natural growth in bankruptcies, have come to pass. In all, the industry has behaved much as proponents of deregulation predicted, providing significant benefits to our economy.

While there is less unanimity on railroad deregulation, it would be fair to say that on average shippers have profited from deregulation. Moreover, once facing bankruptcy and the need for federal aid, the railroads have become a profitable industry able to compete with other modes of transportation. On the whole, partial deregulation has been a great success.

NOTES

[1] Federal Coordinator of Transportation, *Public Aids to Transportation* (Washington, D.C.: U.S. Government Printing Office, 1940), Vol. I, p. 19.

[2] Gabriel Kolko, *Railroads and Regulation 1877–1916* (Princeton, N.J.: Princeton University Press, 1965), pp. 7, 15.

[3] *Ibid.*, p. 7.

[4] Kolko, *op. cit.*, p. 35.

[5] These studies are summarized in Theodore E. Keeler, *Railroads, Freight, and Public Policy* (Washington, D.C.: The Brookings Institution, 1983), Appendix B, pp. 153–164.

[6] Robert M. Spann and Edward W. Erickson, "The Economics of Railroading: The Beginning of Centralizing and Regulation," The *Bell Journal of Economics and Management Science* (Autumn 1970), 104–111.

[7] 41 Stat. 488.

[8] *Buck v. Kuykendall*, 267 U.S. 307 (1925), and *Bush and Sons and Company v. Maloy*, 267 U.S. 317 (1925).

[9] ICC, *Annual Report* (1940).

[10] James C. Nelson, "The Motor Carrier Act of 1935," *Journal of Political Economy*, 44 (August 1936), 464–504; Nelson, "Coordination of Transportation by Regulation" *Southern Economic Journal*, 5 (July 1938), 7–16; Board of Investigation and Research, *Federal Regulatory Restrictions Upon Motor and Water Carriers*, S. Doc. No. 78, 79th Cong., 1st sess. (1945); Walter Adams, "The Role of Competition in the Regulated Industries," *American Economic Review*, 48 (May 1958), 536–537; John R. Meyer, Merton J. Peck, John Stenason, and Charles Zwick, *The Economics of Competition in the Transportation Industries* (Cambridge, Mass.: Harvard University Press, 1959); James C. Nelson, "The Effects of Entry Control in Surface Transport," *Transportation Economics* (New York: Columbia University Press for the National Bureau of Economics Research, 1965), pp. 381–422; and Thomas Gale Moore, *Freight Transportation Regulation: Surface Freight and the Interstate Commerce Commission* (Washington, D.C.: American Enterprise Institute and the Hoover Institution, 1972).

[11] James R. Snitzler and Robert J. Byrne, *Interstate Trucking of Fresh and Frozen Poultry Under Agricultural Exemption* (U.S. Department of Agriculture, 1958), Marketing Research Report No. 224; and *id.*, *Interstate Trucking of Frozen Fruits and Vegetables Under Agricultural Exemption* (U.S. Department of Agriculture, 1959), Marketing Research Report No. 316.

[12] Thomas Gale Moore, "Deregulating Surface Freight Transportation," in Almarin Phillips (ed.), *Promoting Competition in Regulated Markets*, (Washington, D.C.: The Brookings Institution, 1975), pp. 55–98.

[13] Thomas Gale Moore, "The Beneficiaries of Trucking Regulation," *The Journal of Law and Economics*, 21 (October 1978), 327–343.

[14] Stewart Joy, "Unregulated Road Haulage: The Australian Experience," *Oxford Economic Papers*, n.s. Vol. 16 (July 1964); and Thomas Gale Moore, *Trucking Regulation: Lesson from Europe* (Washington, D.C.: American Enterprise Institute and Hoover Institution, 1976), Chap. 1.

[15] The Week's Committee, chaired by Secretary of Commerce Sinclair Week under President Dwight Eisenhower, had recommended a greater reliance on competitive forces in transportation, a cutback in rail rate regulation, but an increase in control of trucking competition.

[16] *Traffic World* (October 17, 1977), 33.

[17] *New York Times* (October 30, 1977), 18.

[18] U.S. Department of Transportation, "A Prospectus for Change in the Freight Railroad Industry" (October 1978).

[19] *Congressional Quarterly* (December 9, 1978), 3422.

[20] *Wall Street Journal* (May 24, 1979), 12.

[21] *Wall Street Journal* (October 23, 1979), 8.

[22] *The New York Times* (March 5, 1980), D3.

[23] *Washington Star* (December 21, 1980), B 5.

[24] "Background on Transportation" Association of American Railroads (July 20, 1981).

[25] *Traffic World* (February 1, 1982), 11.

[26] *Transporation in America,* Interstate Commerce Commission, March 1983 and Table 1.

[27] *Traffic World* (March 26, 1984), 10.

[28] *Traffic World* (October 18, 1982), 19–20.

[29] Statement on The Motor Carrier Act of 1980 by Marcus Alexis, Acting Chairman, Interstate Commerce Commission, before the Subcommittee on Surface Transportation of the House Committee on Public Works and Transportation (June 10, 1981), pp. 3, 4, 11, 12.

[30] *Report on Harbridge House Survey of the Impact of Transportation Deregulation on Major U.S. Manufacturing Firms* (June 1981).

[31] *Ibid.*, p. 1.

[32] Office of Policy Analysis, Interstate Commerce Commission, *The Effect of Regulatory Reform on the Trucking Industry: Structure, Conduct and Performance,* Preliminary Report (June 1981).

[33] *Ibid.*, p. 3.

[34] *Ibid.*, p. 5.

[35] Denis A. Breen, "Regulatory Reform and the Trucking Industry: An Evaluation of the Motor Carrier Act of 1980," Bureau of Economics, Federal Trade Commission (March 1982).

[36] *Small Community Service Study,* Office of Transportation Analysis, Interstate Commerce Commission (September 1, 1982), p. 3.

[37] Donald V. Harper, "Consequences of Reform of Federal Economic Regulation of the Motor Trucking Industry," *Transportation Journal* (Summer 1982), 42.

[38] *Ibid.*, p. 43.

[39] *Ibid.*, p. 48.

[40] *Ibid.*, p. 49.

[41] *Ibid.*, p. 51.

[42] *Ibid.*, p. 52.

[43] *Ibid.*, p. 54.

[44] *Traffic World* (January 30, 1984), p. 41

[45] *Ibid.*, p. 42.

[46] Much of this material appeared in Thomas Gale Moore, "The Record on Rail and Truck Reform," *Regulation Magazine* (November/December 1983).

[47] See Moore, "The Beneficiaries of Trucking Regulation," *op. cit.*

[48] *The Effect of Regulatory Reform on the Trucking Industry* (ICC, 1981).

[49] Computed from ICC, *Transport Statistics of the United States* (various years).

[50] Manufacturing production fell about 10.4 percent from 1973 to 1975 and declined the same percentage from 1979, the previous peak, to 1982. See *Economic Report of the President* (February 1983), p. 210.

[51] *The 1981 Dun & Bradstreet Business Failure Record* (1983), p. 2.

[52] Moore, "Deregulating Surface Freight Transportation," *op. cit.*, 1975.

[53] For total ton-miles carried in intercity movements, 1973–1975 data are from the ICC *Annual Reports* and the 1979–1982 data are from ICC *Transportation in America* (March 1983); for federal regulated motor carriage they are from ICC *Annual Reports*.

[54] ICC, *Small Community Service Study* (1982).

[55] ICC, *The Effect of Regulatory Reform on the Trucking Industry* (1981).

[56] *ICC Annual Reports*.

CASE 2

The Changing Airline Industry

Daniel P. Kaplan
Congressional Budget Office

INTRODUCTION

In the mid-1970s academics and policymakers began calling for less economic regulation in a number of basic industries. The airline industry quickly came to the top of the list, because a test of the marketplace's effectiveness in disciplining airline behavior had been in progress for more than twenty years. Intrastate airlines operated outside the jurisdiction of the Civil Aeronautics Board (CAB) and had more latitude in determining fares and routes. Markets in California and Texas served by these carriers had significantly lower fares than similar interstate markets and the intrastate carriers were profitable.[1]

The case for regulatory reform was first made in academia and ultimately gained support from Congress and Presidents Ford and Carter. In 1976 the Board began changing the regulatory course it had steered for nearly forty years.[2] The effects of these changes were unambiguously positive and led to the passage of the Airline Deregulation Act in October 1978. This legislation phased out the government's authority to regulate the routes that carriers could serve in domestic air transportation as well as the fares they could charge.[3]

The case against regulating airfares and routes was clearly enunciated in congressional hearings as well as in a study done by the Board's staff.[4] And indeed the industry has become far more com-

Much of the material in this paper is based on Elizabeth E. Bailey, David R. Graham, and Daniel P. Kaplan, *Deregulating the Airlines* (Cambridge, Mass.: The MIT Press, 1985). The views expressed are the author's and do not necessarily represent those of the Congressional Budget Office.

petitive and efficient without the government's guiding hand. However, many of the developments in the deregulated industry were not anticipated at the time the Airline Deregulation Act was passed.

A BRIEF HISTORY OF AIRLINE REGULATION

Regulation of the airline industry began in the 1920s when the government began to award contracts for the carriage of mail.[5] Since mail was the major source of revenues in the early days of the industry, the U.S. Post Office and the Interstate Commerce Commission (ICC), which assumed the Post Office's contracting authority in 1934, played a decisive role in the development of the airline industry's structure. Ironically, as the demand for air transportation by passengers and shippers increased, a number of carriers were experiencing financial problems, largely because of the ICC's policies. Specifically, the ICC encouraged carriers to carry mail at rates well below cost in order to secure additional routes. The failure of the existing regulatory scheme coupled with the increasing importance of the passenger service led Congress to establish the CAB in 1938.

The CAB was granted extensive regulatory authority over airlines providing interstate airline services. It inherited the ICC's authority over mail rates and also was given the explicit authority to award routes, to regulate fares, and to assure safe airline operation. (The regulation of safety was transferred to the Federal Aviation Administration in 1958.) The Board was also given a broad mandate to encourage the development of the air transport system.

The decision to establish the CAB and to grant it broad regulatory powers was rooted in the fundamental skepticism of the time about the ability of the free market to function effectively. There was an underlying fear that the unchecked forces of competition would lead to fares that were chronically below costs, which would prevent the fledging airline industry from growing and prospering.

Under the CAB's regulatory control the airline industry did indeed grow rapidly. For example, between 1949 and 1969, passenger traffic (as measured by the number of miles passengers flew or revenue passenger miles) increased more than thirteenfold, at an average annual rate of 14 percent.[6] Moreover, the average fare per mile in 1969 was 2 percent lower than it had been in 1949. The consumer price index, meanwhile, had increased by 50 percent.

However, technology, not regulation, was the key to the industry's growth. Long-haul pressurized propeller aircraft were introduced in the late 1940s; jet aircraft were in wide use by the mid-1960s. Both types of aircraft were larger and faster than the aircraft they replaced. Because they could be flown at higher altitudes, they were also more comfortable for passengers. The introduction of these aircraft improved the convenience of air travel and thus stimulated demand. They were also much less costly to operate. Between 1949 and 1969 airline costs fell by 22 percent, a substantially greater decline than average carrier fares.[7] In fact, in the late 1960s fares in markets served by intrastate carriers were as much as 45 percent below the levels the CAB permitted in comparable markets. These disparities led to increasing questions about the efficacy of Board regulation despite the industry's rapid growth.[8]

The Civil Aeronautics Board's Regulatory Policies

At the time the CAB was established the route authority of the sixteen existing airlines (which became known as the trunks) was "grandfathered."[9] Before an airline, whether an operating carrier or a new entrant, could begin service in a market, it had to obtain the requisite route authority from the Board. Prior to the passage of the Airline Deregulation Act, the CAB did not allow one new entrant to begin service on a major route.[10] In fact, despite the enormous increase in the size of the industry, mergers had actually reduced the ranks of the trunks to eleven carriers by the time the legislation was enacted.

Even for incumbent carriers, securing additional route authority was a costly, time-consuming, and uncertain process. Routes were awarded on a case-by-case basis, and the carrier seeking authority had to show that the proposed service was in the public interest and that it would not harm the incumbent carriers. If more than one carrier sought the same authority, the route award proceeding could take more than two years. Nevertheless, the Board sometimes awarded a lucrative route to strengthen a financially weak carrier instead of basing its decision on the carriers' service proposals. Moreover, a carrier often was unable to get the CAB to institute a route award proceeding for a market it wished to enter. In fact, the Board had unofficial limits on the number of carriers it would authorize to serve a given route.

The Board was more flexible in granting authority for carriers to begin service to small communities. In the late 1940s the Board began permitting a number of new carriers to enter small community markets, many of which were receiving subsidized service. (The Board's subsidy program originated in the airmail contracts of the 1920s, but after World War II these subsidies were directed at promoting small community air service.) The fourteen local service carriers quickly took over all the subsidized service and in 1955 were granted permanent authority.[11] The local service carriers were initially prohibited from competing with the trunk carriers. However, to limit the growing subsidies, in the late 1960s the Board began allowing them to serve major routes within their regions. The local service carriers evolved into regional jet air carriers and became less and less the small community specialists that they were created to be. Nevertheless, no local service carrier was able to become as large as a trunk airline.

In regulating fares the Board's primary concern was carrier profitability. Fares were generally adjusted across-the-board rather than on a market-by-market basis. The cost per passenger mile of providing air service declines with distance, and the CAB used distance as the primary determinant of differences in fares among markets.[12] As new aircraft technologies were introduced, the disparity in the cost of providing short-haul and long-haul service increased. The Board made only minor adjustments to reflect these changes. In fact, throughout its history the Board deliberately kept fares in long-haul markets above what it believed to be the cost of service, while fares in short-haul market (especially in thin short-haul markets) were kept below costs. This policy of cross-subsidization was intended to promote air service.

Although it did not allow carriers to charge lower prices in dense markets, the CAB did permit more carriers to serve them. Since carriers could not compete on the basis of price, they offered elaborate service amenities and scheduled extra flights to attract passengers. With prices fixed, adding extra flights in a market tends to drive down the percentage of seats that are filled (the load factor), thus increasing costs.[13] Therefore competition among carriers dissipated the higher profits they were expected to earn in the dense long-haul markets.

The Board did permit carriers to introduce a variety of discount fares as more efficient equipment entered service. These discounts, which included youth standby fares and family fares, were a major reason for the decline in the average price of air travel. However, between 1960 and 1969 the growth in capacity exceeded the growth in traffic and the trunks' load factor declined from 59.3 to 50.3. In the late 1960s the conversion to jet aircraft was completed, and costs began to increase. Faced with declining profits, the carriers petitioned the Board for fare increases. In 1970 the Board instituted the first systematic analysis of its fare policies in the *Domestic Passenger Fare Investigation* (DPFI).[14]

As a consequence of the DPFI, the Board corrected a number of the distortions caused by its regulations. Most important, by no longer permitting a decline in load factor as a basis for a fare increase, it reduced the incentives for carriers to engage in scheduling competition. However the DPFI continued to set fares based on distance and to subsidize below-cost short-haul fares with higher long-haul fares. Moreover, it further limited the ability of carriers to offer discount fares. In the early 1970s the Board also established an unofficial route moratorium, during which it virtually ceased awarding competitive route authority.[15]

In 1975, amid growing questions about the Board's regulatory policies, the Senate Judiciary Committee held hearings and subsequently published a report on the effects of CAB regulation. Simultaneously, the Board itself formed a special advisory task force to explore the merits of regulatory reform. Both reports concluded that increased competition was warranted. Shortly thereafter the Board began to adopt a more liberal regulatory stance that was ultimately ratified by Congress when it passed the Airline Deregulation Act.

Toward a More Liberal Regime

In 1976 the Board took its first significant step toward a more flexible regulatory regime when it relaxed operating requirements for charters. By requiring only advance-purchase and minimum-stay requirements, charters became a readily available, low-fare alternative to scheduled service.[16] Recognizing the increased threat of competition from charters in the New York to Los Angeles and San Francisco markets, American Airlines applied for authority to make a limited number of seats available at fares up to 45 percent below coach fares. To qualify for the reduced fare, passengers had to meet a thirty-day advance-purchase and a seven-day minimum-stay requirement. The restrictions were designed to limit the number of time-sensitive business travelers who could qualify for the lower fare. The Board approved these "Super Saver" fares in the spring of 1977, even though they did not qualify under the standards for discount fares enunciated in the DPFI. The fares created a surge in traffic in the New York–Los Angeles and the New York–San Francisco markets: during the third quarter of 1977 traffic increased by 61 and 44 percent, respectively, over the previous year.

Given the success of the initial experience with fare flexibility, the CAB continued to approve requests from carriers to offer discount fares, and by March 1978 the regulated air carriers were offering restricted discount fares virtually systemwide. In the spring of 1978 the Board proposed that carriers be allowed to set fares as much as 70 percent below and ten percent above the DPFI formula fare.

Beginning in the spring of 1977, the Board took a number of procedural steps to give carriers greater discretion to determine the routes they serve. The Board began to consider carrier fare proposals in making route awards and to award route authority to more than one carrier in a market. The following year the Board proposed awarding route authority without subjecting carriers to long and costly route proceedings. Moreover, carriers that received such authority were not required to use it.

The airline industry prospered in 1978. Despite an increasing rate of inflation in the economy, airfares (in current dollars) declined for the first time since 1966, and air traffic (in revenue passenger-miles) expanded at a faster annual rate than it had in more than ten years. In addition, carrier profits also increased significantly (Figure 1). While public support for the deregulation of the airline industry grew, most airlines opposed it. They asserted that deregulation would lead to destabilizing, destructive competition and ultimately to widespread market power shared by a handful of airlines.

Amid the positive developments in the industry, Congress enacted the Airline Deregulation Act (ADA) in October 1978. The ADA ended the Board's authority over routes in December 1981 and its authority over fares in January 1983. In the interim it made significant changes in the Board's regulatory authority. It legislated a fare flexibility policy that was similar to the one the Board had already adopted. The ADA shifted the burden of proof in route cases, thereby essentially ratifying the more liberal route award procedures that the Board had proposed only a few months before. At the time this policy was the subject of a lawsuit in a federal court of appeals. The ADA gave air carriers almost complete freedom to stop service on a route, although in cities served by one or two carriers, ninety days' notice of a service suspension decision was required. The ADA also established an Essential Service Air Program to replace the existing small community subsidy program. Finally, the ADA abolished the CAB effective at the end of 1984 and transferred, primarily to the Department of Transportation, the CAB's continuing responsibilities for antitrust and international regulatory matters.[17]

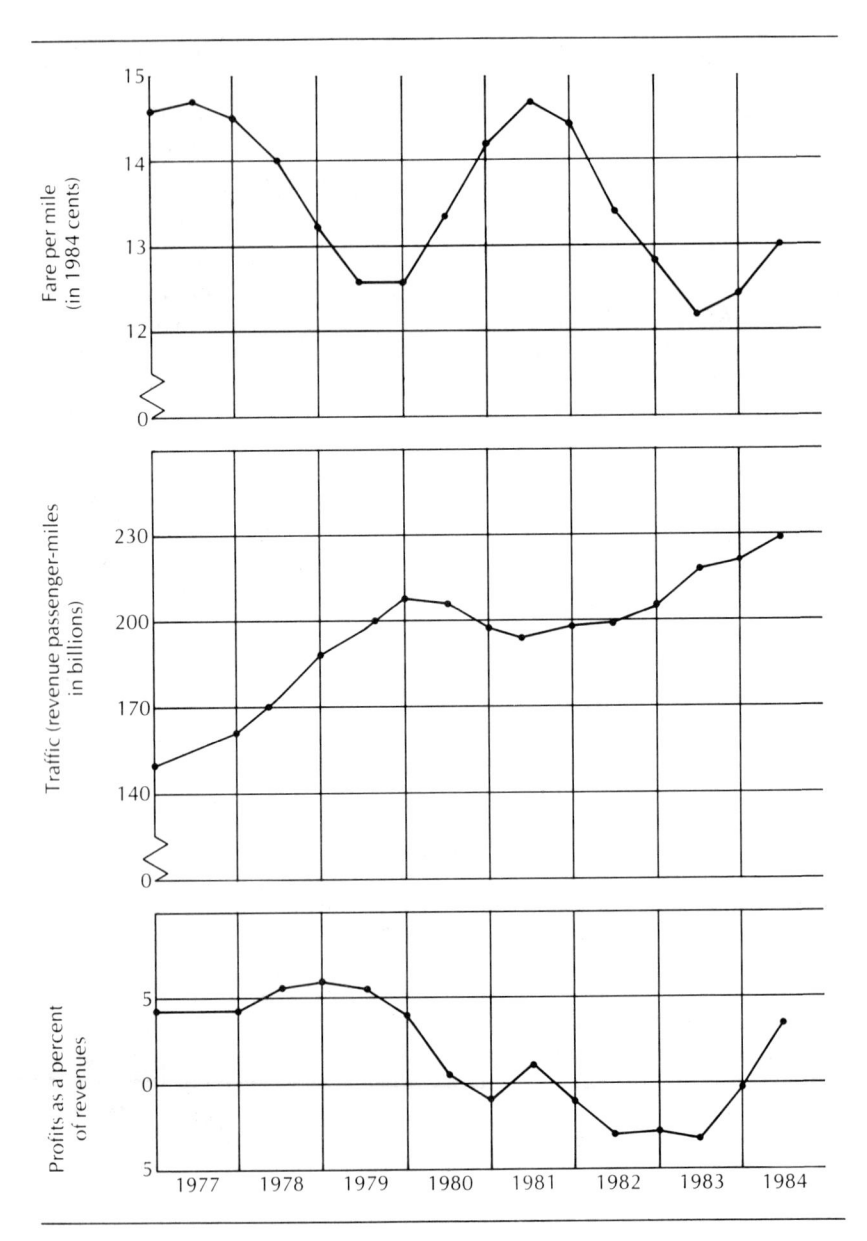

Figure 1. Domestic Yields, Traffic, and Operating Profit Margins for Twelve Months Ending December 1976 Through June 1984

THE AIRLINE DEREGULATION ACT AND AN OVERVIEW OF ITS EFFECTS

Implementing the ADA

The years following the passage of the ADA have been tumultuous. In the spring of 1979 world oil prices skyrocketed, driving up airline operating costs. In 1978 jet fuel was 40 cents a gallon and constituted less than 20 percent of airline operating costs. By the fall of 1982 the price of jet fuel had increased by more than 150 percent and was the primary force behind a more than 50 percent increase in the average airline operating costs. The rapid increase in the price of oil undoubtedly contributed to a decline in growth of the economy, which by early 1980 had slipped into a recession.

The Board adjusted its fare ceilings every two months so that carriers could increase fares to keep pace with rising costs. However, air travel is sensitive to price as well as economic growth, and the combination of higher fares and the recession led to a decline in traffic. Profits quickly followed suit (Figure 1). Although the zones of flexibility were designed to give carriers some pricing discretion, carriers were almost universally setting their coach fares at the ceiling rate. Coupled with the wide availability of discount fares, the Board concluded that additional pricing flexibility was warranted. Thus in May 1980 the Board increased its fare ceilings in most markets by roughly 25 percent. In short-haul markets, where the Board held fares below cost, the Board granted even greater flexibility. This was essentially the only transition policy the Board adopted before its regulatory authority over fares lapsed in 1983. Although in a number of markets some fares were at the ceiling during this transition, for the most part the Board's regulation of airfares ended in May 1980.

The end to route regulation came even sooner. The ADA included two provisions designed to provide a three-year transition to open entry.[18] However, by shifting the burden of proof in route cases from the potential entrant to the incumbent, the ADA allowed the Board to implement the liberal route award policy it had proposed. Under this policy a carrier was usually able to begin serving a route within sixty days of its application for authority. Coupled with the liberal provisions for exiting a route, this policy afforded carriers the freedom to reshape their route networks within a few months after enactment of the ADA.

The more liberal market entry proceedings also enabled new carriers to begin scheduled interstate service with jet equipment. The former intrastate carriers in California and Texas instituted service in neighboring states, and Air Florida began offering service between the Northeast and Florida. World and Capitol, which were restricted to providing charter service under regulation, began scheduled transcontinental service.

In addition, entirely new carriers were formed: the first was Midway Airlines.[19] It was followed in 1980 by New York Air (of which two-thirds of the stock was owned by Texas International, a local service carrier) and in 1981 by People Express. More than a dozen other newly formed jet carriers followed. These carriers operated at substantially lower costs than the formerly regulated carriers, principally because of lower labor costs. Regulation allowed employees to secure relatively generous compensation from the airlines.

Trends in the Deregulated Industry

The introduction of meaningful competition in the airline industry, coupled with rapid cost increases and two recessions in quick succession (in 1980 and again in 1981–1982), led to significant financial difficulties for many carriers and a number of bankruptcies. Financial distress was not unknown in the industry, yet no regulated line had ever gone bankrupt. By acquiring a distressed firm a carrier secured valuable operating rights without going through long, cumbersome, and uncertain Board proceedings. Throughout its history, the CAB presided over a number of such mergers.[20]

If firms are assured that they will not be permitted to fail, their incentives to reduce costs are substantially reduced. It was significant, therefore, that the government did nothing to prevent Braniff Airlines, a profitable trunk carrier during regulation, from declaring bankruptcy and ceasing operations in the spring of 1982. Another trunk, Continental Airlines, filed for bankruptcy in the fall of 1983. Continental, however, continued to operate and by the end of 1984 was profitably providing more service than it had prior to filing for bankruptcy. In declaring bankruptcy Continental abrogated its labor contracts and rehired many of its former employees at lower wages and with more flexible work rules. Over a weekend, Continental literally transformed itself into a low-cost carrier. Continental's experience highlights the increasing importance of paring costs to become a successful competitor in the deregulated industry. Braniff also resumed operations in 1984. Unlike Continental, however, the "new" Braniff was in fact a new carrier, with ownership and management from the "old" Braniff that had ceased operating two years earlier. In addition to the two former trunk carriers, a number of new entrants and Air Florida, a former intrastate carrier, went bankrupt.

The Airline Deregulation Act

Competition has also changed the structure of the industry. The share of the former trunk airlines, whose route authorities were grandfathered when the CAB was created, still had nearly 90 percent of the domestic traffic (measured in revenue passenger-miles) forty years later. By 1984 their share had fallen to less than 75 percent (Table 1).[21] Meanwhile the share of the former local carriers account-

Table 1. Shares of Scheduled Domestic Passenger Service

	12 Months Ending September 1978		12 Months Ending June 1984	
	Market Share	Profit Margin	Market Share	Profit Margin
Former trunks				
United	19.6	7.9	18.7	8.7
American	13.9	3.9	13.7	9.2
Eastern	12.1	3.6	11.1	0.8
Delta	11.6	10.5	10.6	4.4
Trans World	9.2	1.7	6.2	−5.7
Continental[a]	5.2	7.6	3.2	−7.4
Western	4.7	7.3	3.7	−0.9
Pan American[a]	4.7	−0.1	2.7	−38.9
Northwest	4.6	10.9	4.1	4.6
Braniff	3.7	7.3	—	—
Total	89.3	5.5	74.0	3.2
Former local service carriers				
USAir	2.1	8.0	3.4	11.7
Republic[a]	2.6	7.7	3.7	6.2
Frontier	1.2	7.3	1.9	−1.1
Ozark	0.8	9.6	1.1	3.6
Piedmont	0.7	5.5	2.5	11.2
Total	7.4	7.6	12.6	9.2
Others				
Intrastates	2.4		4.0	
Charters	—		1.2	
New jet carriers	—		6.7	
Regionals	1.0		1.5	
Totals	3.4		13.4	

Source: CAB Form 41 and various company reports.

[a]The 1978 figures include data for firms acquired between 1978 and 1984 as follows: Continental — Texas Air; Pan American — National; Republic — North Central, Southern, Hughes Air West.

ed for more than 12 percent of domestic traffic in 1984, an increase of 70 percent over their share before deregulation. The new entrants, which include former charter and intrastate carriers in addition to the new carriers, expanded to 12 percent of industry traffic in 1984 from the 2.4 percent intrastate share in 1978.

Although none of the ten former trunk carriers had as large a share of traffic in 1984 as it had in 1978, the smaller trunks were the most adversely affected. In fact, only one of the smaller six former trunk carriers, Northwest, actually had an increase in domestic traffic between 1978 and 1984,[22] and as a group, their share of traffic declined by nearly 40 percent to less than 20 percent. In addition, the two largest carriers were the only former trunks whose profit margins were larger in 1984 than in 1978.[23] However, two of the five local service carriers had even higher profit margins, and as a group, the former local carriers' profitability was higher than it was in 1978.

At the time the ADA was passed, most of the trunks were not prepared to compete in the deregulated environment. Not only did they have high labor costs but their fleets consisted primarily of large aircraft that could not be easily redeployed in response to market developments. For example, a third of their capacity consisted of wide-bodied aircraft, like the B-747 and the DC-10, which could only be efficiently used in dense long-haul markets. These markets largely consist of discretionary travelers whose demand for air travel was most adversely affected by the recession. Also, 25 percent of their capacity consisted of fuel-inefficient aircraft that became uneconomical as the price of fuel increased.[24] Finally, the dense markets they served under regulation attracted a significant amount of entry. In contrast, the local service carriers had fleets of smaller aircraft that were better suited for the competitive environment. The local service carriers moved quickly to develop the hub-and-spoke route networks that have increased the convenience of air travel for many passengers.

The decline in industry concentration is reflected in an increase in the number of carriers providing nonstop service between city-pairs. Because efficient aircraft are large relative to the number of passengers traveling between most cities, most airline markets remain relatively concentrated. While there was a 30 percent increase in the average number of carriers providing nonstop service in a market since July 1978, the average number of carriers was only 1.8 in July 1983.[25] Even between major cities the average number of carriers providing nonstop service in 1983 was less than three. However, competition in a market also is generated by carriers that provide service with an intermediate stop, sometimes with a change of planes. For example, although only one carrier offered nonstop service between

New York and San Diego in 1984, there were six others that offered one-stop service. This source of increased competition is directly attributable to carrier route realignments in the deregulated environment. Similarly, many markets without nonstop service are served via an intermediate stop by several carriers.

Increased competition has led to fare moderation. Between 1976 and June 1984 the average airfare increased by 59.3 percent in contrast to an 80 percent increase in the consumer price index. (Largely because fuel constitutes a substantial share of airline costs, the prices of the inputs required to produce airline services went up by a greater amount than the consumer price index.) At the same time air traffic increased by 53 percent, an average annual increase of 5.8 percent. Airfares have fluctuated more cyclically than under regulation. For example, airfares fell during the recession of 1982 and then increased during the recovery. Also, carriers are now more likely to offer lower fares during off-peak periods. Despite the moderation in average fares, not all markets have had the same experience. Most notably, fares in short-haul markets have risen relative to fares in long-haul markets.

THE GROWTH OF HUB-AND-SPOKE ROUTE NETWORKS

There can be little doubt that the airline industry, in the absence of government control over carriers routes and rates, has become more competitive and, as a result, more efficient. Moreover, the carriers have employed a wide variety of strategies in their attempt to seize the opportunities created by the new environment. Many of their decisions concerning pricing, route design, and marketing were not anticipated when the merits of deregulation were being debated. Yet the effects of these decisions have fundamentally changed the industry.

By its very nature economic regulation substitutes the judgment of the regulator for the judgment of the marketplace. By a process of trial and error the market guides firms to provide goods and services efficiently. Even the most prescient management cannot fully anticipate the impact of its strategic decisions. If a strategem is successful, other firms will follow the innovator's lead. Conversely, if a strategem is not successful, it will eventually be abandoned. The regulator is not subject to any such test; regulatory policies are enforced by the government and consequently tend to persist. No matter how carefully the regulator analyzes the hypothesized effects of a proposed decision, it cannot be assured of the consequences.

While regulating the industry, the CAB had a clear perspective on how the route networks should be structured. Trunks provided service between major cities. These routes were, for the most part, relatively long and heavily traveled. In contrast, the local service carriers were to provide service within the various regions of the country. Although this route design seemed reasonable, developments in the market quickly showed that it did not represent an efficient use of the industry's resources.

There are roughly 50,000 city-pairs between which passengers travel within the United States. Because of economies of scale in aircraft, only 2,000 or so of these markets have nonstop service. In most markets passengers have to make an intermediate stop and frequently change planes en route to their ultimate destinations. Such routings are most common for passengers traveling to and from small and midsize cities where there is inadequate traffic to justify nonstop service to many destinations. For example, passengers from Syracuse, New York, have nonstop service to many of the major cities in the Northeast but not to the South or the West. Smaller cities, like Erie, Pennsylvania, have nonstop service to only one or two major cities.

Under regulation, passengers from medium and small communities were often served by a local service carrier. A passenger from Syracuse could fly to Pittsburgh or Chicago and proceed to Los Angeles on a trunk airline. Since the flights to and from the intermediate point were not operated by the same airline, schedules were not always well coordinated and such journeys could entail long layovers. Moreover, passengers often had to face long walks between terminals at large airports, and there was greater risk that baggage transferred between airlines would be lost. Not having to change airlines reduces difficulties with connecting service.

With deregulation the local service carriers began to expand their operations by offering longer haul service from their regional hubs. For example, USAir's operations were centered at Pittsburgh. Under deregulation USAir began serving cities such as Phoenix, Houston, and Fort Lauderdale, which were well beyond the scope of its traditional service area. Other local service carriers followed similar strategies.[26]

These new services proved to be profitable. In the first place, passengers preferred single carrier service. The local service carriers were also aided by the equipment they inherited from the regulated regime. Because they served many thin short-haul markets, they operated smaller aircraft than the trunks. Two-engine jet equipment such as the DC-9 and the B-737 were the predominant aircraft in their fleet. Larger aircraft generally have lower average operating costs. However, on stage lengths up to about 1,000 miles, two-engine aircrafts do not have significantly higher average cost per available seat-mile than the three-engine B-727, which was the mainstay of the trunks' fleet.[27] Smaller aircraft require two instead of three pilots, and they also are more fuel efficient. In addition, during the economic downturns of the 1980s the smaller size of these aircraft allowed the carriers to tailor their capacity to market demand. Thus the local service carriers were well positioned to expand into traditional trunk routes.

Ironically, several of the local service carriers feared that they would not be able to operate successfully under deregulation. USAir, then Allegheny, testified at the Senate hearings in 1975 that it would not be able to compete effectively against the larger trunks with their more developed route systems. In fact, USAir has been one of the most successful carriers in the deregulated era, and a critical factor in their success has been the development of its Pittsburgh hub.

The local service carriers did not originate the concept of the hub-and-spoke route network; United and Delta, both trunk airlines, had hubs at Chicago and Atlanta, respectively, under regulation. United, however, began dropping many of its shorter haul "feeder" routes soon after the ADA was enacted. The initial success of the local service carriers encouraged the trunks to follow their lead, and they began developing hub-and-spoke operations at major airports throughout the country. In some cases, like American at Dallas–Fort Worth, this involved a major redeployment of assets. Between 1978 and 1984 American more than doubled the number of flights it offered at that airport — to more than 300 a day.[28] As many as forty of American's flights are scheduled to arrive and then depart at the Dallas airport within a relatively short period of time in order to provide ample connecting possibilities. All of the formerly regulated carriers have centered their operations around at least one hub airport. United, essentially reversing its earlier decision, expanded and revamped its hub operations at Chicago as well as Denver. As a consequence, a high proportion of a carrier's flights now originate or terminate at an airport where it operates a hub. The trunks also began to acquire fleets of two-engine equipment to better service the shorter haul routes.

These route alignments have dramatically changed the carriers serving particular routes. For example, United Airlines provided nonstop service in only 5 percent fewer city-pairs in July 1983 than it did in 1978. However, less than 40 percent of the city-pairs it served in 1978 were still served by it in 1983. United's experience was fairly typical.[29]

The importance of connecting traffic coupled with passenger preference for single carrier service makes a hub-and-spoke network virtually a competitive necessity. A large fraction of the passengers have a destination or an origin other than the cities between which the nonstop flight operates. For example, on a route such as Pittsburgh-to-Chicago over 60 percent of the passengers make a connection at Pittsburgh or Chicago. Since these passengers prefer single carrier service, a carrier relying only on traffic between Pittsburgh and Chicago would have difficulty in sustaining its operation in that market. Over half the passengers traveling on that route would rarely consider using the services of an airline if it did not provide connecting service to other points. While many markets have small proportions of continuing passengers, few routes have negligible connecting traffic.[30]

Most major cities have at least one, and in a few cases as many as three, carriers operating a hub at their airport. The residents of these cities frequently have direct flights to a wide variety of destinations. People traveling to or from small- and medium-size communities generally have flights to one or more of these hubs where they can receive convenient connecting service to their ultimate destination.

The growth of hub-and-spoke operations led to a large increase in the number of departures at large cities. Also, a larger proportion of flights from small communities are destined for large and medium cities; hence small community residents are able to take advantage of an increasing array of connecting services. Not surprisingly, the percentage of passengers receiving single carrier service has increased sharply. For example, in the second quarter of 1978, before the ADA was enacted, 40 percent of passengers that changed planes en route to their ultimate destinations changed airlines; by 1983 this figure had been reduced to less than 15 percent. At the same time the percentage of passengers receiving single plane service increased. In fact, the 1,947 markets receiving nonstop air service in 1983 were 5 percent greater than the number that received such service in 1978.[31]

Although residents of small communities have benefited from the growth of hub-and-spoke route systems, the jet service at many smaller towns has declined significantly. Seventeen percent fewer small community markets had jet service in 1983 than in 1978. This was expected because jets are generally not economical to operate in thin short-haul markets. In fact, in most respects service has improved because of the change in equipment. On short routes jets are not significantly faster than turbo-prop equipment, and because commuter aircraft is smaller, the number of flights has increased in many of these markets. A larger share of the flights from small communities is now destined for large and medium hubs where there is ample service to a wide variety of destinations. Markets between small and large communities have experienced a greater percentage increase in weekly flights than have markets between large cities. And many of the commuter airlines have entered into interline agreements with jet carriers to coordinate schedules and provide other attributes of single carrier service to passengers of commuter airlines. Although the increased reliance on commuter aircraft has led to a significant improvement in service quality, many residents of small communities consider the loss of jet service to be one of the major adverse effects of deregulation.

THE NEW ENTRANTS AND THE TREND TO LOWER COSTS

Labor Costs under Regulation

The CAB's policies led to the relatively high labor costs of the formerly regulated carriers. During the 1960s airline operating costs decreased more than regulated fares declined, and this disparity, as was noted earlier, encouraged various forms of nonprice competition. The combination of technological change and regulatory inertia also enabled labor to capture a significant share of the efficiency gains from the new technologies.[32]

The industry's labor agreements with the pilots illustrate these developments. The jets were larger and faster than the turbo-props they replaced; as a result, the number of passenger-miles per pilot hour, or pilot productivity, increased dramatically. Pilots negotiated contracts in which they were not only paid more for flying the jet aircraft but were also required to fly fewer hours per month. By the late 1970s the average number of hours per month that pilots flew declined to less than fifty from more than sixty in the early 1970s. Moreover, the wage rates and working conditions of pilots employed by regulated carriers were vastly more favorable than those offered by the military or elsewhere in the private sector.

The pilots were not the only labor group that benefited from regulation; in a number of other occupations, airline employees had higher wage rates than employees in other industries. It required half as many employees to provide a given amount of a service in 1970 than in 1960. Yet over the same period labor's share of the trunk's total operating expenses remained at 45 percent.

Several of the intrastate carriers, whose labor contracts were less affected by the CAB's regulatory policies, had significantly lower costs than the formerly regulated carriers. For example, Southwest's cost of operating a Boeing 737 on a 200-mile route was estimated to be one-third less than Piedmont's cost. Its cost advantage over United was even greater.[33]

The New Entrants' Strategies

The experience of Southwest (in Texas) and PSA (in California) demonstrated that when low costs were translated into low fares, air traffic increased dramatically. Consequently, with the passage of the ADA, they, along with the other intrastate carriers and former charter carriers, introduced low-fare service into the interstate markets that they had been prevented from serving. In addition, a host of totally new carriers, all with costs substantially below those of the formerly regulated carriers, began entering the industry. Like the former intrastate carriers, these new entrants stressed no-frill service and offered fares that were well below those that prevailed prior to their entry.

The new entrants to interstate markets tended to serve markets where perceived demand was most price elastic, that is, where a given percentage reduction in fares would produce the greatest increase in traffic. These were generally believed to be short-haul markets, where low fares encouraged people who normally traveled by surface modes to fly instead, and tourist markets, where low fares were most apt to stimulate increased travel. In addition, they frequently used underutilized airports in major cities so they could limit competition with the established carriers.

Initially, the incumbent carriers allowed the new entrants to price below their fares. However, when consumers demonstrated little brand loyalty and flocked to the lower priced carriers, the incumbents began matching them.

With no price difference, passengers tended to select the established carrier with a proven service record. If the reduced price did not substantially increase traffic in the market, the new entrant could not fill sufficient seats to earn a profit. In more price-elastic markets an incumbent had to increase capacity to prevent successful entry. At the incumbent's higher costs, adding capacity at the reduced fare was expensive. Nevertheless, incumbents were able to prevent the successful entry by low-cost rivals in a number of cases. For example, Air Florida introduced and aggressively expanded low-priced service between the Northeast and Florida. Though these operations were initially successful, the incumbents eventually reacted, which ultimately forced Air Florida to retrench its operations and eventually to declare bankruptcy. In the face of the incumbents' aggressive response to low prices, some new entrants elected to use their cost advantage to provide increased leg room and better food service. In fact, both New York Air and Midway Airlines, the first of the newly formed carriers, abandoned their low-frill strategies in 1982 and increased on-board amenities along with their fares.

Most of the dozen or more carriers that began interstate air service after enactment of the ADA have not been able to achieve consistent profitability, and several of them have been forced to cease operations (Table 2). Many of these carriers are still developing their route systems and can be considered start-up operations. A number of them will undoubtedly become profitable; People Express and Southwest have already been notable successes.

Southwest prospered by extending its successful low-fare, high-frequency service outside of Texas. People Express also offers high-frequency, low-fare service and has grown rapidly. By the end of 1984 it was providing more service than Western Airlines, a former trunk carrier. The effect of such operations can be seen by comparing the performance of markets entered by People Express and Southwest with otherwise similar markets (Table 3). The People Express and Southwest markets enjoyed substantial fare reductions and realized marked increases in passenger traffic, while in the control markets fares increased dramatically and traffic, in most cases, declined.

Like many of the other new entrant carriers, People Express centered its operation at an underutilized airport, in its case Newark, New Jersey. It took no-frills service to a new extreme by charging for normally complimentary beverages such as coffee and soft drinks. They even charged passengers for checking their baggage. Initially, like Southwest in Texas, People Express concentrated on serving relatively short-haul markets where low fares would encourage passengers to travel by air instead of surface transportation. They also served several tourist points in Florida. In 1984 they began serving Chicago, Minneapolis, Houston, Los Angeles, and San Francisco. Newark has become a significant hub where passengers along the East Coast can make connections to travel throughout the country. For example, when People Express entered the Newark-Chicago market they offered Washington, D.C.–Chicago passengers willing to make a connection at Newark a significant fare reduction. As a result, carriers providing nonstop service between Washington and Chicago began making a limited number of seats available at comparable fares.

Table 2. New Entrant Airlines to Interstate Scheduled Jet Service

			12 Months Ending June 1984	
Type of Carrier	Inauguration of Service	Suspension of Service	Operating Profit Margin	Revenue Passenger-Miles (Millions)
New jet carriers				
Midway	1979	—	−8.4	720.7
New York Air	1980	—	4.6	772.1
People Express	1981	—	5.9	4,547.8
Muse	1981	—	4.6	811.4
Jet America	1982	—	12.5	690.7
Pacific Express	1982	1984	—	—
Northeastern	1982	1984	−3.6	1,125.9
Pacific East	1982	1984	—	—
American International	1982	1984	−41.5	502.3
Hawaii Express	1982	1983	—	—
Air One	1983	1984	−67.1	204.2
Sunworld	1983	—	−8.8	143.9
America West	1983	—	−17.2	699.9
Frontier Horizon	1984	—	−7.8	266.2
Florida Express	1984	—	−16.0	117.9
Air Atlanta	1984	—	−88.9	55.2
Braniff (New)	1984	—	−67.9	647.6
Former intrastate carriers				
Air Cal	1979	—	9.6	1,439.9
Air Florida	1979	1984	−2.6	1,165.7
PSA	1979	—	1.8	3,132.8
Southwest	1979	—	13.3	4,394.0
Former charters				
Capitol	1979	1984	−5.5	1,109
World	1979	—	−6.4	2,351

The Response of the Formerly Regulated Carriers

Although low costs are not sufficient to assure success, they have certainly been critical to the rapid growth of the new entrants. In the newly competitive environment the established carriers have had

Table 3. Performance of Markets Entered by People Express or Southwest with Otherwise Similar Markets (First Quarter 1980 and 1984)

Market	Distance	1980 Passengers	1980 Fare	Percentage Change in Fare	Percentage Change in Passengers
New York–Buffalo[a]	282	100,832	$48	−25%	179%
Boston-Philadelphia	281	100,590	$52	53%	2%
New York–Norfolk[a]	284	51,800	$48	−30%	264%
Chicago-Columbus	284	50,460	$48	103%	12%
Dallas–Little Rock[b]	303	23,650	$59	−17%	123%
Atlanta-Mobile	303	17,340	$56	56%	−8%
Albuquerque-Phoenix[b]	329	23,550	$61	−27%	160%
Columbus–Washington, D.C.	322	25,420	$53	96%	−18%
El Paso–Phoenix[b]	346	11,110	$74	−41%	178%
St. Louis–Tulsa	351	12,100	$60	83%	−20%
Houston-Tulsa[b]	453	38,930	$74	−23%	83%
Philadelphia-Detroit	453	40,880	$65	53%	−7%

Source: Origin and Destination Survey.
[a]Market entered by People Express; data include all New York City metropolitan airports.
[b]Market entered by Southwest.

some success in renegotiating their labor agreements. Restrictive work rules have been relaxed, a greater number of part-time workers are now employed, and some wage rates have declined. In return for these changes the employees at a number of carriers have been granted significant equity positions in their companies. In the fall of 1983 the employees of Eastern Airlines were granted nearly 25 percent of the outstanding shares of the company. Profit-sharing has become an important part of many compensation packages.

Another important change in the labor agreements has been the institution of two-tiered wage structures, in which new employees are paid substantially less than existing employees. For example, captains of American Airlines 727-200s, the predominant aircraft in its fleet, can receive a maximum monthly salary of $9,057; the maximum rate for someone hired after November 1, 1983, is one-half as much.[34]

As a result, wages paid by the formerly regulated carriers have only kept pace with inflation since deregulation. An increasing fraction of the formerly regulated carriers' employees have lower pay scales, assuring that labor costs will continue to moderate. At the same time employee productivity, especially since the end of 1981, has increased dramatically. Since 1981 available ton-miles[35] per employee of the major carriers (the former trunks plus the two largest local service carriers) has increased at an average annual rate of 6.4 percent (Figure 2). Nevertheless, the new entrants' cost of operations remains substantially lower than the formerly regulated carriers. People Express, for example, had an average cost of roughly 5.25 cents per available seat-mile in 1983, which was almost 40 percent lower than the average cost of the five formerly regulated carriers with the most comparable stage lengths. Moreover, the average employee productivity for Southwest and People Express is more than three times greater than for the average of the major carriers.[36] These data suggest that the new entrants will have a cost advantage for some time to come.

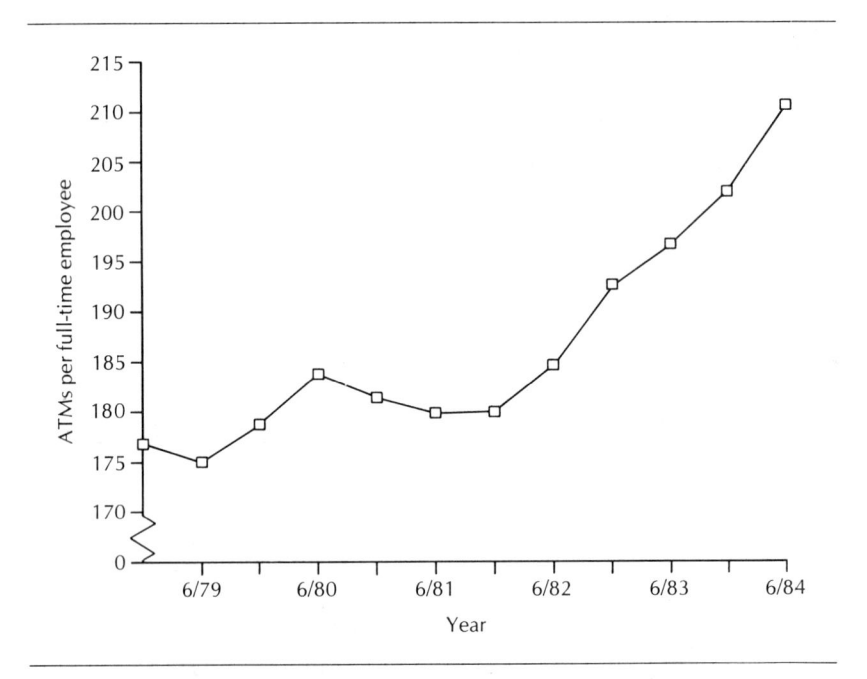

Figure 2. System Majors Employee Productivity (12 Months Ended)

PRICING POLICIES IN THE DEREGULATED INDUSTRY

Relationship of Fares among Markets

Given the growth of low-cost carriers and the improved efficiency of the industry, airfares undoubtedly have been lower than they would have been had regulation continued. However, not all markets have shared equally in the relatively lower fares. In particular, fares in thin markets are now generally higher than fares in dense markets. Moreover, fares in short-haul markets tended to be above levels prescribed by the CAB, while fares in longer haul markets tend to be below those levels. This is demonstrated in Table 4, which shows fares as a percentage of the Board's cost-adjusted DPFI formula for nearly 1,000 markets grouped by distance and density.[37] Since the Board set fares in short-haul and thin markets below what it believed to be the cost of service, this change in the relationship of fares among markets was expected. Moreover, the CAB apparently underestimated the cost of serving thin short-haul markets.

The airline's cost of an extra passenger in an otherwise empty seat will be little more than a meal and a travel agents' commission. The cost of the aircraft, the crew, landing fees, and maintenance are independent of the number of people on the flight; even the amount of fuel consumed is scarcely affected by an increased number of passengers. Prior to the DPFI, if nonprice competition decreased load factors, the resulting decline in profits was justification for fare increases. In the DPFI the CAB decided to establish fares on the assumption that carriers' load factors were equal to 55 percent, and a decrease in load factors was no longer a basis for an increase in fares.

Table 4. Fares as a Percent of DPFI Fare Formula for Year Ending June 1983

Market Distance (Miles)	Market Size (O&D Passengers Per Day)			
	10–50	51–200	201–500	501+
1–400	114	112	95	71
401–1,500	110	97	87	80
1501+	[a]	75	65	60

Source: Origin and Destination Survey. Includes markets with nonstop flights.
[a] Too few markets to provide reliable comparison.

The assumption that all markets should have the same load factor is not justified. For example, air carriers could minimize the average cost, as well as the price of air service, by operating large aircraft at very high load factors. However, in most markets such service would not be responsive to consumer demands. The fewer the number of flights in the market the less likely there will be a flight at or near a passenger's desired departure time. In addition, the higher the load factor the greater the likelihood that passengers will not get reservations on preferred flights.[38] The load factor that would be optimal for passengers depends in large part on the market's characteristics.

The principal advantage of air travel is that it saves time; thus the time sensitivity of passengers is a critical factor affecting a market's optimal load factor. Between most city-pairs the out-of-pocket cost of driving is less than the airfare. A consumer would elect to travel by air if the value of the time saved by flying exceeded the added expense. In short-haul markets, where surface transportation is a viable option for many, carriers expect to operate their aircraft at load factors substantially below those achieved in other markets. Since passengers in short-haul markets tend to place a premium on time, they prefer convenient high-cost service. Dense markets, however, can be expected to have higher load factors. Many passengers in largely tourist markets would gladly exchange frequent flights for low fares, and large aircraft with high load factors could be expected in these markets.

This is precisely what is observed: load factors increase with respect to distance and density in the deregulated industry. In the short-haul markets the average load factor was forty-six for the year ending June 1983, while in the densest long-haul markets the average load factor was sixty-seven.[39] In dense long-haul markets dominated by tourists the load factor was also sixty-seven, but the average aircraft size was more than 25 percent larger than in other dense long-haul markets. By not fully considering the nature of demand for air transportation the CAB had seriously understated the differences in costs among markets. This is undoubtedly an important factor in explaining the difference between the relationship among fares that now prevails from that which the CAB had prescribed.

The Importance of Discount Fares

The low cost of serving an additional passenger on a flight explains another important feature of airlines' pricing policies in the deregulated industry: airlines have substantial incentives to increase the number of passengers on a flight. One way to do this is by reducing the fare. However an across-the-board reduction in fares may lead to a reduction in revenues if the percentage increase in traffic is less than the percentage decrease in the fare. That is, price reductions will not be profitable if demand is price inelastic.[40] In any case it may be more profitable to reduce fares only for a subset of passengers. American Airlines' original Super Saver fares, for example, offered fare reductions only for passengers who could meet both an advance-purchase and a minimum-stay requirement. These restrictions were designed to distinguish business travelers — who frequently cannot make travel plans well in advance of their departure and generally do not spend very much time at their destination — from discretionary travelers, whose demand is more price elastic.

The use of restricted discount fares did not begin with American's Super Saver fares; throughout its history the CAB allowed carriers to introduce a wide variety of discount fares. What distinguished American's proposal was that it controlled the number of passengers traveling on discount fares on each flight. By limiting the number of seats available at the discounted fares, an airline reduces the probability that a passenger willing to pay the full coach fare cannot get a seat on a preferred flight. For example, demand for air transportation is generally the greatest during the late afternoon and evening. During those periods the percentage of seats available to passengers traveling on discount fares will typically be reduced.

The use of these capacity-controlled discount fares means that there are wide differences in average fares among flights. The CAB had traditionally limited the use of peak-load pricing. This prohibition promoted a high variation in load factors among flights, because demand for air travel varies considerably by day of the week as well as by time of day. By varying the proportion of discount passengers on each flight as well as the fare levels, airlines have presumably been able to reduce this load factor disparity. Also, peak-load pricing allows carriers to provide a given level of service with a smaller stock of aircraft, reducing average costs.

Although a passenger traveling at the higher fare may sit next to a passenger paying a lower fare, the higher fare passenger receives better service by having had greater flexibility to select his flight. It is the time-sensitive traveler who is primarily responsible for the frequent flights that increase the cost of service in a market. To a considerable extent the differences in passenger fares are cost-related.[41]

The use of minimum-stay and advance-purchase restrictions is an imperfect method for distinguishing between time-sensitive and discretionary passengers. There are undoubtedly a substantial number of consumers who would travel at the lower but not at the higher fare and cannot meet the restrictions that are attached to the lower fare. If an airline attracts a small share of the passengers paying the higher fare, it might benefit from reducing or even removing the restrictions on the discount fare. The loss in revenue from the passengers who would have paid the higher fare can be more than offset by the increased number of passengers that will fly on an unrestricted low fare. For example, new entrants, many of whom provide fewer amenities, do not use restricted discount fares as extensively as the formerly regulated carriers. Rather they often charge the same fare for all passengers that fly on a given flight. Most, however, offer lower off-peak fares for flights after 7:00 P.M. and on weekends. Similarly, when Continental resumed service after declaring bankruptcy, it used only unrestricted fares.

THE COMPETITIVE ENVIRONMENT

Despite the influx of new carriers and the expansion of many of the incumbents, deregulated airline markets remain relatively concentrated. Advocates of deregulation argued that entry and the threat of entry limit the ability of carriers, even in concentrated markets, to charge prices substantially above the cost of service. The large amount of entry occurring in the deregulated industry would seem to support these claims. Yet as we have demonstrated, markets with similar characteristics in the first quarter of 1980 had dramatically different fares four years later if People Express or Southwest had entered one of them. Moreover, statistical studies confirmed that, on average, markets served by new entrant carriers had fares that were about 25 percent less than fares in otherwise similar markets. These studies further indicated that after controlling for factors including market distance, density, and the presence of a new entrant, carriers in concentrated markets charge somewhat higher fares than carriers in less concentrated markets.[42]

However, the ability of carriers in concentrated markets to price above their costs is limited by several factors. First, as previously noted, surface transportation is a viable substitute for air service in short-haul markets. In longer haul markets one-stop or connecting services are frequently competitive with nonstop service. In fact, the difference in fares between relatively concentrated and relatively unconcentrated markets is estimated to be less than 10 percent. Nevertheless, it is possible that market power is partly responsible for the relatively higher fares that are observed on thin short-haul routes.

Connecting service is less viable as market distance declines. Also, thin routes are most efficiently served by a carrier operating a hub, which limits somewhat the number of potential entrants.

While airlines in certain markets have some pricing discretion, the distortions being caused in the marketplace are far fewer than those introduced by the CAB's regulatory process. For example, any attempt to control fares in thin short-haul routes will undoubtedly produce a significant and costly decline in service quality, and travelers in these markets are most likely to value high-quality service. Moreover, travelers to small communities have benefited most from the increased convenience of hub-and-spoke operations.

One frequent criticism of the CAB's regulatory policy was that it encouraged non-price competition by limiting price competition. But in the deregulated environment not only has price competition increased markedly but costly scheduling competition has declined. Most notably, the industry's average load factor in the deregulated environment has been greater than it has been since the mid-1960s. Even in the early 1980s, when the economy was quite sluggish, load factors were at historically high levels. In addition, the impact of market structure on load factor has been significantly reduced. After controlling for market distance and density, the number of airlines serving a market still had a negative impact on load factor; however, it is apparently much smaller than it had been under regulation.[43]

Deregulation has led to a number of other changes in the competitive environment. As previously noted, competition has encouraged carriers to reduce their costs, and much of this effort has been aimed at paring labor costs. Those formerly regulated carriers who have had the greatest difficulty adapting to the deregulated marketplace have generally been the most successful in securing concessions from employees. In the future there will be a wider disparity in labor costs among carriers than existed under regulation. The tendency for financially weaker carriers to secure more advantageous labor agreements will enable a number of them to adjust to the competitive environment.

In addition, frequent flyer programs, which award free trips to passengers regularly using a particular airline, are now quite common. These have been especially beneficial to carriers with extensive route networks. These programs are most attractive to passengers who travel a lot on business: the business traveler selects the flight and receives the travel bonus, but does not pay for the trip.

Because of the more complicated fare structure, passengers are increasingly relying on travel agents in the deregulated environment, and most airlines offer a variety of financial incentives to encourage agents to book passengers on their flights. Moreover, a number of carriers have developed computer reservation systems for travel agent use. These were designed, in part, to encourage agents to book passengers on flights of the carrier who marketed the reservation system. These systems proved to be so effective that the CAB, in its waning days, adopted a rule designed to limit the extent to which they influence travel agent recommendations to their clients.[44]

SUBSIDIZING SERVICE TO SMALL COMMUNITIES

Promotion of civil air transportation was one of the goals that Congress set for the CAB when it established the agency in 1938. This mandate was reflected in its regulatory policies toward small communities. For example, the Board deliberately employed a policy of subsidizing below-cost fares in thin short-haul markets with above-cost fares in other markets. Throughout its history the CAB also employed a variety of subsidy schemes to encourage service to small communities. Perhaps its most significant action in this regard was its decision to establish the local service carriers shortly after World War II.

The Board's subsidy programs did not work well. The decision to subsidize the fares in short-haul markets fostered higher costs in other markets. Its direct subsidy programs were geared more toward the profits of the carriers than toward the quality of service provided for small communities. A carrier's subsidy was based on the number of eligible cities it served and the number of flights it offered to these small communities.[45] Consequently, carriers faced incentives to provide frequent flights at not particularly convenient times. North Central, for example, offered five flights from Pellston, Michigan, in 1975: one at 1:16 A.M., one at 6:23 A.M., and the other three clustered between 12:53 and 2:35 P.M. By scheduling service to small communities at off-peak times, the carriers' equipment was available for more lucrative markets during peak periods.

Despite a variety of steps by the CAB to reduce the subsidy bill, it was paying the local service carriers at an annual rate of roughly $70 million in the mid-1970s. This was greater than its nominal payments in the early 1960s. Moreover, the number of communities receiving subsidized service was declining. Between 1965 and 1975 the Board allowed the regulated carriers to cease service to small communities at the rate of approximately one a month.[46] The fact that a regulated carrier ceased operations at a small community did not necessarily

Subsidizing Service to Small Communities

imply that the community lost all air service. In many cases a commuter carrier instituted service. Operators of aircraft of less than thirty seats were exempt from Board regulation.

As early as 1972 the CAB proposed that the existing system of subsidizing small communities be replaced by one in which subsidized service to a small community would be based on a low-bid contracting system. Under this proposal service levels and aircraft size would be specified according to the isolation of the community and the expected levels of traffic. Essentially, the Board would enter into a fixed price contract with the carrier that agreed to provide the required service at the lowest cost. The amount of subsidy would not vary if traffic levels or costs were higher or lower than forecast. This proposal was designed to assure that the air service to a community was geared to the community's air service requirements. It also provided carriers with strong incentives to provide efficient service. If the profitability of the route was higher than forecast, the subsidy was not reduced, nor was it increased if the airline made less profit than it anticipated.

The ADA gave carriers an unprecedented opportunity to enter and exit markets. Hence there was concern that there would be a substantial reduction in the number of communities receiving scheduled air service. Consequently, as part of the ADA, Congress established the Essential Air Service Program to maintain service to small communities included in carriers' certificates at the time the legislation was enacted.[47] This program was scheduled to last ten years, at which time government subsidy of air service to small communities would end.

The Essential Air Service program was, in most critical respects, the same as the CAB's 1972 proposal. However, in making carrier selections, the Board was required to consider the quality of the carriers' service on other routes and the community's preferences, in addition to the carriers' subsidy and service proposal.

In many ways the Essential Air Service Program has been a success. In 1978 the Board subsidized 392 points at a cost of over $75 million. In 1984, under the Essential Air Service Program, 145 communities received subsidies at a total cost of $36 million. At the same time the exodus of air service from small communities served by certificated carriers has been halted. These communities are now served by more flights, albeit with smaller aircraft. In addition, there has been a dramatic increase in service to large and medium hubs.

Although the Essential Air Service Program is a substantial improvement over the system it replaced, it is far from ideal. Nearly half of the communities that were subsidized in 1983 were less than 100 miles from a hub. Many passengers at these communities have found it less expensive, and in some cases more convenient, to drive to the nearby hub rather than to fly there. In other cases the community's economic base has shrunk considerably since air service was inaugurated. It seems imprudent to subsidize service to a community that by historical accident happened to be listed on a carrier's certificate in 1978. But fundamentally, there seems good reason to question the wisdom of a national policy to subsidize scheduled air service. The Essential Air Service Program is scheduled to expire in 1988. There are, however, residents in at least 145 communities who would like to see it continued.

AIRPORT ACCESS: A CONTINUING REGULATORY ISSUE

Even without the CAB's regulation of routes and rates there are still some potential limits to competition on the horizon. Perhaps the most notable is airport access. Certain airports currently do not have sufficient capacity to handle airline demand; they simply do not have the runway and control tower capacity to handle the number of operations the airlines want to schedule. Moreover, the number of such capacity-constrained airports is expected to grow.

In addition to its authority to oversee carrier routes and rates, the Board had substantial antitrust responsibilities, which included the authority to grant antitrust immunity for carrier agreements. This authority was central to the allocation of airport access at congested airports. These antitrust responsibilities were transferred to the Department of Transportation after the Board's demise.

In the late 1960s carriers began experiencing flight delays with increased frequency at Chicago O'Hare, Washington National, and the two New York City airports, LaGuardia and Kennedy.[48] In order to limit congestion the Federal Aviation Administration developed hourly quotas to restrict the number of landings and takeoffs permitted. The CAB granted the airlines antitrust immunity to decide among themselves how these landing and takeoff rights ("slots") were to be allocated. It required, however, that an agreement be adopted unanimously by the airlines who desired to operate at each airport. The Board prohibited carriers from discussing their operations at other airports at each airport's "scheduling committee."

In a tightly regulated environment the scheduling committee system worked fairly smoothly. Since the CAB was not particularly generous with new route authority, the scheduling committees did not have to accommodate much entry. Carriers undoubtedly found the arrangement profitable because it limited their ability to engage in schedule competition. Not surprisingly, with open entry the scheduling committees have had increasing difficulty in reaching agreements. In the first few years after deregulation incumbents with large shares of the slots were willing to cede some to the new entrants in order to preserve the arrangement. Eventually, however, such cooperation began to unravel under the strain of new entry. The simple fact is that slots at congested airports are valuable, and there is a limit to how much any carrier is willing to concede.

Obviously, at any given time an airport has some maximum capacity. Moreover, because of environmental concerns there may be a limit to how much any given airport can be expanded, and in any case airport expansion is quite expensive. Although, by using larger aircraft, lines can use air traffic control and ground facilities more efficiently, it is likely that existing facilities at an increasing number of airports will not accommodate demand at present zero slot prices.

Whatever its initial merits, the scheduling committee mechanism no longer appears to be a viable method of allocating access to congested airports. In a market economy, scarce resources are generally allocated on the basis of price: those who will pay the most for a resource get it. In the case of scarce landing and take off rights, the existing policy excludes the price mechanism and can thereby prevent an efficient operator from entering or expanding. In fact, a carrier can prevent entry by simply making unreasonable demands in order to deadlock the scheduling committee. If carriers had to pay the market value of the landing and takeoff rights that they were using, some airlines would undoubtedly decide that they could more profitably use their aircraft by serving less congested airports, allowing other carriers to enter or expand their services.

There is substantial opposition to the use of the price mechanism to allocate airport access. Many of the incumbents are understandably reluctant to pay for something that they currently receive for substantially less than its market price. However, any expansion of the existing mechanism to allocate scarce landing and takeoff rights would seem to be a major impediment to the development of an efficient and competitive industry. Carriers would be precluded from offering services that consumers desire, while efficient carriers would be prevented from growing.

CONCLUSION

Competition has flourished in the deregulated airline industry, and the industry has changed dramatically as a result. Overall, consumers are receiving better service at lower fares than they would have received if the industry were still regulated. Moreover, a number of trends seem certain to persist. Hub-and-spoke route systems will continue to dominate carrier route planning, and the industry should continue to record significant increases in productivity.

While the larger carriers have seen their shares of traffic decline, the two largest have become quite profitable. In fact, American is aggressively adding aircraft to its fleet and has announced an ambitious expansion plan. However, a variety of the smaller carriers are also quite profitable, and they too are expanding rapidly. Meanwhile the less successful carriers are trying to develop market niches as they strive to reduce their costs. Consumers seemed destined to reap continued benefits from this process.

At the same time that fare increases have been moderate and service quality has improved, the industry has demonstrated a remarkable safety record. The rate of fatal accidents on scheduled commercial flights by operators of jet equipment has remained quite low. While commuter air carriers continue to have higher rates of fatal accidents than operators of jet equipment, there has been a significant improvement since deregulation (Table 5). Any concerns about the adverse effect of competition on safety have proved unwarranted.

Although competition has proved a better regulator of the marketplace than government, it has not been perfect. For example, there are undoubtedly markets where carriers have been able to charge fares well in excess of costs, and some communities are receiving less service than perhaps they warrant. However, few industries are perfectly competitive and few products or services are priced precisely at costs and perfectly rationed. The relevant question is whether any regulatory policy would eliminate distortions without creating others that are even greater. In the case of the airline industry the answer would appear to be a resounding no.

Table 5. Fatalities in Scheduled Passenger Service (1975–1984)

| Year | Operators of Jet Equipment ||||| Commuter Air Carriers |||||
| | Fatal Accidents | Fatalities | Fatal Accident Rates || | Fatal Accidents | Fatalities | Fatal Accident Rates ||
			Per 100,000 Aircraft Hours	Per 100,000 Departures				Per 100,000 Aircraft Hours	Per 100,000 Departures
1975	2	122	0.037	0.043		12	28	1.28	0.82
1976	2	38	0.036	0.041		9	27	0.93	0.59
1977	1	70	0.017	0.020		9	32	0.78	0.52
1978	4	159	0.066	0.080		14	48	1.08	0.70
1979	2	347	0.030	0.037		16	67	1.37	0.85
1980	0	0	0.0	0.0		8	37	0.68	0.45
1981	0	0	0.0	0.0		9	34	0.73	0.49
1982	3	233	0.047	0.060		5	14	0.38	0.25
1983	1	1	0.015	0.020		3	21	0.20	0.13
1984	0	0	0.0	0.0		7	45	0.40	0.26

Source: National Traffic Safety Board. Published fatality statistics for carriers operating under fourteen CFR 121 (airlines) have been adjusted to remove accidents that involved all-cargo operations, helicopter operations, and only airline employee fatalities. There were ten such accidents. Two accidents involving commuter carriers operating under fourteen CFR 121 have been reclassified as air commuter aircraft operators and reported with fourteen CFR 135 (commuter air carrier) statistics.

NOTES

[1] See, for example, Levine (1965), Jordan (1970), and Keeler (1972).

[2] The CAB was an independent regulatory agency that consisted of five members appointed by the President and confirmed by the Senate. President Ford appointed John Robson Chairman in 1975, and he became a strong advocate of regulatory reform. In 1977 President Carter appointed Alfred Kahn Chairman and Elizabeth E. Bailey a member. Both were prominent economists who strongly advocated a greater reliance on the market to determine carrier fares and routes.

[3] Domestic air cargo was deregulated by an act of Congress in 1977. International aviation is governed by bilateral aviation agreements between the United States and more than eighty other nations. Although the U.S. government has renegotiated a number of these agreements to achieve a more liberal and competitive international environment, it still has regulatory responsibilities.

[4] See U.S. Congress (1975) and Pulsifer et al. (1975). Also see Breyer (1982).

[5] For a more detailed discussion of the early history of regulation, see Levine (1965) and Keeler (1981) and the references therein.

[6] The data used in this paper are largely based on carrier reports to the CAB on financial and traffic performance.

[7] Average cost is measured by operating expense per available ton-mile (ATM). ATM is a measure of capacity and is derived by multiplying aircraft capacity by the number of miles the aircraft are flown. Most aircraft carry cargo in their bellies, and this measure of capacity includes both passengers and cargo. As discussed subsequently, costs are not appreciably affected by the amount of passengers or cargo an aircraft actually carries.

[8] See, for example, Keeler (1972, 1981).

[9] These carriers' route systems were largely parallel to one another rather than competitive. At the time the CAB was created, passenger fares were set at first-class pullman railroad rates, which were proportional to distance.

[10] Between 1950 and 1974 the CAB blocked entry by seventy-nine applicants desiring to create newly certificated airlines. See U.S. Congress (1975).

[11] For a discussion of the effectiveness of the local service carrier experiment, see Eads (1972).

[12] The CAB largely ignored factors other than distance in regulating fares. For example, there are economies of scale in providing air service: the more passengers that travel in a market the lower the cost of providing a given level of service. The CAB, however, did not consider market density in setting fares. Also, demand for air transportation varies by time of day and day of the week; yet the Board gave carriers only a limited ability to employ peak-load pricing.

[13] Although additional flights in a market increases demand, the percentage increase in traffic is generally less than the percentage increase in flights,

see DeVany (1975). Douglas and Miller (1974) modeled the incentives that this regulatory process gave carriers to engage in scheduling competition and provided evidence on its effect.

[14] See U.S. CAB (1974).

[15] It went a step further by granting eight carriers antitrust immunity to discuss the possibility of reducing capacity on eighteen routes. The carriers managed to agree to such capacity reductions on only three of the routes.

[16] Throughout its history the CAB allowed airlines that were not certificated for passenger service to provide nonscheduled service. In order to limit the competitive effect of charters on scheduled service, the CAB placed a variety of restrictions on the ability of charter operators to offer low fares.

[17] The ADA shifted antitrust responsibilities to the Department of Justice, but in the "CAB Sunset Act of 1984," These responsibilities were transferred to the Department of Transportation. The 1984 legislation also transferred the CAB's consumer protection responsibilities and its existing rules to the Department of Transportation; the ADA had been silent on these matters.

[18] The dormant route authority program enabled a carrier to enter a market that was not being serviced by the carrier that held the authority. The ADA also gave carriers the right to enter one market a year without going through a route proceeding.

[19] It was a successful applicant in the Board's Midway Low Fare Route Proceeding, which was completed before the ADA was enacted.

[20] The sixteen trunk carriers had been reduced by merger to eleven by the time the ADA was enacted. The original fourteen local service carriers had merged to form eight carriers. After the ADA was enacted, Pan American acquired National, North Central and Southern merged to form Republic, which subsequently acquired Hughes Air West. In 1981 Texas International acquired Continental. In the subsequent discussion of market shares it is assumed that the mergers had taken place prior to the ADA. This assumption does not affect any of the conclusions.

[21] In addition to the trunk and local service carriers, the CAB certificated a number of other carriers to provide regional service. The largest of these operated within Alaska and Hawaii.

[22] Northwest was unique among the trunk carriers in its efforts to maintain low costs in the regulated environment. For example, in 1978 its average cost per available ton-mile was 35 percent lower than Trans World Airlines, which had roughly the same stage length, and like Northwest, provided international as well as domestic service. Since costs per mile decline with stage length, it is appropriate to compare costs of carriers with comparable stage lengths.

[23] Operating profit margin is defined as operating revenues minus operating expenses divided by operating revenues. Expenses do not include interest on long-term debt or corporate income taxes. Although United and American were profitable in 1983 and 1984, they recorded losses in the three previous years. As a group, the local service carriers were profitable in each year since the ADA was enacted.

[24] See Bailey et al. (1985), p. 143.
[25] See U.S. CAB (1984), p. 14.
[26] Piedmont established a hub at Charlotte, North Carolina; Frontier expanded at Denver; Ozark at St. Louis; and Republic at Minneapolis. See Carlton et al. (1980) for an estimate of the value of single carrier service.
[27] See Bailey et al. (1985), p. 51.
[28] For a list of carriers' major hubs and their changes in operations at them, see Bailey et al. (1985), p. 79.
[29] See U.S. CAB (1984), p. 29.
[30] Markets between major population centers, and especially those that are short-haul, like Dallas to Houston or New York to Boston, can generally support service that caters to passengers that do not continue their journey beyond the route segment. In addition, a number of tourist markets, like New York to Fort Lauderdale, can support such service.
[31] See U.S. CAB (1984). For changes in service at different sized communities see the "Report on Airline Service, Fares, Traffic, Load Factors, and Market Shares," which was published bimonthly beginning in 1979 by the staff of the CAB. For example, between June 1978 and June 1984, departures at large hubs increased by 37 percent, at medium hubs by 34 percent, at small hubs by 18 percent, and at nonhubs by 9 percent. The number of nonhubs receiving scheduled service declined by 16 percent during this period, so the average number of flights at nonhub communities actually increased by 28 percent. A large hub is defined as a city in which 1 percent of total revenue passengers are enplaned; medium hubs have between 0.25 and 0.99 passengers; small hubs 0.05 and 0.24; and nonhubs less than 0.05. There are roughly twenty-five large hub airports and thirty-three medium hubs. In this discussion we consider small hubs and nonhubs to be small communities.
[32] See Bailey et al. (1985), Chapter 5, for a fuller discussion of the effect of regulation on labor costs.
[33] These calculations are based on a costing methodology the CAB developed for the DPFI. United's cost disadvantage partly stemmed from its contract that required three crew members to operate the two-engine aircraft. Nontrunk airlines used a two-man cockpit crew to fly the aircraft. United and Western, the only other trunks that operated the B-737, were able to amend their agreements and began to use two-man crews in 1981. For further discussion see Bailey et al. (1985), p. 94.
[34] See *Aviation Daily* (December 26, 1984).
[35] Available ton-miles are discussed in note 7.
[36] People Express' stage length in 1983 was 457.4 miles. Frontier had a 423.2 mile average stage length, and its cost per mile was 8.32. For Piedmont it was 334.9 miles and 7.91 cents, for USAir it was 354.4 miles and 9.96 cents, for Ozark it was 398 miles and 8.53 cents, and for Republic it was 370 miles and 8.11 cents. People Express and Southwest contract out a significant number of services, hence their relative productivity may be somewhat overstated.
[37] Fare and traffic data come from the CAB's origin-and-destination survey. Fares are a weighted average of all non–first-class passengers. The data include only origin-and-destination passengers; they do not include passen-

gers who travel between the two city-pairs en route to their ultimate destination.

[38] Essentially, passengers are assumed to try to minimize their cost of travel, which includes the fare and the value of time. This model was developed by Douglas and Miller (1974).

[39] See U.S. CAB (1984), p. 23.

[40] Even if demand is price elastic, a fare reduction may not be profitable if carriers must provide additional capacity. In that case the price reduction will be profitable if the additional revenue exceeds the cost of the additional capacity.

[41] Although it is less costly to serve discretionary passengers, such a pricing strategy is also consistent with price discrimination and may indicate that airline markets remain monopolistically competitive. For further discussion on this issue see Schmalensee (1977), Frank (1983), Borenstein (1983), and Bailey et al. (1985).

[42] See, for example, Graham et al. (1983) and Bailey et al. (1985). Unpublished statistical work by the author, using later data, confirms the results of these earlier studies.

[43] See Graham et al. (1983). Load factors for the formerly regulated carriers were 1976, 55.5; 1977, 55.8; 1978, 61.0; 1979, 62.7; 1980, 58.3; 1981, 57.1; 1982, 58.5; 1983, 59.7; and 1984, 57.8.

[44] The flights of the owners of computer reservation systems were more likely to be prominently displayed. If a travel agent requested flights that departed at 10 A.M., the sponsoring carrier's 10:30 flight might be listed before another carrier's 9:50 flight. The CAB's rule prohibited such bias in flight displays. For further information see the Board's Notice of Proposed Rulemaking as well as its final rule in Carrier-Owned Computer Reservation Systems (Docket 41686). This rule transferred to the Department of Transportation after CAB was dissolved.

[45] See Eads (1972) as well as Bailey et al. (1985). Also see U.S. CAB (1984).

[46] See, for example, U.S. DOT (1975).

[47] The ADA also continued the existing subsidy program for the local service program. This program was terminated in 1983.

[48] For a review of airport access issues see U.S. Airport Access Task Force (1983).

BIBLIOGRAPHY

Air Transportation Association, *Consequences of Deregulation of the Scheduled Air Transport Industry: An Analytical Approach*. Washington, D.C.: Air Transport Association, 1975, 29 pp.

Bailey, E. E., Graham, D. R., and Kaplan, D. P., *Deregulating the Airlines*. Cambridge, Mass.: The MIT Press, 1985.

———, and Panzar, J. C., Jr., "The Contestability of Airline Markets during the Transition to Deregulation," *Law and Contemporary Problems* (Winter 1981), 125–145.

Borenstein, S., "Price Discrimination in Free Entry Markets," Ph.D. dissertation, Massachusetts Institute of Technology, 1983.

Breyer, S., *Regulation and Its Reform*. Cambridge, Mass.: Harvard University Press, 1982.

Carlton, D., Landes, W., and Posner, R., "Benefits and Costs of Airline Mergers: A Case Study (Market Share Due to Single-Carrier Service in North Central-Southern Merger)," *Bell Journal of Economics* (Spring 1980), 65–83.

Caves, D. W., Christensen, L. R., and Tretheway, M. W., "Productivity Performance of U.S. Trunk and Local Service Airlines in the Era of Deregulation," *Economic Inquiry*, 21 (July 1983), 312–334.

DeVany, A. S., "The Effect of Price and Entry Regulation on Airline Output, Capacity and Efficiency," *Bell Journal of Economics* (Spring 1975), 327–345.

Douglas, G. W., and Miller, J. C., III, *Economic Regulation of Domestic Air Transport: Theory and Policy*, Washington, D.C.: Brookings Institution, 1974.

Eads, G. C., *The Local Service Airline Experiment*. Washington, D.C.: Brookings Institution, 1972.

Frank, R. H., "When are Price Differentials Discriminatory?" *Journal of Policy Analysis and Management*, 2 (Winter 1983).

Graham, D., Kaplan, D., and Sibley, D., "Efficiency and Competition in the Airline Industry," *Bell Journal of Economics*, 14(1) (Spring 1983), 118–138.

Jordan, W. A., *Airline Regulation in America: Effects and Imperfections*. Baltimore: The Johns Hopkins University Press, 1970.

Kahn, A. E., "Applications of Economics to an Imperfect World," *American Economic Review*, 69 (May 1979), 1–13.

Kahn, M. L., "Collective Bargaining on the Airline Flight Deck," in H. Levinson, L. M. Rehmur, J. P. Goldberg, and M. L. Kahn (eds.), *Collective Bargaining and Technological Change in American Transportation*. Evanston, Ill.: Northwestern University, 1971.

Keeler, T., "Airline Regulation and Market Performance," *Bell Journal of Economics* (Autumn 1972), pp. 399–424.

———, "The Revolution in Airline Regulation," in L. Weiss and M. Klass (eds.), *Case Studies in Regulation: Revolution and Reform*. Boston: Little, Brown & Company, 1981.

Levine, M., "Is Regulation Necessary? California Air Transportation and National Regulatory Policy." *Yale Law Journal*, 74 (July 1965), 1416–1447.

MacAvoy, P. W., and Snow, J., *Regulation of Passenger Fares and Competition among the Airlines*. Washington, D.C.: American Enterprise Institute, 1977.

Meyer, J., and Oster, C. V., Jr., *Airline Deregulation: The Early Experience*. Boston: Auburn House Publishing Company, 1981.

Northrup, H. R., "The New Employee-Relations Climate in Airlines." *Industrial and Labor Relations Review*, 36 (January 1983).

Pulsifer, R., Keyes, L. S., McMahon, J. A., Eldridge, P., and Demory, W. L., *Regulatory Reform Report of the C.A.B. Special Staff*. Washington, D.C.: Civil Aeronautics Board, 1975.

Schmalensee, R., "Comparative Static Properties of Regulated Airline Oligopolies." *Bell Journal of Economics* (Autumn 1977), 565–576.

U.S. Airport Access Task Force, "Report and Recommendations," March 10, 1983.

U.S. Civil Aeronautics Board. *Domestic Passenger Fare Investigation: January 1970 to December 1974*. Washington, D.C.: U.S. Government Printing Office, 1976, 976 pp.

———, *Report to Congress on Implementation of the Provisions of the Airline Deregulation Act of 1978*. Washington, D.C.: Civil Aeronautics Board, January 31, 1984.

———, "Employment, Productivity and Unit Cost, System Majors 1978–1984," Office of Economic Analysis Report. Washington, D.C.: Civil Aeronautics Board, April 2, 1984.

U.S. Congress, Senate, *Committee on the Judiciary Oversight of Civil Aeronautics Board Practices and Procedures*. Washington, D.C.: U.S. Government Printing Office, 1975.

U.S. Department of Transportation, *Air Service to Small Communities*. Washington, D.C.: Department of Transportation, 1976.

CASE 3

The Rise and Fall and Rise of Cable Television Regulation

Bruce M. Owen
Paul D. Gottlieb
Economists Incorporated

INTRODUCTION

Television is the major entertainment industry in America. The A. C. Nielsen Company estimates that the average American family watches more than six hours of television per day. More than 98 percent of all households in the United States have at least one TV set. Billions of dollars are spent yearly on TV advertising and TV program production. Viewers would be willing to pay billions more in order to retain even the current level of programming.

Since 1955 the number of cable TV subscribers has grown at an average rate greater than 20 percent per year. In 1984 one out of three households subscribed to cable service. The explosive growth of cable in the 1960s and 1970s led to a major con ontation among several industries, refereed by the Federal Communications Commission (FCC). The history of cable TV regulation during this period is a story rooted in economic conflict between cable TV operators, TV stations and networks, and Hollywood program producers.

The broadcast industry and its allies saw cable as a destructive force that threatened to diminish their profits and the public interest in "free" over-the-air broadcasting. Cable TV companies and most outside observers saw cable as an opportunity to achieve a vast increase in consumer service, freedom of viewer choice, and economic competition in broadcasting. By the late 1970s cable proponents had

Introduction

largely prevailed, and a host of federal restrictions on cable had been removed. But in 1984 cable regulation began to rise again from the ashes of the deregulation movement.

The cable TV industry, despite its rapid growth, is still comparatively small. There are about 30 million cable subscribers, and the industry has revenues of about $8 billion per year.

Figure 1 shows the physical design of a cable system. The typical older system has twelve channels, devoted mainly to rebroadcasting local TV signals in order to improve the quality of reception. Some systems carry a local origination channel, programmed mostly with time and weather forecasts. Most systems also carry from distant cities

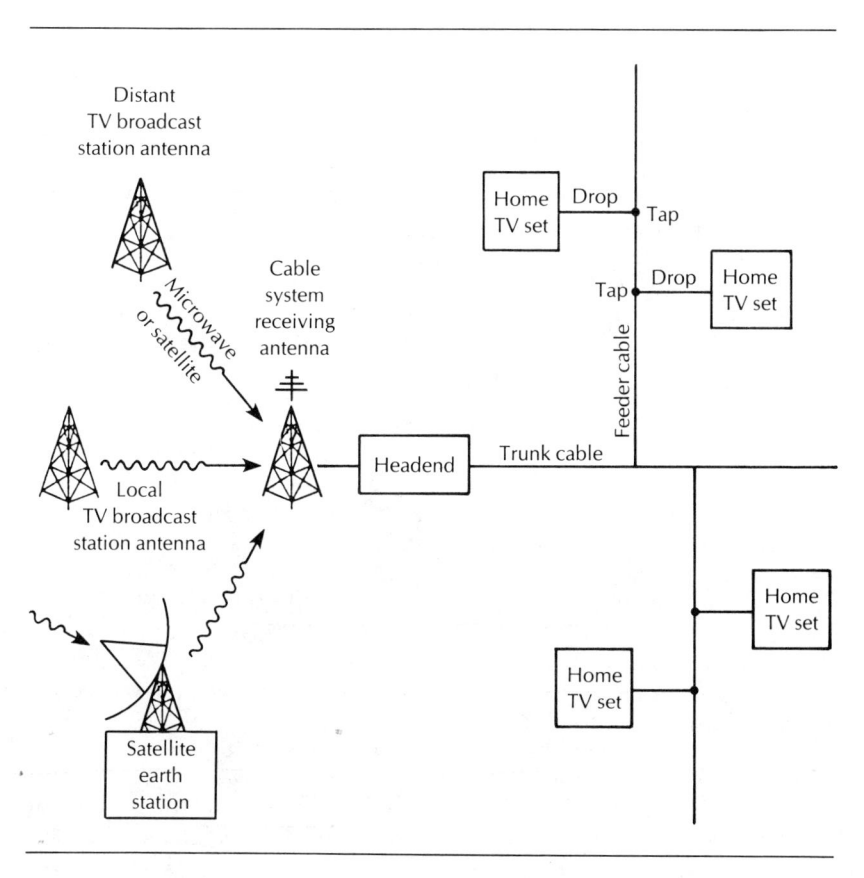

Figure 1. Physical Design of a Cable System

TV signals that cannot be received by rooftop antennas in the area. These signals are "imported" by microwave relay or by communication satellites. A growing number carry one or more special channels with new movies, for which a separate charge is made. These are "pay TV" channels, whose operation was severely restricted by the FCC until 1977. About 66 percent of all cable subscribers subscribe to pay TV services.

New systems often have several dozen channels composed of satellite-delivered networks, with separate charges for each tier. Basic service on such systems typically consists of local over-the-air signals as well as a variety of free services, including time, weather, news, and public affairs channels.

A few entrepreneurs are providing other innovative program services. For example, C-SPAN, Inc., provides live satellite feeds of sessions of Congress and other public affairs events to hundreds of cable systems. The largest cable system in the country is in San Diego, with about 235,000 subscribers. The top fifty cable companies (multiple-system operators) serve more than 80 percent of all cable subscribers. The largest such company is TCI, with more than two million subscribers.

The TV rating services list over 200 TV markets in the United States, defined roughly by the coverage areas of broadcast TV stations assigned to a city or adjacent cities. Most TV station revenues and profits go to VHF network affiliates in the top 100 markets. This is not surprising, given the distribution of population: about one-third of all TV households are in the top ten markets, two-thirds in the top fifty, and 86 percent in the top 100. TV stations are in the business of selling audiences to advertisers. The larger the audience the more advertisers are willing to pay. Therefore TV revenues are greater in larger cities than in smaller ones. Of course, there are important differences within TV markets, some of which are quite varied internally, so that the quantity and quality of TV service and the extent of economic demand for cable is not a constant within markets or from one local market to another.

Cable systems are often regarded as having the characteristics of natural monopolies in their local areas. Recent research confirms that costs decline as the number of subscribers within a given area increases. The higher the ratio of subscribers to homes passed by the cable the lower the cost per subscriber. Nevertheless, the cost advantages of a single system are not so great as to preclude the possibility of beneficial head-to-head competition in certain cases. The financial viability of a cable system depends on population density, income levels, quality of over-the-air reception, number of over-the-air signals, and so on, all of which may vary considerably within a TV market. Hence cable may be viable in some parts of a market and not in other parts.

HISTORY OF CABLE REGULATION

The historical development of federal regulation of cable television can be understood only in the broader context of radio and television regulation. In 1927 Congress nationalized the radio spectrum and in 1934 granted regulatory authority over wire and radio communications to the FCC. As demand for TV programs grew after the war, the FCC was faced with the problem of allocating spectrum to this new service.

At first the Commission seriously underestimated demand for TV channels and allocated only twelve VHF channels (two through thirteen) to the new service. Moreover, it continued its policy of localism in allocating these channels, attempting to maximize the number of localities served by a station rather than the number of signals available to the population. Assigning a frequency to a city meant that that frequency could not be assigned to nearby cities without causing interference. This created an excess demand for licenses, which began to change hands at prices reflecting substantial scarcity rents.

The undersupply of spectrum to TV service had a number of effects, aside from the production of excess profits for VHF licensees. First, the market responded with supplementary technologies: boosters, satellite stations, translators, and cable TV systems, all means of improving reception in rural areas. Second, the FCC responded by allocating a relatively large number of new channels to TV service. Unfortunately, these channels were allocated in the UHF band, where stations were at a technical disadvantage compared with VHF stations. Not only did most TV sets manufactured in the fifties and early sixties lack UHF tuners, but UHF signals do not travel as far or as clearly as equally powerful VHF signals. This "UHF handicap" has been gradually diminished by the FCC's efforts and by cable carriage. (The FCC's efforts included a requirement that all TV sets have UHF tuners and, later, that they have "click-stop" tuning dials.) It is generally agreed that the FCC made a serious error in its UHF decisions. If the Commission had shifted all TV broadcasting to the UHF band, or if it had not mixed UHF and VHF stations in the same markets, the resulting abundance of channels might have reduced the need for cable television. This would have eliminated the handicap that UHF stations had in competing with VHFs. However, by the late 1950s, when the implications of the FCC's error became apparent, the VHF broadcasters were politically too powerful to dislodge. An effort to "deintermix" the VHF and UHF stations was abandoned.

The net result of these events was that TV viewers in most cities were limited to three or four channels and that VHF TV broadcasters were practically guaranteed substantial profits because of the scarcity of channels.

The supplementary technologies that grew up in the fifties were designed to bring TV signals to rural fringe areas where the primary signals were weak or plagued with interference. Boosters, satellites,* and translators received these weak signals and rebroadcast them with greater power. Cable TV systems do the same but use wires rather than rebroadcasting the signals. Cable TV systems are much more expensive than satellite antennas and translators for small numbers of channels, but they have two overwhelming advantages: (1) because they use wire, cable companies can at relatively little expense charge consumers for the service they provide by excluding those who don't pay and (2) because of the technical characteristics of coaxial cable, they can carry a large number of channels.

The selling point of cable systems during the fifties was the provision of clear signals. This service was uncontroversial and even welcomed by broadcasters because it increased their audiences. In 1959 the FCC refused to accept regulatory jurisdiction over cable, asserting that it was neither a broadcast facility nor a wire common carrier.

Between 1959 and 1966 the situation changed radically. Cable operators discovered that they could increase the demand for their service by importing distant TV signals using microwave relay systems. Subscribers were willing to pay to receive these additional non-local signals, and the coaxial cable had the capacity. Distant-signal importation aroused the ire of broadcasters, because by increasing the choices available, it fragmented their audiences. This reduced local advertising revenues. The new audiences gained by the distant station were of little value to the imported station's own local advertising clients. Local advertising accounts for a third of the revenue of non-network VHF stations and about half of the revenue of nonnetwork UHF stations. Also, for the first time cable began to grow in the big cities where the most profitable stations are found.

*These were terrestrial antennas that retransmit signals, not orbiting communication satellites.

In opposing cable, broadcasters employed two strategies: (1) they pressed the FCC for restrictions on cable television and (2) they challenged cable in the courts, on the grounds that distant-signal importation infringed on the copyright of program producers. The FCC first asserted jurisdiction over the microwave relay systems used to import distant signals (1962), and then in 1965–1966 asserted full regulatory jurisdiction over cable television, freezing all such systems in the largest 100 TV markets and forbidding importation of additional signals. These actions were upheld in the courts. The copyright challenge did not go so well for the broadcasters. In 1968 the Supreme Court held that cable systems had no copyright liability for retransmitted local signals and in 1974 ruled similarly with respect to distant signals.

The years of the freeze were characterized by intense pressure for the industry and for the Commission. Despite the freeze, cable systems grew rapidly. The political strength of the cable industry grew as well, in part because the more spectacular potential services that cable might offer caught the imagination of a number of writers, who produced a growing flood of literature and interest in cable. These "blue sky" services included free public soapbox channels, channels for education, the arts, government, electronic voting, shopping, meter reading, and access to electronic program libraries with limitless possibilities. A major criticism of broadcast television has been the difficulty of access and the scarcity of channels. Cable was called the "medium of abundance."

In 1971 intense negotiations among the trade groups under the auspices of FCC Chairman Dean Burch and Office of Telecommunications Policy Director Clay T. Whitehead resulted in a compromise solution. This compromise included a formula for payment of royalties for distant signals and a specified limit (varying with market size and other factors) to the number of such signals that could be imported. The compromise was intended to be embodied in a massive set of FCC rules promulgated in 1972. These rules, in addition to regulating the number and type of distant signals that might be imported, imposed a number of requirements on cable systems. Among these were local origination, the provision of free channels for various uses, and technical, capacity, and access rules designed to ensure the more rapid development of the "blue sky" services.

The 1972 rules discussed below were truly a compromise in the sense that the FCC convinced itself and the cable industry that they were the minimum conditions required to get cable moving, while not irreparably harming the broadcasters. The free channels and other requirements imposed on cable systems were designed to ensure that cable lived up to its promise of abundance, rather than simply existing on the retransmission of broadcast signals. These requirements were on the whole technically and financially unrealistic and were relaxed as their effective dates approached. In an important sense the public service and capacity requirements were necessary to get the vote of "liberal" commissioners, particularly Nicholas Johnson.

After 1972 the major issues in cable regulation were pay television, copyright, pole rentals, and federal versus state and local jurisdiction over cable. The FCC rules against pay television on cable systems (as well as over-the-air) were gradually relaxed but still remained highly restrictive until 1977, when they were struck down by the courts. In 1976 Congress passed an omnibus copyright bill that included compulsory licenses for distant signals allowed by the FCC, with royalties paid to a central pool for distribution to copyright owners by a federal Copyright Royalty Tribunal.

In 1974 the Cabinet Committee on Cable Communications issued a report that outlined a new regulatory framework for cable, based on the separation of transmission and content functions. Under the Committee's proposal cable would be a common carrier with no federal regulation of content. The rationale was that local cable transmission is a natural monopoly, which for competitive and First Amendment reasons ought not to be translated into a monopoly of control over content. If all cable channels were competitively programmed, there would be no scarcity and less need for federal regulations, such as the fairness doctrine, which impinge on freedom of expression. The policy proposals of the Cabinet Committee were endorsed in an influential 1976 House Communications Subcommitee Staff Report.

During the Ford administration a domestic council regulatory review group headed by economist Paul MacAvoy considered the problem of cable television and came to the unexpected conclusion that the proponents of cable deregulation had failed to sustain the burden of proof necessary to make out a case for abandoning the rules. In fact, a certain amount of political courage would have been required to overcome broadcast industry opposition to deregulation of cable — courage that the Carter administration was later to muster. Nevertheless, of the half-dozen major attempts to conduct objective reviews of the cable regulations undertaken by government committees and private commissions in the 1970s, the MacAvoy effort was the only one that failed to conclude that the rules were unduly restrictive on cable development. By 1979 the FCC itself had gradually abandoned nearly all of its 1972 rules restricting cable growth, except for those limiting distant-signal importation. On April 25, 1979, the Commission, chaired by Charles Ferris, issued a massive economic study of the effects of cable regulation, concluding that regulation was not necessary and releasing a proposal to abolish its distant-signal restrictions. The Commission adopted these proposals in July 1980, and FCC cable TV regulation ended — for a while — just eighteen years after it began.

CABLE REGULATION AT FULL FLOOD

The cable regulations adopted by the FCC in 1972, although ending the five-year freeze on cable growth in the top 100 television markets, were highly restrictive in a number of respects. After 1972 these rules were slowly but steadily abandoned, either by voluntary FCC action or by court order. The FCC's authority to regulate cable was reinforced in 1968 and 1972 by Supreme Court decisions. After 1972 the tide of judicial endorsement of FCC jurisdiction receded, most markedly in a 1977 court of appeals decision striking down the pay TV rules.

The 1972 rules were enormously complicated, a state of affairs resulting at least in part from the technical and legal (and in several cases uninterpretable) language employed. The following is a summary description.

Certificate of Compliance. Cable systems that retransmit broadcast signals could not operate legally without, in effect, a license from the Commission.

Franchising Standards. Licenses were not granted unless the cable system had a franchise meeting certain standards. Requirements were imposed on both cable systems and franchising authorities. Franchises were limited to fifteen years; construction had to begin within one year; the local authority was required to regulate rates; due process was required in franchise awards; franchise fees were limited; and local authorities were preempted on most other matters.

Signals. Cable systems were required to carry local signals and over-the-air signals that, although nonlocal, were "significantly viewed" in the market (that is, had a specified minimum share of the local audience). In addition, systems might import at least two signals, and as many more as were necessary, so that after taking account of local signals:

1. Systems in the largest fifty markets had three independents plus three networks.

2. Systems in the second-largest fifty markets had two independents plus three networks.

3. Systems in markets smaller than the top 100 had one independent plus three networks.

4. Systems outside TV markets had no restrictions.

These rules can be illustrated by the following example. Suppose a cable system serves one of the largest fifty markets. First, it must carry all the local stations. Second, it must carry any nearby station that manages to obtain 5 percent or more of the local over-the-air audience. It might then, in addition, import from distant cities two stations and enough others to carry at least three network stations and three independent stations. However, the imported signals were subject to two further limitations.

First, the "antileapfrogging" rule (also called the "leapfrogging" rule) required cable systems to import the nearest qualified distant signals. The leapfrogging rule was apparently meant to encourage localism, since the natural tendency of a cable system would be to import the stations that had the best programming, which are likely to be independent VHF stations in the largest cities. If these stations were widely imported, they might begin to form the basis for regional TV networks, capable of tapping regional advertising markets. To a certain degree this had already taken place. Oakland's KTVU, for example, was extensively imported to the intermountain west. The leapfrogging rules discouraged this, often by forcing cable systems to pick up nearby underfinanced independent UHF stations. This policy benefited the imported station and the local broadcasters but hurt viewers and the cable system.

Second, local stations' exclusivity rights were protected by blacking out, on any imported signal, program material for which a local station had broadcast rights. The leapfrogging and exclusivity rules varied by size of market, the latter rules also by type of programming.

Origination. The 1972 rules required cable systems to create their own programming on at least one channel and to make available free channels for public free access, local government, and the local school system, respectively. Channels not devoted to retransmission of TV stations were subject to the FCC broadcast content regulation, including the fairness doctrine, equal-time provisions, and obscenity rules.

Capacity. The 1972 rules imposed a minimum channel-capacity constraint (twenty channels) and a two-way communications requirement. The 1972 regulations also contain the so-called $n + 1$ rule:

Cable Regulation at Full Flood 87

Whenever all of the channels described in subparagraphs (4) through (7) of this paragraph are in use during 80 percent of the weekdays . . . for 80 percent of the time during any consecutive 3-hour period for 6 consecutive weeks, such system shall have 6 months in which to make a new channel available. . . .

This rule, apparently designed to ensure adequate capacity without regulating prices, would perhaps have made sense to one of the characters in *Alice in Wonderland*. The FCC made no attempt to enforce it.

Leased Channel Programming. Systems were required to lease their remaining channels to others, relinquishing all control of program content. The effect of this rule was negligible, since the smaller systems common in 1972 rarely had channels remaining after fulfilling requirements for local programming and exercising their own distant-signal and origination rights.

Ownership. Cable systems could not be owned by telephone companies, TV stations in the same market, or TV networks.

Pay Television. The FCC required that cable systems carrying per-program or per-channel pay television meet the following guidelines on the pay channels:

1. No advertising.

2. Maximum of 90 percent combined sports and movies.

3. No sports programs if the event had been broadcast in the market within the past five years; new events could not be shown for five years after their first occurrence.

4. No movies made between the past four and ten years.

The purpose of these rules was to prevent pay TV channels from bidding away programs that would otherwise have been shown on free over-the-air television. Since they were meant to prevent such siphoning of programs to pay television, they were called antisiphoning rules. For instance, most movies then shown on television were between four and ten years old. Pay TV systems could not bid on such movies, though they could show newer ones, competing with theatrical exhibitors. The practical effect of the FCC's pay TV rules was to deprive viewers of certain programs and to artificially lower the price that TV stations had to pay for programs, sports, and movies.

The general thrust of the cable rules was to limit the growth of cable by direct constraint and by the imposition of various regulatory taxes. The beneficiaries of this policy were broadcast stations, networks, and those viewers (if any) who might be harmed by cable growth. The costs of cable restraints were borne by cable operators and those viewers who were deprived of the opportunity to subscribe to cable services.

In addition to the FCC's 1972 regulations, various state regulations were and are imposed.

Various state governments have created special cable regulatory commissions or awarded such jurisdiction to their public utility commissions. Vermont, Massachusetts, New York, and Connecticut are particularly active in this area. The line between federal and state jurisdiction was not clearly drawn until enactment in 1984 of the federal legislation discussed below.

DISTANT SIGNALS AND COPYRIGHT LIABILITY

A number of studies have examined the effect of the FCC rules on the growth of cable systems, the profitabilty of TV stations, and the welfare of viewers. These studies, which are summarized in the FCC's 1979 report, focus on the impact of varying the number and type of distant signals allowed under some assumptions about copyright liability.

Providing distant signals in big cities was probably a necessary step in establishing cable's economic viability. It increased demand for the system's services at relatively low cost, which may have allowed the operator to achieve sufficient penetration of the market to make other services profitable, notably pay TV channels offering movies. More exotic and specialized services, such as alarm systems, meter reading, and electronic shopping, were heralded. It was argued that these exotic services could not be offered until cable systems had a high penetration and that distant signals were a necessary preliminary step. Some studies suggested that in large cities with good over-the-air signals, distant signals would be just enough to make cable systems marginally profitable. The amount of copyright payment and the costs of services required by regulators could make the difference. Thus, although none of the industry groups denied the necessity for copyright liability, it took many years to arrive at the particular formula contained in the Copyright Act of 1976.

Similarly, industry groups debated the extent of exclusivity (geographical and temporal) that copyright owners might grant to stations that buy their programs.

The issue of copyright liability for distant signals is complex since transactions costs under various policies, the elasticity of program supply, and possible changes in patterns of TV advertising are purely speculative. One straightforward approach is to dispense with copyright liability. Cable operators could import an unlimited number of distant signals, paying only the cost of physical transmission. The distant stations being imported would attract additional audiences, additional advertising revenue, and in the end would be more profitable for program suppliers.

On the other hand, copyright liability for distant signals may be necessary if the market for programs is to operate effectively. Program suppliers rent their products to TV stations and networks for "runs" that include geographic and temporal exclusivity provisions; this presumably increases the value of the program to the station (because most of the local audience will not have seen the program before) and therefore increases the revenue that the program supplier can expect. If cable systems had a right to import any distant signals without copyright liability, then a given program would be relatively unproductive to local stations, and the program suppliers might not be able to sell it to more than a few powerful independent VHF stations. But distant local audiences are worth less to the imported station than to the local station in terms of advertising revenue. Therefore the revenues of program suppliers, who are highly competitive, might decrease. The absence of copyright liability with widespread distant-signal importation might thus result in a decline in the supply of program material, depending on the amount of economic rents in program supply. Ideally, cable systems would bargain with distant stations over the fees to be paid for importation. These payments would then be reflected in the market prices paid for programs by stations. However, stations themselves hold only an exhibition license to the programs, not a copyright. Direct bargaining between cable systems and program suppliers is arguably too expensive, because transactions costs are high relative to the value of the material being traded. Giving cable systems a compulsory license to import signals subject to freely negotiated "reasonable" copyright fees might be feasible if stations seeking revenues from importation were to compete with each other. Then program producers would be able to charge imported stations a price that reflected the royalty payments made to the station by cable systems. Even this approach may be flawed, however, if the physical transmission costs of importation are insufficient to overcome the tendency of competing distant stations to bid down the royalty rate charged to the systems they are serving.

The copyright issue was settled for the time being with the passage of the General Revision of the Copyright Law in 1976. The Act made retransmissions by cable companies of broadcast programming subject to copyright law. It required compulsory licenses for all unaltered retransmissions authorized by the FCC, provided that proper statements of identity and accounts are filed and royalty fees are paid. All large cable systems must pay a royalty fee based on gross revenues, which gives them the right to import such distant signals as the FCC allows. The royalties are accumulated by the Copyright Office and distributed once a year by a newly created Copyright Royalty Tribunal to copyright owners whose programs were retransmitted as distant signals. There is an annual struggle among the lawyers for various interest groups who seek a share of such royalties.

Congress presumably imposed the compulsory license royalty pool solution on the assumption that transaction costs in a free market would be prohibitive, and thus cable systems would be unable to bargain for distant signals. There was and is insufficient empirical evidence to support this assumption. The marketplace has responded in other, far more problematical, areas with institutions that appear to cope adequately with transactions costs problems. One example is the use of blanket licenses for musical performances, which are provided by voluntary private associations in response to transactions costs problems far more difficult than those that would be faced by cable systems in negotiating for TV signal carriage rights.

WHY WAS CABLE DEREGULATED?

Over the course of two decades the FCC first regulated and then gradually deregulated cable. The FCC's activities generally paralleled those of the federal courts, though it is hard to see which institution, if either, was the leader. Although Congress passed no significant legislation affecting cable before 1984 other than the Copyright Act, it continued to oversee FCC actions, many of which were heavily influenced by the perceived positions of the communications subcommittees in both houses. In short, the FCC did not act alone.

Two alternative theories explain the phenomenon of cable regulation and deregulation. The first is the FCC's own official version, contained in its 1979 Report on the Inquiry into the Economic Relationship between Television Broadcasting and Cable Television. This version holds that, as it became apparent that cable might present a significant economic challenge to TV broadcasting, cable regulation was imposed by the FCC and upheld by the courts to protect both broadcasters and their viewers from harm. As the Commission gradually acquired more information about the nature of the risks and the likely economic effects of cable growth, the regulations were relaxed. The motives of the government were entirely benevolent. So long as any individual member of the viewing public might be disadvantaged by cable, the government was justified in retarding the diffusion of cable among those who might benefit from it. Better information acquired through studies and experience allowed the FCC increasingly to discount the risks of significant harm, and by 1979 the restrictions were abandoned entirely. In assessing this theory, one might ask not whether the FCC and the courts made minor errors of judgment in timing, but instead whether the government has a right to protect consumers and corporations from the risks associated with marketplace forces and technological change by directly retarding the change. Since few changes benefit everyone, progress will nearly always claim some victims. Sometimes the victims are impossible to predict or identify, making compensation impossible. In such cases delay is the only protection available.

The second theory of the government's behavior is more cynical. Cable television may have been regulated simply to protect the excess profits of TV broadcasters because TV stations have significant political power. According to this theory, claims about the need to protect viewers from the risk of harm are merely rhetoric, designed to rationalize the government's behavior. This theory is bolstered by the indisputable fact that the most draconian cable restrictions, the freeze and later the distant-signal rules, were imposed in those cities where the most powerful and profitable TV stations were located, not in the markets where cable posed the greatest threat to TV station viability. Cable television is a greater threat to the economic viability of small-market VHF network affiliates, but large-market VHF affiliates were the greatest beneficiaries of protection.

The cynical theory would presumably explain the gradual deregulation of cable by pointing to the steadily increasing political power of the cable industry and the growing body of public opinion favoring cable development. Alternatively, cable may gradually have been perceived as a less serious economic threat by the broadcast lobby, or the industry may simply have gained the time it needed to make its own adjustments. One such adjustment has been the purchase of cable systems by broadcasters. Under the July 1980 order TV stations were still prohibited from owning cable systems in their viewing areas, but they could own them elsewhere. A third explanation of deregulation is that "good people" took control of the FCC and sought to remedy previous sins.

The "good guys, bad guys" approach to explaining these events is almost certainly fruitless. The FCC was fenced in by congressional and judicial constraints, and these too changed markedly between the period of regulation and the period of deregulation. Perhaps better information and the effects of public opinion affected large numbers of public officials in all three branches.

Which of the two theories is valid? The facts are consistent with both. Perhaps a more general hypothesis would incorporate elements of both theories. Industries vying for government largesse offer public-interest rationales for their proposals. The "protecting viewers from risk" rationale for cable regulation is not absurd in principle, merely in practice. But it certainly was not obvious to reasonable people in, say, 1968, that cable regulation would in practice be absurd. Nor was it obvious to the Carter administration deregulators in 1980 that by 1984 Congress would put the FCC back into the cable regulation business.

CABLE TELEVISION SINCE THE 1980 DEREGULATION

The growth of cable television in the period of deregulation has been phenomenal by any measure. Since 1980 the number of subscribers has doubled, while cable penetration has grown from 20 to 36 percent of TV households. A majority of subscribers now rely on cable for original entertainment and information services rather than the simple rebroadcast of local and nearby stations.

Cable regulation was justified on the basis that without it multiple imported channels might force broadcasters off the air. This simply did not happen. As predicted, the UHF stations' positions improved. The total number of UHF channels being broadcast increased from 229 to 365 between 1980 and 1985. The number of VHF channels also increased — from 517 to 539 — and a search by several persons inside and outside the FCC in November 1985 did not yield a single case of a VHF channel broadcast in 1980 that was not still on the air in 1985. In general, the FCC's limits on cable between 1965 and 1980 did virtually nothing for viewers.

The TV marketplace since 1980 has been characterized primarily by the advent of new technologies that have changed the regulatory picture from broadcast versus cable to one of "every man for himself." Chief among these technologies is the videocassette recorder (VCR), which, unlike cable, has few limits to penetration. Videocassette recorder sales have increased at a rate of 70 percent per year since 1978, and 18 percent of American TV households now have at least one machine.

Broadcasters who worried that their audiences were fragmented by the importation of distant signals must now deal with the VCR's fragmentation of audiences over time as well as space. The effect of this time-shifting, absent other factors, is ambiguous. At the very least it reduces the predictability and measurability of broadcast audiences, on which advertising rates are based. It allows people not only to watch programs they would otherwise miss but also (to the ad man's horror) to delete the commercials.

Cable programs can be taped as well. To the extent that cable programs consist of premium movies and sporting events, they are perhaps more likely to be taped than broadcast offerings. In this way, as consumers attempt to accumulate high-quality video libraries, the growth of VCRs enhances the demand for cable and vice versa. And since many cable services are not supported by advertising, they are unlikely to feel threatened by time-shifting.

When the existence of large numbers of VCRs is accompanied by the rental of first-run movies at a low enough price, however, the effect on broadcasters and cable operators is almost certain to be adverse. There is some evidence that movie fans regard videocassettes as good substitutes for pay cable. They may therefore regard the VCR as a substitute, rather than complement, to cable service. The decision about which to buy depends not only on comparative prices but also on the ability of each medium to obtain good movies quickly. This in turn is controlled by the movie studios' decisions regarding the timing of release of motion pictures.

One important development on the electromagnetic frontier is a technology called Multi-channel Multipoint Distribution Service (MMDS). MMDS currently involves the transmission of a small number of channels in the microwave band direct from a central station to subscribers. The advantage of MMDS over cable is its low construction cost. While the nation's eighty-five or so operating single channel MDS systems now serve mostly hotels and apartment buildings, decreases in the cost of reception equipment have brought MDS well within the reach of private homeowners. The FCC has increased the number of channels allocated to MDS in the top fifty markets from two to twenty; forecasts of the number of eventual MMDS subscribers range as high as twelve million in 1990.

Other breakthroughs in technology promise to expand the boundaries of traditional broadcast television. On the high end, CBS is experimenting with terrestrial TV broadcasting at 12 billion cycles per second (12 GHz). And low-power television, formerly relegated to translator service for full-power TV signals, is now the subject of some 20,000 applications at the FCC. A number of new, low-power TV stations are already on the air in urban areas.

Nor has technological progress left the established TV broadcast industry untouched. Improved UHF reception and growing demand have led to an increase in total UHF stations of 29 percent between 1980 and 1984, compared to 10 percent between 1976 and 1980. The net effect of cable was almost certainly to enhance rather than to reduce the viability of UHF stations (Figure 2).

It would be difficult to overestimate the impact of new satellite services on the growth of cable television. As the FCC began to permit the construction of receive-only satellite earth stations in the mid-1970s, cable operators seized the opportunity to improve their ability to import distant signals for distribution to subscribers. The number of pay cable services doubled. Cable Network News and the "Super-

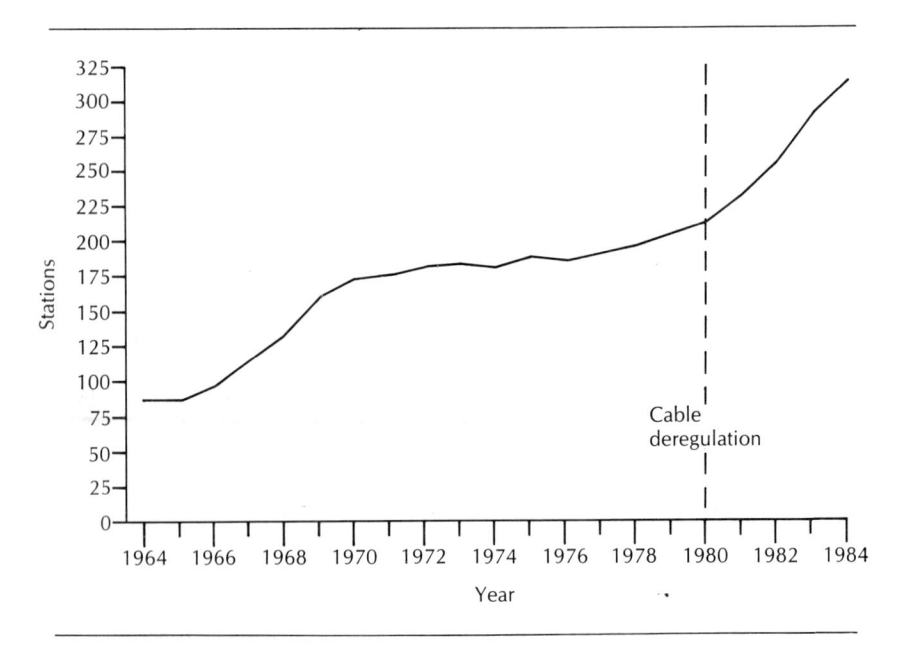

Figure 2. UHF Commercial Stations, 1964–1984.

stations" were born, resulting in the formation of national cable networks.

The new cable networks relied on cable operators picking up programming from satellites and distributing it to their subscribers by wire. As the cost and size of satellite receivers decreased, however, cable's role in this process began to be challenged.

The first step in this direction was Satellite Master Antenna Television (SMATV). Sometimes called "private cable," SMATV collects and delivers satellite-fed programming to apartments, hotels, and other buildings. Like MDS, SMATV has significant cost advantages over traditional cable and is likely to emerge as the delivery system of choice for high-density housing.

The logical end result of the new satellite technology is the direct broadcast satellite (DBS), which transmits video signals directly to small earth stations installed on residential rooftops. Attractive particularly in rural areas, DBS is an expensive, exotic service not expected to threaten cable in the near future. But DBS represents a long-term competitive force in the video marketplace, as evidenced by the issuance of eight construction permits (with five pending) in 1982.

Telephone Versus Cable

The video marketplace has entered a period of fluidity and competition. This is in sharp contrast to the other arena in which cable competes.

Cable systems offer various two-way interactive services, such as burglar alarm systems and videotex. In these applications cable's main competitor is local telephone service. The one salient point about the recent AT&T consent decree, from cable's point of view, is that the local telephone monopoly has been left intact. Thus cable's fight to provide many of its most promising services is as much a legal fight as a technological one. Its enemies include not only the telephone companies but local regulators who are accustomed to controlling every aspect of interactive in-home communications.

Since the 1960s, for example, telephone companies have severely limited cable systems' access to their telephone poles. While telephone poles are arguably not the essential facilities for which access is generally guaranteed by law, the phone companies have made no secret of their desire to retard cable's growth. In cases where cable companies could contract for pole attachments, telephone companies often specified that the poles not be used for purposes other than the retransmission of broadcast signals. The FCC has long chastised local authorities for not correcting such abuses.

When telephone companies cannot stop cable, they frequently attempt to enter the business themselves. This phenomenon is potentially serious: (1) because it would allow the phone companies to preempt what may be their principal local competitive threat, thus preserving a monopoly that has become outdated, and (2) because of the influence that many telephone companies have on local authorities. With their economic power and political sophistication, phone companies may have the inside track on franchise awards.

There is little doubt that telephone companies have a substantial amount of experience building communication facilities along residential streets. On the other hand, both telephone companies and cable companies frequently hire outside contractors to do the actual installation work. The question is whether the eventual cost of letting telephone companies into the cable business outweighs any efficiencies. Both the FCC and local authorities have addressed this question by permitting telephone companies only an indirect stake in local cable systems.

A telephone company may legally act as a facilities subcontractor, or it may "lease back" much of its channel capacity to a franchiseholder. In either case a cable system operator must be involved. The city of Palo Alto recently refused to continue negotiating with Pacific Bell over the construction of a cable system until a cable operator had been selected. The FCC likewise closed Pacific's application for a Section 214 certificate until "an agreement with the successful franchisee is reached."

The District of Columbia City Council recently awarded a cable franchise to District Cablevision, Inc., with the understanding that construction was to be carried out by the Chesapeake & Potomac Telephone Company. A losing bidder promptly sued, arguing that an agreement between District Cablevision and C&P amounted to an unfair advantage because of the phone company's local monopoly power.

The D.C. case summarizes many of the fears arising out of telephone company involvement in cable television. Such fears are strictly local. An interesting provision of the 1982 AT&T consent decree permits AT&T to offer "electronic publishing services" after seven years. While this provision might permit AT&T to regain, through cable, the local distribution facilities that it divested, it would now enter the market as a *competitor* of the local telephone operating companies. Regulators will continue to be concerned about the effect such ownership has on the local control of information. By that criterion the entry of AT&T into cable may be less worrisome than the entry of local newspapers and local television stations.

More Legal Issues, More Economic Realities

The lawsuit against District Cablevision raises another issue: the extent to which cities may be held liable for franchise decisions that appear to violate the antitrust laws. In its 1982 *City of Boulder* decision the Supreme Court stated that cities could be held liable for antitrust violations growing out of cable franchise awards. In October 1984 Congress passed, and the President signed, a bill that prohibits claims for damages in antitrust suits against cities, effectively neutralizing the *Boulder* decision.

But the issue of franchising authority goes beyond the momentary reversals of legal fortune. It is questionable whether there is any economic justification for the awarding of single cable TV franchises in the first place — short of preventing the unchecked ravaging of city streets. Evidence is accumulating that cable companies can compete effectively with one another. Companies with adjacent service areas compete along the border to sign up subscribers. This threat of competition "on the margin" is a fundamental spur to economic efficiency. There are also a surprising number of cases in which cable companies compete down the same streets to provide essentially the same service. The evidence does *not* support the view that economies of scale make these "overbuild" situations inefficient in all cases.

More important, restricting cable competition to the franchising procedure has led to delays and probably to corruption in scores of cities. Local authorities often hold up cable development while bargaining (frequently in pork barrel terms) over the franchise award. In contrast, two directly competing cable operators in Phoenix, Arizona, installed cable at an average rate of 150 miles per month in 1981–1982. Consumers, rather than favored companies or political factions, benefited by having access to cable television much sooner than their counterparts in other cities.

To the extent that cable's status as a natural monopoly is called into question, so too is the justification for additional varieties of cable regulation. Many of the special committees and task forces set up to study cable in the 1970s recommended that cable systems have a common-carrier access obligation, so that the transmission monopoly would be separated from the programming function. This usually translated into something known as "mandatory leased channel access." Cable operators were required to lease all or part of their channel capacity to applicants at nondiscriminatory rates.

It was felt that mandatory leased channel access would prevent cable operators from controlling program content on all the channels of the medium they monopolized. As a side effect, leased access would obviate the need for any federal regulation of program content. This argument, though well intentioned, rests on the assumption that cable is a unique kind of service with no substitutes and few likely competitors among its own or other media. This proposition has become increasingly controversial because of the new technologies.

Cable operators have also begun to claim for themselves the First Amendment protection that mandatory leased access would reserve only for others. The selection of programming, they argue, is an editorial function subject to the same protection afforded newspapers and magazines.

Some cable operators have even gone so far as to challenge, on First Amendment grounds, a city's right to select a single operator to use public and private rights of way. They have met with some success. Preferred Communications Incorporated (PCI), a California cable operator, sued the city of Los Angeles in 1984 alleging both antitrust and First Amendment violations. Los Angeles awards exclusive franchises in various sectors of the city by means of an auction. Winning bidders are required to offer a variety of fees and public access facilities to the city government and to accede to stringent regulatory oversight. PCI attempted to make arrangements with private and public utilities for pole attachments in South Central Los Angeles, but decided to bring legal action rather than submit to the auction procedure.

The district court rejected both claims by the cable operator, but the Ninth Circuit Court of Appeals reversed the First Amendment portion of that decision. It is not clear, argued the court, that cable television — even with its need for utility conduits — exhibits any of the characteristics of scarcity that permit the government to license the broadcast media. In fact, the court used another analogy entirely. It argued that "allowing a procedure such as the City's would be akin to allowing the government discretion to grant a permit for the operation of newspaper vending machines located on public streets only to the newspaper that the government believes 'best' serves the community, a practice which we find clearly invalid."

The common carrier–First Amendment debate has raged for as long as cable has provided original programming. One difference is that now cable's twenty to 100 channels look less and less like the only game in town. Issues remain — among them the potential for newspaper-cable combinations that may restrict the flow of the kind of community-oriented information that so concerns policymakers. Nor do we know when — if ever — new delivery technologies such as

MDS or DBS will achieve the scale and penetration they require to become profitable.

Still, in the absence of evidence to the contrary, the technologies ought to be allowed to fight it out in the marketplace. Deregulation was good for cable, for consumers, and even for UHF. There is no reason to assume it will be bad for the newer kids on the block.

THE CABLE COMMUNICATIONS POLICY ACT OF 1984

Cable television was not deregulated completely in 1980. The FCC's more restrictive rules, most notably those concerning distant-signal importation, were abandoned. Capacity, access, and rates remained subject to regulation, primarily through local franchise requirements.

Through most of this period Congress has waited on the sidelines. In the absence of strict FCC guidelines, however, cable operators have grown increasingly frustrated at what they view as the arbitrariness of the local franchising process. Meanwhile city governments — especially in the wake of the *Boulder* decision — have begun to feel insecure about their right to regulate cable television. Both sides lobbied Congress. The result, whatever the lobbyists intended, was the effective reregulation of cable television at the federal level.

The objectives of the Cable Communications Act of 1984 are (1) to clarify local, state, and federal jurisdiction of cable television, (2) to assure diversity of cable programming, (3) to eliminate some of the arbitrariness of the franchise and renewal process, and (4) to "promote competition in cable communications and minimize unnecessary regulation that would impose an undue economic burden on cable systems" (that is, the regulation of rates and imposition of taxes and franchise fees).

In practice, the Act returns to the FCC many of the powers it relinquished in 1980.

Encouraging Competition

The Act's key "regulatory reform" provision states that basic cable system rates may not be regulated except in "circumstances in which a cable system is not subject to effective competition." The FCC is charged with drawing up nationwide standards by which effective competition can be measured. The Commission may then prescribe local rate regulation for markets that fail the test.

In arriving at this formulation, Congress has taken the view that the existence of new technologies in the national marketplace does not eliminate the possibility that some local cable companies, by virtue of certain geographic or economic advantages, will still be able to monopolize video delivery in their service areas. Such companies might need to be regulated as natural monopolies.

The problem with this portion of the Act lies not in the theory, but in the application of that theory to public policy. No simple federal criterion can ever take into account all of the local variations that bear on the question of "effective competition." The result is likely to be case-by-case FCC determination of local conditions in a highly litigious context. The FCC's natural aversion to such an approach has led it, not surprisingly, to propose a simple numerical count of the number of over-the-air broadcast stations that cable subscribers could view without benefit of cable. Proposals to combine broadcast with other available delivery systems or to use cable channel capacity as a measure of the degree to which an existing system can foreclose competition were rejected by the Commission.

More difficult to measure, but central to the question of effective competition, is the extent to which new technologies might enter a market in response to a cable operator's monopoly profits. The FCC is unwilling to try to measure this potential, and will fall back on a static, rather than dynamic definition of effective competition.

To cable operators the value of the Cable Act's rate provision is that it steers a middle course between two less palatable alternatives: the blanket regulation of rates specified by the 1972 rules and the "chaotic" regulation of rates by a variety of jurisdictions in the post-1980 period.* Only time will tell whether this compromise serves consumers' interest in the rapid expansion of video services. One likely outcome is an avalanche of litigation in 1986, the first year that existing franchisees will begin to be subject to the new rate rule.

1972 Revisited

Other provisions of the Cable Act of 1984 lack even the pretense of regulatory reform. The result is a potential renewal of the regulatory framework of 1972 — with one large exception. Since pay television and other national sources now provide the bulk of cable program-

*The FCC relaxed its rate regulation requirement in 1976.

ming, the importation of nearby broadcast signals is not considered important enough to require regulation. And the cable network's political clout is such that few contemplate the reimposition of rules on pay TV content.

The general thrust of the Cable Act is toward regulation of the local cable loop, the basic service tier, and the allocation of channels to local information sources in an attempt to realize the medium's "blue sky" potential. The separation of content from transmission is not as complete as some would like, and in other respects the Act clearly gives the impression of 1972 revisited.

Two examples are educational channels and mandatory leased access.

Educational Channels. The Act confirms the right of franchising authorities to force channels to be set aside for public, educational, or governmental use.

Mandatory Leased Access. The Act provides a numerical formula for determining the number of channels a cable operator must lease to unaffiliated users. For a system with thirty-six or more channels, 10 percent of the channels not already designated by law for specific uses must be leased. An operator with fifty-five channels must designate for lease 15 percent of the channels that remain after fulfilling other requirements. Of 100 or more channels, 15 percent must be leased. In the future systems with fewer than thirty-six channels will not be subject to mandatory access.

From an economic point of view, the exact formulation of the mandatory leased access requirement has important consequences for the goal of information diversity. Stanley Besen and Leland Johnson discussed these consequences in an important 1982 Rand Corporation study. Besen and Johnson's findings indicate that the method chosen by Congress might have an adverse impact on small programmers. First, if channels are required to be leased at nondiscriminatory rates, small programmers now benefiting from discriminatory (in some cases implied) access fees will leave the system. Second, if access fees are not regulated, the Act's proposal to set aside only a portion of capacity for lease may lead to higher access fees than would otherwise be the case. This is because, in the words of Besen and Johnson, "in setting the access fee for the channels he must lease [the cable operator] will take into account the effect of competition from lessees on the profits from his own channels."

Regulation of access fees can reduce these problems, but only at the cost of increased administrative burden and political intervention in cable system operation.

One of the primary objectives cable operators had in seeking the 1984 legislation was to lend some predictability to the franchising process. The 1972 rules set up standards for initial franchise awards. As renewal dates approach in many communities, Congress has found it expedient to regulate that procedure as well. Under the provisions of the Act a cable operator may now:

- Apply for the modification of a franchise requirement for reasons of financial hardship and obtain a decision from the franchising authority within a period of 120 days.
- Apply for renewal at any time during the current franchise.
- Three years before a renewal date, request public hearings on the performance of the system and on the community's cable needs.
- At the end of such a proceeding submit a proposal for renewal to be answered within 120 days by the franchising authority.
- If renewal is rejected, enter into a public administrative proceeding at which witnesses and evidence are presented.
- Appeal the final decision to the courts.

Under the Act a franchising authority may not deny renewal on the basis of a violation of the franchise unless the cable operator was given amply notice and an "opportunity to cure" the problem.

The net effect of the franchising provision is that renewal may not be denied without substantial and expensive due process. "The result," according to one FCC official, is "a statute that provides security to incumbent cable systems and poses great, if not insurmountable, difficulty to any challenger to the incumbent." The Act not only affirms the city's right of franchise, it closes off an important opportunity for competition at renewal time.

Some other notable provisions of the Cable Act are as follows:

1. Cable systems may not be owned by broadcasters or telephone companies serving the same area. Ownership by newspapers is not expressly prohibited.

2. It is illegal to use special technological means to steal cable service, but the right to own and use private satellite dishes without liability is protected.

3. Annual franchise fees are limited to 5 percent of cable operators' gross revenues.

4. The FCC will regulate pole attachment fees in the face of state inaction.

5. A state or the FCC may require the filing of informational tariffs for common carrier services other than those traditionally known as "cable (video) service."

The most important aspects of the Act, however, remain its rate and franchising provisons. On balance, the Cable Act codifies a regulatory status quo in which cities and the FCC have the ability to play a much greater role than market forces.

PROSPECTS FOR FUTURE DEREGULATION

A number of factors affect the prospects for the deregulation of cable over the next several years.

One of the most favorable factors is the pro-competitive position of the FCC. The Commission has come full circle since 1972. Its studies now provide highly respected support for the free market view of telecommunications regulation. It will be interesting to see how the FCC handles the new cable responsibilities given it by Congress.

The Department of Justice, normally the federal agency most concerned with encouraging competition, has given a number of indications that it sides with the cities on cable TV regulation. In comments before the FCC on the Cable Act's effective competition standard, the Department proposed guidelines that would bring more cable systems under local regulation than standards proposed by the Commission. The Department also decided not to block a proposed "swap" of cable systems between the Times Mirror Company and Storer Communications, Inc. One effect of this swap will be a consolidation of overbuilt systems in Phoenix and Paradise Valley, Arizona. Where Storer and Times-Mirror have built duplicate facilities down the same Arizona city street, Times Mirror will now own and operate both. The Department of Justice has announced that in cases of this kind, it will not enforce the federal antitrust laws but will instead defer to the wishes of the franchising authority.

More ominous is the role that the cable industry itself played in the drafting of the cable bill. The bill is essentially a mandate for stability over competition: it contains the presumption that franchises ought be renewed and implicitly accepts the natural monopoly hypothesis. Thus it protects the "haves" among cable system operators, rather than the "have-nots" among consumers and potential competitors. The danger here is that the cable industry will join trucking, telephone, broadcasting, and a long line of industries which, upon reaching maturity, found it easier to compete in the regulatory arena than in the marketplace.

Finally, in July 1985 the D.C. Circuit Court of Appeals struck down the last of the FCC's 1972 cable rules — cable systems no longer must carry all local broadcast signals, although they retain a statutory compulsory copyright license to do so. How this decision will affect the balance between broadcasters and cable operators in the marketplace — and in Congress — will become apparent over the next few years.

BIBLIOGRAPHY

Besen, Stanley M., and Johnson, Leland C., *An Economic Analysis of Mandatory Leased Channel Access for Cable Television*. Santa Monica, Calif.: Rand Corporation, 1982.
Cabinet Committee on Cable Communication, *Cable, Report to the President*, Washington, D.C., 1974.
Federal Communications Commission, *Cable Television Report and Order*, 36 F.C.C. 2d 143 (1972).
_____, *Report on the Inquiry into the Economic Relationship Between Television Broadcasting and Cable Television*, 71 F.C.C. 2d 632 (1979).
Levy, Jonathan D., and Pitsch, Peter K., *Statistical Evidence of Substitutability Among Video Delivery Systems*. Washington, D.C.: Federal Communications Commission, 1984.
Lloyd, Frank, "Cable Television's Emerging Two-Way Services: A Dilemma for Federal and State Regulators," *Vanderbilt Law Review*, 36 (1983), 1045.
MacAvoy, Paul W. (ed), *Deregulation of Cable Television*. Washington, D.C.: American Enterprise Institute, 1977.
Noll, Roger G., Peck, Merton J., and McGowan, J. J., *Economic Aspects of Television Regulation*. Washington, D.C.: The Brookings Institution, 1973.
Owen, Bruce M., Beebe, Jack, and Manning, W. G., Jr., *Television Economics*. Lexington, Mass.: Lexington Books, 1974.
Shapiro, George, Kurland, Philip, and Mercurio, James, *Cablespeech: The Case for First Amendment Protection*. New York: Harcourt Brace Jovanovich, Inc., 1983.
U.S. Congress, House Committee on Commerce, Subcommittee on Communications, Staff Report, "Cable Television: Promise Versus Regulatory Performance," Committee Print, January 1976.
_____, Senate Committee on Commerce, Science and Transportation, Report on S. 66, "Cable Telecommunications Act of 1983," 98th Cong., 1st Sess. (April 27, 1983).

CASE 4

Petroleum Regulation and Public Policy

R. Glenn Hubbard
Northwestern University and the National Bureau of Economic Research

Robert J. Weiner
Harvard University

INTRODUCTION AND BACKGROUND

Focus

The petroleum industry is the largest in the world and one of the most visible. Oil companies dominate the "ten biggest" list of America's giant industrial corporations. Petroleum is highly concentrated geographically, both in the United States and worldwide. Government intervention in the industry consequently has high political and economic consequences. Winners and losers are apt to be strongly affected and easily identifiable.

Public concern over petroleum industry practices dates back to the last century. Standard Oil was the dominant company from the industry's early days until its dismemberment by the U.S. Supreme Court on antitrust violations in 1911. Domestic oil production was

---

Parts of this paper reflect research supported by the Energy and Environmental Policy Center at Harvard University, the National Science Foundation (SES-8408805), and the U.S. Department of Energy. We are grateful to Ronald Braeutigam, Michael Klass, and Leonard Weiss for helpful comments and suggestions.

restricted by state governments in Texas and Oklahoma from the early 1930s to the early 1970s. Federal regulations kept domestic crude oil prices below market-clearing levels from 1971 until 1981. The present era is the first in fifty years that the industry has faced market forces without strong government intervention. In this paper we will analyze recent regulation and the trend away from government control of the petroleum industry.

After reviewing conditions under which government intervention might improve economic efficiency, we will evaluate "efficiency" and "nonefficiency" motivations for price controls on domestic crude oil, the most visible form of government regulation of the industry in the 1970s. The analytical part of this discussion illustrates how simple tools of microeconomics can be used to assess the effects of price regulation on economic efficiency, oil consumption, oil prices, and income transferred abroad to pay for additional imports. We close with an examination of the current, price-decontrolled environment. Given the rationale for a public policy in the petroleum sector, what types of actions can maintain economic efficiency and at the same time protect the economy from oil supply disruptions?

Motivations for Policy Intervention

Market Failure and Economic Efficiency. Focusing first on economic efficiency, we assume that the goal of policymakers is to advance the economic welfare of the citizenry to the maximum extent possible. This has two dimensions. The first is long-run industry structure and behavior. Second, the oil market has been subject periodically to sharp fluctuations — the Suez Crisis of 1956–1957, the Arab embargo of 1973–1974, the Iranian revolution of 1978–1979, and the present Iran-Iraq war. According to the well-known "invisible hand" proposition first put forth by Adam Smith, national economic welfare is maximized when governments allow markets to operate freely. Only when some sort of *market failure* is present is there justification for public intervention. An *efficiency* case for *any* energy policy — price controls, tariffs, public stockpiles, energy conservation, or anything else — requires a demonstration of market failure.

A long-standing argument for governmental intervention is domestic monopoly. The petroleum industry has been the object of considerable government scrutiny and public mistrust over the years, in large part because of industry structure. Around the turn of the century, Standard Oil achieved notoriety for its monopolization of the industry. Three of its offspring — Exxon, Mobil, and SoCal — along with two other American (Texaco and Gulf) and two foreign giants

(British Petroleum and Royal Dutch Shell) came to be known as the "majors." These multinational companies dominated the international oil trade from the 1920s to the 1960s. The sheer size of these companies brought them into the public limelight.

Table 1 shows the concentration of United States companies in the petroleum industry. Like many mineral industries, petroleum can be divided into vertical stages. *Production* entails extraction of crude oil from existing reserves, development of newly discovered sources, and exploration. *Refining* consists of processing the crude oil by heat and chemical means into usable products. *Distribution* consists of marketing these products as well as service to consumers through gasoline stations and fuel oil deliveries.

Table 1 shows that the petroleum industry is not highly concentrated by United States standards (see Scherer, 1980, Chapter 3). Moreover, entry into the production, refining, and distribution segments of the industry is relatively easy. On the other hand, the large firms in the industry appear to face little threat from entrants. For example, only three of the largest twenty refining companies in 1980 entered the industry since World War II. All three entered by acquiring existing refineries. The largest firm to enter in the postwar period through constructing a new refinery ranked forty-fifth in 1980.

Vertical integration is prevalent in the industry. Sixteen of the twenty largest United States refiners in 1980 also appeared on the list of the twenty largest producers. An exact measure of vertical integra-

Table 1. Concentration of United States Companies in the Petroleum Industry

	Percent of Total		
	Largest Four Companies	*Largest Eight Companies*	*Largest Twenty Companies*
Production			
Crude oil extracted	25	41	60
Ownership of reserves	35	53	70
Refining			
Capacity	29	49	74
Crude oil processed	31	54	81
Distribution			
All products	28	46	65
Gasoline	28	49	65

Source: American Petroleum Institute (1981b).

tion is difficult to construct, since the majors exert influence over foreign production sources that they do not actually own. Much of the government intervention in the petroleum industry has been directed toward preserving competition between non-vertically integrated, "independent" refiners, and their larger brethren.

The majors' dominant position in the industry gradually eroded in the 1960s. Until that time, demand fluctuations had been smoothed within their vertically integrated chains, and prices had been declining slowly in real terms with discoveries of low-cost Middle Eastern oil. The entry weakened the companies' bargaining position with the Organization of Petroleum Exporting Countries (OPEC), which was founded in 1960. Crude oil prices rose in the early 1970s and then jumped substantially during the "oil embargo" of 1973–1974.

The transfer of control from the majors to OPEC in the 1970s raised a question for domestic oil regulation: What role could it have? The crude oil market is international, as low transport costs enable cargoes to travel long distances. If the price of crude oil is set in the world market, the existence of alleged monopoly power at home becomes less relevant. Domestic price controls on a freely traded international commodity have very different consequences than controls on nontraded goods; most important, excess demand is no longer allocated through rationing, queues, and the like, but through additional imports. Thus domestic regulation spills over into the international market.

Short-run fluctuations in the oil market present a different set of issues. The arguments for government intervention during a short-term supply disruption on the grounds that the interests of private agents and the nation are not identical are as follows:

1. *Macroeconomic losses.* Such losses have been substantial in the past (Fried and Schultze, 1975; Mork and Hall, 1980; Hickman and Huntington, 1984). A large, unanticipated increase in the price of oil generates economic losses for oil-importing nations through cyclical losses in aggregate demand, deteriorating terms of trade, and reduced potential output. The first effect is transitory, traceable primarily to downward inflexibility of nominal wages and non-oil prices and to demand-management problems. Related demand-side costs may stem from the redistribution of income among sectors, possibly affecting aggregate demand because of differences in propensities to spend.

The last two effects are more long term. As oil is a major input to the economy's production process, an oil price increase resulting from a supply shock will reduce potential output, that is, the output attainable with all resources fully and efficiently employed. Conserva-

Introduction and Background

tion of energy and substitution of other production factors (for example, capital and labor) in a free market will reflect adjustments to higher energy costs, but the reduction in energy consumption may lower capital and labor productivity.

2. *Monopsony power.* The United States is a large player in the world petroleum market, since its actions affect market outcomes. An example is the price control and entitlements program that subsidized oil imports in the 1970s, thereby putting upward pressure on world oil prices. Imported oil thus has an additional cost associated with it (sometimes called the "monopsony premium") inasmuch as increased United States imports result in higher prices and greater wealth transferred abroad.

3. *Vulnerability.* The level of national preparedness could affect the likelihood of a disruption (Balas, 1980; Kinberg et al., 1978). This argument clearly applies only to the case of deliberate action taken by foreign powers against the United States.

4. *National security.* The nation's security objectives may cause it to incur foreign policy and military costs, regardless of whether a disruption is deliberate. A potential example is the cost of the Rapid Deployment Force.

Two additional efficiency arguments for public intervention are based on imperfections in other markets. *Information* is the basis for the first. The government could gain access to confidential intelligence information regarding future supply conditions and thus be in a position to make better decisions than private agents (Marchand and Pestieau, 1979). The second is based on *insurance*. Private agents may fear to act in their own best interests because they cannot ensure there will not be a public outcry for additional government regulation or taxation (for example, windfall profits tax) during the disruption, and because of past behavior, the government cannot credibly commit itself to avoid such actions (Wright and Williams, 1982).

The importance of each of these arguments is empirical and will vary according to circumstance. Those who believe that the best energy security policy is to let the market be the determining factor, however, are obliged to reject them all.

Price Controls and Economic Efficiency. In this study we examine in detail the impacts of crude oil price controls on the behavior of domestic producers, refiners, and consumers. Price controls are direct and highly visible and thus politically attractive. The experience in the United States in the 1970s resulted in unhappiness with price controls

(Kalt, 1981). Economists' arguments against price controls (apart from innate professional distaste) in a disruption fall into three categories. First, they discourage additional supply. This argument is weak unless supply is elastic in the short run, which seems unlikely. Second, they discourage conservation when it is most needed. Like the previous argument, this depends on a short-run elasticity (in this case, of demand). There is an important additional consideration, however; the United States is not autarkic. Given imports as the marginal supply source, increased United States demand exerts upward pressure on *world prices,* which in a disruption are very sensitive. Since only domestic prices are controlled, demand pressure can raise world prices sufficiently that even the controlled domestic price eventually exceeds the price that would prevail in a free market (Hubbard and Fry, 1982). Finally, price controls redistribute substantial income, which serves to create beneficiary groups (in the past, United States refiners and consumers), making rescission difficult after the emergency has passed.

Nonefficiency Motivations for Price Controls. Price controls and subsidies dominated the regulatory pattern of the 1970s. Thus it is pertinent to consider two nonefficiency motivations for controls: "fear of inflation" and "consumer protection." The term "nonefficiency motivations" is in no way designed to minimize their importance. Indeed, one of the reasons rising energy prices have been accompanied by such political attention is the enormous size of the associated (domestic and international) transfers of income and wealth. For example, the price of crude oil imported into the United States rose from $2 in 1970 to $12 in 1974.

As general economy-wide price controls were being phased out in 1973, it became apparent that domestic oil prices would rise markedly to the level of oil prices. At the same time the fear of rekindling inflation pervaded the policymaking community. Indeed, even with price controls on domestic production, the rate of inflation accelerated sharply in 1974 and 1975. While not all of the increase in inflation was traceable to the oil supply shock of 1973–1974, one contemporary econometric study claimed that roughly 28 percent of the total increase in inflation was a result of higher energy prices (see Fried and Schultze, 1975). Further compounding the problem, as higher energy prices reduced aggregate production, the demand for labor fell, contributing to the previously unknown condition of "stagflation" — high inflation and unemployment rates.[1]

Even in the face of such an alarming connection between higher energy prices and slower economic growth, arguments for maintaining price controls in the long run are questionable. Substantial domestic welfare costs are incurred because of overconsumption and underproduction of crude oil, and the controls slow down the economy's adjustment to rising oil prices during oil supply disruptions. If price controls were given preexisting distortion, there might be ample argument for phased deregulation to minimize macroeconomic side effects, but that is certainly no cause for their reimposition in the future.

Because of the importance of oil (and energy in general) in both production and consumer expenditure and because of limited possibilities for substitution in the short run, oil price increases can be expected to reduce real living standards and effect large transfers of income and wealth.[2] The particular system of price controls used throughout most of the years of petroleum price regulation in the United States transferred income from domestic producers to consumers.[3] As a point for economic analysis, however, to the extent that such transfers affect the decisions of the players involved (producers, refiners, and consumers), losses in economic efficiency result. We take up later the question of the relative efficiency of using price controls to affect consumers.

PUBLIC INTERVENTION IN THE OIL INDUSTRY: BACKGROUND[4]

Intervention Prior to 1973

Public intervention has long played an important role in the domestic petroleum industry, although the source of concern (and hence the means of intervention) has varied over time. Except for the Standard Oil case and the imposition of price controls on crude oil in the 1970s, public policy could be fairly described as "proproducer," with a wide variety of protective interventions, including (1) restrictions on domestic production, (2) favorable tax treatment for oil producers, and (3) official barriers against foreign competition.

Policies of the first type were typically embodied in state "prorationing" or "conservation" schemes, which acted to restrict domestic production by allowing each well to operate a given number of days per month. Formal federal intervention to achieve cartel-type restriction of production came with the passage of the Connally Hot Oil Act (1935), under which state prorationing schemes were coordinated.[5]

Favorable tax treatment for oil producers is as old as the income tax itself, with a "depletion allowance" of 5 percent of the value of annual production written into the Revenue Act of 1913. By 1926 the allowance had reached 27.5 percent, and it stayed there for more than forty years.

National security interests ostensibly led to the announcement of a voluntary oil import restriction program in 1957. When the voluntary program failed to reduce imports significantly, it was replaced by President Eisenhower in 1959 with an official Mandatory Oil Import Program (MOIP). With some exceptions (for example, imports to the West Coast), the program restricted imports to a set percentage of domestic producton. "Import tickets," or rights to import oil, were allocated to domestic refiners roughly according to size, though (as was typical of future intervention as well) small refiners were favored. Tickets could be bought and sold on a white market, at a price equal to the spread between domestic and imported prices.

As there was no clear efficiency rationale for the MOIP, transfers to domestic producers could be expected to be accompanied by substantial welfare costs. Such deadweight losses stemmed from the increase in the price of oil in the United States above the world price and the resulting underconsumption of oil and overproduction of domestic oil. Economic studies have indicated that such losses were quite large.[6]

The onset of the 1970s brought substantial criticisms of the MOIP both from groups concerned with its labyrinthine administration and from policymakers concerned about inflation. Though the MOIP was not eliminated until April 1973, restrictions started to be phased out in 1970.

By the early 1970s restrictions on oil imports were removed, the depletion allowance was substantially reduced (and later removed), and prorationing controls were eliminated. For the first time, however, public intervention switched to price controls. Controls were imposed on all stages of the industry as part of the economy-wide anti-inflation program announced by President Nixon in 1971.[7]

Emergency Petroleum Allocation Act

Though controls were phased out for most of the economy by the end of 1973, regulation of oil prices continued. These "Phase IV" regulations were ratified in the Emergency Petroleum Allocation Act of 1973 (EPAA). Operationally, EPAA controls separated domestic oil into two tiers, "old oil" and "new oil." Prices for old oil were set at substantially lower levels than prices for new oil. Output levels for 1972 were established as "base period control levels." Any amount by which production from a given well fell below this control level was added to the well's "current cumulative deficiency." The first tier, "old oil," was composed of the base period control level and the current cumulative deficiency. Three other complications were introduced: (1) producers could release a barrel from the "old oil" category for each barrel of new oil produced from pre-1972 wells; (2) output from wells not brought into production until after 1972 was classified as "new oil;" and (3) output averaging less than ten barrels per day from a well was classified as "stripper oil." By the end of 1973 new, stripper, released, and import prices were not subject to controls.

Regulation soon expanded beyond price controls per se, as competition for access to controlled oil led to the imposition of allocation regulations and the virtual freezing of vertical (buyer-seller) transaction arrangements. Allocation of crude oil was controlled under the "Buy/Sell" program, which required refiners with ratios of crude oil to refining capacity in excess of the national average to sell to crude-short refiners.

In addition to the fear of shortages, an obvious byproduct of EPAA-styled price regulation were differences in average crude costs paid by refiners. That is, refiners with access to price-controlled oil would have lower average costs than those purchasing only decontrolled oil. To equalize these interrefiner differences, Congress adopted an "old oil entitlements" program in late 1974. Under this program the number of entitlements given to a particular refiner was equal to the number of barrels of controlled oil it would have used in the previous month assuming national-average proportions of controlled and uncontrolled oil. If a refiner used more price-controlled oil than the national average, it was required to purchase entitlements to refine the excess. The "entitlement price" reflected the spread between the acquisition costs of uncontrolled and old oil across refiners. We discuss the impact of the entitlements program on marginal incentives in a later section. The introduction of the entitlements program effectively eliminated the need for the Buy/Sell program.

Many exceptions to the entitlements program were made under the EPAA tenure, primarily to give extra entitlements to favored groups. Principal categories included (1) the Small Refiner Bias program, (2) the Exceptions and Appeals Relief system, and (3) the United States Strategic Petroleum Reserve. Under the Small Refiner Bias program, extra entitlements were given on a sliding scale with fewer entitlements given as refinery throughput increased up to

175,000 barrels per day.[8] The Exceptions and Appeals Relief system conferred additional entitlements on refiners with "hardships." In practice, the program was an administrative nightmare.[9]

Energy Policy and Conservation Act

The Ford administration favored deregulation upon expiration of the EPAA in early 1975. Congress, however, passed the Energy Policy and Conservation Act (EPCA), which took effect in February 1976, and maintained domestic petroleum price regulation. The introduction of a three-tier pricing program extended controls to almost all domestic production exempted from controls under the EPAA.

Under the original EPCA legislation, authority for price controls (except for emergency standby status) was to expire on September 30, 1981. The EPCA defined all output from a property less than its base period control level plus current cumulative deficiency as "lower tier oil." Any output from wells brought into production after 1975 and output from pre-1976 wells greater than assigned lower tier output became "upper tier oil." Finally, stripper oil and imported oil prices were not subject to controls. Upper tier oil sold for its price on September 30, 1975, less $1.32, plus adjustments for inflation (and for incentives). Lower tier oil sold for its price on May 15, 1973, plus $1.35, with additional inflation and incentive adjustments. EPCA amendments in 1976 eased these controls by allowing average domestic prices to rise by at least 10 percent per annum (irrespective of inflation). Average prices in 1976 were roughly $5 for lower tier oil, $11.50 for upper tier oil, and $12 for stripper oil.

Deregulation

On June 1, 1979, President Carter began (under legislative authority from EPCA) a gradual decontrol of domestic crude oil prices. Ostensibly to capture most of the income transfers from domestic consumers to domestic producers, the Crude Oil Windfall Profit Tax Act of 1980 was also enacted under the Carter administration. The tax is not at all a profits tax. Rather, it is an excise tax on the difference between the market price of a barrel of crude oil and a predetermined base price. We discuss the implications of such a tax for producer behavior in the next section.

Three tiers of oil are categorized under the Act for tax purposes. Tier One consists of recently decontrolled upper tier oil and all lower tier and upper tier oil under the EPCA. Its base price is equal to the ceiling price in May 1979, adjusted for inflation. Stripper and Naval Petroleum Reserve crude oil constitutes Tier Two, the base price for which is about a dollar higher than the Tier One base price. The tax rates on the first two tiers are 70 and 60 percent, respectively. Tier Three oil includes oil from post-1978 wells, heavy crude oil, and incremental oil from tertiary recovery. Its base price is $2 above the May 1979 upper tier ceiling price, and its tax rate is 30 percent. A small amount of oil is exempt from "windfall profit" taxation on the grounds of exceptionally high cost of production or ownership by nonprofit organizations.

The windfall profit tax will be phased out beginning January 1988 or the first month (but no later than January 1991) after the federal govenment has collected $227 billion from the tax. To evaluate the impact of the tax on producer revenues, note that in conjunction with existing corporate income taxes, the windfall profit tax will collect more than 70 percent of crude oil price increases during its tenure. While the elimination of price controls and entitlements subsidies got rid of the regulation-induced distortion of consumption decisions, the excise tax system enacted under the Crude Oil Windfall Profit Tax Act will continue to distort producer behavior. The revenues from the tax (about $66 billion as of 1984) have been assigned to a variety of energy assistance, research, and subsidy programs.

ECONOMIC ANALYSIS OF GOVERNMENT INTERVENTION

Price Controls and Economic Efficiency

The level of demand for oil would be *efficient* if oil were used in such a way that its economic value was no less than the price of imports. Depending on their implementation, price controls can create distortions in both the domestic demand for and supply of oil. These distortions in turn can lead to substantial deadweight losses for the economy as a whole — losses above transfers among consumers, producers, and refiners. Departures from efficiency are measured in terms of these deadweight losses — reductions in the size of the national economic pie. In addition, to the extent that the United States is not a price taker in the world oil market, distortions in domestic demand and supply can influence the world price. As a first step we follow Kalt (1981) in making two assumptions about market structure: (1) domestic refining and production of oil is assumed to be undertaken competitively (Table 1) and (2) the United States is assumed to have no monopsony power in the world oil market. We relax the second assumption later.

Contemporary popular claims notwithstanding, the original EPAA-type price controls did not distort refiner marginal costs (and hence, given our "competitive refiners" assumption, consumer prices and demand). To see this, note the description of the domestic refining market in Figure 1. D_d and S_d represent the domestic demand for and supply of crude oil, respectively. Given the price-taking assumption (that is, changes in United States oil imports do not affect world oil prices), the supply of imports is represented by the horizontal line S_m at world price P_m. $\overline{P}_d$ represents the controlled domestic price. In the absence of price controls, producers within the United States

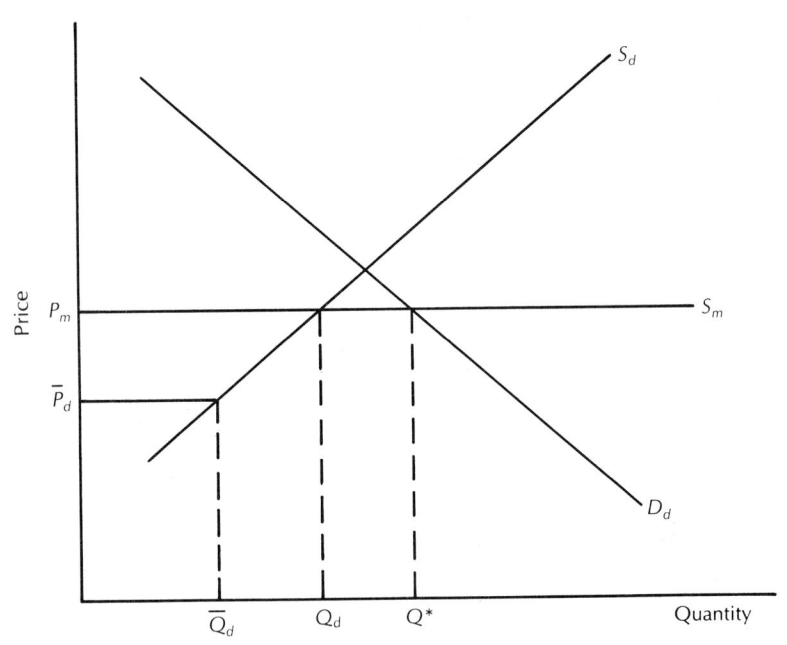

NOTE: Figure 1 is simplified by assuming that all domestic oil is price controlled at the same level, as under EPAA.

Figure 1. Market Equilibrium with Price Controls

would produce Q_d, and refiners would purchase Q^*, with $Q^* - Q_d$ coming from imports. With domestic price controls at P_d, domestic producers reduce their quantity supplied to $\bar{Q}_d$, and imports widen to $Q^* - \bar{Q}_d$. Total refinery purchases do not change (only the split between domestic production and imports), because the marginal cost of crude oil is still the (unchanged) import price. Thus there are no demand-side distortions. There are, however, *supply-side* distortions because the difference in domestic production $Q_d - \bar{Q}_d$ could have been produced at less than the world price.

As Figure 1 indicates, rents on the inframarginal (price-controlled) barrels were captured only by refiners with access to controlled crude oil. A major reallocation of those property rights occurred in November 1974, with the introduction of the entitlements program. Again, simply put, rights to controlled crude oil (entitlements) were granted as an equal proportion of each refiner's total input. Most important for our purposes, the program not only redistributed rents but also lowered refinery *marginal costs* and production decisions. This is because the purchase of additional barrels allowed a refiner additional entitlements to lower priced oil, partially offsetting the cost.

The entitlements program under the EPAA is best understood as the system of taxes and subsidies depicted in Figure 2. The entitlements program equalized (subject to the exceptions mentioned in section II) the marginal cost of crude oil across refiners as the weighted average cost of all oil refined domestically. That is, the weighted average price P_s in Figure 2 corresponded to

$$P_s = mP_m + (1 - m)\bar{P}_d$$

where m represents the fraction of domestic consumption coming from imports. Of course, $P_s < P_m$, with the difference being the value of the per unit entitlement subsidy.

The program implicitly taxes away the rents on controlled oil $\bar{R}[(P_m - \bar{P}_d) \times \bar{Q}_d]$, redistributing them (the area $(P_m - P_s) \times Q^{**}$) to all refiners — even those without access to controlled oil. Two results can be distinguished from the previous case of price controls without entitlements: (1) a subsidy (equal to $P_m - P_s$) is generated, lowering refiner marginal cost, and (2) as a consequence, total refinery purchases increase (from Q^* to Q^{**}). Since the refining sector is assumed to be competitive, the marginal price faced by consumers of petroleum products declines.[10] The resulting increase in final demand (and refinery purchases) increases imports and the nation's oil import bill.

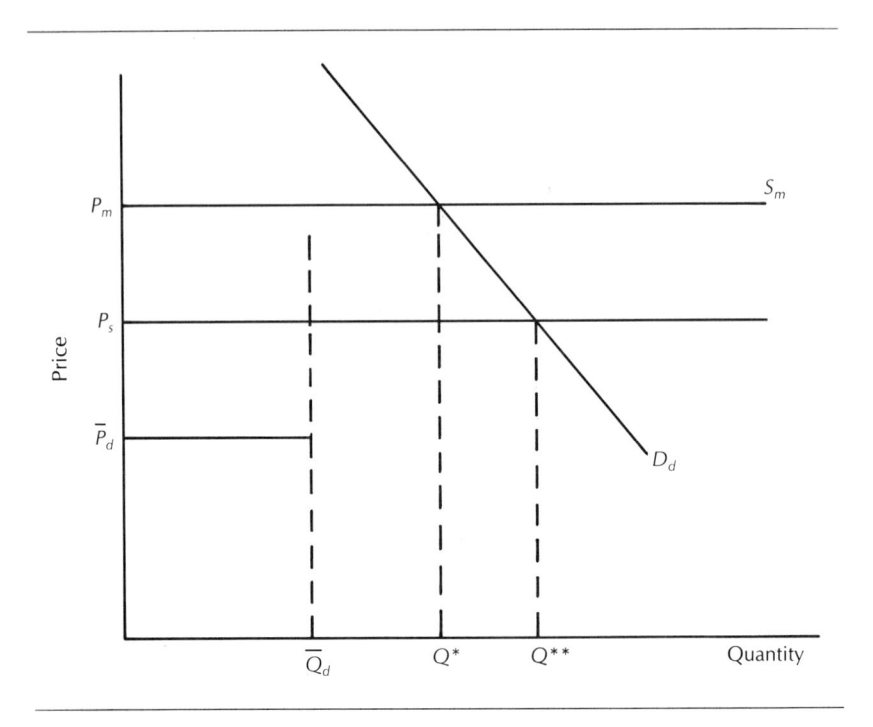

Figure 2. Crude Oil Price Controls and Entitlements

After the passage of the EPCA, the entitlements program changed to accommodate the new three-tier pricing system in February 1976. New entitlements had to be created for upper tier oil, since upper tier oil prices were reduced below market levels. The existence of multiple tiers complicates the diagram in Figure 2, but the qualitative points about the redistribution of rents on the controlled oil remain.

As part of the original provisions of the EPCA, ultimate decontrol of crude oil prices was scheduled for the fall of 1981. Designed to capture the price increases on oil already under production, President Carter's Crude Oil Windfall Profit Tax Act in reality imposed excise taxes on domestic oil production. As such, the taxes prolong the system of multi-tier price regulation, even though crude oil prices are now decontrolled.

Measuring the Welfare Costs of Crude Oil Price Controls

Our next step is to examine the impacts of petroleum price regulation on efficiency in production and consumption. Such information will help us to quantify the benefits of crude oil price decontrol. Price controls effected a massive redistribution of rents (associated with controlled oil) away from producers to refiners and consumers. Even though the windfall profit tax superseded price controls, it continues to forestall significant transfers of wealth to crude oil producers.

We first calculate the efficiency losses due to price controls under the continuing assumption that the United States is a price taker in the world oil market. The marginal social cost in the calculations is the price of an extra barrel of imported oil, since this measures foreign producers' claim on United States output. As shown in Figure 3, the operation of the price controls-cum-entitlements subsidy program increases domestic demand from Q^* to Q^{**}, creating a welfare cost on the consumption side equal to the area ABC. On the supply side, the controls reduce domestic production from Q_d to $\bar{Q}_d$. This reduction is made up with imports, which cost United States refiners P_m per barrel (Figure 3), when United States producers could produce them at a lower marginal cost (as represented by the S_d function). Hence an additional welfare cost represented by the area DEF is created. How significant these welfare costs are to society depends on assumptions about the shapes (elasticities) of the D_d and S_d curves.

Trends in world oil prices and the difference between the world price and the marginal cost of oil to domestic refiners (because of the entitlements subsidy program) are reported over the period from the first quarter of 1974 to the second quarter of 1984 in Table 2.[11] The peak in world oil prices occurred at about the same time as crude oil prices were decontrolled in the United States, as world demand decreased (because of a slowdown in output growth in most industrial countries and the lagged effects of higher oil prices) and supply conditions improved.

Kalt (1981) provides some estimates of the deadweight losses from domestic overconsumption and underproduction for the years during which the entitlements program operated. His calculations are summarized in Table 3. Constant-elasticity demand and supply relationships were assumed, with a (one year) price elasticity demand of -0.5 and a set of supply elasticities for production from existing wells and new production (see Kalt, 1981, pp. 195–205). The calculations in Table 3 make clear the size of the annual welfare costs involved —

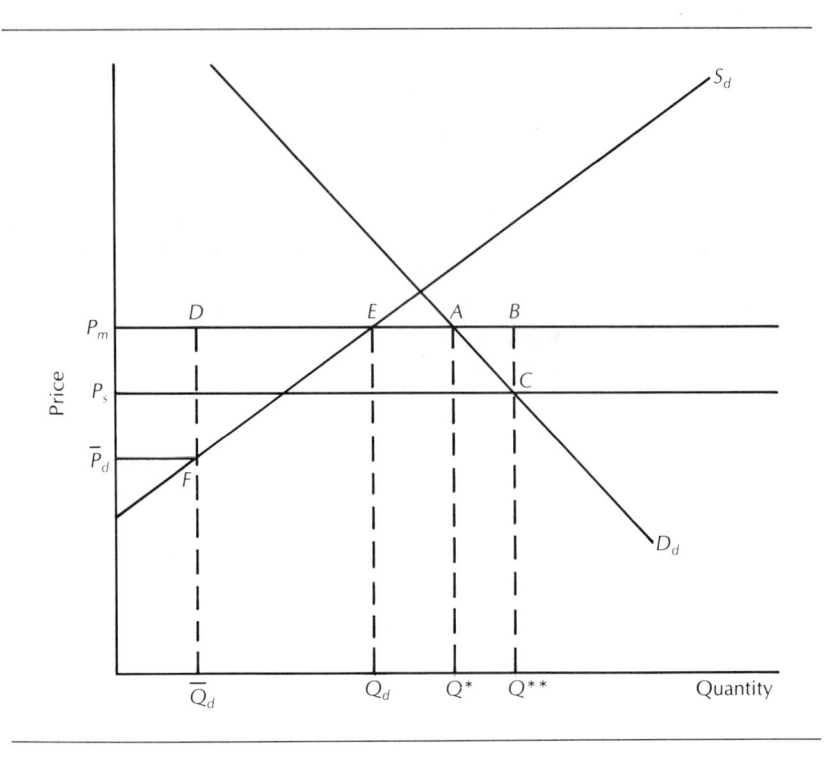

Figure 3. Measuring the Welfare Costs of Price Controls

typically in excess of $1 billion (1980 dollars). Expenditures on additional oil imports were on the order of $15 to $20 billion per year.

There are likely to be further costs to the economy (over and above these distortions in consumption and production) from crude oil price regulation, stemming from (1) a gap between the private and social costs of imported oil and (2) feedback effects from changes in United States demand to prices in the world market.

With respect to the first point, in addition to possible "national security externalities" associated with dependence on foreign oil, the structure of the United States economy leads to the creation of a "macroeconomic" externality in the presence of a large and unanticipated increase in the price of crude oil (see the statistical evidence in Hamilton, 1983). The inability of wages and non-oil prices to adjust downward in response to an oil supply shock exacerbates the effects of the shock on inflation, real output, and unemployment.

When the United States is a price taker, the price relevant for the

Table 2. Price Regulation and the Marginal Cost of Oil to Domestic Refiners, 1974–1984[a]

Year	Quarter	World Price	Domestic[b] Marginal Cost	Year	Quarter	World Price	Domestic[b] Marginal Cost
1974	1	11.59	—	1979	1	15.32	13.65
	2	12.93	—		2	18.41	15.90
	3	12.65	—		3	25.22	21.48
	4	12.60	11.25		4	30.39	26.03
1975	1	13.03	10.62	1980	1	34.05	28.90
	2	13.56	10.73		2	34.72	29.14
	3	14.11	11.19		3	33.45	29.01
	4	14.84	11.76		4	32.28	29.87
1976	1	13.42	10.72	1981	1	36.54	—
	2	13.56	10.83		2	35.91	—
	3	13.60	11.16		3	34.42	—
	4	13.79	11.60		4	34.27	—
1977	1	13.77	11.48	1982	1	33.05	—
	2	13.79	11.36		2	31.20	—
	3	14.27	12.02		3	31.53	—
	4	14.54	12.45		4	31.78	—
1978	1	14.44	12.47	1983	1	29.62	—
	2	14.51	12.84		2	28.61	—
	3	14.46	13.04		3	28.87	—
	4	14.54	13.18		4	28.94	—
				1984	1	28.76	—
					2	28.79	—

[a]Prices are in United States dollars per barrel. A dash means that the two prices are equal (for example, no entitlements subsidy).
[b]See note 12 for definition.

calculation of efficiency losses increases from P_m to $\hat{P}_m$ to reflect the negative externalities associated with imported oil. The analogue to Figure 3 is Figure 4. The welfare loss due to distortions in consumption increases by the area $IJAB$ to area CIJ, and the welfare loss due to distortions in domestic production increases by area $GHDE$ to area FGH.

When the United States is no longer assumed to be a price taker in the world oil market, the increase in United States demand caused by the price controls-cum-entitlements subsidy program will lead to an increase in the world price. We can construct a world demand

Table 3. Welfare Costs of Entitlements Subsidy, 1975–1980
(Millions of 1980 Dollars)

	Demand Side			Supply Side		
	Dead-weight Loss	Additional Crude Imports (MMB)	Expenditure on Additional Imports	Dead-weight Loss	Additional Crude Imports (MMB)	Expenditure on Additional Imports
1975	1037	491	9602	963	99	1948
1976	852	477	8764	1046	344	6288
1977	654	433	8052	1213	455	8444
1978	300	305	5285	816	348	6034
1979	627	361	9200	1852	331	8444
1980	1038	373	14,261	4616	530	20,214

Source: Kalt (1981), Tables 5.1 and 5.2.

curve for oil imports by adding the import demands of other countries to that of the United States. (The United States import demand curve is the difference between the domestic demand and supply curves.) In Figure 5 we combine the import demand relationships with the upward-sloping import supply function of oil exporters.[12]

Consider the impact of the price controls and entitlements in this case. Since domestic price controls increase the level of demand for imports at any given world price, the import demand curve shifts to the right to D'_m. In addition, to the extent that the United States is a large player in the world market, the slope becomes steeper, since United States import demand is less sensitive to changes in the world price because of the entitlements subsidy. The entitlements subsidy in effect dilutes the effects of changes in the world price on United States consumption because an increase in the world price raises the value of an entitlement.

It is this latter modification that is likely to have the most serious consequences during oil supply disruptions (in which the S_m curve shifts back and to the left), since demand response to world price changes will not be as great as in the "no controls" case. These qualifications introduced by potential monopsony power of oil-importing countries increase the social cost of additional crude oil imports, raising the domestic welfare costs of price controls.

Removing the assumption that the United States is a price taker in the world oil market and replacing it with an upward sloping import supply curve, we can recalculate the deadweight losses sketched in

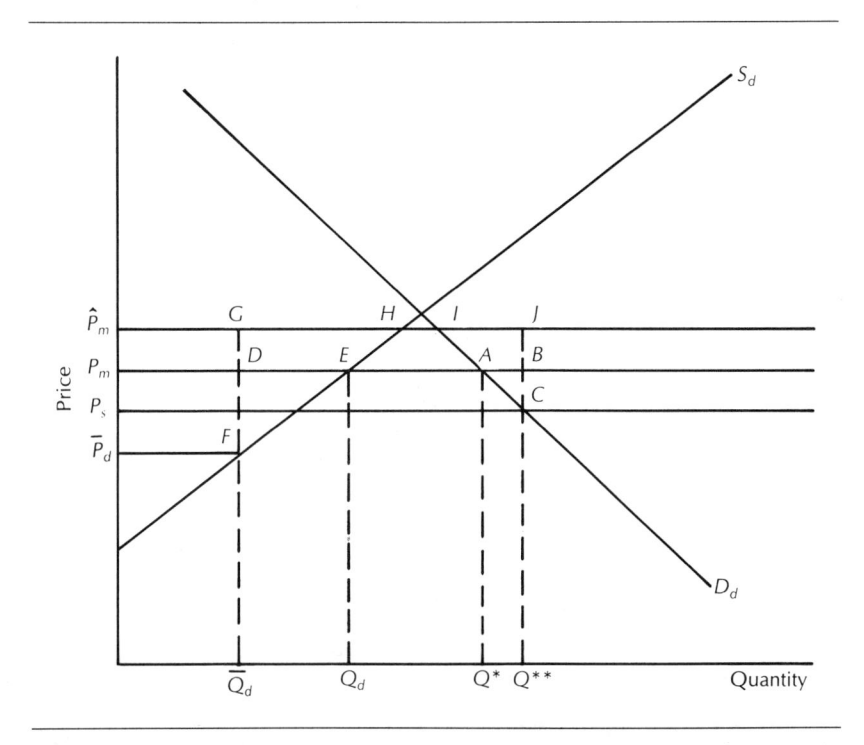

Economic Analysis of Government Intervention 123

Figure 4. Welfare Costs of Price Controls When Oil Imports Have Negative Externalities

Figure 3 resulting from the operation of the domestic price controls-cum-entitlements subsidy program. To focus on distortions in consumption, we consider the simple case wherein domestic supply is perfectly inelastic at Q_d. The marginal cost of oil to domestic refiners (MC_d) is less than the world price because of the entitlements subsidy, but as imports become relatively more important, the per unit subsidy diminishes. Hence MC_d approaches S_m, the import supply curve, as quantity demanded increases. These relationships are depicted in Figure 6.

The domestic subsidy raises United States demand from Q^* to Q^{**}, increasing the world price by $P_m^{**} - P_m^*$, and raising imports by $Q^{**} - Q^*$. The deadweight loss due to the extra domestic consumption is represented by the region ADE. This loss per se is smaller than when the United States was assumed to be a price taker, because the attendant increases in the world price and the weighted-average re-

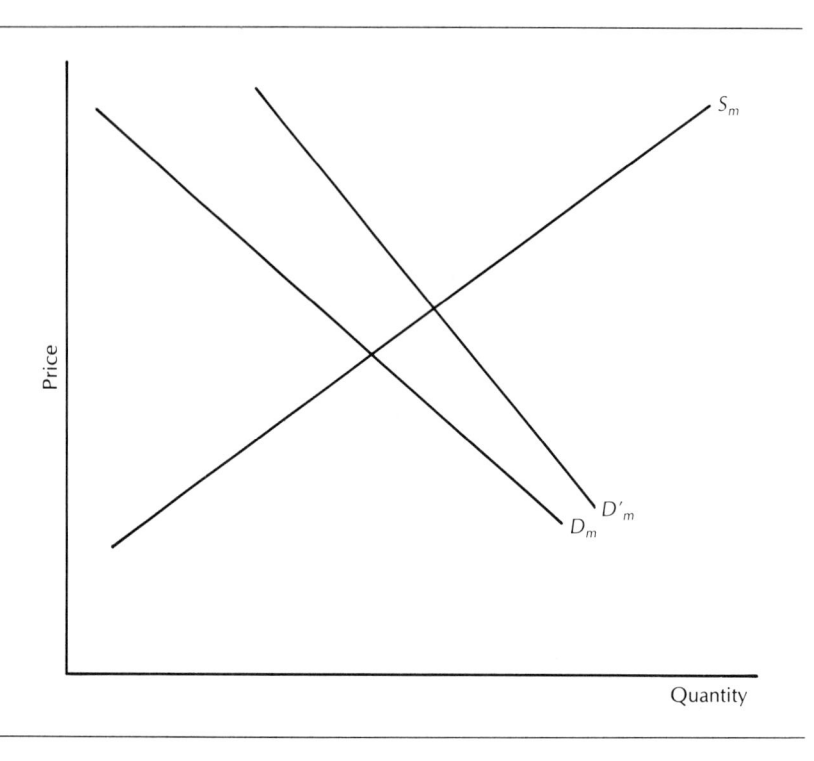

Figure 5. U.S. Policies and World Oil Prices

finer's acquisition cost reduce consumption. There is, however, an additional loss (represented by *AEC*) corresponding to the inefficient extra foreign production.

The rectangle *ABGF* represents an incremental wealth transfer from the United States to foreign oil producers, a deadweight loss from the point of view of the United States economy alone, but not from the point of view of the world economy. This wealth transfer is likely to be large, since it reflects the price increase the United States must pay on *all* imports, not just the additional imports due to the regulations. Even this transfer may involve second-order welfare costs because of the macroeconomic externalities accompanying oil price increases discussed before.

In addition to losses imposed on the United States economy, a negative externality is created for all oil-importing countries because of the higher world price. Such losses could be substantial for most major Organization for Economic Cooperation and Development

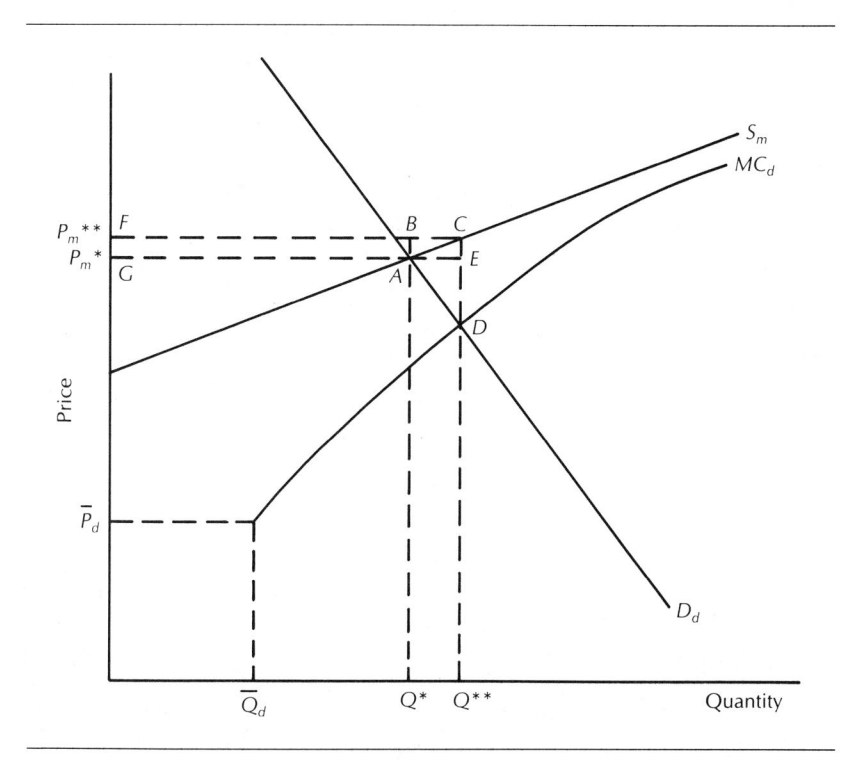

Economic Analysis of Government Intervention 125

Figure 6. Welfare Costs of Domestic Controls When United States Is Not a Price Taker

(OECD) countries, whose impost demand elasticities are likely to be much lower in absolute value than in the United States.[13]

In Table 4 we modify the Kalt estimates of the deadweight loss on the demand side under the assumption that the United States faces an upward-sloping supply schedule in the world market. Four alternative values of the elasticity of that import supply curve (ϵ_m) are used: 0, 0.5, 1.0, and 5.0. Of course, the size of the deadweight loss depends on the magnitude of the supply response. In all cases, though, the deadweight loss is reduced, because additional imports due to entitlements are less a result of the upward-sloping foreign supply curve. The additional loss from excess foreign production is too small to offset this. These losses do not include possible costs from macroeconomic externalities associated with higher oil prices or the cost to other countries of higher oil prices.

Table 4. Deadweight Loss from Entitlements Subsidy,
1975–1980 (Millions of 1980 Dollars)

	$\epsilon_m = \infty$	$\epsilon_m = 5.0$	$\epsilon_m = 1.0$	$\epsilon_m = 0.5$	$\epsilon_m = 0.0$
1975	1037	903	571	415	0
1976	852	742	469	275	0
1977	654	570	360	262	0
1978	300	261	165	120	0
1979	627	545	345	251	0
1980	1038	904	570	415	0

Elasticity of Import Supply Curve

NOTE: First column is from Table 3. Other columns are based on calculations from data in Table 3.

Although an upward-sloping foreign supply curve results in lower deadweight losses, it causes a wealth transfer from the United States to foreign oil exporters, as shown in Table 5. This is because the demand resulting from the entitlements program raises the price artificially. The transfer is a loss to the United States economy and a corresponding gain to the economies of oil-exporting countries. The more inelastic foreign supply, the greater is the loss. Thus in a disruption, when supply is very inelastic, the entitlements program is particularly harmful — it raises price further and causes large transfers abroad.

Summary

The price controls and entitlements program imposed substantial costs on the United States economy. It increased consumption and decreased domestic production, thereby fueling import demand and world oil prices. Yet the government's desire to do something about the "energy crisis" — the swift and steep run-up in oil prices — cannot be dismissed on economic or political grounds. The goals of controlling inflation and averting a massive wealth transfer from oil consumers to producers led to price ceilings on domestic crude oil production. Unequal access to low-priced oil by refiners led to the entitlements program, which effectively used the rents generated by these ceilings to subsidize imports.

The unfortunate consequences of past regulatory programs do

Table 5. Wealth Transfers Abroad Due to Entitlements Subsidy, 1975–1980 (Millions of 1980 Dollars)

	$\epsilon_m = \infty$	$\epsilon_m = 5.0$	$\epsilon_m = 1.0$	$\epsilon_m = 0.5$
1975	0	1720 (5.8%)	5660 (19%)	8610 (28.9%)
1976	0	1540 (4.3%)	5070 (14.3%)	7690 (21.7%)
1977	0	1420 (3.2%)	4670 (10.4%)	7090 (15.8%)
1978	0	930 (2.3%)	3060 (7.6%)	4630 (11.5%)
1979	0	1630 (2.7%)	5340 (8.8%)	8130 (13.4%)
1980	0	2510 (3.4%)	8290 (11.3%)	12,540 (17.1%)

NOTE: Calculations are based on data in Tables 3 and 4. Figures in parentheses are percentage increases in world oil prices resulting from the United States entitlements program. Transfers from oil importing countries outside the United States are not included.

not imply that pure laissez-faire is the best solution, however. The failure of explicit price regulation to satisfy desires for both economic efficiency and consumer protection leads naturally to a consideration of policies designed to influence the *world* oil price itself rather than creating an artificial difference between domestic and world prices. The final section looks at the problems the oil market faces in the post-decontrol era and possible government policies to address them.

ENERGY POLICY AFTER PRICE DEREGULATION

The failure of crude oil price regulation to address the most significant economic problem in the oil market — short-run instability of world oil prices and accompanying macroeconomic fluctuations caused by oil supply disruptions — suggests a search for new channels for government intervention.[14] Considering the principal sources of market failure in the short run to be macroeconomic externalities and monopsony power of oil-importing countries, we focus on three policy options widely discussed since oil prices were decontrolled: (1) imposition of oil import tariffs, (2) use of public strategic stockpiles, and (3) participation in coordinated policy agreements with other major oil-importing nations.[15]

Tariffs

To the extent that the marginal social cost of imported oil exceeds its market price, a policy entirely opposite from price controls and subsidies suggests itself — namely, tariffs. As a long-run proposition, tariffs force consumers to "internalize" the social cost of imported oil and may lower the world price if (1) the United States has monopsony power in the world oil market and (2) producers do not retaliate strategically (see the discussion in Bohi and Montgomery, 1982). Tariffs, however, transfer income to domestic oil producers, an action likely to be unpopular.

On the other hand, if periodic oil supply disruptions are the primary source of concern, the design of a short-term, or "disruption," tariff, tax, or quota poses a different problem. Again, by restricting imports, downward pressure is exerted on world oil prices. In an economy free of macroeconomic rigidity these are "first-best" policies for correcting market externalities and thus improving social welfare. Although such policies are well suited to the objective of easing oil market conditions, they do so at the expense of raising domestic prices still further, thereby aggravating the macroeconomic harm associated with a disruption, and ought to be viewed with extreme skepticism.[16] Nevertheless, they have been proposed (Verleger, 1982; Hogan, 1982).

Public Stockpiles: The United States Strategic Petroleum Reserve

Ten years ago the U.S. Congress authorized the creation of the Strategic Petroleum Reserve (SPR) with the intent of bolstering energy security. As of this writing, the reserve stands at over 450 million barrels of oil (about thirty days of domestic consumption) — a large and potentially powerful policy instrument.[17] Economic issues surrounding the SPR center principally around its optimal size and drawdown behavior in the event of an oil crisis.[18]

The benefits stemming from a reserve must be compared with its costs in order to determine the optimal size. These costs comprise the purchases of oil to be stored, the possible increase in world oil prices resulting from these purchases, the interest paid on capital borrowed to make the purchases, the purchase or development of storage capacity, and the operation and maintenance costs of the storage program.

Some have suggested that releasing SPR oil would serve to replace oil imports during an embargo. This assumption — that embargoes against particular countries and "access" to oil supplies make sense — is simply unbelievable in a market as large and liquid as world oil. The 1973–1974 shock was spread about evenly across importing countries (Stobaugh, 1976). Warnings of dire consequences resulting from increasing "rigidities" since then (Neff, 1981) have a curious "Chicken Little" aspect to them. Since an analytical framework is lacking, it is even unclear what constitutes supporting evidence.

Given the diverse assumptions and methodologies used in engineering and economic studies, it is encouraging, as well as surprising, that the recommendations regarding SPR allocations fall in a relatively narrow band. A survey by the National Petroleum Council (1981) found that of twenty studies conducted in the 1970s, all but two suggested figures between 500 and 1,000 million barrels, with the more recent recommendations in the upper half of this range. Analyses conducted in the early 1980s, when the climate appeared most menacing, recommended sizes of 750 to 2,000 million barrels (Chao and Manne, 1982; Hogan, 1983; Rowen and Weyant, 1982; U.S. Department of Energy, 1982).

Issues surrounding drawdown are perhaps the most difficult part of analyzing the SPR. The effectiveness of the SPR will depend on assumptions about (1) market structure, (2) expectations (about the likelihood of future shocks or the duration of present ones), and (3) the reaction of domestically held private stocks and foreign public stockpiles to announced and unannounced SPR policy.

As a stylized description of the use of public stocks to exploit short-run monopsony power in the oil market, there are three channels through which SPR releases affect world oil prices. The *direct* effect is to ease price increases as the SPR release reduces the demand for OPEC output during a crisis. A *feedback* effect occurs, because holding down the world price serves to hold down domestic prices at home and abroad as well, thus reducing the cutbacks in United States and foreign consumption. The feedback effect clearly works against the direct effect. The *interaction* effect depends on the reaction of domestically held private stocks and foreign stocks to SPR releases.

Cooperation (on the part of private stocks or foreign stockpile authorities) serves to magnify the benefits of the SPR release, while competition serves to mitigate them.

The importance of oil inventories, which fell during the last shock but climbed sharply during the previous two, is widely acknowledged. A satisfactory explanation for inventory behavior remains elusive, yet is critical in assessing the private sector's response to public intervention. For example, expectations about changes in oil price controls may affect private stockpiling.[19] Moreover, the government's SPR will be rendered impotent if its releases are hoarded by private stockholders.

Simulation studies have found significant benefits in terms of reduced oil prices during shocks (Hubbard and Weiner, 1983b).[20] Recent theoretical work has emphasized the importance of market structure, expectations, and United States monopsony power as determinants of the success of the SPR in reducing oil price increases and their attendant macroeconomic costs (Hubbard and Weiner, 1984).

International Coordination of Energy Policies: Using Public Stockpiles

A broad consensus holds that international cooperation in meeting oil shocks is both essential and terribly difficult. Prospects for coordination are perhaps greatest for stockpile intervention. Among the OECD countries, this cooperation is under the aegis of the International Energy Agency (IEA).

It is not our task here to provide a detailed critique of past IEA actions; suffice it to say that consumer cooperation has not always been a resounding success. Indeed, it has sometimes proved difficult to detect. The relevant regulations are codified in the International Energy Program, signed by the United States in 1974. The details are too involved to present here (see U.S. Senate, 1974), but the salient points are three. First, countries are required to hold buffer stocks in proportion to their imports. Second, the agreement is dormant until a determination of emergency is made. The emergency is signaled as a quantity shock, which must be sufficiently large in absolute value to reduce supply by 7 percent compared to its pre-shock value. (In practice, the time unit is the quarter, and the pre-shock value is a moving average of the previous four quarters.) Third, the agreement calls for countries to "restrain demand" by 7 percent (through such means as taxes, tariffs, regulation, and exhortation) and substitute buffer stock releases in making up any remaining loss in supply (for example, a 10 percent reduction in quantity supplied calls for 3 percent to be made up by stockpile releases in addition to the 7 percent demand restraint). The scheme's monopsonistic intent is clear.

One problem with the IEA agreement is that the 7 percent threshold corresponds to a severe disruption. Assuming Free World oil consumption of roughly fifty mb/d (million barrels per day) and taking the IEA share of consumption as constant, a loss of 3.5 mb/d (net of increased exports by other producers) is necessary to trigger the emergency mechanism. The Iranian crisis, during which oil prices more than doubled, was of considerably lesser magnitude. Second, demand restraint proved to be easier said than done. The March 1979 agreement to cut consumption by 5 percent was honored more in the breach than in the observance.

Among the lessons to come out of the 1979 and 1980 supply shocks was that while high stockpile *levels* are a sine qua non for the functioning of international sharing agreements, it is the *drawdown* (or buildup) behavior that is likely to spell the difference between containment and disaster. Another is that actions taken in a so-called sub-trigger disruption (one falling beneath the threshold) may serve to avert a 1979-style catastrophic price run-up. Demand restraint having failed, the economic damage attending a sub-trigger disruption has called forth proposals for coordinated drawdown programs.

As it figures prominently in current policy discussions, we focus here on the impact of international coordination in the evaluation of SPR drawdown strategies. How effective would SPR draw be in relieving pressure in the world oil market if other IEA members do not do likewise? Or, even worse, what it some countries fill while others draw?

Since the oil market is international, the use of a buffer stock by one country has spillover effects on others, further emphasizing potential benefits from international policy coordination. The supposed merits of such coordination notwithstanding, issues of whether such an outcome would occur in the absence of an agreement and of what type of institutional mechanisms might facilitate cooperation have been largely ignored.

That cooperation can reap benefits begs the question of how it might be achieved. Regulation at the international level is difficult to enforce. Since there is no regulator with the power to require compliance, the incentive question naturally arises. While import restriction is clearly in the interest of the group as a whole, the effectiveness of the regulatory rules in attaining the cooperative outcome is not evident. It is in the interest of each individual country to be a "free rider," taking advantage of import restrictions by others.

Summary

Much of the failure of previous domestic intervention stems from its inability to address the most serious problem — the instability of world oil prices in the short run and accompanying economic fluctuations caused by oil shocks. We analyzed some policy options discussed in the wake of price deregulation to deal with these issues — namely, the use of oil import tariffs or public strategic stockpiles either by the United States alone or in an internationally coordinated agreement. Such policies, by their design to influence world (rather than just domestic) oil prices, avoid many of the distortions introduced by price regulation.

CONCLUSION

Government intervention in the domestic petroleum industry is almost as old as the industry itself. Even after the decontrol of domestic crude oil prices in 1981, public policies on "windfall profit" taxation, maintenance of an SPR, and participation in international agreements in the event of oil crises continue to affect market outcomes. The task for economists and decision-makers is to isolate sources of market failure (in the short run or the long run), and design policies accordingly.

Close to the heart of economists, the pursuit of economic efficiency in domestic energy markets carries real benefits. The programs of United States petroleum price regulation during the 1970s were accompanied by significant deadweight losses — losses not offset by gains to consumers, refiners, or domestic and foreign producers. Because of the size of the oil trade, any recurrence of "shocks" will generate distributional concerns. Those concerns are best addressed, however, through conventional macroeconomic policies and through systematic energy policies designed to influence world oil prices.

Past experience has taught policymakers that price controls, instead of mitigating the effects of foreign oil supply disruptions, acted to exacerbate them, as well as imposing substantial losses on the economy. In the mid-1980s we have available policy instruments such as the SPR that are more appropriate for addressing the problem at hand.

NOTES

[1] A recent study of econometric models of the United States economy by the Stanford University Energy Modeling Forum found substantial effects on inflation, output, and unemployment from oil price shocks; see Hickman and Huntington (1984).

[2] See, for example, the studies in Landsberg and Dukert (1981).

[3] We will discuss this system in detail in the section on government intervention.

[4] More detailed histories of various facets of United States energy policy can be found in Goodwin (1981), Kalt (1981), Weimer (1982), and Vietor (1984).

[5] Kalt (1981, p. 5) notes that the Federal Oil Conservation Board (1924–1929), the National Recovery Act's Petroleum Administration (1933–1935), and the Department of the Interior (after World War II) backed similar anticompetitive measures.

[6] For example, Bohi and Russell (1978) found that the MOIP reduced the consumer surplus of oil users by $5.4 billion during 1969, while augmenting producer rents domestically by $2.3 billion and transferring import rights worth $0.8 billion to chosen refiners. The resulting deadweight loss is $2.3 billion, or about 43 percent of the reduction in consumer surplus.

[7] For a detailed discussion of the Nixon price controls as they applied to the oil industry, see Kalt (1981).

[8] Of the 290 refineries operating in the United States in 1978, roughly 265 (over 90 percent) had refining capacities of less than 175,000 barrels per day (American Petroleum Institute, 1981a). These "small" refineries accounted for 20 to 25 percent of industry capacity (American Petroleum Institute, 1980).

[9] Kalt (1981, p. 62) notes: "In the first twelve months of the entitlements program, for example, only about $85 million (1980 dollars) were distributed through Exceptions and Appeals. By the late 1970s, several hundred million dollars per year were being distributed through Exceptions and Appeals."

[10] We assume that imports are not an important factor in the United States market for refined products. For evidence on this, see Kalt (1981). If this is not the case, imports of products are reduced to offset the additional crude imports.

[11] Various regulations have complicated the definition of the marginal cost to domestic refiners. From the first quarter of 1974 (1974:1) through 1974:3, the imported price (which exceeded the domestic price because of price controls) was the marginal cost. From 1974:4 through 1976:3, the marginal cost faced by American refineries is measured as the import price less the value of crude oil entitlements to refineries (which effectively acted to reduce the marginal cost). From 1976:4 through 1980:4, the uncontrolled price of domestically produced stripper oil was used as the marginal cost. After decontrol, the world price is again used to represent the marginal price.

[12] The diagram in Figure 5 is drawn under the assumption that oil suppliers are competitive; adding monopoly elements would complicate the analysis, but the qualitative conclusions remain.

[13] Even if total demand elasticities were identical across countries, the fact that the United States has significant domestic production gives it a substantially higher net import demand elasticity than, say, Japan or West Germany.

[14] As discussed in the previous sections, price controls were most likely imposed because of distributional concerns. Cushioning the impact of rapidly rising energy prices for particular groups (for example, the poor) can be implemented through modifications of existing transfer programs without relying on sweeping domestic energy policies.

[15] The use of conservation measures is also frequently discussed in policy circles. However, emergency mandatory conservation and fuel-switching combine the negative aspects of price regulation and demand restriction. That is, they are not only inefficient — since there is no reason to believe that those who can most economically conserve will do so — but also lead to macroeconomic costs.

[16] In principle, monetary policy could accommodate the added price increase. The goals of monetary policy are broader, however, and such a response may conflict with other objectives.

[17] The SPR need not, of course, be both owned and managed by the government. See the discussion of different options and institutions in Hubbard and Weiner (1985).

[18] For a detailed discussion of the SPR as an economic policy instrument, see Hubbard and Weiner (1985).

[19] Controls may even increase stockpiling initiatives (for the wrong reasons) — for example, the anticipation of higher price ceilings. Indeed, domestic privately held inventories rose sharply relative to trend in the months prior to President Reagan's decontrol of crude oil prices in January 1981; see Hubbard and Weiner (1983a).

[20] Releasing SPR oil on the spot market is not the only way in which stockpile intervention might occur. Devarajan and Hubbard (1984) consider the case of selling oil through futures contracts, finding that futures sales (1) achieve much of the price-reducing benefits in the early stages of a disruption and (2) lead to a lower price trajectory overall when compared with spot market sales.

[21] Given a specification of the optimizing behavior of the public stockpiles of consuming countries, we can estimate the benefits of stockpile coordination using "game-theory" methods in economics. Theoretical analyses of the benefits of public stockpile coordination (Hubbard and Weiner, 1984) have found that whether member countries to an agreement drew down more stocks at the onset of a shock than if there had been no agreement depends on (1) the expected persistence of the shocks and (2) the heightened monopsony power made possible by coordinated buyer behavior.

BIBLIOGRAPHY

American Petroleum Institute, "Trends in Refinery Construction in the U.S.," Discussion Paper No. 20, September 1980.
_____, "Entry and Exit in U.S. Petroleum Refining, 1948–1978," Research Study No. 21, April 1981a.
_____, "Market Share and Individual Company Data for U.S. Energy Markets: 1950–1980," Discussion Paper No. 14R, October 1981b.
Balas, E., "Choosing the Overall Size of the Strategic Petroleum Reserve," in W. Ziemba, S. Schwartz, and E. Koenigsberg (eds.), *Energy Policy Modeling: U.S. and Canadian Experiences*. The Hague: Martinus Nijhoff, 1980.
Bohi, D. R., and Montgomery, W. D., *Oil Prices, Energy Security, and Import Policy*. Baltimore: Johns Hopkins University Press, 1982.
_____, and Russell, M., *Limiting Oil Imports*. Baltimore: Johns Hopkins University Press, 1978.
Chao, H. P., and Manne, A. S., "An Integrated Analysis of U.S. Oil Stockpiling Policies," in J. Plummer (ed.), *Energy Vulnerability*. Cambridge, Mass.: Ballinger Publishing Co., 1982.
Devarajan, S., and Hubbard, R. G., "Drawing Down the Strategic Petroleum Reserve: The Case for Selling Futures Contracts," in A. L. Alm and R. J. Weiner (eds.), *Oil Shock: Policy Response and Implementation*. Cambridge, Mass.: Ballinger Publishing Co., 1984.
Fried, C. R., and Schultze, C. L. (eds.), *Higher Oil Prices and the World Economy*. Washington, D.C.: The Brookings Institution, 1975.
Goodwin, C. D. (ed.), *Energy Policy in Perspective*. Washington, D.C.: The Brookings Institution, 1981.
Hamilton, J. D., "Oil and the Macroeconomy Since World War II." *Journal of Political Economy*, 91 (April 1983):228–248.
Hickman, B. G., and Huntington, H. G., *Macroeconomic Impacts of Energy Shocks: An Overview*, Stanford University Energy Modeling Forum, 1984.
Hogan, W. W., "Oil Stockpiling: Help Thy Neighbor." *Energy Journal*, 4 (July 1983):49–71.
_____, "Policies for Oil Importers," in J. M. Griffin and D. J. Teece (eds.), *OPEC Behavior and World Oil Prices*. London: Allen & Unwin, 1982.
Hubbard, R. G., and Fry, R. C., "The Macroeconomic Impacts of Oil Supply Disruptions," Discussion Paper E-81-07, Energy and Environmental Policy Center, Kennedy School of Government, Harvard University, 1982.
_____, and Weiner, R. J., "Oil Supply Shocks and International Policy Coordination," mimeograph, Northwestern University, 1983a; *European Economic Review* (in press).
_____, and _____, "The 'Sub-Trigger' Crisis: An Economic Analysis of Flexible Stock Policies." *Energy Economics*, 5 (July 1983b):178–189.
_____, and _____, "Inventory Optimization in the U.S. Petroleum Industry: Empirical Analysis and Implications for Energy Emergency Policy," mimeograph, Harvard University, 1984; *Management Science* (in press).

_____, and _____, "Energy Policy in a Market Setting: Managing the Strategic Petroleum Reserve," *Annual Review of Energy*, 10 (1985).
Johany, A. D., *The Myth of the OPEC Cartel*. Chichester, West Sussex: John Wiley & Sons, Ltd., 1980.
Kalt, J. P., *The Economics and Politics of Oil Price Regulation*. Cambridge: The MIT Press, 1981.
Kinberg, Y., Shakun, M. F., and Sudit, E. F., "Energy Buffer Stock Decisions in Game Situations," *TIMS Studies in the Management Sciences*, 10(1978): 109–127.
Landsberg, H. H., and Dukert, J. M., *High Energy Costs: Uneven, Unfair, Unavoidable?* Baltimore: Johns Hopkins University Press, 1981.
Marchand, M., and Pestieau, P., "Tarification et Anticipations Divergentes." *Annals Pub. Coop. Economy*, 50 (1979):111–136.
Mork, K. A., and Hall, R. E., "Energy Prices and the U.S. Economy in 1979–1981," *Energy Journal*, 1 (April 1980):41–54.
National Petroleum Council, *Emergency Preparedness for Interruption of Petroleum Imports into the United States*, Washington, D.C., 1981.
Neff, T. L., "The Changing World Oil Market," in D. A. Deese and J. S. Nye (eds.), *Energy and Security*. Cambridge, Mass.: Ballinger Publishing Co., 1981.
Rowen, H. S., and Weyant, J. P., "Reducing the Economic Impacts of Oil Supply Interruptions: An International Perspective." *Energy Journal*, 3 (January 1982):1–34.
Scherer, F. M., *Industrial Market Structure and Economic Performance*, 2d ed. Chicago: Rand McNally, 1980.
Stobaugh, R. B., "The Oil Companies in the Crisis," in R. Vernon (ed.). *The Oil Crisis*. New York: W. W. Norton & Co., Inc., 1976.
U.S. Department of Energy. *Domestic and International Energy Preparedness*, DOE/EP-0027, Washington, D.C., 1981.
_____, *Report to the President and the Congress on the Size of the Strategic Petroleum Reserve*, DOE/EP-0036, Washington, D.C., 1982.
U.S. Senate, Committee on Interior and Insular Affairs, *International Energy Program Hearing*, Washington, D.C., 1974.
Verleger, P. K., *Oil Markets in Turmoil*. Cambridge, Mass.: Ballinger Publishing Co., 1982.
Vietor, R. H. K., *Energy Policy in America Since 1945*. New York: Cambridge University Press, 1984.
Weimer, D. L., *The Strategic Petroleum Reserve*. Westport, Conn.: Greenwood Press, 1982.
Wright, B. D., and Williams, Jr., "The Roles of Public and Private Storage in Managing Oil Import Disruptions." *Bell Journal of Economics*, 13 (Autumn 1982):341–353.

CASE 5

Natural Gas: The Regulatory Transition

Ronald R. Braeutigam
R. Glenn Hubbard
Northwestern University

INTRODUCTION

One of the most significant pieces of legislation dealing with deregulation in American industry is The Natural Gas Policy Act of 1978 (NGPA).[1] This legislation marked the culmination of an extended debate over the regulation of the price of natural gas at the wellhead (the point at which natural gas comes out of the ground to be sold to pipeline delivery systems). The intensity of the policy debate over the NGPA was and is fueled by the sizes of the attendant transfers from consumers to producers.[2]

The contemporary gas industry may be characterized as having three segments: production, pipeline delivery, and local distribution. Natural gas is produced either in fields that primarily yield natural gas or from fields that produce gas and oil together.[3] Producers gather the gas at the wellhead and sell it under contract to pipelines, from which the gas is delivered to various markets. A pipeline may sell the gas directly to a large end-user (such as an industry) or to a local distribution company, which in turn delivers it to an end-user (typically a residential or commercial customer). Since the NGPA does not deal with the regulation of the pipelines or of the local distribution companies, the focus of this case is on the regulation and deregu-

Parts of this chapter draw closely on Braeutigam's discussion of natural gas regulation in the previous edition. Portions reflect research done by Hubbard under a grant from the National Science Foundation (SES-8408805). We are grateful to Michael Klass and Leonard Weiss for helpful comments and suggestions.

lation of the price at which a producer sells gas to a pipeline at the wellhead.

Natural gas is a vital part of America's total energy supply. This clean-burning fuel's share of the total energy used in the United States has grown from only 14 percent in 1948 to about 27 percent in 1983 (Table 1). Approximately one-quarter of the yearly gas supply is used by residential consumers, and nearly half is consumed by American industry.

In one sense the industry has come nearly full circle. In the early part of this century there was no federal regulation of natural gas. Wellhead prices of natural gas then became regulated following a combination of legislative and judicial events that took place over an extended period (1938–1954). During the next two decades, regulators struggled with the difficulties of controlling wellhead prices for thousands of productive wells. The regulatory tasks became further complicated in the 1970s as shortages developed and as costs of production changed rapidly. The regulatory turmoil of the 1970s led to the passage of the NGPA in 1978, which specified a phased deregulation of most (but not all) wellhead prices.

We begin with a brief examination of the history of the natural gas industry, including the origin, evolution, and economic consequences of regulation. Prior to the NGPA, discussions of the effects of regulation focused on several areas, including the administrative difficulties of controlling prices, shortages of gas in interstate markets, potential imperfections in wellhead markets, income transfers under

Table 1. Percentage of Total Energy Produced by Type[a]

Source	1948	1963	1978	1983
Coal	48	26	25	28
Natural gas (dry)	14	31	32	27
Petroleum	33	35	30	30
Natural gas plant liquids	2	4	4	4
Hydropower	4	4	5	6
Nuclear power	0	1	5	5
Geothermal and other	0	0	—[b]	—[b]
Total gross energy produced (quadrillion BTU)	35.99	46.15	61.00	61.18

Source: Annual Report to Congress (1978), Vol. II, Energy Information Administration, Department of Energy, p. 5; and *Monthly Energy Review,* Department of Energy (various issues).

[a] Totals do not equal 100 percent because of independent rounding.
[b] Less than 0.5 percent.

regulation, and regulation-related incentives for inefficient utilization of energy resources. We then describe the forces that led to deregulation, particularly the changing market conditions of the 1970s that made it impossible for regulators simultaneously to hold down wellhead prices and avoid shortages of gas.

Finally, the discussion turns to the provisions of the NGPA and indicates some of its consequences. Soon after the passage of the NGPA there was concern that rapidly rising world oil prices might cause gas prices to "fly up" dramatically as phased deregulation approached more complete deregulation in the middle of the 1980s, although concerns of this sort all but disappeared as the Organization of Petroleum Exporting Countries (OPEC) weakened and world oil prices fell in 1983 and 1984. More recently, attention has centered on the nature and effects of long-term contracts between gas suppliers and pipelines as both make costly long-term investments under the increased uncertainty of a competitive environment. Under new contracts, deregulated prices may be based on the price of Mexican or Canadian gas (an "imported gas" clause) or a percentage of the energy-equivalent price of fuel oil (an "oil reference" clause). Contracts may require the pipeline to pay for some or all of the gas under contract, even if the pipeline has no market for that gas (a "take-or-pay" clause), or allow the pipelines to offer the producer a lower price than the contractually established price (a "market-out" clause) if, for example, the gas cannot be sold at the contractual price.[4] We will describe these recent developments and their potential consequences in some detail.

THE REGULATION OF NATURAL GAS

Several factors led to the federal regulation of natural gas. In the 1930s many new large oil and gas fields were found in regions far from the large city markets, particularly in the Southwest. Improved drilling and exploration techniques aided in the discovery of fields. The development of seamless pipe, which greatly reduced the problems with leakage posed by the high pressures required in the transport of gas, made it possible to move the gas from these remote fields to large markets. Thus natural gas moved across state lines to become an important source of energy.

Until 1938 state and local regulators had no power to control the price distributors paid for gas imported from other states. The Supreme Court had held that the interstate pipelines were beyond their reach.[5] After lengthy consideration, Congress passed The Natural Gas Act of 1938, declaring "that the business of transporting and selling natural gas for ultimate distribution to the public is affected with a public interest, and that Federal regulation in matters relating to the transportation of natural gas and the sale thereof in interstate and foreign commerce is necessary in the public interest."[6] The Act brought the interstate transmission of natural gas and its sale for resale under the control of the Federal Power Commission (FPC). It exempted the gathering of gas and its retail distribution. The rates for transmission and sale were to be "just and reasonable" and without "undue" preferences.[7] Pipelines were required to publish and adhere to published tariff schedules and to give advanced notice of proposed tariff changes.[8] The Commission was empowered to suspend proposed changes, conduct hearings, order refunds to consumers when warranted, and issue orders to ensure that reasonable rates would prevail.[9] The law differed from earlier similar legislation for the electricity industry (The Federal Power Act of 1935) in one important respect. It did not authorize the FPC to order interconnections among pipelines.

After World War II the federal regulation of wellhead prices became an increasingly important issue. Before pipeline networks were established, gas was often produced as a worthless byproduct of oil production. Often it was burned (flared) at the wellhead. With the advent of pipelines, its value went up rapidly. Prices in new contracts rose. Prices for gas already in production at that time increased as a result of "most favored nation" clauses, which required a purchasing pipeline to pay the producer a price equal to the highest price paid to any other producer within a given area by that pipeline, or in some cases by any pipeline in that area. The pipelines responded by submitting proposals for price increases that they in turn charged to local distributors.

Until 1954 the FPC had assumed (amid spirited debate) that it did not have jurisdiction over the price at which gas was sold at the wellhead. This belief was based on a clause in the 1938 Act stating that the Act "shall not apply . . . to the production or gathering of natural gas," even though these were sales to pipelines for resale.[10] Several states in the gas-consuming areas of the North felt that the FPC should have regulated wellhead prices, while the gas-producing states of the Southwest opposed this view.

The issue came to a head in 1954 in a famous case, *Phillips Petroleum Company v. Wisconsin et al.*[11] Phillips was the largest of the independent gas producers. After Phillips had raised the price of its natural gas, the State of Wisconsin, along with the cities of Milwaukee, Detroit, and Kansas City, complained before the FPC. When the Commission declined to act, the case went to court.

During the testimony on the *Phillips* case, the Wisconsin consumer representatives stated that they felt Phillips had monopoly power in the market for natural gas sales to pipelines, and they were concerned that this power led to excessively high prices at the wellhead and, in turn, for the consumer. Phillips strongly denied the existence of monopoly power. It pointed out that in 1946 and 1947 there were approximately 2,300 independent producers or gatherers supplying gas to the pipelines, so that the supply of gas was in fact quite competitive.[12]

Ultimately the Supreme Court ruled that, while the production activities of Phillips were not regulated within the scope of the Act, the sales of Phillips to pipelines intending resale did fall under its provisions. The Court assigned to the FPC the duty to adjudge the reasonableness of prices for gas sold by Phillips.

The controversy surrounding this ruling arose for two main reasons. First, as already described, it was certainly not clear that Congress intended that the law be interpreted to include regulation of wellhead prices. Second, the nature of any market imperfection that one might cite as a basis for regulating wellhead prices was never made clear. Did producers have sufficient monopoly power to warrant the extension of regulation to them? Kahn points out by analogy that in the electric power industry the assumption has been that suppliers of fuel oil or coal to electricity generating companies have been sufficiently competitive to protect the consumer, and "that as long as they have remained financially independent, the regulated monopolists had no incentive to pay more than the competitive price."[13] In any case, sixteen years after the enabling legislation, regulation was in fact extended to the wellhead.[14]

Regulation in Practice

Following the *Phillips* decision, the FPC began to regulate wellhead prices. Between 1954 and 1960 "the Commission had accumulated some 11,091 rate schedules and 33,231 supplements to those schedules from 3,372 independent producers," and by 1960 "there were 3,278 producer rate increase filings under suspension and awaiting hearing and decisions."[15] The Commission was confronted with the impossible task of making thousands of individual rate determinations using methods traditionally employed in rate cases for public utilities. The Commission estimated that it would not finish its 1960 caseload until the year 2043.[16]

The impossibility of regulating individual wellhead prices meant that a more pragmatic procedure was necessary. In 1960 the Commission decided to divide the country into twenty-three geographic areas and then set uniform prices for each of them, based on prices in the 1956–1958 period. In 1965 the FPC set its first rate for the Permian Basin area, including parts of New Mexico and Texas. There were really two ceiling prices, one for gas already being produced ("old gas") and for gas associated with oil and the second (higher) price for gas not associated with oil, which was classified as "new gas." New gas referred to gas that was either discovered or first committed to interstate commerce after a date specified by the FPC. The justification for this two-level system of prices was that it "was both undesirable and unnecessary to extend that higher price to old gas, undesirable because to do so would confer windfalls on the owners of reserves discovered and developed at lower costs in the past (a noneconomic argument) and unnecessary because the investments in the old gas had already been made (an economic consideration)."[17] This procedure, called area-wide ratemaking, was soon challenged in court, and in the 1968 Permian Basin Area Rate Cases, the Supreme Court upheld the FPC order.[18]

As the first years of the 1970s passed, it became apparent that the new ratemaking approach was simply too cumbersome to permit the Commission to react promptly and responsively to changing conditions in wellhead markets. By 1974 the FPC had completed proceedings in less than half of the twenty-three geographic areas, and changing market conditions meant that some of the rates already set needed revision. These prospects, along with an increasing gas shortage, led the Commission to reassess its ratemaking practices. On June 21, 1974, the FPC extended the concept of area rate regulation to establish "a uniform just and reasonable national base rate of 42 cents per thousand cubic feet [Mcf] at 14.73 psia [pounds per square inch, absolute pressure], for interstate sales of natural gas."[19] Thus, instead of setting rates by areas, the FPC moved to a policy of establishing nationwide rate ceilings. This procedure was called "nationwide ratemaking."

CONSEQUENCES OF REGULATION

The Shortage in Interstate Markets

Before 1970 no "shortages" of gas were observed either in the interstate or intrastate markets. This means that the amount of gas produced nationally was sufficient to meet the contractual demands for shipment by pipelines. Since producers of natural gas in new gas fields often had the option of selling in either the regulated interstate market or an unregulated intrastate market, one would have expected sales to occur in these markets so that the prices observed were about equal. Table 2 shows that weighted average prices in interstate and intrastate markets were within $0.02 per Mcf of one another.[20] (As noted earlier, actual individual transactions occurred at different prices. A weighted average price indicated in the table is determined as the price that, when multiplied by the total sales volume, would yield the same revenue as did the sum of all of the individual transactions at their respective actual prices.)

However, during the 1970s, production in interstate markets began to fall short of contractual demands by greater amounts each year. Pipeline shipments were curtailed; that is, they delivered less than the contractually agreed-upon amounts to downstream customers.[21] For the period from September 1976 to August 1977, net curtailments of contracted interstate gas deliveries amounted to about 3.77 trillion cubic feet (Tcf), a significant amount considering that the total supply of natural gas was about 19 Tcf for that period.[22] Consequently, some industries cut back production, some users went without service, and many people temporarily lost their jobs. Prospects of increasing shortages helped to push the debate over natural gas to the national forefront during the 1970s.

Among other major concerns was the continual decline in proven

Table 2. Comparison of Intrastate and Jurisdictional Weighted Average Prices ($/Mcf)

Date of Contract	Intrastate	Jurisdictional (Interstate)
1966[a]	$0.168	$0.185
1967[a]	0.173	0.191
1968[a]	0.175	0.192
1969[a]	0.180	0.198
First half, 1970[a]	0.207	0.202
July 1, 1970, to Sept. 14, 1971[a]	0.241	0.284
Sept. 15, 1971, to Sept. 14, 1972[a]	0.316	0.286
1975	0.60 (est.)[b]	0.40[c]

[a]*Source:* FPC data as presented in Report No. 94-732 (House of Representatives, 94th Congress, first session), p. 6.

[b]*Source:* No hard data are available, but this figure was named as a consensus estimate by Chip Schroeder of the House Energy and Power Subcommittee Staff. See L. Kumins, "Cost of S. 3422's Pricing Provisions," Senate Report 94-907.

[c]*Source: FPC News,* 8:35 (week ending August 29, 1975), 1, 5.

reserves. Gas reserves include all the gas that actual drilling has proven to exist and that is therefore potentially available for production. As Table 3 shows, proven reserves declined from 291 Tcf in 1970 to 209 Tcf in 1977. Thus throughout the 1970s the rate of extraction of natural gas exceeded the rate of discovery of new reserves.

There can be little doubt that changing economic conditions, including a higher demand for energy, rising oil prices, declining reserves, and increasing shortages generated pressure on regulators to raise wellhead prices during the 1970s. As Table 3 indicates, by 1972 regulators were holding interstate wellhead prices below the levels observed in the unregulated intrastate markets, and increasingly so over time. This trend toward diverging wellhead prices is even more

Table 3. Natural Gas Supply, Average Wellhead Price, and Consumption

Year	Total Energy Production (Quadrillion BTU)[a]	Natural Gas (Dry) Produced Quadrillion BTU[a]	Tcf[a]	Proved Reserves (Dry Gas) (Tcf)[a,b]	Average Wellhead Value (¢/Mcf)[c]	Total Consumption (Tcf)[a]
1948	36	5.1	4.9	173	6.5	4.7
1949	31	5.4	5.2	180	6.3	5.0
1950	35	6.2	6.0	185	6.5	5.8
1951	38	7.4	7.2	193	7.3	6.8
1952	37	8.0	7.7	193	7.3	6.8
1953	37	8.4	8.1	210	9.2	
1954	36	8.7	8.4	211	10.1	8.1
1955	39	9.3	9.0	223	10.4	8.7
1956	42	10.0	15.2	237	10.8	9.3
1957	42	10.6	10.3	245	11.3	9.9
1958	39	11.0	10.6	253	11.9	10.3
1959	41	12.0	11.6	261	12.9	11.3

[a]*Source: Annual Report to Congress* (1978), Energy Information Administration, Department of Energy, Vol. 2, pp. 5, 33, 77; and *Monthly Energy Review*, Department of Energy (various issues).

[b]*Source:* Proved reserves are defined to be "the estimated quantities of natural gas, which geological and engineering data demonstrate, with reasonable certainty, to be recoverable in the future from known natural oil and gas reservoirs, under existing economic and operating conditions." See *Annual Report to Congress* (note [a] above), p. 169.

[c]This column is generated "by dividing the sum of total values of natural gas produced in all States by the sum of total quantities of natural gas produced in all States." See *Annual Report* (note [a] above), p. 85.

Table 3. Natural Gas Supply, Average Wellhead Price, and Consumption—cont'd

Year	Total Energy Production (Quadrillion BTU[a])	Natural Gas (Dry) Produced Quadrillion BTU[a]	Tcf[a]	Proved Reserves (Dry Gas) (Tcf)[a,b]	Average Wellhead Value (¢/Mcf)[c]	Total Consumption (Tcf)[a]
1960	42	12.7	12.2	262	14.0	12.0
1961	42	13.1	12.7	266	15.1	12.5
1962	44	13.7	13.3	272	15.5	13.3
1963	46	14.5	14.1	276	15.8	14.0
1964	48	15.3	14.8	281	15.4	14.8
1965	50	15.8	15.3	287	15.6	15.3
1966	53	17.0	16.5	290	15.7	16.5
1967	55	18.0	17.4	293	16.0	17.4
1968	57	19.1	18.5	287	16.4	18.6
1969	59	20.5	19.9	275	16.7	20.1
1970	63	21.7	21.0	291	17.1	21.1
1971	62	22.3	21.6	279	18.2	21.8
1972	63	22.2	21.6	266	18.6	22.1
1973	62	22.2	21.7	250	21.6	22.1
1974	61	21.2	20.7	237	30.4	21.2
1975	60	19.6	19.2	228	44.5	19.5
1976	60	19.5	19.1	216	58.0	20.0
1977	60	19.6	19.1	209	79.0	19.5
1978	61	19.3	18.9	208	91.9	19.4
1979	64	20.1	19.6	201	118.0	20.2
1980	65	19.9	19.4	199	159.0	19.9
1981	64	19.7	19.2	202	198.0	19.4
1982	64	18.3	17.9	202	246.0	18.1
1983	61	16.5	16.1	—	259.0	15.5

easily observed if one examines the prices in new gas contracts over the period (instead of weighted average prices). "During 1969–1975, interstate natural gas prices for new contracts rose by 158 percent, from approximately $0.198 per Mcf to over $0.51 per Mcf. However, during the same period, intrastate natural gas prices rose at an even greater rate, from approximately $0.18 per Mcf in 1969 to in excess of $1.35 per Mcf in 1975, a 650 percent increase."[23] At the time of the passage of the NGPA in 1978, average intrastate prices for new contracts and for renegotiated or amended contracts were often over $2 per Mcf.

As the difference between prices of new gas sold in the two markets increased over the first half of the 1970s, producers were given incentives to commit newly found reserves to an intrastate (rather than the interstate) market. In the 1964–1969 period producers dedicated 67 percent of their new reserves to the interstate market, but this figure fell to less than 8 percent over the 1970–1973 period.[24]

Income Redistribution

Figure 1 depicts a supply schedule for producers and a demand schedule for consumers of natural gas in the interstate wellhead market. The regulated price, P_R, is below the unregulated price, P_E. As a result, only Q_S is actually supplied to customers, while the demand for $(Q_D - Q_S)$ remains unsatisfied. Under these conditions pro-

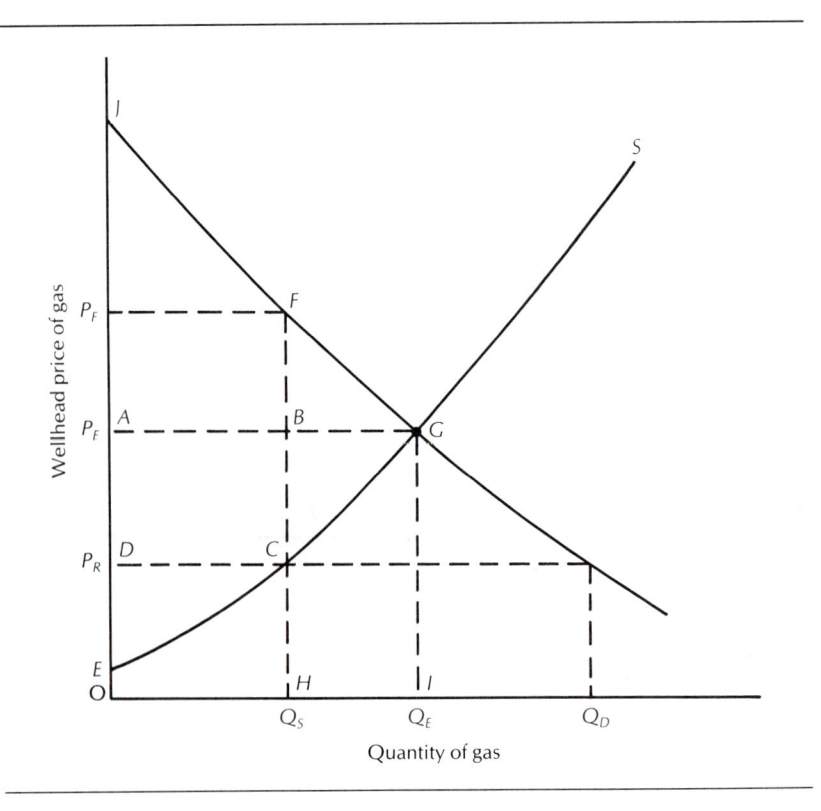

Figure 1. The Interstate Wellhead Market

ducers realize dollar revenues corresponding to the area *DCHO* and incur costs of *OECH*, leaving them with dollar profits represented by the area *CDE*. If those consumers who were successful in obtaining the quantity Q_S had paid the unregulated price, P_E, then producer profits would be increased by the amount *ABCD*, and consumer expenditures would be increased by the same amount. In short, regulation effectively transfers *ABCD* from producers to consumers. (In discussing the estimated size of these transfers, however, we will see that there is some doubt that the income redistribution is adequately measured by *ABCD* alone.)

Since the unregulated intrastate and regulated interstate prices were approximately equal until 1970, there was relatively little income redistribution from price regulation at that time. However, since interstate and intrastate prices diverged significantly by the mid-1970s, the effects of income redistribution became quite large. Table 3 shows that approximately 19 Tcf were produced in 1975. About two-thirds of this (say, 13 Tcf) was sold in interstate commerce. Table 2 shows that the weighted-average price was thought to be about 20 cents per Mcf higher in intrastate than in interstate markets. It is not unreasonable to believe that virtually all of this difference resulted from regulation. Thus the amount of income redistribution can be approximated as the product of 13 Tcf and 20 cents per Mcf, or about $2.6 billion for the year. While this is only an approximation, it serves to emphasize that the redistribution may well have been in the billions of dollars annually during the middle of the 1970s.[25]

Helms (1974) has suggested an additional aspect of income redistribution occurring under regulation. He noted that while some consumers were "fortunate" enough to be able to purchase gas, other consumers were not able to acquire gas at all. Those consumers were forced to seek alternative sources of energy, including imported gas, at much higher prices. His conclusion is that while regulation may have redistributed income from producers to those fortunate consumers, a large amount of income was also redistributed away from other consumers, in many cases to foreign instead of domestic suppliers.

Economic Efficiency

Since a demand schedule shows how much gas buyers would like to purchase at any announced price in the market, it can be used to determine the value of a given quantity of gas to consumers. For example, in Figure 1, suppose Q_S were provided to all consumers willing to pay at least P_F.[26] Then the gross value of that gas can be represented in dollars by the area $OHFJ$.[27] However, since it costs producers an amount $OHCE$ to produce the gas, then the net economic benefit of producing Q_S is the area $ECFJ$. How this net economic benefit (or, as it is often called, net surplus) is divided between consumers and producers depends on the price charged. If the regulated price, P_R, is in effect, then the consumer surplus is $DCFJ$, and the producer surplus is ECD.

Now suppose that regulation were removed, so that the price in the market could move to P_E (at which the market clears). The quantity of gas offered for sale would increase by the amount $(Q_E - Q_S)$. A measure of the gross value of this additional gas is the area $HFGI$. The costs to producers of providing this additional gas would be $HCGI$. Note that $HFGI$ is larger than $HCGI$. Therefore a net benefit increase would be realized if regulation were removed, where the size of the net additional value is represented by the triangular area CFG. In other words, regulation may prevent the market from allocating $(Q_E - Q_S)$ to consumers even though the benefits they attach to the additional gas exceed the costs of producing that gas. Economists therefore say that gas is not being produced or allocated efficiently under regulation, and they call the net benefit loss CFG an "efficiency loss."

There are reasons to believe that the efficiency losses under regulation were even larger than CFG. To understand this, recall that at the regulated price, P_R, only Q_S will be supplied to customers. There is no guarantee that the customers who actually get the gas value it the most. Restated, gas may not be allocated so that customers get the most benefit from it. It may very well be that some people valuing the gas less than P_E, indeed as low as P_R, are receiving gas under regulation. At the same time others willing to pay very high prices (even higher than P_E) may be rationed out of the market. All one can say is that CFG places a lower bound on the deadweight loss due to regulation.

MacAvoy (1975) proposes a slightly different way of looking at efficiency losses to define a better lower bound on them. It is worthwhile developing that notion here, since he has provided some empirical estimates using this method. He notes that the demand for gas can be considered in two parts, as depicted in Figure 2. There is one set of consumers who are able to purchase gas at regulated prices. Typically, those consumers who have had access to gas in one year will continue to have access in the next year. One could represent the demand schedule for this group of consumers by D' in the figure.

As time passed, many new would-be consumers were not able to purchase gas because of the shortage. If the demand of this unfortunate group were added to D', the actual demand for gas could be

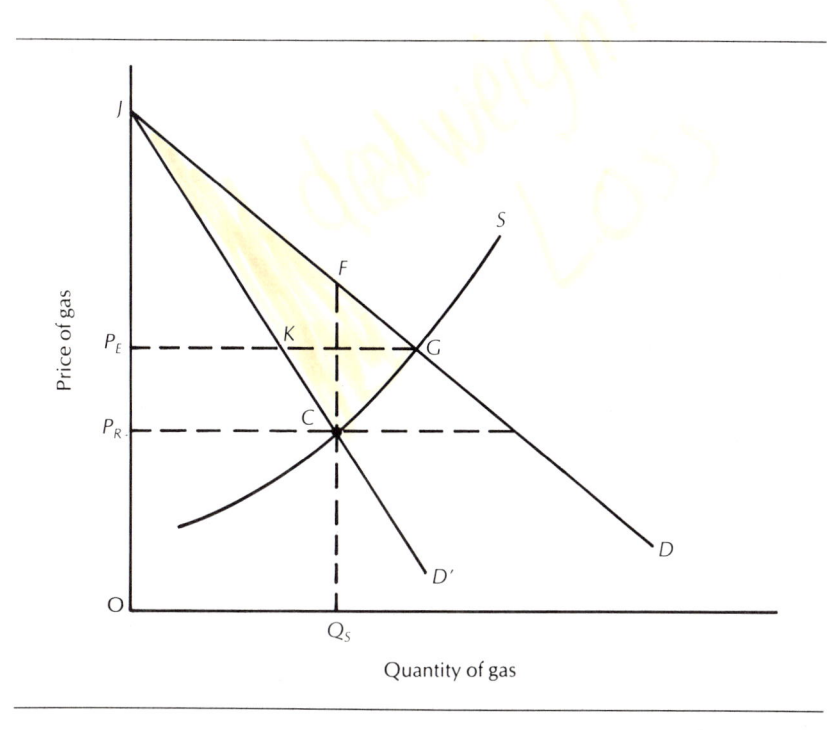

Figure 2. Efficiency Loss: Two Consumer Groups

represented by *D*. (In Figure 2 it is assumed that neither existing nor potential customers would purchase any gas at a price higher than that represented by point *J*.) Most of the burden of the shortage will be borne by new would-be consumers who cannot get gas at all, since existing customers will be served first. Thus, in addition to the efficiency loss *CFG* (in Figure 2), there is an additional loss of *CFJ*. The loss *CFJ* arises because some prospective consumers who are not able to get gas value it more than some of the "fortunate" consumers who can purchase it. Thus gas is not being allocated to the consumers who place the highest value on it.

MacAvoy and Pindyck (1975) estimated that if regulation were to have continued at the 1974 prices for the rest of the decade, then the efficiency loss would have been more than $2.5 billion in 1978 and more than $5.8 billion in 1980. To our knowledge no one has attempted to reestimate the size of the loss given that the increases in regulated prices and intrastate prices were more rapid than MacAvoy and Pindyck assumed. Further, their procedure requires extensive assumptions about the nature of the demand for natural gas in order to calculate the size of the area *CGJ* in Figure 2. MacAvoy and Pindyck assumed the demand schedule was linear, a procedure that could introduce significant error if incorrect, since the difference between regulated and unregulated prices is quite large.[28]

WELLHEAD MARKET STRUCTURE

As the debate about deregulation became more intense in the 1970s, it was natural that investigators should ask whether the wellhead market structure was conducive to competition. That is, if there were substantial anticompetitive behavior at the wellhead level, some justification for field price regulation might exist. Space does not allow more than a brief summary of the evidence here. Although the issue of monopoly power was raised in the *Phillips* case, subsequent analyses have cast doubt on the proposition that monopoly power was in fact a problem in the industry. The existence of literally thousands of independent producers alone makes such an argument difficult to accept.

The possibility of monopsony power by pipelines was frequently highlighted in the studies. This argument states that if, for example, only one pipeline were buying gas from a given field, it might not act as a wellhead price taker. Rather, it might perceive and exploit the fact that the wellhead price varied directly with the amount of gas it purchased. The most famous studies of wellhead market structure in the 1950s were by MacAvoy (1962, 1970a, 1970b) and Neuner (1960). MacAvoy constructed statistical tests designed to see if observed variations in wellhead prices across field (that is, wellhead) markets significantly depended on the number of pipeline buyers in the market. He concluded that monopsony power was not pervasive, although in a few areas there was some evidence of its existence.[29]

Empirical testing of monopoly and monopsony power in the period after regulation was implemented will be difficult for at least two reasons. First, interstate market prices were controlled, so that variations in prices over regions result from many factors addressed in regulatory proceedings rather than monopoly or monopsony power. Second, until the NGPA, the only remaining markets in which price fluctuated without regulation were the intrastate markets, and data have only recently been recorded at the Department of Energy on a consistent reporting basis. This is somewhat unfortunate, since it is reasonable to suppose that any markets that were to some extent monopsonistic in the past would be presumably less so now than just before regulation, as natural gas markets have grown and new entrants have appeared.[30]

THE NGPA: PROVISIONS AND CONSEQUENCES

The NGPA represented a major change in the structure and direction of regulation in the natural gas industry. In three areas the Act entails significant changes from the past. First, the Federal Energy Regulatory Commission (FERC) was granted regulatory control over intrastate as well as interstate wellhead prices. Second, the Act contained a time schedule for the deregulation of new and old gas produced from "high-cost" sources (see the description of production categories in Table 4), and it indicated a set of wellhead prices to be in effect for new gas during the transition to deregulation. Old gas prices will remain regulated indefinitely. Third, the Act provided a set of rules under which the interstate pipelines must pass along the higher costs incurred with the purchase of "high-cost" gas to selected large industrial customers. This is known as the "incremental pricing" provision of the Act.

In addition, the NGPA empowers the President to declare a natural gas emergency if a shortage that would endanger supplies to certain high-priority users exists or is imminent. In such an emergency the President can authorize pipelines and local distributors to purchase gas at any price he believes to be appropriate. If these emergency purchases are insufficient to meet designated high-priority needs, the President can reallocate gas supplies as necessary under some circumstances.[31] The Act also provides guidelines for a system of curtailments during times of shortage.

A convenient summary of the price ceilings set by the NGPA has been provided by the FERC and appears in Table 4. As noted earlier, the NGPA extends regulation to include intrastate markets. Together with the already numerous categories of interstate gas defined by regulators before the Act, there existed an even more complicated set of categories after its passage. As Table 4 shows, the old gas is not to be deregulated. However, several categories of gas were deregulated in January of 1985, with still more to be deregulated in 1987. The Act specified a set of transition prices between 1978 and the middle of the 1980s when regulation was to be phased out of many of the categories of gas. As world oil prices rose more rapidly than expected during the late 1970s and early 1980s, there was concern that the transition path of prices specified in the Act was not high enough, and that in 1985 a

Table 4. Maximum Gas Price Ceilings Set by the NGPA

Section of the Act	Price per Million BTUs[a]	Category of Gas	Date of Deregulation
102	$1.75 + inflation[b] and escalation[c] ($2.07)[d]	*New Natural Gas* New outer continental shelf (offshore) leases (on or after 4/20/77) New onshore wells (1) 2.5 miles from the nearest marker well[e] (2) If closer than 2.5 miles to a marker well, 1,000 feet deeper than the deepest completion location of each marker well within 2.5 miles New onshore reservoirs	1/1/85
		Gas from reservoirs discovered after 7/27/76 old (pre-4/20/77) offshore continental shelf	Not deregulated
103	$1.75 + inflation ($1.97)[d]	*New Onshore Production Wells* (Wells, the surface drilling of which began after 2/19/77, that are within 2.5 miles of a marker well and not 1,000 feet deeper than the deepest completion location in each marker well within 2.5 miles)	
		Gas produced above 5,000-foot depth	7/1/87
		Gas produced from below 5,000-foot depth	1/1/85
104	$1.45 + inflation ($1.63)[d]	*Gas Dedicated to Interstate Commerce Before The Date of Enactment* (Rates previously set by FPC) From wells commenced from 1/1/75–2/18/77	Not deregulated

	$0.94 + inflation ($1.06)[a]	From wells commenced from 1/1/73–12/31/74
	$0.295 + inflation ($0.33)[a]	From wells commenced prior to 1/1/73
	Applicable FERC rate + inflation	Other gas (gas produced by small producers, gas qualifying for special relief rates, etc.)
105	Contract price[f]	*Gas Sold Under Existing Intrastate Contracts* If contract price is less than Section 102 price, it may escalate, as called for by contract, up to Section 102 price If contract price exceeds Section 102 price, then contract price plus annual inflation factor or Section 102 price plus escalation applies, whichever is higher	1/1/85 — if contract price exceeds $1.00 by 12/31/84; if lower, not deregulated
106	$0.54 or other applicable FERC price + inflation ($0.61)[a]	*Sales of Gas Made Under "Roll-Over" Contracts* (An expired contract that has been renegotiated) Interstate	Not deregulated

Source: FERC Fact Sheet (November 1978).

[a] Under the NGPA, if natural gas qualifies under more than one price category, the seller may be permitted to collect the higher price. The ceiling prices set by the NGPA do not include state severance taxes.

[b] These prices include an "annual inflation adjustment factor" in order to adjust prices for inflation. The price for a given month is arrived at by multiplying the price for the previous month by the monthly equivalent of the annual inflation factor. Since most of the prices set by the NGPA are as of April 20, 1977, the adjustment for inflation begins in May 1977.

[c] These prices will escalate monthly, in addition to the inflation adjustment factor, by an annual rate of 3.5 percent until April 1981, after which they will escalate by 4 percent.

[d] The estimated maximum ceiling price as of October 1978, due to operation of inflation and escalation adjusters.

[e] A marker well is any well from which natural gas was produced in commercial quantities after January 1, 1970, and before April 20, 1977, with the exception of wells the surface drilling of which began after February 19, 1977.

[f] The average price reported to the FERC for intrastate gas sales contracted for during the second quarter of 1978 was approximately $1.90.

Continued.

Table 4. Maximum Gas Price Ceilings Set by the NGPA—cont'd

Section of the Act	Price per Million BTUs[a]	Category of Gas	Date of Deregulation
	The higher of expired contract price or $1.00 + inflation ($1.13)[a]	Intrastate	1/1/85 if more than $1.00
107	$1.75 + inflation + escalation[c] ($2.07)[a]	*High-Cost Natural Gas* Production from below 15,000 feet from wells drilled after 2/19/77	Deregulated on effective date of FERC incremental pricing rule called for by the Act (approximately one year after enactment)
		Gas produced from geopressurized brine, coal seams, Devonian shale	
	Applicable rate under the Act or higher incentive rate as set by FERC	Gas produced under other conditions the FERC determines to present "extraordinary risks or costs"	Not deregulated
108	$2.09 + inflation (after 5/78) + escalation[c] ($2.21)[a]	*Stripper Well Natural Gas* (Natural gas not produced in association with oil, which is produced at an average rate less or equal to 60,000 cubic feet per day over a 90-day period)	Not deregulated
109	$1.45, or other "just and reasonable" rate set by FERC, + inflation ($1.63)[a]	*Other Categories of Natural Gas* Any natural gas not covered under any other section of the bill	Not deregulated
		Natural gas produced from the Prudhoe Bay area of Alaska	

"fly up" of prices would be experienced as decontrol took place. However, with the sharp decline in world oil prices after 1981, the fear did not materialize.

New gas prices can now be expected to approximate marginal costs, since regulatory control does not apply to that gas. Since old gas prices are still controlled, the weighted average price of gas at the wellhead will still be below marginal cost, and some incentive for inefficient utilization of gas will remain.[32] The extent of this incentive will diminish as new gas constitutes an even greater portion of gas production streams.

Another potential source of inefficiency arises from the NGPA specification of ceiling prices that differ by type of well. Consider the following example as illustrative of this type of inefficiency. Suppose that regulation imposes a ceiling of 40 cents per Mcf on gas produced by well A and $1.80 per Mcf on gas from well B. A substantial increase in the rate of production might be obtained from well A by any of a number of technological processes (such as water flooding, fracturing the formation to improve the rate of flow, and chemical treatment) that might raise the marginal cost of production to, say, 50 cents per Mcf. These improvements will not be made, however, since regulation allows only 40 cents per Mcf. At the same time well B is producing gas that costs as much as $1.80 per Mcf. Thus it is quite likely that the total cost of producing any given amount of gas is significantly higher under the NGPA than it would be if differential price ceilings were not in force.[33]

REGULATION AND CONTRACTING IN NATURAL GAS MARKETS

Regulation and Contracting: An Explanation

Producer-Pipeline Contractual Arrangements. In the mid-1980s many gas consumers began to question deregulation when they found their gas rates rising in spite of generally falling energy prices. They were told that this was due to certain contracts — especially "take or pay" contracts — that the pipelines had signed. Many were suspicious. Actually, these contracts were quite normal arrangements that had been in use for decades, dating back to before regulation, although the regulatory environment of the 1970s had encouraged their wider use. As discussed, analyses of natural gas regulation have closely reflected the perception of the problem at the time — from studies of horizontal structure and conduct in the industry in the 1950s and 1960s to concerns in the 1970s over the shortage of natural gas induced by wellhead price regulation. The passage of the NGPA focused attention on future increases in wellhead prices as price ceilings were phased out. Both producers and pipelines had reason to believe that the demand for gas by final users would be strong, given the history of excess demand for gas (because of binding price controls) and of the high and rising price of oil, a major substitute.

Reflecting this emphasis on information in addition to that contained in current prices, policy focus has recently shifted to the impact of changes in regulation on contracts between wellhead producers and pipelines. This is important. Studies of regulation in the natural gas market have almost totally focused on impacts on wellhead prices. However, "price" is only one of many provisions negotiated in the complicated contracts between producers and pipelines. The dominance of long-term contracts (often of at least twenty years' duration) with both "price" and "non-price" provisions widens the scope of the effects of wellhead price regulation — and deregulation.

This so-called contracts problem is now a major policy issue as wellhead price ceilings are being lifted. We summarize the problem briefly below and describe it in detail later. In the late 1970s, as oil prices rose rapidly, pipeline companies found themselves constrained from competing for supplies by wellhead price ceilings, and bargained more on non-price provisions instead. Chief among these was the guarantee to purchase a minimum quantity each year, regardless of downstream demand — the so-called "take-or-pay" clause.

Expectations about future events figure prominently in contract negotiations in two respects: (1) anticipation of wellhead price decontrol in the future and (2) forecasts of the future price of oil. The former should elicit contractual concessions from pipelines trying to compete for additional future supplies. The latter is a major source of uncertainty about future gas prices, as in our earlier discussion of the predicted "fly up" in wellhead prices in the 1980s. Expectations that the increase in oil prices during the late 1970s would be permanent again suggests increased compensation of producers in new contracts.

However, in the early 1980s, as price ceilings were being phased out, gas prices did not rise as much as expected, largely as a result of the decline in world oil prices. Saddled with contracts reflecting the hope of rising gas prices, many pipelines face take-or-pay obligations that exceed the value of their assets. Some pipelines confront the choice between contract abrogation and bankruptcy.[34] Congress has considered legislative measures that would release pipelines from their contract commitments, on the grounds that their predicament is itself due largely to federal regulation.

The extent to which price regulation is responsible for the current contract imbroglio requires an explanation of the use of non-price provisions in producer-pipeline contracts both in the absence and presence of regulation. In the following discussion we draw heavily on the recent theoretical and empirical study of producer-pipeline contractual arrangements in Hubbard and Weiner (1984).

Transactions costs (Williamson, 1975) provide a basic reason for contracting in the gas market. Because of the "specific capital" (that is, capital useful only in the particular transactional arrangement involved in individual producer-pipeline relationships), trade organized through spot exchange is costly. "Opportunism" is likely to be a serious problem when uncertainty is great and when the cost of failure to come to terms is high.[35] Once the initial gas well development costs are sunk, a pipeline faces the temptation to appropriate some of the rents (revenues above production costs) from production unless the producer has an alternative means of sale. Realizing this, the producer demands a long-term contract with adjustment clauses beforehand. The pipeline is itself a form of specific capital; once constructed, it would be prohibitively expensive to move. Since it is best operated near full capacity, a long-term contract "guaranteeing supplies" is in the buyer's interest as well.

Wellhead price regulation may provide an additional motivation for long-term contracting. If pipelines are not free to offer market-clearing prices in order to obtain additional gas, they may sidestep the regulation by granting more generous non-price concessions. Take-or-pay provisions, which specify a minimum lump-sum payment per year from pipeline to producer, are a good example.

Of course, not all variables affecting the contract can be anticipated by the transacting parties. In general, contracts specifying only price are not efficient, because in the absence of future markets, prices allocate both risk and commodities. Signatories can in many cases obtain efficient contracts by making the payment rule conditional on a few key variables such as output and general prices indices easily verified by both parties.

One case is particularly instructive. Suppose that the dominant source of uncertainty stems from the demand side (for example, because of fluctuations in the price of oil). Given this assumption, the efficient contract involves both a take-or-pay provision (essentially a lump-sum payment) and "price payment" equal to the marginal cost of production for gas taken.[36] The contract will leave the choice of output to the pipeline, with a payment rule combining "price" and "non-price" provisions so as to leave producers indifferent to the level of production. The lump-sum guarantee offers producers insurance against fluctuations, while payments on the margin are efficient. This arrangement is appropriate for the demand uncertainty case, since it is the pipeline that faces downstream fluctuations in demand and can adjust takes accordingly. Interestingly, take-or-pay requirements were used extensively in producer-pipeline contracts even before the 1954 advent of wellhead-price regulation. Indeed, MacAvoy (1962) notes that a typical contract specified a take-or-pay of about 80 percent of wellhead capacity, even in the early 1950s.

Thus, even in the absence of wellhead price controls, an expectation of rising oil prices would lead pipelines to increase the total compensation to producers in new contracts (because of the resulting anticipation of higher gas prices). That such price expectations turn out to be wrong later on vitiates neither the desirability of the contract nor its efficiency.

Now consider the case wherein price controls are imposed. Under binding field price control regulation there is a gap between the marginal willingness to pay for new supplies and the marginal opportunity cost of production at the controlled price. Going back to the "demand uncertainty" case above, to the extent that field price controls are binding, there will be excess demand for gas, and uncertainty materializes in demand fluctuations. Equilibrium production is no longer efficient, as pipelines would be willing to raise producer prices to attract more gas, but price regulation stops them from doing so. This situation persists as long as controls remain. Price regulation, then, introduces no new dimensions per se to the negotiation problem producer and pipeline, though it may alter the relative reliance on different provisions.

Deregulation and the "Contracts Problem." Understanding the nuts and bolts of the "contracts problem" in the early 1980s requires an analysis of contracting during the transition from regulation to total deregulation. While contract provisions may be similar in the two extremes, a period of transition can bring unanticipated gains or losses to parties as long as market conditions are uncertain. The magnitude of those gains and losses depends on the type of deregulation — immediate decontrol versus phase deregulation.

Consider for example the events of the late 1970s and early 1980s. A demand shock from an increase in the price of oil caused an increase in the market-clearing price-quantity combination. If decontrol were immediate and total, wellhead prices would increase. There would be no need to increase reliance on non-price provisions — that is, no significant change in price escalators or take-or-pay requirements.

However, given phased decontrol — or, in general, anticipated future decontrol — competition for new supplies in the current period requires an increase in "other payments" (such as higher future prices or take-or-pay requirements). As long as the oil price increase is expected to continue, the pipeline should be willing to grant concessions, as with the anticipated price change due to future deregulation.

For example, by increasing the take-or-pay requirement, the pipeline in effect extends additional insurance to the producer. That is, if the demand for gas declines (because of a decline in economic activity or the price of oil), the producer's revenue is still stabilized because of the take-or-pay provision. The producer obtains this "downside protection" at no cost, because if demand is high, he still receives the additional revenue from greater output.

A "contracts problem" can arise under phased decontrol if, contrary to expectations, the demand shock is not permanent — particularly if non-price contract provisions include high take-or-pay requirements or rigid downward prices. Suppose for example that the oil price increase is temporary and subsequently oil prices decline. As a result of the oil price decline, at the agreed-upon price, the gas may not be marketable downstream. Pipelines incur losses on the high take-or-pay requirements to which they agreed on the anticipation of higher future prices. Such losses do not imply that contracts are necessarily inefficient but reflect the hazards of operating via contracts in a market subject to shocks.

This does not imply that natural gas price regulation is "blameless" in causing the contracts problems. First, the excess demand for natural gas accompanying a binding price ceiling will lead to increased reliance on contract provisions other than current-period price, leaving pipeline profits more vulnerable to external forces — such as changes in the price of oil or in economic growth.

Second, the type of transition from regulation to laissez-faire is important. Immediate decontrol will focus the negotiation of new contracts on price changes (marginal compensation), while anticipated phased decontrol will require increases in concessions not related to current prices (inframarginal compensation) — for example, take-or-pay provisions, which increases vulnerability to market shifts. With respect to public policy, discussion of the second point involves a comparison of the benefits of phased decontrol with the costs imposed by contract rigidities.

Policy concern extends beyond the contracting parties. For example, as noted in a recent study by the U.S. General Accounting Office:

An increase in gas prices at the wellhead, because of the operation of contract clauses, will increase a pipeline's average acquisition costs for all of its gas supply and, thus, increase the cost of gas to its customers. As these increased acquisition costs plus normal charges for transportation and distribution push the retail price of gas to where it approaches or exceeds the price of residual fuel oil, price sensitive industrial and electric utility consumers could switch to this alternative fuel. Such a drop in industrial and electric utility demand for natural gas and subsequent loss of pipeline load could in turn lead to further increases in residential prices (1983, pp. iii–iv).

The temporary losses faced by some market participants as a result of previous contractual commitments do not negate the importance and desirability of wellhead price deregulation. First, while the interaction of market uncertainty and past regulation contributed to the current "contracts problem," continuing regulation would extend the distortions in natural gas production and consumption. Second, contracting parties are proving to be flexible as economic conditions in the gas market change; new contracts carry less restrictive provisions than those signed a few years ago, and many existing contracts are being renegotiated. Public policy should facilitate this market transition, rather than overturning all existing contracts or reimposing wellhead price controls.

Regulation and Contracting: Evidence

Below we present some summary evidence on the impact of regulation on the structure of long-term contracts based on contract surveys conducted by the Energy Information Administration. Table 5 illustrates the sensitivity of minimum-purchase provisions to current and anticipated demand conditions. A striking pattern occurs in the percentage "take" requirements across contracts of different vintages. Take-or-pay requirements rose by nearly 50 percent between the pre-1973 period and the period between 1973 and 1977. The second period witnessed the anticipation of field price deregulation and the excess demand for gas caused by the explosion in oil prices. As the excess demand situation began to reverse, the average minimum-purchase provision declined somewhat, but remained high relative to the pre-oil-shock level.

In addition to take-or-pay provisions, natural gas contracts typically include a set of price-escalator provisions and a set of buyer-protection provisions. The former divide into both "definite" and "indefinite" (indexed to the price of oil or to the highest price paid for gas in the same area) components. Moreover, "minimum-price" provisions set a floor to the price paid or to a price increase. The latter category is typified by "market-out" clauses allowing the pipeline to default on contractual obligations if the gas is not marketable at the agreed upon price and by "maximum-price" provisions, which set a ceiling on the price paid.

For example, patterns similar to those for take-or-pay require-

Table 5. Take-or-Pay Provisions by Contract Vintage

Contract Vintage	Take-or-Pay Requirement (%)[a]
Pre-1973	59.6
1973 to April 20, 1977	85.9
April 21, 1977 to November 8, 1978[b]	82.3
November 9, 1978–1979	82.5
1980	78.3

Source: U.S. Energy Information Administration (1983), p. ix.
[a]Weighted-average percentage minimum-purchase requirement (take-or-pay) based on percentage of deliverability or capacity.
[b]The Natural Gas Policy Act was enacted on November 9, 1978.

ments reported in Table 5 exist for other non-price provisions reported in the studies by the Energy Information Administration. Splitting new contracts signed in the pre-NGPA period into two intervals (pre-1973 and 1973 to April 20, 1977), "minimum-price" provisions covered 69 percent of the volume of gas traded by the second period, as opposed to 39 percent before. Coverage by "market-out" provisions declined from 12 percent to roughly zero.

Perhaps the most convincing evidence on the impact of regulation on take-or-pay provisions and the "contracts problem" comes from a sample of producer-pipeline contracts we obtained from a survey conducted in 1982 by the Energy Information Administration. These contracts cover sales of natural gas in interstate commerce from 615 producing wells in the continental United States. The survey selected contracts signed after 1978, grouping them by "sections" assigned by the NGPA. Specifically, gas sold under Sections 102 ("new" natural gas), 103 ("new" onshore production wells), and 107 ("high-cost" gas from deep wells, Devonian shale, tight sands, or geopressurized brine) was included.

In Table 6 we present the average take-or-pay percentages for the three sections in our sample. Since gas sold under Section 107 was not subject to price controls, we would predict that the mean take-or-pay requirement would be lower than that for Section 102 gas. Technically, price ceilings were lower for Section 103 gas, but because it was produced at a much lower cost than Section 102 gas, price controls were relatively more binding on Section 102 gas. Hence the prediction would be that the take-or-pay percentage for Section 103 would be less than that for Section 102. These predictions are corroborated by the data.[37]

Table 6. Average Take-or-Pay
Requirements by *NGPA* Section
(Post-1978 Contracts in 1982 *EIA* Survey)

NGPA Section	Take-or-Pay Requirement (%)
102	92.2
103	84.4
107	82.7

Source: Hubbard and Weiner (1984).

The anticipation of wellhead price decontrol and high future demand for gas because of rising world oil prices gave producers the upper hand in negotiating new contracts with pipelines during this period. The same data indicate further non-price concessions to producers of controlled gas (NGPA Sections 102 and 103) through more infrequent use of "buyer-protection" clauses. Specifically, "maximum-price" provisions appeared in 37 percent of the Section 107 contracts versus 6 percent for Section 102 contracts and 4 percent for Section 103 contracts. "Market-out" provisions were also much less common in contracts signed under Sections 102 (16 percent) and 103 (16 percent) than under Section 107 (36 percent).

This approach of considering the effects of federal regulation on the contractual arrangement as a whole and not just on the wellhead price assumes continued importance in analyzing policy proposals and new market arrangements in the era of price deregulation. The transition to the deregulated environment will be much slower than would be predicted by looking only at dates of legislation. The great majority of gas produced from post-NGPA wells is sold under contracts not expiring until after 1985; 43 percent do not expire until after 1990, and 28 percent do not expire until after 1995.

The contractual problems arising during this lengthy transition period are already leading to extensive litigation. Between 1981 and the beginning of 1984, at least sixteen interstate pipelines exercised "market-out" provisions in their contracts for high-cost gas (U.S. Energy Information Administration, 1983b). Other pipelines, seeking to avoid loss of load downstream from industrial fuel-switching, have invoked *force majeure* clauses to obtain relief. Perhaps most sweeping in its potential impact, some distribution companies have sued to block pipelines' ability to pass through high purchased gas costs to consumers (see the *Columbia Gas Transmission Corporation* case, 1982).

New Market Arrangements

Current inflexibility in producer-pipeline contracts is stimulating both policy discussion and new market arrangements. In 1983 the Reagan administration[38] put forth a renegotiation proposal allowing either party to "market out" of a gas contract that has not been renegotiated by January 1, 1985. The proposal would have reduced take-or-pay obligations by declaring take-or-pay requirements greater than 70 percent of field capacity to be legally unenforceable (a feature shared by some congressional proposals).

The administration's proposal also encouraged a change in the producer-pipeline relationship by providing incentives (through higher allowed markups) for "contract carriage," in which pipelines would no longer hold title to the gas they transport. In addition, many other proposals would have increased incentives for pipelines to consider contract carriage by making it more difficult to pass through exceptionally high purchased gas costs.

The higher risks of operating in a deregulated market also create the potential for changes in market structure — for example, vertical integration of pipelines and producers or joint ventures. Such developments would require new research to assess the competitiveness of different segments of the gas market. Another mechanism for enhancing short-run flexibility would be the operation of spot and futures markets in natural gas (see the discussion in U.S. Energy Information Administration, 1983b).[39]

Vertical integration can be a cause for policy concern. Even if pipelines continue to be regulated as they presently are (except for wellhead price regulation), and even if a producer delivering gas to an affiliated pipeline is surrounded by other competing producers, there is reason to be wary. If regulators of the pipeline were not observant, the affiliated producer could conceivably charge a higher-than-competitive wellhead price to the pipeline, thereby making excessive profits, and the pipeline might in turn try to pass the excessive prices it paid for gas through to its customers as a cost it had incurred. Note that even competitive wellhead markets would not eliminate these incentives.

Although one possible solution would be to prohibit pipelines and producer affiliates in the same wellhead markets, one should not leap from this warning to a proposal for disintegration. After all, there are a number of potential economic efficiencies that may be gained by vertical integration, including possibly the opportunity for affiliated firms to share risks and negotiate contracts in a less costly fashion. The point of the argument is simply to indicate that at the minimum some problems of a regulatory nature may remain under the NGPA.

In particular, the incentives for inefficiency we have described under vertical integration might be controlled if the pipeline regulator could recognize and disallow any excessively high prices charged by a producer affiliate — prices exceeding those charged by nonaffiliated producers. The drawback here is evident: the regulator would have to be watchful, and the task would not be easy, since as we have shown, gas contract provisions can be quite complicated.

CONCLUSION

The natural gas industry has been neither completely regulated nor deregulated at the wellhead since 1938. Between The Natural Gas Act of 1938 and the *Phillips* decision of 1954, the statutory basis for such regulation was evidently in place, but it was not until the *Phillips* decision that regulation was enforced. Even then intrastate wellhead prices were uncontrolled, and there were serious administrative problems in regulating interstate prices. The best evidence available suggests that regulators had no real effect in holding interstate wellhead prices down below the levels that would have prevailed in the absence of regulation, at least until about 1970. During the 1960s no shortages were evident, and wellhead prices in interstate markets were approximately the same as the prices in the uncontrolled intrastate markets.

When the 1970s arrived, however, with a rising demand for energy and increased world oil prices, the FPC did hold interstate wellhead prices below the levels that would have been observed absent regulation. Shortages occurred. Natural gas reserves declined. The FPC was forced to let new gas prices rise to avert worse shortages. The clamor for deregulation of wellhead prices led to many proposals that were rejected amidst intense debate before the passage of the NGPA.

This new Act forms the framework for the deregulation of certain categories of natural gas at the wellhead. But deregulation is not complete. Old gas in interstate markets will not be deregulated, even after 1985. Neither will gas from stripper wells, from the Prudhoe Bay in Alaska, or from certain offshore areas.

It is not an easy task to analyze a piece of legislation that appears to have as many objectives as the NGPA. In one rather lengthy fell swoop it apparently seeks to promote efficiency in the use of energy resources, to provide at least a partial solution to the problem of gas shortages, to remove the incentives to dedicate new reserves only to intrastate markets wherever possible, to decrease reliance on imported energy, and to do all these things without large inflationary consequences.

We have concluded that the Act will lead to reduced shortages, both in the interim period and after 1985. The Act will lead to substantial improvements in the efficiency with which natural gas is used. However, it will not totally eliminate the old incentives for inefficiency, and it has introduced some new incentives for inefficiency.

As a recent development in the post-NGPA period, we discuss the "contracts problem" of the early 1980s. With the phased decontrol embodied in the NGPA, many individual producers and pipelines entered into long-term contracts in that period expecting high world oil prices and demand for natural gas in the future. Because of price controls still in effect, pipelines could not compete for additional supplies with higher prices, and instead offered non-price concessions to producers. With the collapse of world oil prices, the inflexibility in the contracts because of these concessions led to inefficiency in pipeline purchases and fears that some pipelines might go bankrupt. Policy proposals to deal with such contract problems must distinguish between poor contracting practices and the more general difficulty of negotiating long-term contracts under conditions of uncertainty.

Finally, two areas in which current developments in the gas market are taking place are the increased interest in spot markets in natural gas and proposals for vertical integration of producers and pipelines. With respect to the former, the development of a well-functioning spot market would facilitate the operation of futures markets, greatly increasing the flexibility of adjustments in long-term contracts. Vertical integration in response to recent contract difficulties between pipelines and producers is not without its problems, however, because of potential supra-normal transfer payments between affiliated producers and pipelines, even though the supply at the wellhead is competitive. Close scrutiny by pipeline regulators will be required.

NOTES

[1] This legislation became effective in November 1978.

[2] For example, in a 1981 study Loury estimated that gross transfers from decontrol (in 1981 dollars) would rise from $9 billion in 1981 to $37 billion in 1984.

[3] Gas found in conjunction with oil is termed "associated gas."

[4] See, for example, *Information On Contracts Between Natural Gas Producers and Pipelines Companies,* Report of the Comptroller General of the United States, GAO/RCED-83-5, February 22, 1983.

[5] See, for example, *Barrett v. Kansas Natural Gas Co.,* 265 U.S. 298 (1924).

⁶*Natural Gas Act*, 52 Stat. 821 (1938), 15 U.S.C.A. et. seq., Section 1(a). No particular market failure or other problem was cited, however.
⁷*Ibid.*, Sections 4(a) and 4(b).
⁸*Ibid.*, Sections 4(c) and 4(d).
⁹*Ibid.*, Section 4(e).
¹⁰*Ibid.*, Section 1(c).
¹¹*Phillips Petroleum Company v. Wisconsin et al.*, 342 U.S. 672 (1954).
¹²MacAvoy (1970a) p. 154.
¹³Kahn (1971), Vol. 11, p. 31.
¹⁴If there were no market imperfection or, particularly, no significant monopoly power, there could be no efficiency gain from the regulation.
¹⁵*National Gas Survey* (1975), Vol. 1, p. 85.
¹⁶See *In re Phillips Petroleum Company*, 24 FPC 537 (1960).
¹⁷This justification was suggested by Kahn (1970), Vol. 1, p. 43.
¹⁸*Permian Basin Area Rate Cases*, 390 U.S. 747 (1968).
¹⁹*Federal Power Commission Annual Report* for 1974, p. 41.
²⁰In fact, the table suggests that intrastate prices may have actually been less than interstate prices before 1970, although they were virtually the same.
²¹*The Economics of the Natural Gas Controversy*, Staff study of the Subcommittee on Energy of the Joint Economic Committee, Congress of the United States, September 19, 1977, p. 16.
²²See, for example, *An Analysis of the Impact of the Projected Natural Gas Curtailments for the Winter of 1975–76*, a report of the Office of Technology Assessment, November 4, 1975.
²³United States House of Representatives, Report No. 94–732, p. 6.
²⁴Specifically, in the 1964–1969 period, additions to interstate reserves were 11.4 Tcf, while additions to intrastate reserves were 5.6 Tcf. In the 1970–1973 period, the corresponding additions were respectively 0.7 and 8.4 Tcf. See the *House of Representatives, Report No. 94-732* (94th Congress, 1st Session), p. 56.
²⁵This simple calculation supports the more detailed study of MacAvoy and Pindyck (1975), who also measured an income transfer in excess of a billion dollars annually in 1975.
²⁶This analysis assumes competition in gas supply.
²⁷As a technical point, the use of consumer surplus exactly measures the welfare change for an individual if there are zero income effects associated with the demand schedule. However, Willig (1976) has shown that even if there are nonzero income effects, the measure may serve to approximate the actual welfare change.
²⁸For a more detailed critique of the MacAvoy and Pindyck approach, see Braeutigam (1978).
²⁹See, for example, MacAvoy (1970a), p. 160. Note that if monopsony were the principal problem, minimum rather than maximum wellhead prices might be set.
³⁰For a more extensive discussion of wellhead market structure in the 1970s, see Braeutigam (1978).
³¹See Title III of the NGPA.
³²This incentive for inefficient gas utilization due to weighted-average

pricing is similar to that observed under the "entitlement system" accompany crude oil price controls; see the discussion in Case 4.

[33] For more on this point see *Pricing Provisions of the Natural Gas Policy Act of 1978*, Energy Policy Study, Vol. 3, Energy Information Administration of the Department of Energy, pp. 15–17.

[34] An extended discussion of contracting and deregulation is available in U.S. Energy Information Administration (1981–1983a, 1983b). A discussion of related legal issues can be found in Pierce (1983).

[35] A major source of uncertainty here is variation in the price of oil, a substitute for gas for many users.

[36] See the theoretical discussions in Hall and Lilien (1979) and Hubbard and Weiner (1984).

[37] In formal econometric tests, Hubbard and Weiner (1984) found that the effect of the price ceilings was to raise the average take-or-pay requirement by about 5 percentage points. While this represents a significant increase, take-or-pay requirements are predicted to be large even in contracts for gas not subject to price controls.

[38] Descriptions of the bills are contained in U.S. Energy Information Administration (1983b).

[39] The world oil market, for example, operates on a two-price system, with trades carried out both under long-term contracts and spot market transactions.

BIBLIOGRAPHY

An Analysis of the Impact of the Projected Natural Gas Curtailments for the Winter of 1975–76, Report of the Office of Technology Assessment, November 4, 1975.

Braeutigam, Ronald R., "An Examination of Regulation in the Natural Gas Industry," *Study on Federal Regulation*, Appendix to Vol. VI, United States Senate Committee on Government Operations, December 1978.

Breyer, S. G., and MacAvoy, P. W., *Energy Regulation by the Federal Power Commission*. Washington, D.C.: The Brookings Institution, 1973.

———— and ————, "The Natural Gas Shortage and the Regulation of Natural Gas Producers," *Harvard Law Review*, 86, 6 (April 1973), 941–987.

Columbia Gas Transmission Corporation, Docket Nos. TA81-1-21-001 and TA81-2-21-001, reported at 21 FERC S. 63, 100.

Helms, Robert B., *Natural Gas Regulation, An Evaluation of FPC Price Controls*, American Enterprise Institute for Public Policy Research, 1974.

Hubbard, R. Glenn, and Weiner, Robert J., "Regulation and Bilateral Monopoly: Long Term Contracting in Natural Gas," mimeograph, Northwestern University, 1984.

Information on Contracts Between Natural Gas Producers and Pipeline Companies, Report of the Comptroller General of the United States, GAO/RCED-83-5, February 22, 1983.

Kahn, Alfred E., *The Economics of Regulation: Principles and Institutions*, Vols. I and II. New York: John Wiley & Sons, Inc. 1971.

Loury, Glenn C., "Efficiency and Equity Impacts of Natural Gas Deregulation," study for the Natural Gas Supply Association, 1981. Reprinted in Robert H. Haveman and Julius Margolis, *Public Expenditure and Policy Analysis*, 3d ed. Boston: Houghton Mifflin, 1983.

MacAvoy, Paul W., "The Regulation-Induced Shortage of Natural Gas," *Journal of Law and Economics*, 14, 1 (April 1971), 167–199.

——, *Price Formation in Natural Gas Fields*. New Haven, Conn.: Yale University Press, 1962.

——, "The Reasons and Results in Natural Gas Field Price Regulation," in Paul MacAvoy (ed.), *The Crisis of the Regulatory Commissions*. New York: W. W. Norton & Co., Inc., 1970 (reference 1970a).

——, "The Effectiveness of the Federal Power Commission," *Bell Journal of Ecnomics* (Spring 1970) (reference 1970b).

——, and Pindyck, Robert S., "Alternative Regulatory Policies for Dealing wth the Natural Gas Shortage," *The Bell Journal of Economics and Management Science*, 3 (Autumn 1973).

Natural Gas Curtailments, 1975–76 Heating Season, National Gas Task Force, Federal Energy Administration, October 1975.

"Natural Gas Policy Act of 1978: Interim Regulations," Federal Energy Regulatory Commission, *Federal Register*, (December 1, 1978), Part VIII.

National Gas Survey, United States Federal Power Commission, 1975.

Neuner, Edward J., *The Natural Gas Industry*. Norman, Okla.: University of Oklahoma Press, 1960.

Pierce, Richard J., "Reconsidering the Roles of Regulation and Competition in the Natural Gas Industry." *Harvard Law Review*, 97 (December 1983): 345–385.

Pricing Provisions of the Natural Gas Policy Act of 1978, Energy Policy Study, Vol. 3, Energy Information Administration of the Department of Energy.

U.S. Energy Information Administration. "An Analysis of the Natural Gas Policy Act and Several Alternatives," Part I (December 1981), II (June 1982), III (September 1982), and IV (May 1983a), Washington, D.C.

——, "Structure and Trends in the Natural Gas Wellhead Contracts," Document DOE-EIA-0419, Washington, D.C., November 1983b.

U.S. General Accounting Office, "Information on Contracts Between Gas Producers and Pipeline-Companies," Document GAO/RCED-83-5, February 22, 1983.

Williamson, Oliver E., *Markets and Hierarchies*. New York: The Free Press, 1975.

Willig, R. D., "Consumer's Surplus Without Apology," *American Economic Review*, 66, 4 (September 1976), 589–597.

CASE 6

The Partial Deregulation of Banks and Other Depository Institutions

Lawrence J. White
New York University

INTRODUCTION

Commercial banks and other depository institutions — savings and loan associations, mutual savings banks, and credit unions — are extensively regulated by the federal government and by the fifty state governments. They may be the most heavily regulated institutions in the American economy after electric utilities.

Depository institutions are subject to both economic regulation and "social" regulation, and both forms of regulation have substantial consequences for the performance of this industry. The economic regulation includes federally imposed limits on the interest rates they can pay on various kinds of deposits (price controls), state-imposed limits on the interest rates they can charge on some types of loans (price controls), state and federally imposed limits on who can establish new banks and other depository institutions or even branches of existing institutions (entry controls), and federally imposed limits on the activities (financial and nonfinancial) in which these institutions can engage (entry controls). The social regulation includes government efforts to ensure that these institutions are safe, that they pro-

---

The author would like to thank John Ballantine, Stephen Cecchetti, Jeffrey Gordon, Thomas Huertas, Juliana Nelson, A. Kendall Raine, Lawrence Uhlick, and Leonard Weiss for helpful suggestions and comments on an earlier draft of this paper. He also thanks Linda Canina for her research assistance.

vide extensive information to loan customers, and that they practice no discrimination in their loan practices.

The extensive regulations affecting financial institutions reflect the important position of financial intermediaries in the economy. They are virtually the only providers of checking account services (until the 1970s commercial banks were the sole providers of such services) and of savings accounts — a relatively safe and liquid investment vehicle for small savers. They are major providers of credit to borrowers. Tables 1 and 2 provide some summary statistics on these institutions.

Though regulation of financial institutions has been pervasive, its extent and character has changed over time. In particular, in the early 1980s economic regulation of deposit rates was modified and substantially loosened, other forms of economic regulation for these depository institutions were modified, and major efforts at further deregulation were being discussed widely.

This paper will deal with the regulation and deregulation of depository institutions, focusing primarily on economic regulation.[1] The history of regulation and its rationale will be discussed, followed by an analysis of the consequences of that regulation and then a discussion

Table 1. Depository Institutions in the United States, as of December 31, 1983

Type of Institution	Number	Number of Offices (Includes Branches)	Assets[d] (Billions of Dollars)	Deposits (Billions of Dollars)
Commercial banks[a]	15,047	55,960	$2,027.3	$1,535.1
Mutual savings banks[b] } "Thrifts"	534	3,233	249.1	219.0
Savings and loan associations	3,513	21,611	771.7	634.1
Credit unions[c]	20,000	—	88.9	81.0

Sources: U.S. Federal Deposit Insurance Corp. (1984b), pp. 6, 21; U.S. League of Savings Institutions (1984), pp. 46-47, 54-56; and U.S. Department of Commerce (1984), p. 515.

[a] Includes 142 nondeposit trust companies.

[b] Includes mutual savings banks insured by The Federal Savings and Loan Insurance Corporation.

[c] As of December 31, 1982.

[d] Assets are largely loans, mortgages, and debt securities.

Table 2. The Size Distribution of Banks, as of December 31, 1983[a]

Size (in Dollars)	Number	Assets (Billions of Dollars)	% of Total Number	% of Total Assets
Less than 5 million	658	$ 1.3	4.3%	0.1
5.0–9.9 million	1,312	10.1	8.6	0.5
10.0–24.9 million	4,189	71.3	27.6	3.2
25.0–49.9 million	3,773	135.1	24.9	6.1
50.0–99.9 million	2,709	187.3	17.8	8.5
100.0–299.9 million	1,720	275.3	11.2	12.4
300.0–499.9 million	300	113.9	2.0	5.1
500.0–999.9 million	226	157.7	1.5	7.1
1.0–4.9 billion	239	486.9	1.6	22.0
5.0 billion or more	56	772.9	0.4	34.9
Total	15,182	$2,211.8	100.0	100.0

Source: U.S. Federal Deposit Insurance Corporation (1984b), p. 21.
[a] Includes mutual savings banks.

of the events and circumstances that led to the regulatory reform of the early 1980s. Those deregulatory actions themselves, and their consequences, will be analyzed. An assessment of the current (mid-1980s) regulatory structure, which is still pervasive and remains an important influence on the industry, concludes the discussion.

THE HISTORY OF REGULATION

The Nineteenth and Early Twentieth Centuries

The history of depository institutions in the United States is characterized by economic regulation from the beginning.[2] In the early nineteenth century commercial banks were licensed by the individual states; charters usually required a separate law by the state. The bank's scope and authority were usually confined to the state of chartering. Thus began a tradition of state regulation and confinement that has persisted to the present day. In the late 1830s, however, a number of states began to loosen their controls on entry into banking substantially.

The first major federal initiative of lasting consequence occurred in the 1860s, with the enactment of the National Currency Act of 1863 and the National Bank Act of 1864. (Table 3 summarizes the major federal regulatory legislation.) These acts established a system of federally chartered commercial banks to be chartered and regulated by the newly created Office of the Comptroller of the Currency. These acts also included a tax on (and were thereby intended to eliminate) the state chartered banks, but the latter devised strategies that permitted them to survive and prosper.

With both national and state chartered banks flourishing, a second distinctive characteristic of the American banking sector, the dual regulatory structure, was established. This dual regulatory structure meant that new, and even existing, bank owners could choose their chartering agency and thus choose their regulatory structure. Since they tended to choose the regulatory regime that, on balance, was less onerous, a form of competition between the federal regulators and the state regulators developed. Neither side could allow significant differentials in regulatory requirements to develop, for fear of losing too many bank charters from their regulatory domain. This dual

Table 3. Summary of Important Federal Legislation Affecting Economic Regulation of Depository Institutions

Year	Legislation	Important Regulatory Provisions
1863	National Currency Act	Established national bank charters; established Office of the Comptroller of Currency
1864	National Bank Act	
1913	Federal Reserve Act	Established Federal Reserve System
1927	McFadden Act	Allowed national banks to branch within home cities (if state law permitted); reaffirmed and strengthened the ability of national banks to deal in securities
1932	Federal Home Loan Bank Act	Established Federal Home Loan Bank Board
1933	Banking Act (including Glass-Steagall Act)	Established Federal Deposit Insurance Corporation; established federal deposit insurance for banks; established deposit interest rate ceilings for commercial banks; restricted commercial banks from investment banking; allowed national banks to branch statewide (if state law permitted)

Table 3. Summary of Important Federal Legislation Affecting Economic Regulation of Depository Institutions — cont'd

Year	Legislation	Important Regulatory Provisions
1933	Home Owners' Loan Act	Established federal charters for savings and loan associations
1934	National Housing Act	Established Federal Savings and Loan Insurance Corporation; established deposit insurance for S&Ls
1934	Federal Credit Union Act	Established national charters for credit unions
1935	Banking Act	Restricted entry into banking
1956	Bank Holding Company Act (including Douglas Amendment)	Restricted bank holding companies (controlling two or more banks) to activities related to banking; prevented bank holding companies from owning banks across state lines
1966	Interest Rate Control Act	Extended deposit interest rate ceilings to S&Ls and mutual savings banks
1970	Bank Holding Company Act Amendments	Extended provision of 1956 Act to one-bank holding companies
1978	International Banking Act	Brought domestic branches of foreign-owned banks into regulatory conformance with domestic banks
1980	Depository Institutions Deregulation and Monetary Control Act	Permitted all depository institutions to offer NOW accounts; authorized orderly elimination of all deposit interest rate ceilings (except on demand deposits); expanded asset powers and activities of federally chartered thrifts; preempted state usury laws for some loans; allowed Federal Reserve to set reserve requirements for all depository institutions
1982	Garn–St Germain Depository Institutions Act	Directed that a depository account competitive with money market mutual funds be created; expanded asset powers and activities for thrifts; allowed state chartered thrifts to offer variable rate mortgages; authorized federal charters for new mutual savings banks; permitted failing depository institutions to be bought by an out-of-state bank or thrift

regulatory structure and the competition among regulators is a feature that has persisted to the present day.[3]

The next major federal initiative occurred in 1913, with the passage of the Federal Reserve Act and the creation of the Federal Reserve System. For the first time the United States had a central bank that could carry out an active monetary policy and act as a lender of last resort to banks. Congress hoped that the Federal Reserve would mean the end of financial panics and would provide greater stability for the banking system and for the overall economy. All national banks were required to join the Federal Reserve System and to keep deposits in the Reserve, and thus they were subject to regulatory supervision by "the Fed." It was hoped at the time that all or most state chartered banks would join the Reserve (which they could do while maintaining their state charters), but few did. Looser state regulatory regimes (and, especially, lower state reserve requirements on deposits) provided a strong incentive for state banks to stay out.

One important feature of state regulation began to gain prominence in the early twentieth century: rules with respect to branching of state chartered banks. The states varied widely in their branching rules. Most, like Illinois and Texas, were "unit banking" states that allowed a bank to operate at only one physical location. A few others, like Florida, Massachusetts, and New York, allowed some branching but imposed some within-state geographic limitations on branching.[4] One, California, allowed statewide branching for its banks.

National banks were limited to single locations, regardless of state regime. During the nineteenth century this limitation on national banks was comparatively unimportant, since poor transportation and telecommunications limited the advantages of operating a branch system. As both transportation costs and telecommunications costs fell rapidly in the first quarter of the twentieth century, this restriction on national banks seemed more of a disadvantage. In 1927 the McFadden Act allowed national banks to establish branches within their same city of operation, if the law of that state also permitted state chartered banks to do the same.[5] Six years later, the Banking Act of 1933 extended the branching privileges of national banks to bring them into complete conformity with the rules that applied to state chartered banks in each state. Interstate branching was still not possible, because of the state chartering laws.[6]

Though many states have eased their branching restrictions over time, divergent state policies with respect to intrastate branching (and the ban on interstate branching) have persisted into the mid-1980s. Table 4 provides a summary of these policies as of 1983.

Table 4. State Branching Regulations, as of 1983

Unit banking[a] (9)
  Colorado, Illinois, Kansas, Minnesota, Missouri, Montana, North Dakota, Texas, Wyoming
Limited branching (20)
  Alabama, Arkansas, Florida, Georgia, Indiana, Iowa, Kentucky, Louisiana, Massachusetts, Michigan, Mississippi, Nebraska, New Mexico, Ohio, Oklahoma, Pennsylvania, Tennessee, Virginia, West Virginia, Wisconsin
Statewide branching (21)
  Alaska, Arizona, California, Connecticut, Delaware, Hawaii, Idaho, Maine, Maryland, Nevada, New Jersey, New York, New Hampshire, North Carolina, Oregon, Rhode Island, South Carolina, South Dakota, Utah, Vermont, Washington

---

Source: Golembe and Holland (1983), p. 120.
[a] Some states allow bank holding company networks.

The 1930s to the 1970s

The stock market crash of 1929 and the steep decline in economic activity that followed ushered in the Great Depression of the 1930s and created a genuine crisis in the banking system. As Table 5 indicates, the number of bank failures increased sharply in the years from 1930 to 1933, as compared with the previous decades. One of the first acts of office of the new President, Franklin D. Roosevelt, in early March 1933 was to declare a "bank holiday," to stop the runs on banks and to restore confidence in the banking system. Most banks reopened about a week later, and the runs largely stopped, but Congress was convinced that major reform of the banking system was necessary. The Banking Act of 1933 followed within a few months.

In Congress it was widely believed that "excessive" competition among banks had contributed to their vulnerability and to the demise of those that failed. The Comptroller of the Currency and the states had been relatively unrestrained in chartering new banks during the previous half century. Many banks had competed vigorously in offering to pay interest on various types of deposits. Further, Congress believed that the securities activities (such as underwriting of new securities and dealing in existing securities) in which many banks engaged[7] had exposed those banks to excessive risk and, again, had contributed to their problems.[8] Finally, Congress believed that a national insurance system for depositors was necessary.

Table 5. Bank Failures[a]

Year(s)	Number of Failed Banks (Annual Average)	Deposits of Failed Banks (Billions of Dollars) (Annual Average)	Annual Average of Failed Banks as a % of All Banks at Beginning of Period (%)	Annual Average of Failed Bank Deposits as a % of All Bank Deposits at Beginning of Period (%)
1864–1870	6.7	n.a.	0.4	n.a.
1871–1880	50.8	n.a.	2.6	n.a.
1881–1890	30.8	n.a.	0.9	n.a.
1891–1900	129.3	n.a.	1.6	n.a.
1901–1910	82.4	n.a.	0.6	n.a.
1911–1920	95.4	n.a.	0.4	n.a.
1921–1929	634.9	0.2	2.1	0.5
1930	1,352	0.9	5.3	1.5
1931	2,294	1.7	9.5	2.8
1932	1,456	0.7	6.5	1.2
1933	4,004	3.6	20.7	7.9
1934	61	0.04	0.4	0.1
1935	32	0.02	0.2	0.04
1936–1940	71.4	0.1	0.4	0.2
1941–1950	7.3	0.01	0.05	0.01
1951–1960	4.3	0.01	0.03	0.01
1961–1970	6.3	0.03	0.04	0.01
1971–1980	8.3	0.5	0.06	0.1
1981	10	3.8	0.07	0.3
1982	42	9.9	0.3	0.4
1983	48	5.4	0.3	0.4
1984	79	2.9	0.5	0.2

Sources: U.S. Department of Commerce (1975), pp. 1019, 1020, 1038; U.S. Department of Commerce (1984), pp. 510, 513; U.S. Federal Deposit Insurance Corporation (1984a), p. 53; U.S. Federal Deposit Insurance Corporation (1984b), pp. 6, 21; and New York Times (December 27, 1984), D–1.

[a]Includes mutual savings banks.

The Banking Act of 1933 addressed all three concerns. First, the Act specifically forbade all banks from paying interest on demand deposits (checking accounts), and it gave the Federal Reserve the power to set the rates for all other deposits. The Federal Reserve subsequently codified these restrictions in a set of rules that have come to be known as "Regulation Q." Two years later, further dampening competition, the Banking Act of 1935 specifically instructed the Federal Reserve, the Comptroller, and the newly established Federal Deposit Insurance Corporation (FDIC) to tighten the controls on entry into banking. Before the Reserve could admit a new state bank for membership, before the Comptroller could charter a new national bank, and before the FDIC could insure a new state bank, each was required to consider the financial history and condition, the adequacy of the capital structure, its future earning prospects, the general character of its management, and the *convenience and needs of the community to be served by the bank*. This last requirement, especially, gave the agencies great power over entry (even of state banks, since most state banks wanted FDIC insurance), as they were easily convinced that the existing banks in an area were adequately serving the area's needs.

Second, in four clauses of the Banking Act of 1933 that subsequently came to be known as the Glass-Steagall Act, Congress divorced commercial banking from investment banking by forbidding commercial banks from underwriting most securities or dealing in them for their own accounts.[9]

Third, the Banking Act of 1933 created the FDIC and established a system of deposit insurance. All members of the Federal Reserve were required to join. Nonmember state banks were encouraged to join, and most did so. Initially, the first $2,500 of an individual's (or organization's) deposits were covered; the amount was raised in subsequent years until, in the mid–1980s, it was $100,000. The insurance has been financed by annual levies of $1/12$ percent on the domestic deposits of all banks covered by insurance.[10] As part of its insurance function, the FDIC was given extensive supervisory powers vis-à-vis insured banks. The FDIC also acquired extensive insurance and regulatory powers vis-à-vis mutual savings banks (MSBs): state chartered savings institutions that originally had been designed to encourage thrift by "the working classes."

The success of these measures — especially FDIC insurance — in ending bank runs and bank failures can be seen in Table 5. Since 1933, bank failures have been a small fraction of their previous levels. With their deposits insured, depositors need not worry about the safety and liquidity of those deposits, so the motives for runs on banks have largely disappeared. In the early 1980s, though, with the failure of a few medium-size banks and the near-collapse of one large bank yielding actual or prospective losses for large, uninsured depositors, concern about bank failures and about possible runs by large depositors resurfaced. We shall return to this problem later.

In the 1930s federal regulation was extended to savings and loan associations (S&Ls). First established in the nineteenth century, these state chartered institutions originally had been designed to use members' deposits to make housing mortgage loans to other members. Over time the "cooperative" nature of the associations diminished, but their specialized functions of using depositors' funds for mortgage loans persisted.

The severe financial and economic decline of the early 1930s caused many S&Ls to fail along with commercial banks. Again, Congress saw a need for federal action. The Federal Home Loan Bank Act of 1932 established the Federal Home Loan Bank Board, with a structure and regulatory powers vis-à-vis S&Ls that paralleled that of the Federal Reserve System. The next year the Home Owners' Loan Act provided for federal charters for S&Ls, and in 1934 the National Housing Act created the Federal Savings and Loan Insurance Corporation to provide deposit insurance for S&Ls, comparable to FDIC insurance for commercial banks. And, as was the case for banks, the chartering of the S&Ls was expected to be restrictive, to prevent "excessive" competition.

Also in 1934 the Federal Credit Union Act permitted credit unions — state chartered institutions developed at the beginning of the twentieth century to encourage thift and make consumer loans to members, with membership based on a common bond of affiliation, organization, or location — to acquire federal charters. Regulation of credit unions passed among a number of agencies, including the FDIC from 1942 to 1947. Only in 1970 did Congress establish the National Credit Union Administration (giving it regulatory powers over interest rates paid on deposits) and create a deposit insurance system for credit unions.

By the mid-1930s, then, federal involvement in and regulation of the banking system, covering all depository institutions, had increased substantially. This regulatory structure has persisted, relatively unchanged, into the 1980s.

One "loophole," left relatively untouched by the 1930s legislation, was the operations of bank holding companies. Although the charters of commercial banks specifically limited their activities and brought them within the ambit of the regulatory system, the owners of banks could form holding companies and transfer the ownership of the bank to the holding company. The holding company could have other, nonfinancial subsidiaries, the activities of which were largely unregulated.[11] These subsidiaries could also include other banks in the same state or even in other states. Thus the bank holding company provided a vehicle for partially evading state branching restrictions and for allowing interstate banking.

The Bank Holding Company Act of 1956 substantially closed this loophole. The Act applied to all holding companies controlling two or more banks. One portion of the Act (frequently referred to as the Douglas Amendment) prevented holding companies from controlling banks in more than one state, unless the laws of the relevant states explicitly permitted interstate banking (though interstate networks existing at the time were "grandfathered" and were not required to dissolve). The Act also limited the activities of bank holding companies to those that were closely related to banking and a proper incident thereto, with the Federal Reserve acquiring the necessary regulatory powers. Thus, among the activities permitted to bank holding companies, were consumer finance companies, financial advising, mortgage finance, credit card operation, courier services, and data processing related to financial or economic data.[12]

Holding companies controlling one bank only were not covered by the 1956 act. As their number grew in the 1960s, concern about their nonbanking activities also grew, and one-bank holding companies were finally brought into the regulatory fold by the Bank Holding Company Act Amendments of 1970.

As wage and price inflation gathered steam in the 1960s, the general level of interest rates in the American economy began to rise as well. The two phenomena were related, since lenders would be expected to try to take into account expected inflation when calculating the interest rate that they require to yield an adequate "real" (inflation-adjusted) return.

The secular increase in interest rates posed a severe problem for S&Ls and MSBs (frequently described collectively as "the thrifts"). Their assets were largely mortage loans that had been made in previous years. The mortgages were long-lived (as long as thirty years) and carried the relatively low interest rates that were representative of those earlier years (and the interest rates on those mortgages were fixed for the term of the mortgage). But the thrifts' liabilities were largely deposits that could be withdrawn on short notice. Many thrifts found themselves competing with each other (and with other depository institutions and even with other borrowers) to retain their deposits. The primary form of competition, naturally enough, was higher interest rates paid on those deposits. But the higher interest rates paid could not be covered by the interest earned on those long-lived mortgages, threatening losses for some thrifts.

Congress' "solution" to this problem was to pass the Interest Rate

Control Act of 1966, which extended regulatory controls on interest rates to thrifts' deposits for the first time and gave this regulatory power to the Federal Home Loan Bank Board (for S&Ls) and the FDIC (for MSBs). For the next fifteen years those agencies and the Federal Reserve adjusted and coordinated the rates that depository institutions were permitted to pay. We shall return later to the questions of the success and wisdom of these actions.

One other federal regulatory initiative is worthy of note. The United States branches of foreign banks had largely escaped the regulatory structures that governed domestically chartered banks. (They were not, for example, restricted from interstate branching.) The inequity of applying different rules to foreign and domestic banks finally became too obvious, and the International Banking Act of 1978 brought the regulation of foreign banks' United States operations into close conformance with the regulation of domestic banks.

Although much regulatory attention has been focused on the deposit side of depository institutions' activities, the lending side also has received substantial regulatory attention. Some of this regulation would qualify as "social" regulation, such as federal requirements that lenders provide adequate information to borrowers or not practice discrimination in their lending practices. Depository institutions are limited in the loans that they can make to their owners, officers, and directors and in the fraction of their portfolio that can be lent to any single borrower. Depository institutions must also meet minimum paid-in capital requirements. These limitations presumably increase the safety and soundness of the institution, providing depositors with a safer "product" in the same way that the actions of the Food and Drug Administration or the Consumer Product Safety Commission yield safer products for consumers.

Until 1980, thrifts were limited only to home mortgage loans. This severe restriction was eased in the early 1980s. Since it was part of Congress' effort to encourage home ownership, this limitation could be considered social regulation. However, there were economic regulation aspects in that the limitation prevented thrifts from competing with other lenders for nonmortgage loans.

Two other economic regulatory restrictions on loans are noteworthy. First, until the late 1970s, depository institutions were not allowed to make mortgage loans that carried variable or adjustable interest rates. Apparently, Congress feared that the mortgage lender, once the mortgage was granted and the borrower "locked in," would unscrupulously adjust the rates upward.

Second, throughout the history of banking in the United States, regulatory authorities (mostly state, but occasionally federal) at various times and places have imposed usury ceilings on the interest rates that lenders could charge on loans. There seems to be no good way of cataloging the incidence and prevalence of these ceilings, but they have clearly had binding effects at times for some types of loan customers. The justification for this type of ceiling is usually that borrowers need to be protected from the exercise of market power by lenders and/or that ill-informed borrowers will be "fleeced" by opportunistic lenders.

REGULATION AS OF THE 1970s AND ITS CONSEQUENCES

A summary of the major facets of the economic regulation that affected depository institutions in the mid- to late 1970s provides a useful picture of the regulatory regime that was eventually modified in the 1980s. The rationale for this regulation and a critique will then follow, highlighting the consequences of the regulation for this industry and for the economy.

The Picture

Prices (Interest Rates). Regulation Q, and its extension to other depository institutions, meant that commercial banks could not pay interest on checking accounts and that all depository institutions were limited in the rates that they could pay on most other deposits. As the general level of interest rates fluctuated over time, the regulators tried to adjust the ceiling rates to protect the thrifts while trying to avoid keeping rates so low that depositors abandoned the depository system entirely. (To help prevent abandonment, the Federal Reserve in 1970 increased the minimum denomination of Treasury bills from $1,000 to $10,000, making them a less easily available alternative; and in 1974 Congress prevented bank holding companies from issuing floating or adjustable interest rate obligations in small denominations.)

An elaborate schedule of ceilings developed, with differentials for size of deposit, length of deposit, and type of institution. Thrifts for example, could pay a ½ percent higher rate — later diminished to ¼ percent — on passbook deposits than could commercial banks; this was designed to offset the thrifts' alleged disadvantage in attracting depositors, since they could not offer checking accounts or other commercial bank services.

On the loan side of the balance sheet, depository institutions in some states faced usury ceilings on the rates they could charge borrowers. And they could not offer variable or adjustable rate mortgages.

Entry. Entry by new firms into the depository field was controlled by the various federal and state regulators. Entry was not totally blocked — new firms did enter, and the severity of entry controls varied over the years and across states — but the flow of new firms into the field was clearly below that which an unregulated market would have yielded.[13]

Further, the combined effects of state chartering, the McFadden Act, and the Douglas Amendment meant that existing banks could not branch across state lines. (The same limitations applied to thrifts.[14]) And state laws determined whether (and to what extent) existing banks could branch within states. (Again, this also applied to thrifts.)

These geographic limitations, however, applied only to the establishment of branch locations that both accepted deposits and made commercial loans. Banks were free, in principle, to lend to anyone at any location and could even establish "loan production offices" at out-of-state locations. They were free to receive deposits from anyone residing at any location.[15] They could establish branches in foreign countries to provide banking (and even nonbanking) services in those countries. Banks could establish "Edge Act" offices across state lines to provide banking services related to international trade and foreign investment. And the authorized activities of bank holding companies could (except for banking itself) extend across state lines.

In essence, the geographic limitations imposed by regulation created impediments, but not absolute barriers, for banks that wished to serve customers in other geographic locations. The severity of the impediment varied with the service and the customer. Banks, regardless of location, could and did compete nationwide to provide loans to major corporations or to receive large-denomination deposits. But the geographic restrictions clearly restricted the ability of out-of-area banks to compete locally for checking or savings account customers or for loans to small businesses, since physical proximity and familiarity with customers are usually crucial for these services.

Limitations on entry meant that thrifts could not encroach on much of the commercial banks' product territory. Thrifts could not offer checking accounts; they could not make commercial loans; and they were largely limited to residential mortgage loans.

Finally, the Glass-Steagall Act and the Bank Holding Company Acts limited the ability of banks to enter other fields. The Glass-

Steagall Act kept them out of most of investment banking; the Bank Holding Company Acts kept them out of nonfinancial areas generally.

The Rationale

Part of the rationale for much of the economic regulation surrounding depository institutions stemmed from (and continues to stem from) the financial debacle of the early 1930s. The massive bank failures of those years were a searing experience. "Never again" has been the watchword of Congress and the regulators. Limitations on entry meant reduced competitive pressures that might otherwise lead to the failure of some banks and thrifts. Interest rate ceilings on deposits more directly dampened competition. The Glass-Steagall Act kept commercial banks out of allegedly more risky investment banking. The Bank Holding Company Acts kept them from entering into nonfinancial areas where their lack of expertise might cause them trouble.

There were other rationales for the regulatory restrictions as well. The geographic restrictions on interstate and intrastate branching has reflected the states' wishes to protect local depository institutions. This protection has usually been justified by an amalgam of claims that local institutions will somehow serve the local community's needs better than will out-of-area institutions, general fear of the economic and social power of large financial institutions, and a specific fear of predatory behavior. In this scenario one or a few large, out-of-area depository institutions will "invade" the local area, decrease prices so as to drive out the local institutions, and then raise prices to monopoly levels.

A similar amalgam has frequently been offered as a justification for keeping commercial banks out of investment banking and out of nonfinancial areas generally.[16] Further, it has been feared that banks would make loans only if the borrower purchased other products or services from the bank, thus giving banks an unfair competitive advantage in these other products or services. Also, because banks have a supply of zero interest checking deposits available to them, it is frequently claimed that they have an unfair cost advantage vis-à-vis other firms that have to pay market interest rates for this capital; hence banks again have an unfair competitive advantage. Finally, another rationale for keeping banks out of investment banking has been that corporate securities underwriting would pose conflicts of interest that would harm bank depositors and/or their underwriting customers. A bank might sell securities of a weak company to the public to bolster loans it had made to the company; or the bank might lend funds to prop up a weak company whose securities it had previously underwritten, to maintain its underwriting reputation.

Congress' desire to encourage a supply of "affordable" housing for the nation has provided a special rationale for the economic regulation of depository institutions.[17] Thrifts were seen as special institutions designed to ensure a supply of capital for housing; hence the restrictions that kept their portfolios devoted to residential mortgages were essential. Further, the efforts to buffer the thrifts from the effects of the secular rise in interest rates during the late 1960s and the 1970s were a logical part of this scheme. And, it was sometimes argued that keeping down the interest rates that thrifts paid would also mean lower rates on the mortgages the thrifts issued.

Finally, as was noted above, usury ceilings have often been justified by claims that lenders have market power and/or that opportunistic lenders would take advantage of ill-informed borrowers.

A Critique

Though the rationales for economic regulation of depository institutions have some surface plausibility, they are fundamentally flawed by weak economic logic and the absence of supporting empirical evidence. And, as we shall see, the events of the marketplace eventually made interest rate ceilings especially untenable and forced their abandonment.

Bank Failure. From the preceding discussion it is clear that much of the economic regulation surrounding depository institutions has been (at least partially) designed to prevent "excessive" competition and avoid the wave of bank failures that marked the early 1930s. Unfortunately, most (if not all) of this effort is misdirected. First, aside from the occasional anecdote, there is no reliable evidence to link the bank failures of the 1930s to "excessive" competition. Those failures were almost entirely caused by the banks' exposure to a sharp and unprecedented decline in economic activity, compounded by counterproductive policies of the Federal Reserve and by a series of runs on banks.[18] Neither theory nor evidence suggests that financial institutions competed too aggressively at the time nor that they thereby exposed themselves to excessive risks.[19]

Second, and more important, since the 1930s deposit insurance has provided the major bulwark against bank runs and hence against failures that might be precipitated by runs. With deposit insurance, the major public policy concern surrounding bank failures that might motivate restrictions on competition — the concerns that a run at one bank will lead to a series of runs on banks and/or that individuals (and small businesses) will lose a significant amount of their assets (such as "nest eggs" and life savings) — no longer hold. (Deposit insurance, though, has a set of problems of its own, to which we shall return in the last section.)

Third, by narrowing the scope for banks to diversify the geographic and product scope of their operations, branching restrictions and product diversity restriction may well have increased the risks of bank failures. The experience of the 1920s and early 1930s indicated that unit banks, restricted to one geographic area, were more likely to fail than were branch banks; the same was true for bank failures in the 1960s and 1970s.[20]

Fourth, in many geographic areas — especially urban areas — the restrictions on interest rate competition did not stifle all competition among existing depository institutions. When market interest rates rose in the late 1960s and the 1970s and interest ceilings prevented banks and thrifts from paying those market rates to attract and retain deposits, many of these institutions turned to other, non-price forms of competition. They offered special up-front "prizes" such as toasters, radios, and tennis rackets to new depositors. When state laws permitted, they opened extra branches, stayed open longer hours, or provided other customer services (for which they did not charge) in competitive efforts to provide more convenience to actual and potential customers. It is no accident that the federal regulators, after the extension of interest rate ceilings to the thrifts in 1966, had to set limits on the values of the prizes that banks and thrifts could use to reward new depositors.

But this non-price competition was less effective and less efficient than direct competition would have been. Depositors wanted higher interest rates; instead they got toasters and tennis rackets. Many depositors turned to substitutes such as stocks, bonds, real estate, coins, and "collectibles" that would yield a market return. Companies went to great lengths to economize on their cash balances held in nonyielding checking accounts. Money market mutual funds (MMMFs) came into being in the early 1970s and grew rapidly in the late 1970s and early 1980s. These were financial intermediaries that allowed small- and medium-size investors to pool their funds and obtain shares of a liquid portfolio of short-term and large-denomination obligations of banks, large corporations, and the federal government. The yields from these funds were higher than most investors could get from a bank, the shares were easily cashed in (most MMMFs provided check-like services), and the investor got substantial diversification from the fund's portfolio (though the shares did not carry deposit insurance). By the early 1980s the aggregate assets of MMMFs had climbed to over $200 billion.

These alternatives were inefficient in the sense that depositors would not have turned to them — or certainly not in the same volume — if banks and thrifts had been able to offer market rates of interest. A comparison with the Canadian banking system is instructive: Canadian banks were not forbidden from paying market interest rates to depositors, and MMMFs never became an important part of Canada's financial structure.[21] (Also, after United States banks and thrifts were allowed to pay market rates of interest on "money market accounts" in 1982, the aggregate assets of MMMFs grew at a much slower rate and even declined for a year or so.)

Fifth, to the extent that entry and branching limitations meant that competition among banks and thrifts in financial services markets was impeded, the protected institutions frequently charged higher-than-competitive rates for local loans and paid lower rates on deposits. The appropriate geographic markets for banking services vary with the service. For loans to large companies, the appropriate market is nationwide, or perhaps even worldwide. And it is clear that there are more than enough large institutions to provide vigorous competition. As can be seen in Table 2, in 1983 there were 295 banks (commercial banks and MSBs) in the United States with assets of $1 billion or more. But for loans to small- and medium-size companies and for checking account services, the appropriate market may be an urbanized area or a rural county. And these markets are, on average, quite concentrated. As seen in Table 6, the combined market shares of the leading three banks in the localized markets in 1979 were, on average, in the range of 50 to 75 percent.

Numerous studies have been conducted that have examined statistically the relationship between banking market concentration and loan rates or deposit rates. Most have found that in markets with higher concentration (and restricted entry), banks charge higher rates on loans or pay lower rates on deposits.[22] And entry restrictions generally have meant that it has been more difficult for newcomers with fresh ideas, innovations, new ways of doing things — in sum, more efficient ways of serving customers — to replace the old.

Protecting Local Institutions. A second motive for the restrictions on entry and on branching has been to protect local depository institutions, either because they are thought to serve local needs better or because they might be subject to predatory behavior.

As for the first argument, the evidence cited above with respect to the effects of concentration on loan and deposit rates indicates just

Table 6. Concentration Ratios for Insured Commercial Banks, SMSA[a] Markets, 1979[b]

	Largest Bank (%)	Three Largest Banks (%)	Five Largest Banks (%)
Unit banking states	22.5	49.4	60.2
Limited branching states	29.9	62.5	76.3
Statewide branching states	34.0	67.5	80.3

Source: U.S. Department of the Treasury (1981), p. 48.
[a]Standard metropolitan statistical area.
[b]Weighted averages.

the opposite effect. Depository institutions in protected environments have tended to provide worse service for their customers. Further, studies have also shown that banks in high concentration markets tend to devote a lower proportion of their funds to loans (and devote more to, say, government bonds) — again, an indication that they are probably serving their loan customers less well.[23]

Further, if local institutions really do know and serve their local markets well, they should have little fear of new competition from out-of-area banks.

The predatory behavior argument has its problems as well. For predation to be worthwhile, the predator (in this case the large out-of-area bank) must be able to raise prices (for example, interest rates on loans) to above-competitive levels after it has vanquished the local banks. But those above-competitive rates could be maintained only if future entrants could not come into the market and offer new competition — in essence, only if there are significant barriers to entry. If, for example, large banks had a substantial efficiency edge (that is, had lower costs) over smaller banks, then future entry might be difficult. If smaller banks are not at an appreciable efficiency disadvantage, a predator could not gain much by predation, since entrants would generally be prepared to compete for any excess profits that the predator might try to reap.

A large number of studies of economies of scale (efficiencies of size) of banks have been conducted.[24] The preponderance of the evidence indicates that the advantages of greater size were virtually exhausted at a bank size in the area of $25 million in assets in the mid-1970s. (A bank of equivalent size in the mid-1980s might be around $50 million in assets.) The capital required to start a bank of this size (8 to 10 percent of total assets) could easily be raised by large numbers of companies or groups of wealthy individuals. Also, as Table 2 indicates, as of 1983 there were literally thousands of banks with $50 million in assets or more who might serve as potential entrants (and with loosened branching restrictions many of the smaller banks could bring themselves up to sufficient size). Thus a predator could not reasonably expect any appreciable profit gains for any significant period of time.

One caveat should be entered. The data on which most of these efficiency of size studies are based excluded the largest banks in the United States (those with assets of $1 billion or above). Consequently, little is known about their relative efficiency.[25] But in the states that have eased within-state branching restrictions, the larger banks did not expand rapidly into new areas (contrary to what would have been expected under a greater efficiency of size hypothesis or a predatory scenario). For example, despite liberalization of New York's holding company and branching laws, the large New York City banks were not successful in invading the upstate banking markets. Between 1955 and 1979 the shares of the largest banks' deposits statewide remained virtually unchanged.[26] The same lesson is demonstrated when bank holding companies have bought existing banks: the acquired banks' market shares tend not to change significantly after the acquisition.[27]

In sum, there appears to be little theoretical or empirical support for the fears of predatory behavior.[28] Also, Section 2 of the Sherman Act, which prohibits monopolizing behavior, is available to prevent any truly predatory behavior.

Fear of the political and social power of big institutions — including big banks — has been a powerful force in American political tradition. It is probable that easing restrictions on branching would have led some large banks to expand their operations and become yet larger — although, as the evidence indicates, this expansion might not have been nearly as great as many of the small bank defenders feared. But restrictions on branching also prevented small- and medium-size banks from expanding. As noted, branching restrictions, by preventing geographic diversification, increased the risks of failure by small and large banks. Restrictions on entry prevented new (often comparatively small) firms from offering new competition to existing entities, large and small. And there was a clear efficiency cost to the restrictions.

One irony of the effects of interest rate ceilings on deposits should be noted: to the extent that depositors moved their deposits to money market mutual funds, money generally did not leave the depository system (since the MMMFs tended to invest in commercial bank obligations). But the MMMFs tended to be located in financial centers and generally favored the obligations of larger banks (which tend to be more liquid and, for uninsured denominations over $100,000, less risky). Thus one of the indirect effects of interest rate controls was the growth of large depository institutions over small ones.

This author strongly suspects that much of the protection that has been accorded existing depository institutions has been simply the result of lobbying by these institutions, the owners and managers of which have enjoyed the higher profits and quieter life of the protected environment and have succeeded in cloaking their self-saving arguments for protection with a seemingly more public-spirited rationale.

Preventing Entry of Banks into Other Fields. The Glass-Steagall and Bank Holding Company Act restrictions on banks' entry into other fields are flawed by the same weak rationale as restricting branching. The predatory behavior scenario has little logic or evidence to support it; there have been no charges of predatory behavior made against banks in the limited fields that they have been allowed to enter. The restrictions, by preventing diversification into other fields, have increased the risks of bank failure. And to the extent that banks have had efficiency advantages in entering other (probably related) fields, such as offering consumers "one-stop shopping" for financial services (if consumers wanted it), these limitations have been inefficient.

Further, fear of the ill-effects of banks' tying loans to other services does not seem well grounded. To effect a tie of any significance, a bank must have market power in the tying good (loans). But the market structures of many loan markets have been competitive enough (or would be, in the absence of restrictive regulation) so that many banks would not be able to effect a tie. Further, even if a bank were to have market power, it could usually extract the consequent monopoly profits through the interest charged on the loan itself. There would be no increased "leverage" that it could use to extract extra profits through the tie.[29] Further, the antitrust laws (Clayton Act, Section 3) are always available to support government or private suits to prevent abuses of tying.

Also, banks have not enjoyed a special competitive advantage in other fields because of their access to low-cost deposits. The relevant consideration for competitive advantage was the *marginal cost* (or opportunity cost) of funds. And that marginal cost applied to funds attracted or lent at the margin — usually involving relatively high-cost funds obtained through financial markets (or the marginal costs of attracting deposits through non-price competition). Thus the *opportunity cost* of a bank's undertaking an activity would be the making of a loan to a potential customer who was otherwise turned away, lending the funds to other financial institutions in the financial markets, or obtaining fewer funds from the financial markets. In this important sense the marginal costs of banks were roughly equal to those of other comparably sized institutions,[30] and banks did not possess a special or unfair advantage in undertaking other activities or competing with other firms.[31]

With respect to the Glass-Steagall Act's special restrictions on commercial banks' entry into investment banking, there is no reliable evidence linking the problems of bank failures in the early 1930s with their securities activities.[32] Further, the potential problems of conflicts of interest are no more severe than the problems already faced by commercial banks (between, say, their loan and their trust departments) and by securities firms (between, say, their underwriting and their brokerage or mutual fund operations). A proper concern for the long-run reputation of the institution usually leads to internal operating arrangements (such as "Chinese walls" — instructions that the two sensitive departments not exchange information with each other) that deal adequately with the problem.

Also, the riskiness of one important part of investment banking — corporate securities underwriting — seems quite modest and would not appear to increase commercial banks' risks of failure.[33]

Finally, comparisons of one of the underwriting markets where the Glass-Steagall Act allows commercial banks to compete — the general obligation bonds issued by municipal governments — with similar markets where they are forbidden to enter (most municipal revenue bonds) indicate that increased competition by banks has meant narrower underwriting spreads (margins) and lower borrowing costs for issuers.[34] The extra competition by banks can make a difference.[35]

In sum, the prohibition on banks' entry into other fields, especially other financial fields, has probably meant reduced competition and reduced efficiency, while offering few offsetting gains.

Usury Ceilings. Price ceilings to prevent firms with market power from exploiting that market power are, in principle, a reasonable regulatory tool. They are a standard part of most states' regulation of local electricity, natural gas, and telephone utilities.

But price ceilings ought to be applied only when there is significant market power and even then need to be applied flexibly, with a vast amount of information and regulatory effort required.

This has not been the approach of the states in imposing usury ceilings. The ceilings are usually specified by state law or by administrative fiat, with comparatively little detailed informational support. They apply broadly and inflexibly, usually persisting unchanged for long periods of time, despite changes in financial conditions and market interest rates. Thus they are frequently binding on competitive markets as well as noncompetitive markets and do not allow adjustments for the riskiness of borrowers.

The consequences of usury ceilings appear to be exactly those that elementary economics would predict. Though the ceilings may have prevented some exploitation of market power (but the easing of restrictions on branching and entry would be a far superior means of addressing any market power problem), all too often they have interfered with the efficiency of competitive lending markets. When the ceilings have been below market rates, depository lenders have found other (less efficient) ways of charging interest in disguised forms (such as charging "points" — up-front payments by the borrower of a percentage of the loan). They have also shortened loan terms to reduce their risks, or they have simply reduced their volume of loans and have invested their funds elsewhere.[36] Borrowers, faced by an inability to obtain loans from depository lenders, have turned to lenders who are not covered by usury ceilings (for example, in some instances, consumer finance companies are not covered) or to less formal borrowing arrangements (such as "loan sharks"), or they have not borrowed at all.

In sum, there is little good that can be said about usury ceilings.

Housing and the Thrifts. Encouraging the production of housing and keeping its cost low has been an important goal of Congress. A vast array of sacrosanct tax advantages for building and owning housing has developed in furtherance of this goal. Protecting the thrifts, keeping them focused on housing loans, and trying to keep down the costs of their deposits were part of the package.

It appears, however, that these efforts with respect to the thrifts may have had little net effect. As argued above, the crucial variable for pricing is marginal cost. And thrifts, like commercial banks, faced true marginal costs that were appreciably above the apparent costs of their deposits. Hence low-cost deposits did not mean low-cost mortgage loans. Indeed, the time pattern of the interest rates on newly issued mortgage loans tracks the pattern of market interest rates quite closely.[37] Consistent with this outcome is the fact that other mortgage lenders, such as commercial banks, mortgage bankers (who initiate mortgages and then package them and sell them to other investors), and insurance companies — who did not have access to the thrifts' low-cost funds — nevertheless accounted for a third of new mortgage loans in the late 1960s and the 1970s.[38] In short, mortgage loans appear to have been made largely at market rates, and the special protection for the thrifts appears to have had little or no direct effect on mortgage costs or availability.[39]

Moreover, to the extent that deposits stayed within the thrifts (and commercial banks), depositors were being deprived of market rates of interest. The sums, in aggregate, were large,[40] and the income distribution consequences were not consistent with a policy of favoring lower income individuals relative to those with higher incomes: small depositors (who were least likely to have good alternatives) tended to have comparatively lower incomes; bank and thrift stockholders[41] (and the recipients of new mortgages, if one believes that the ceilings somehow had a favorable effect on mortgage rates) tended to have comparatively higher incomes.[42]

Perhaps most important, the interest rate ceilings on deposits could not solve the fundamental problems of the thrifts, so long as depositors had alternatives. The inherent financial structure of the thrifts was to have long-term, fixed interest rate assets (mortgages) and short-term, easily withdrawn liabilities (deposits). In a stable interest rate environment this structure was viable. But in the environment of the late 1960s and the 1970s marked by large cyclical fluctuations in interest rates and a secularly rising level of interest rates, this structure was not viable, *and interest rate ceilings on deposits could not make it viable.*

In essence, so long as their asset portfolio was filled with fixed rate mortgages made in earlier years, the thrifts faced a Hobson's choice: without deposit rate ceilings, they would have to pay interest rates on deposits that at times exceeded the yields on their mortgage portfolio and consequently would run losses; with ceilings, depositors who had alternatives took their money elsewhere ("disintermediation"), and the thrifts faced a liquidity squeeze. The rise of money market mutual funds in the mid-1970s gave an increasing number of depositors a constantly improving set of alternatives.

It is interesting to note that commercial banks faced a much less painful predicament than did the thrifts. The banks had somewhat greater flexibility in their ability to pay market rates on large denomination deposits. More important, they could adjust the terms and maturity structure of their loan portfolio so as to avoid the "lock in" problem of the thrifts and match the maturity structure of their assets and their liabilities.[43] One indication of the different position of the banks and the thrifts is the time patterns of their profit rates (return on net worth) shown in Figure 1. The banks' profits have been relatively stable; the thrifts' profits have varied more widely (even before the debacle of the early 1980s).

Beyond the effect on the thrifts themselves, the deposit rate ceilings had a negative effect on the housing market. Not only (as argued above) did they not achieve lower mortgage interest rates, but they

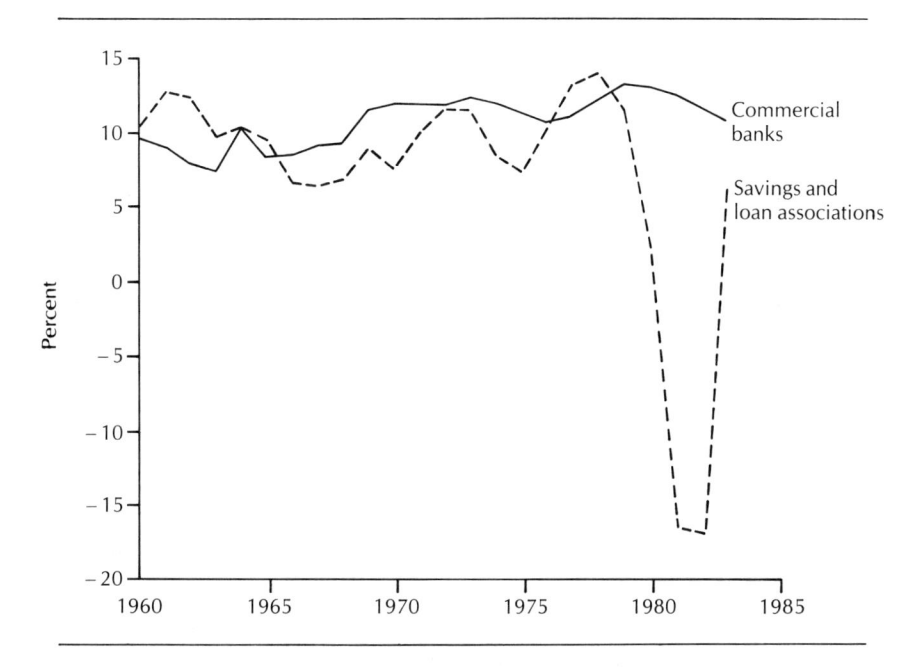

Figure 1. Profitability of Commercial Banks and of Savings and Loan Associations (Net Income as a Percent of Net Worth)

also heightened the cyclical nature and riskiness of the housing industry.[44] A cyclical pattern of market interest rates would have meant a cyclical pattern of housing starts in any event. But, with deposit rate ceilings, when market interest rates rose, the thrifts faced a liquidity squeeze and had less funds to lend. (The binding effects of any usury ceilings that might be present would, of course, compound this effect.) Fewer mortgages were granted, and fewer new homes were bought and sold.[45] This heightened cyclicality and risk meant higher costs for builders and thus higher prices for new homes — surely not what Congress had intended.

In sum, interest rate controls on deposits could not cure the thrifts' problems and could only make the housing industry's problems worse.[46] The experience of the 1970s drove this point home. Congress finally absorbed the lesson in 1980.

DEREGULATION AND ITS CONSEQUENCES

The Actions

From 1966 onward, federal banking regulators faced a difficult, and often impossible, task in setting deposit interest rate ceilings. They had to establish a term structure of maximum rates (extending over deposits with different time maturities) that would keep deposits within the depository system but would not lead to large losses for the thrifts. Depending on the general level of market interest rates, they achieved these goals with greater or lesser success.

As early as 1970, however, they realized that commercial banks in particular needed a "safety valve" to allow them to attract funds and avoid "disintermediation." In that year interest rates on large-denomination deposits ($100,000 and over) were deregulated. For the next decade other experiments in partial deregulation for deposits of some sizes and time durations were tried.

The deregulation of large deposits opened an important loophole in the system of deposit rate controls. Securities firms created money market mutual funds to take advantage of it. As the decade progressed, and especially at times of high market interest rates, the number of funds and their assets grew.

In the early 1970s another loophole developed. Massachusetts authorized its mutual savings banks to offer "negotiated order of withdrawal" (NOW) accounts to individuals. These were accounts that paid interest but that also permitted individuals to write checks on them. (Also, around the same time, credit unions were authorized to offer similar accounts to their members.) The NOW accounts spread to MSBs in the rest of New England and then to New York and New Jersey. Commercial banks in these states complained that they were at a competitive disadvantage vis-à-vis the MSBs. Congress in 1976 authorized commercial banks in New England to offer NOW accounts and extended the privilege to New York banks in 1978 and to New Jersey banks in 1979.

Also, in the mid-1970s, increased use of computers allowed some banks to offer "sweep" or automatic transfer accounts, which would automatically transfer funds back and forth between checking accounts and savings accounts, thus implicitly allowing the banks to pay interest on idle checking account funds. The U.S. Circuit Court of Appeals (D.C. Circuit) in 1979 found this practice to be a violation of the prohibition on paying interest on checking accounts, but gave Congress until January 1, 1980, to pass legislation to authorize it.

Finally, beginning in 1971, a number of governmental commissions, studies, and reports[47] through the decade uniformly recommended that deposit rate ceilings be phased out, that thrifts be allowed to offer variable rate mortgages (to ease their "lock in" problem), and that other regulatory restrictions on competition be eased or abolished.

By the late 1970s, then, with the loopholes to deposit rate ceilings growing and the recommendations mounting, Congress began to realize that some other solution to the problems of the thrifts would have to be found.

The first important action came from the Federal Home Loan Bank Board (FHLBB), with implicit congressional approval. In 1979 and 1980 the FHLBB established regulations that permitted S&Ls to offer variable rate mortgages.[48] A decade earlier, and through the middle 1970s, FHLBB proposals along these lines had met intense congressional hostility and had been withdrawn. This time Congress demurred.

In early 1980 the Depository Institutions Deregulation and Monetary Control Act (DIDMCA) became law. DIDMCA represented the most important banking legislation since the Banking Act of 1933. The DIDMCA contained six major provisions that are relevant to our discussion of economic regulation[49]:

1. All depository institutions were authorized to offer NOW accounts, and commercial banks were also authorized to continue to offer automatic transfer accounts.

2. A Depository Institutions Deregulation Committee (DIDC) — composed of the heads of the Treasury Department, the Federal Reserve, the FDIC, the FHLBB, and the National Credit Union Administration (with the Comptroller of the Currency as a nonvoting member) — were authorized to oversee the orderly elimination of interest rate ceilings on all deposits (except demand deposits offered by commercial banks to businesses) by March 31, 1986. Also, any state imposed ceilings on deposit rates were overridden.

3. Federally chartered S&Ls were authorized to invest up to 20 percent of their assets in consumer loans, commercial paper, and corporate debt securities. They could issue credit cards and offer trust and fiduciary services.

4. Federally chartered MSBs could invest up to 5 percent of their assets in loans to business and could offer demand deposits in connection with those business loan relationships.

5. State usury laws were preempted for residential mortgages and for agricultural and business loans in excess of $25,000 and were partially preempted for other loans made by state chartered banks and by insured S&Ls and credit unions. (The states were given until April 1, 1983, to override the federal preemption and explicitly reinstate their usury laws.)

6. The Federal Reserve gained the power to set reserve requirements for all depository institutions that are federally insured or are eligible for federal insurance.

The first two provisions meant the end of most interest ceilings on deposits. The DIDC, after some hesitation, did improve interest yields on deposits, and it appears that the 1986 target will be met. Business checking accounts remain the glaring exception, though automatic transfer services and other arrangements will allow banks some freedom to circumvent this restriction.

The third and fourth provisions allowed the thrifts to diversify their portfolios somewhat, reducing their narrow dependency on housing. The fifth was simply an expression of the general belief in Congress that the states should not be allowed to "shoot themselves in the foot" by imposing usury ceilings when interest rates had reached all-time highs. (Ironically, however, the preemption was less complete for small loans, where the costs and risks to lenders were proportionally greater and hence where the usury ceilings were more of a problem.) And the sixth provision eased the Federal Reserve's concern that lower reserve requirements offered by states to state chartered institutions might cause more depository institutions to adopt state charters and cause the Federal Reserve to lose control over the money supply.

At the same time that the DIDMCA was promising some deregulation of depository institutions, the Carter administration in March 1980 moved in the opposite direction and (as part of a macroeconomic effort to combat inflation) imposed credit controls on commercial banks, trying to restrict the volume and types of loans they made. Fortunately, the program expired four months later.[50]

The DIDMCA did not provide an instant solution to all of the thrifts' problems (as, of course, it could not). In the high-interest rate environment of 1980 and 1981, large numbers of thrifts continued to be financially troubled, as Figure 1 indicates. In 1982 Congress tried again, this time with the Garn–St Germain Depository Institution Act of 1982. This Act was less revolutionary than the DIDMCA, but it nevertheless had some important provisions affecting economic regulation[51]:

1. The DIDC was instructed to authorize a depository account that would be directly competitive with money market mutual funds (which the DIDC subsequently did).

2. Thrifts were allowed to invest up to 55 percent of their assets in various types of commercial loans and up to 30 percent in consumer loans.

3. Federally chartered S&Ls were permitted to offer demand deposits in connection with business loan relationships.

4. State chartered banks and thrifts were allowed to offer variable rate mortgages.

5. Federal, state, and local governments could hold NOW accounts.

6. Federal charters for new mutual savings banks were authorized (federal charters for existing MSBs were authorized in 1978), and thrifts could more easily change their charters from state to federal (or vice versa) and from S&L to MSB (or vice versa).

7. The federal regulatory agencies were authorized, in instances of a failing bank or thrift, to allow mergers of banks with thrifts or to allow mergers that crossed state lines. This provision formally blessed what the regulatory agencies had already been doing in the previous two years. And it represented a modest breaching of the entry barriers between banks and thrifts and the barriers to interstate banking.

The Garn–St Germain Act, then, continued the process of deregulation that DIDMCA had started.

A few other actions of the early 1980s that eased regulatory restrictions are worth noting. First, the FHLBB began to allow statewide branching for federally chartered S&Ls in all states (regardless of the state rules that applied to state chartered S&Ls). Second, the Federal Reserve authorized commercial bank affiliates to offer discount brokerage services to their customers, concluding that the provision of these services did not violate the Glass-Steagall or Bank Holding Company Acts. Third, the FDIC concluded that state chartered banks that were not members of the Federal Reserve would not violate the Glass-Steagall Act or other federal banking laws if they offered financial services (including underwriting and insurance) through a separate subsidiary.

Fourth, the "nonbank bank" became a potentially important phenomenon. Sharp-eyed lawyers noticed that the definition of a commercial bank in the relevant federal legislation was an institution that offered demand deposits and made commercial loans. A few securities firms bought small banks, sold off their commercial loan portfolios, and operated them as institutions ("nonbank banks," or, as they are sometimes described, "limited service banks") that accepted deposits and made only consumer loans. More important, a number of nationally chartered banks began petitioning the Comptroller of the Currency and the Federal Reserve to permit them to establish "nonbank banks" in states other than their home state. These agencies granted permission for a few such "banks," then issued a moratorium (waiting for Congress to act during the 1984 legislative session), and then began granting permissions again when Congress failed to act.

Fifth, a number of states established regional reciprocal banking arrangements, allowing a bank from another state to purchase or establish a bank in its state if the other state granted similar privileges to the first state's banks. Most of these arrangements excluded New York, because of the local banks' fear of expansion by the large New York banks. (The legality of these regional arrangements was upheld by the Supreme Court in 1985). Thus, again, the barriers to interstate banking have been breached somewhat.

The Consequences

As of early 1985 most of the deregulatory actions are too recent for their full consequences to be observed and analyzed. Deposit rate deregulation, however, has had a clear set of consequences. As depository institutions have been able to pay market interest rates on their deposits, their offerings of noncash prizes for new deposits have largely ceased. The timing of the two phenomena is not coincidental. Further, banks and thrifts have begun to close branches in unprofitable locations, begun charging for services that they previously offered for free, and raised their fees for other services. These actions are in part responses to the higher costs of doing business (primarily higher labor costs) in the 1980s. Mostly, like the end of prizes, they are the consequence of allowing depository institutions to compete directly on price and not having to compete indirectly by not charging (or not charging enough) for other services. The net result for most depositors surely is positive.

It is true that the general level of interest rates in the mid-1980s, though below the rates of 1979–1982, have nevertheless been high by historical standards, especially when measured in real (inflation-adjusted) terms. Is the deposit rate deregulation initiated by DIDMCA responsible for these high rates, as many critics have claimed? The answer is surely no. Interest rates on loans are sensitive to the *marginal* costs of depository institutions, and these marginal costs were always above the deposit rate ceilings. The high level of interest rates in the mid-1980s appears to result mostly from the uncertainties of lenders about the future course of the United States economy, including uncertainties about future inflation rates (inspired by the prospects of large federal budget deficits) and about the abilities of a number of developing countries to pay back loans from banks in the United States and other developed countries.

Also, the entry of commercial banks into discount brokerage has not brought any charges of predatory behavior. Again, the scenario of predatory behavior appears to have had no empirical (or logical) basis.

At the same time the number and size of bank failures has increased substantially, as is indicated by Table 5, and in mid-1984 one of the largest banks in the country (Continental Illinois National Bank and Trust Co.), with over $40 billion in assets, was saved from failing only by a massive rescue operation by the FDIC. Were these failures and near-failures related to the deregulation that has occurred? Perhaps, but only slightly. Deregulation of any industry is likely to lead initially to a higher rate of failure by industry members, as the less efficient among the previously protected firms are outcompeted by the more efficient (and by entrants). This has been true in stock brokerage, trucking, and airlines and will surely be true for banking. But the recent history of banking failures reveals that in virtually all cases the banks failed because their loan portfolios turned sour (frequently, because of loans to energy-sector companies that could not be repaid because oil prices were lower than had been expected). "Excessive" competition does not appear to have played much of a role (if any). Indeed, part of Continental Illinois' problems resulted from restrictive regulation: Illinois unit banking law meant that Continental Illinois could not establish a branching network to attract "retail" deposits or make small business loans; instead, it had turned to "wholesale" deposits of large (uninsured) denominations by institutions who became extremely skittish and started a run on the bank when the first signs of Continental Illinois' loan portfolio problems appeared.

CONCLUSION

Despite the partial deregulation of depository institutions in the early 1980s, this sector is still saddled with a heavy burden of economic regulation:

1. No interest can be paid directly on demand deposits offered to businesses (price controls).

2. Some states have usury ceilings (price controls).

3. De novo entry is restricted by federal and state regulators (entry controls).

4. Interstate branching is illegal or at best very difficult (entry controls).

5. Many states have within-state branching limitations (see Table 4) (entry controls).

6. Depository institutions are restricted in their ability to enter nonbanking fields (entry controls).

7. Thrifts are limited in their ability to compete with commercial banks (entry controls).

The arguments against these forms of economic regulation remain as valid in the 1980s as they were in the 1970s. In essence, deposit insurance is the proper way to deal with the problems of bank failure; restraints on entry and competition are an extremely inefficient means of achieving this end. Usury laws are an inefficient way of dealing with the possible market power of lenders. And geographic and product line restrictions on depository institutions inhibit competition and protect existing (often, inefficient) firms, both within banking and outside it.

Removing these barriers could result in the expansion of some large banks, but their increases in size are not likely to be great. If the large New York City banks could not dominate the Buffalo or Rochester (or even Plattsburgh) banking markets when given the chance in the 1970s, nor dominate (or behave in a predatory fashion) in government bond underwriting or discount stock brokerage activities, they are unlikely to expand voraciously in other geographic or product markets.

In a deregulated environment some depository institutions may take imprudent actions, such as making bad loans at the wrong interest rates, offering the wrong interest rates on deposits, or unwisely entering a nonbanking field. But no regulatory scheme can prevent all imprudent actions, nor should it try. The proper disciplining mechanism is the competitive marketplace, with a properly structured system of deposit insurance providing protection to depositors.

Financial services may well be like retailing in general. There very likely is room in the market for large, multi-service organizations (comparable to large department stores and supermarkets) that may even be part of nationwide chains (comparable to Sears or Safeway) and also room for smaller organizations that specialize in certain lines of business (like clothing boutiques) or in serving the unique requirements of local communities (like specialty food stores or convenience stores).

Further, depository institutions are not the only lenders of funds in the United States economy. In the 1970s and early 1980s depository institutions met only (as a rough average) 50 percent of the economy's lending needs.[52] Other finance sources include providers of retail credit, trade credit, mortgage banking, consumer finance, and industrial finance services and include major firms such as Sears, General Motors, Ford, General Electric, Household Finance, Merrill Lynch, American Express, Metropolitan Life, and Prudential, as well as large pension funds and the tens of thousands of firms providing retail and trade credit to their customers. The bond market and the commercial paper market provide other opportunities for borrowers and nonbank lenders to come together. Also, most money market mutual funds and many brokerage firms offer check-like services for their account holders. Since these lenders and account providers do not operate under the same constraints as do depository institutions, the rationale for restraining the latter becomes weaker still.

Finally, the current system of deposit insurance deserves more attention. A major accomplishment of deposit insurance is that it has put an end to most runs on depository institutions. But there are two remaining problems. First, the premiums that depository institutions pay for the insurance are not sensitive to the risks of the asset portfolios of the institutions. Thus the institutions do not have adequate incentives to avoid incurring excessive risk. Second, deposits above $100,000 are not covered by insurance. Such uninsured depositors, if they fear for the safety of their deposits, may withdraw their funds precipitously, causing a run.

This second problem is, of course, a partial solution to the first. To the extent that uninsured depositors are prepared to flee, they serve as a long-run restraining influence on the depository institution's management (which will rationally try to avoid taking the risks that would lead to the large depositors' flight). But this equilibrating mechanism can never work perfectly, and unintended management mistakes (or extreme lack of luck) can lead to the losses and financial weakness that would lead to some large depositors' flight and to the subsequent run.

"Perfect" regulation and supervision by depository regulators (that is, instantaneous examinations whenever the hint of weakness arises and exactly the right adjustments in portfolio composition and capital requirements) would avoid all depository problems. But perfection in regulation (as elsewhere) is rarely possible.

A superior alternative would be to require full deposit coverage (at least for demand deposits and very short-term deposits), adjust the premiums so that they are sensitive to risk, and open the deposit insurance "market" explicitly to nongovernment insurers.[53] Bank regulators currently assess depository institutions' portfolio risks as part of their examination procedures. The result of the assessment would be a premium determination rather than a regulatory command. Indeed, this is exactly what private insurers would do.

Overall, then, a competitive and efficient, yet relatively stable, depository system is possible. The proper task of public policy is to continue the pace of the deregulation of the early 1980s to achieve this end.

NOTES

[1] Other discussions of the regulation of depository institutions can be found in Phillips (1975a), Kane (1981), Spellman (1982), Johnson and Roberts (1982), Chap. 10, Benston (1983a, 1983c, 1983d), Carron (1983), Golembe and Holland (1983), and Cooper and Fraser (1984).

[2] Other discussions of the history of regulation are found in U.S. Department of the Treasury (1981), Spellman (1982), Chap. 2, Johnson and Roberts (1982), Chap. 10, Benston (1983a), Golembe and Holland (1983), White (1983), Huertas (1983), Cooper and Fraser (1984), Chap. 2, and Luckett (1984), Chap. 16.

[3] As of 1983, there were 10,296 state chartered banks, with $856.7 billion in total assets, and 4,751 national banks, with $1,175.5 billion in total assets.

[4] Typical rules in these limited branching states restrict the establishment of branches to the city or county of a bank's main office or to a group of contiguous counties or to counties in which no other bank has a main office.

[5] The McFadden Act's 1927 limitations also applied to state bank members of the Federal Reserve.

[6] Independent banks in different states could, however, be owned by a common entity, a bank holding company, if the relevant state laws permitted.

[7] The McFadden Act of 1927 had reaffirmed the right of national banks to engage in securities activities.

[8] Some in Congress also believed that the banks' securities activities had been a cause of the stock market crash and the subsequent economic decline.

[9] A major exception was that commercial banks could continue to underwrite the general obligation securities of the federal, state, and local governments. Also, banks could continue their traditional trust activities, which frequently involve large holdings of stocks and bonds.

Notes

[10] The FDIC refunds approximately 60 percent of these levies to the banks, so their effective payments are considerably smaller.

[11] The Banking Act of 1933 provided for slight Federal Reserve power over bank holding companies. And the Glass-Steagall Act specifically applied to bank affiliates.

[12] Further details are found in Golembe and Holland (1983), Chap. 10, Whitehead (1983), and Eisenbeis (1983).

[13] See Peltzman (1965), Edwards and Edwards (1974), and Ladenson and Bombara (1984).

[14] Credit unions were limited by affiliation but could have nationwide (or, as in the case of the credit union of the U.S. Navy, worldwide) branches for that affiliation.

[15] And, as is discussed below, banks in the 1980s realized that "nonbank banks" that accepted deposits but did not make commercial loans were a possible loophole.

[16] For a discussion of some of these issues, see Goldberg and White (1979).

[17] Other evidence of this goal is the plethora of tax advantages that are offered for building and owning residential real estate.

[18] For a further discussion see Flannery (1985).

[19] For a further discussion of competition, regulation, and a risk of failure or of other encroachments on safety, see Golbe (1981, 1983).

[20] See McCall and Lane (1980), U.S. Department of the Treasury (1981), Chap. 5, and White (1983). To the extent that loans can be "packaged" and sold in national markets, however, geographic restrictions may pose less of a diversification problem for banks.

[21] See Landy (1980).

[22] Surveys are found in Heggestad (1979), Rhoades (1981), U.S. Department of the Treasury (1981), Chaps. 2 and 6, and Gilbert (1984).

[23] See McCall (1980b).

[24] See McCall (1980a), U.S. Department of the Treasury (1981), Chaps. 4 and 6, Benston et al. (1982), Benston et al. (1983), Gilligan and Smirlock (1984), Clark (1984), and the other studies cited in those sources.

[25] For an argument that these very large banks may enjoy economies of scale relative to smaller ones, see Peltzman (1984).

[26] See Shull (1972, 1978), Kunreuther (1976), and U.S. Department of the Treasury (1981), Chaps. 2 and 6.

[27] See Goldberg (1979), Savage and Solomon (1980), U.S. Department of the Treasury (1981), Chap. 6, Savage (1982), and Rose and Savage (1982).

[28] Nor is it valid in other, often regulated, industries in which this scenario is frequently raised. See Phillips (1975b), Fromm (1981), Weiss and Klass (1981), Noll and Owen (1983), and the other chapters in this book.

[29] In some instances tying can be used to "meter" demand and effect, a form of disguised price discrimination. But metering does not seem to be a likely motive for the tying of other services to bank loans.

[30] Except for the advantage that banks have in not being required to pay risk-sensitive insurance premiums on deposits.

[31] In essence, banks and other depository institutions enjoyed a windfall that should not have affected their behavior at margin.

[32] See Flannery (1985).

[33] See Giddy (1985).

[34] See Silber (1979).

[35] For a direct application to corporate securities underwriting, see Pugel and White (1985). For a discussion of the Glass-Steagall issues generally, see Goldberg and White (1979), Section IV, Sametz (1981), and Walter (1985).

[36] For a recent summary of the arguments and evidence, see Pettit and McConnell (1984).

[37] See Carron (1983), p. 72.

[38] See Carron (1983).

[39] For further support of this position, see Meltzer (1974), Jaffee (1975), and Benston (1983a, 1983c). It is also worth recalling that, as the 1970s progressed and housing values in many areas soared, a significant fraction of mortgage lending went for second mortgages or the refinancing of existing houses, rather than for new housing. And one can question whether the efforts at special favoritism for housing, at the expense of other social goals, were appropriate social policy.

[40] See Pyle (1974).

[41] Since many thrifts were mutual associations, with no distinct group of stockholders, it is likely that their management absorbed much of the surplus through extra salaries and job-related perquisites.

[42] See Kane (1970).

[43] See Flannery (1981, 1983).

[44] See Hendershott (1979).

[45] If financial markets worked smoothly and instantaneously, the shortage of funds from thrifts need not have meant fewer mortgages, if other lenders were prepared to step quickly into the breach. But institutional adjustments take time, and the cyclical swings were short run and (by definition) unexpected.

[46] For other discussions of the thrifts' problems, see Carron (1982, 1983), Kane (1983), and Balderston (1985).

[47] Among the more influential were the 1971 Hunt Commission Report and the 1975 congressional study of "Financial Institutions and the Nation's Economy" (FINE). See Phillips and Jacobs (1983).

[48] State chartered S&Ls in California had offered them a few years earlier.

[49] The DIDMCA contained many other provisions as well. For a more complete discussion see Brewer et al. (1980), McNeil and Rechter (1980), Johnson and Roberts (1982), pp. 253–257, and Cooper and Fraser (1984), Chap. 4.

[50] For a critique of selective credit controls, see Kane (1977) and Merris and Mote (1980).

[51] Again, this act contained many other provisions. For a more complete discussion, see Garcia et al. (1983) and Cooper and Fraser (1984), Chap. 5.

[52] Cooper and Fraser (1984), p. 3. This percentage varied widely from year to year, with a high of over 70 percent and a low of less than 32 percent.

[53] See Benston (1983a, 1983b, 1983c). But for a negative view of risk adjusted premiums, see Goodman and Shaffer (1984). As of early 1985, mismanagement by one state chartered, privately insured S&L in Ohio led to its demise and to runs on and temporary closure of the other state chartered S&Ls that were insured by the same organization. Some observers claimed that this incident demonstrated the need for a universal federal insurance for all depository institutions. To this author, however, the incident only indicated that not all private insurance arrangements (especially one that was a cooperative arrangement of the insured parties themselves, that was not sufficiently diversified, and that did not have risk-sensitive premiums) are perfect. Also, it appears that mismanagement by Ohio political officials exacerbated the runs and hastened the closures. The issues of *The Wall Street Journal* during March 1985 are a useful source of information on this event.

BIBLIOGRAPHY

Balderston, Frederick E., *Thrifts in Crisis: Structural Transformation of the Savings and Loan Industry.* Cambridge, Mass.: Ballinger Publishing Co., 1985.

Benston, George B., "Federal Regulation of Banking: Analysis and Policy Recommendations," *Journal of Bank Research,* 14 (Winter 1983a), 216–244.

———, "Deposit Insurance and Bank Failures," *Economic Review,* Federal Reserve Bank of Atlanta (March 1983b), 4–17.

———, "The Regulation of Financial Services," in George J. Benston (ed.), *Financial Services: The Changing Institutions and Government Policy.* Englewood Cliffs, N.J.: Prentice-Hall, Inc., 1983c, 28–63.

———, (ed.), *Financial Services: The Changing Institutions and Government Policy.* Englewood Cliffs, N.J.: Prentice-Hall, Inc., 1983d.

———, Hanweck, Gerald A., and Humphrey, David B., "Scale Economies in Banking: A Restructuring and Reassessment," *Journal of Money, Credit and Banking,* 14 (November 1982), 435–456.

———, Berger, Allen N., Hanweck, Gerald A., and Humphrey, David B. "Economies of Scale and Scope in Banking," in *Proceedings of a Conference on Bank Structure and Competition.* Chicago: Federal Reserve Bank of Chicago, 1983, pp. 432–455.

Brewer, Elijah, et al., "The Depository Institutions Deregulation and Monetary Control Act of 1980," *Economic Perspectives,* Federal Reserve Bank of Chicago (September-October 1980), pp. 3–23.

Carron, Andrew S., *The Plight of the Thrift Institutions.* Washington, D.C.: The Brookings Institution, 1982.

———, "The Political Economy of Financial Regulation," in Roger G. Noll and Bruce M. Owen (eds.), *The Political Economy of Deregulation: Interest Groups in the Regulatory Process.* Washington, D.C.: American Enterprise Institute, 1983, pp. 69–83.

Clark, Jeffrey A., "Estimation of Economies of Scale in Banking Using a Generalized Functional Form," *Journal of Money, Credit and Banking,* 16 (February 1984), 53–68.

Cooper, S. Kerry, and Fraser, Donald R., *Banking Deregulation and the New Competition in the Financial Services Industry.* Cambridge, Mass.: Ballinger Publishing Co., 1984.

Edwards, Linda N., and Edwards, Franklin R., "Measuring the Effectiveness of Regulation: The Case of Bank Entry Regulation," *Journal of Law and Economics,* 17 (October 1974), 445–460.

Eisenbeis, Robert A., "Bank Holding Companies and Public Policy," in George J. Benston (ed.), *Financial Services: Changing Institutions and Public Policy.* Englewood Cliffs, N.J.: Prentice-Hall, Inc., 1983, pp. 127–155.

Flannery, Mark J., "Market Interest Rates and Commercial Bank Profitability: An Empirical Investigation," *Journal of Finance,* 36 (December 1981), 1085–1101.

———, "Interest Rates and Bank Profitability: Additional Evidence," *Journal of Money, Credit and Banking,* 15 (August 1983), 355–362.

———, "An Economic Evaluation of Bank Securities Activities Before 1933," in Ingo Walter (ed.), *Deregulating Wall Street: Commercial Bank Penetration of the Corporate Securities Market.* New York: John Wiley & Sons, Inc., 1985, pp. 67–87.

Fromm, Gary (ed.), *Studies in Public Regulation.* Cambridge, Mass.: The MIT Press, 1981.

Garcia, Gillian, et al., "The Garn-St Germain Depository Institutions Act of 1982," *Economic Perspectives,* Federal Reserve Bank of Chicago (March-April 1983), 3–31.

Giddy, Ian H., "Is Equity Underwriting Risky for Commercial Banks?" in Ingo Walter (ed.), *Deregulating Wall Street: Commercial Bank Penetration of the Corporate Securities Market.* New York: John Wiley & Sons, Inc., 1985, pp. 145–169.

Gilbert, R. Alton, "Bank Market Structure and Competition: A Survey," *Journal of Money, Credit and Banking,* 16 (November 1984), 617–645.

Gilligan, Thomas W., and Smirlock, Michael L., "An Empirical Study of Joint Production and Scale Economies in Commercial Banking," *Journal of Banking and Finance,* 8 (March 1984), 67–77.

Golbe, Devra L., "The Effect of Imminent Bankruptcy on Stockholder Risk Preferences and Behavior," *Bell Journal of Economics,* 12 (Spring 1981), 321–328.

———, "Product Safety in a Regulated Industry: Evidence from the Railroads," *Economic Inquiry,* 21 (January 1983), 39–52.

Goldberg, Lawrence G., "Bank Holding Acquisitions, Competition, and Public Policy," in Lawrence G. Goldberg and Lawrence J. White (eds.), *The Deregulation of the Banking and Securities Industries.* Lexington, Mass.: Lexington Books, 1979, pp. 219-242.

———, and White, Lawrence J. (eds.), *The Deregulation of the Banking and Securities Industries.* Lexington, Mass.: Lexington Books, 1979.

Golembe, Carter H., and Holland, David S., *Federal Regulation of Banking, 1983–84.* Washington, D.C.: Golembe Associates, 1983.

Goodman, Laurie S., and Shaffer, Sherrill, "The Economics of Deposit Insurance: A Critical Evaluation of Proposed Reform," *Yale Journal on Regulation*, 2 (1948), 145–162.

Heggestad, Arnold A., "A Survey of Studies on Banking Competition and Performance," in Franklin R. Edwards (ed.), *Issues in Financial Regulation*. New York: McGraw-Hill Book Company, 1979, pp. 449–490.

Hendershott, Patric H., "Deregulation and the Capital Markets: The Impact of Deposit Rate Ceilings and Restrictions Against Variable Rate Mortgages," in Lawrence G. Goldberg and Lawrence J. White (eds.), *The Deregulation of the Banking and Securities Industries*. Lexington, Mass.: Lexington Books, 1979, pp. 71–100.

Huertas, Thomas F., "The Regulation of Financial Institutions: A Historical Perspective on Current Issues," in George J. Benston (ed.), *Financial Services: The Changing Institutions and Government Policy*. Englewood Cliffs, N.J.: Prentice-Hall, Inc., 1983, pp. 6–27.

Jaffee, Dwight M., "Housing Finance and Mortgage Market Policy," in *Government Credit Allocation*. San Francisco: Institute for Contemporary Studies, 1975, pp. 93–122.

Johnson, Ivan C., and Roberts, William W., *Money and Banking: A Market-Oriented Approach*. Chicago: The Dryden Press, 1982.

Kane, Edward J., "Short-changing the Small Saver: Federal Discrimination Against the Small Saver During the Vietnam War," *Journal of Money, Credit and Banking*, 2 (November 1970), 513–522.

———, "Good Intentions and Unintended Evil: The Case Against Selective Credit Allocation," *Journal of Money, Credit and Banking*, 9 (February 1977), 55–69.

———, "Accelerating Inflation, Technological Innovation, and the Decreasing Effectiveness of Banking Regulation," *Journal of Finance*, 36 (May 1981), 355–367.

———, "The Role of Government in the Thrift Industry's Net-Worth Crisis," in George J. Benston (ed.), *Financial Services: The Changing Institutions and Government Policy*. Englewood Cliffs, N.J.: Prentice-Hall, Inc., 1983, pp. 166–184.

Kunreuther, Judith B., "Banking Structure in New York State: Progress and Prospects," *Monthly Review*, Federal Reserve Bank of New York (April 1976).

Ladenson, Mark L., and Bombara, Kenneth J., "Entry in Commercial Banking, 1962–78," *Journal of Money, Credit and Banking*, 16 (May 1984), 165–174.

Landy, Laurie, "Financial Innovation in Canada," *Quarterly Review*, Federal Reserve Bank of New York (Autumn 1980), 1–8.

Luckett, Dudley G., *Money and Banking*, 3d ed. New York: McGraw-Hill Book Company, 1984.

McCall, Alan S., "Economies of Scale, Operating Efficiencies, and the Organizational Structure of Commercial Banks," *Journal of Bank Research*, 11 (Summer 1980a), 95–100.

———, "The Impact of Bank Structure on Bank Service to Local Communities," *Journal of Bank Research*, 11 (Summer 1980b), 101–109.

———, and Lane, John T., "Multi-Office Banking and the Safety and Soundness of Commercial Banks," *Journal of Bank Research*, 11 (Summer 1980), 87–94.

McNeil, Charles R., and Rechter, Denise M., "The Depository Institutions Deregulation and Monetary Control Act of 1980," *Federal Reserve Bulletin*, 66 (June 1980), 444–453.

Meltzer, Allan H., "Credit Availability and Economic Decisions: Some Evidence from the Mortgage and Housing Markets," *Journal of Finance*, (June 1974), 763–777.

Merris, Randall C., and Mote, Larry R., "The Credit Restraint Program in Perspective," *Economic Perspectives*, Federal Reserve Bank of Chicago (July/August 1980), 7–14.

Noll, Roger G., and Owen, Bruce M. (eds.), *The Political Economy of Deregulation: Interest Groups in the Regulatory Process*. Washington, D.C.: American Enterprise Institute, 1983.

Peltzman, Sam, "Entry in Commercial Banking," *Journal of Law and Economics*, 8 (October 1965), 11–50.

———, "Comment," *Journal of Money, Credit and Banking*, 16 (November 1984), 650–656.

Pettit, R. Richardson, and McConnell, John J., "The Impact of Usury Laws on the Effectiveness and Efficiency of the Operation of Small Business," in Paul M. Horvitz and R. Richardson Pettit (eds.), *Small Business Finance: Problems in the Financing of Small Business*. Greenwich, Conn.: JAI Press, 1984, pp. 129–172.

Phillips, Almarin, and Jacobs, Donald P., "Reflections on the Hunt Commission," in George J. Benston (ed.), *Financial Services: The Changing Institutions and Government Policy*. Englewood Cliffs, N.J.: Prentice-Hall, Inc., 1983, pp. 235–265.

———, "Competitive Policy for Depository Financial Institutions," in Almarin Phillips (ed.), *Promoting Competition in Regulated Markets*. Washington, D.C.: The Brookings Institute, 1975a, pp. 329–366.

———, (ed.), *Promoting Competition in Regulated Markets*, Washington, D.C.: The Brookings Institute, 1975b.

Pugel, Thomas A., and White, Lawrence J., "An Analysis of the Competitive Effects of Allowing Commercial Bank Affiliates to Underwrite Corporate Securities," in Ingo Walter (ed.), *Deregulating Wall Street: Commercial Bank Penetration of the Corporate Securities Market*. New York: John Wiley & Sons, Inc., 1985, pp. 93–139.

Pyle, David H., "The Losses on Savings Deposits from Interest Rate Regulation," *Bell Journal of Economics and Management Science*, 5 (Autumn 1974), 614–622.

Rhoades, Stephen A., "Does Market Structure Matter in Commercial Banking?" *Antitrust Bulletin*, 26 (Spring 1981), 155–181.

Rose, John T., and Savage, Donald T., "Bank Holding Company De Novo Entry and Banking Market Deconcentration," *Journal of Bank Research*, 13 (Summer 1982), 96–100.

Sametz, Arnold W. (ed.), *Securities Activities of Commercial Banks*. Lexington, Mass.: Lexington Books, 1981.

Savage, Donald T., "Branch Banking Laws, Deposits, Market Shares and Profitability of New Banks," *Journal of Bank Research*, 13 (Winter 1982), 200–206.

———, and Solomon, Elinor H., "Branch Banking: The Competitive Issues," *Journal of Bank Research*, 11 (Summer 1980), 110–121.

Shull, Bernard, "Multiple-Office Banking and the Structure of Banking Markets: The New York and Virginia Experience," in *Proceedings of a Conference on Bank Structure and Competition*. Chicago: Federal Reserve Bank of Chicago, 1972, pp. 30–40.

———, "Structural Impact of Multiple Office Banking in New York and Virginia," *Antitrust Bulletin*, 23 (Fall 1978), 511–550.

Silber, William L., *Municipal Revenue Bond Costs and Bank Underwriting: A Survey of the Evidence*, New York University Graduate School of Business Administration, Monograph Series in Finance and Economics, No. 1979-3, 1979.

Spellman, Lewis J., *The Depository Firm and Industry: Theory, History, and Regulation*. New York: Academic Press, Inc., 1982.

U.S. Department of Commerce, *Historical Statistics of the United States, Colonial Times to 1970, Bicentennial Edition*. Washington, D.C.: 1975.

———, *Statistical Abstract of the Unitied States, 1984*. Washington, D.C.: 1984.

U.S. Department of the Treasury, *Geographic Restrictions on Commercial Banking in the United States: The Report of the President*. Washington, D.C.: 1981.

U.S. Federal Deposit Insurance Corporation, *Annual Report, 1983*. Washington, D.C.: 1984a.

———, *Statistics on Banking, 1983*. Washington, D.C.: 1984b.

United States League of Savings Institutions, *Savings Institutions Sourcebook, 1984*. Washington, D.C.: 1984.

Walter, Ingo (ed.), *Deregulating Wall Street: Commercial Bank Penetration of the Corporate Securities Market*. New York: John Wiley & Sons, Inc., 1985.

Weiss, Leonard W., and Klass, Michael W. (eds.), *Case Studies in Regulation: Revolution and Reform*. Boston: Little, Brown & Company, 1981.

White, Eugene N., *The Regulation and Reform of the American Banking System, 1900–1929*. Princeton, N.J.: Princeton University Press, 1983.

CASE 7

The Regulatory Change in Telecommunications: The Dissolution of AT&T

Gerald W. Brock
Federal Communications Commission

INTRODUCTION

In the late 1950s the telephone industry was a fully regulated monopoly, and entry into any part of the business was seemingly impossible. Much of the industry appeared to be an obvious natural monopoly, particularly local distribution of final telephone communications. Other parts, especially equipment manufacturing, had no specialized natural monopoly characteristics but were tied into the system by ownership and contractual limitations that effectively prohibited competition.

The controlling company in the system was the American Telephone and Telegraph Company (AT&T), which included as subsidiaries the major Bell operating companies around the country, the Western Electric equipment manufacturing company, and the research and development organization of Bell Laboratories. Many independent telephone companies existed, dating from the period of open competition in local telephone service after the expiration of the original Bell patents in 1894. The independent companies retained monopoly rights to local telephone service in their own areas and

---

The views expressed in this paper are those of the author alone and do not necessarily represent the views of the Commission or other members of its staff. Parts of this paper are adapted with permission from Gerald Brock, *The Telecommunications Industry: The Dynamics of Market Structure*, (Cambridge, Mass.: Harvard University Press, 1981).

interconnected with the Bell System to provide service to other areas. AT&T established standards and took overall managerial responsibility for the telephone network. Toll revenues for calls between an independent telephone company and Bell companies were shared by a formula approved by regulatory authorities. AT&T provided virtually all of the interstate service and approximately 80 percent of the local service, with independent telephone companies providing the remainder of the local service.

The monopolistic industry structure was not an explicit creation of regulatory policy. The basic industry structure and many industry pricing patterns (such as higher prices for business than for residential telephones) had been established during the Bell patent monopoly. After the expiration of the patents, Bell had retained dominance through price competition and the purchase of competitive telephone companies. When early twentieth-century reformers began advocating regulatory control for telephones and other public utilities, the Bell System enthusiastically allied itself with the reformers. In the 1910 Annual Report, then Chief Executive Theodore Vail discussed the benefits of regulation and asserted that a regulated monopoly could provide better and cheaper service than either competition or government ownership. He also explicitly discussed the need for protection from other competition: "If there is to be state control and regulation, there should also be state protection — protection to a corporation striving to serve the whole community ... from aggressive competition which covers only that part which is profitable."[1] Vail echoed the same theme in a 1915 speech in which he said, "I am not only a strong advocate for control and regulation but I think I am one of the first corporation managers to advocate it. It is as necessary for the protection of corporations from each other as for protection to, or from, the public."[2]

Early regulation helped to stabilize the existing structure rather than to seek an optimal structure or price policy. The independent companies that existed then were neither allowed to expand into Bell-controlled territories nor required to yield to Bell companies. Regulators accepted and protected the industry structure of one dominant firm and many small independent companies because it existed when regulation was established, not because some economic analysis indicated that it was a particularly desirable structure. The structure of prices was considered a management decision and was not subject to the regulatory review process so long as the companies did not engage in too much discrimination. The early regulatory agencies imposed rate of return regulation; however, conflicts over the definition of the rate base and other accounting issues together with the complex interrelated structure of the various AT&T-owned

companies prevented the regulators from comprehensively examining company finances. One extensive study of Bell System finances concluded that regulation had little effect on profitability: "For the system as a whole, from 1900 on through the period when the various States, one by one, gave their commissions regulatory power over telephone companies, the earnings continued at about the same rate. . . ."[3] AT&T's interstate long-distance service was placed under the jurisdiction of the Interstate Commerce Commission in 1910 and then transferred to the newly created Federal Communications Commission (FCC) in 1934. Both agencies accepted the industry structure as it was, and neither sought to regulate AT&T's actions in detail nor to determine the optimal industry structure. Neither agency adopted a specific policy of prohibiting new entry into long-distance telecommunications, but the effect of their actions was to prevent entry and to protect the status quo.

In recent years the telecommunications industry has become far more competitive than it was during the 1950s. Telephone instruments made by various manufacturers now can be purchased at retail stores and plugged in like other electric appliances. Before competition, they were the property of telephone companies and were wired into the system by telephone company technicians. Consumers now have a choice of long-distance carriers instead of being connected automatically to AT&T for long-distance calls. Businesses now have a variety of specialized services available from competing companies and are not limited to the services of a regulated monopolist. These changes have been associated with an increased emphasis on competition and a decreased emphasis on the traditional regulatory tools to promote the public interest.

The regulatory change has not been brought about by a specific reform plan but instead has occurred as a gradual response to the implications of key court decisions together with regulatory responses to the actions of the companies involved. The pro-competitive efforts can be seen as the FCC's attempt to achieve traditional goals of equity and procedural justice when faced with new circumstances. Economic analysis has played a minimal role in the regulatory changes. There has been no explicit analysis of the costs and benefits of competition versus regulation, of the extent of economies of scale or economies of scope to be lost through competition, or of the social benefits and costs of using profits from some services to subsidize other services.

In part, this is due to the extreme difficulty of gathering reliable information. Economic analysis requires extensive amounts of information, but there is not agreement on even such basic facts as the change in average costs with change in the volume of output. Instead, interested parties present information and assertions they think are likely to cause the Commission to support the policies the parties desire. However, the limited role of economic analysis in telecommunications regulatory changes goes beyond this. It is also a function of legal standards that give procedural justice a key role. Procedural justice emphasizes the process used to arrive at a result rather than the result itself. It is the basis for much of the legal system. If a person is convicted of a crime by a properly chosen jury and with no procedural irregularities, most people believe the convict is guilty — not because they have any personal knowledge of his or her guilt or innocence but because they believe that the established procedure generally leads to a correct result. Similarly, in the regulatory process, using the correct procedure to reach a decision is legally more important than an analysis of the economic effects of the decision and may lead to decisions very different from those the economist would determine as economically justified.

This paper explores the evolution of telecommunications regulation with the gradual introduction of competition. More emphasis is given to legal and procedural issues than to an economic analysis of the costs and benefits of the changes, because the author believes that the legal and procedural issues were the controlling forces. Of course, the changes had major economic implications, but those implications were often minimized in the actual decision process rather than emphasized as the rationale for introducing more competition. Three key court decisions based on traditional legal principles rather than conscious attempts to change telecommunications regulatory structure implied a dramatic change in the methods used by the Commission to regulate the industry.

EQUIPMENT COMPETITION AND REGULATORY CHANGES

The transformation of the "customer premises equipment market" (CPE) from a part of the regulated monopoly to full competition evolved from a dispute over a minor item known as the Hush-A-Phone. The Hush-A-Phone was a cuplike device that snapped onto the telephone instrument to provide speaking privacy and shield out surrounding noises. It was a passive nonelectrical device that directed the speaker's voice into the instrument. However, the AT&T tariffs at the time prohibited attachment of any device not furnished by the telephone company to telephone equipment. AT&T informed customers and distributors of the Hush-A-Phone that its use violated the

AT&T tariff. Hush-A-Phone appealed to the FCC for protection from AT&T harassment, but the Commission upheld AT&T's right to prohibit the device. Hush-A-Phone then appealed the Commission's decision to the appeals court, where it won a crucial victory and established the key legal point that the telephone company may not interfere with the right of a telephone subscriber to use the telephone in any way he or she chooses so long as it does not harm other subscribers. AT&T had argued that if a telephone subscriber wanted privacy, he should cup his hand around the telephone receiver instead of using the Hush-A-Phone cup. The court ruled:

> The question, in the final analysis, is whether the Commission possesses enough control over the subscriber's use of his telephone to authorize the telephone company to prevent him from conversing in comparatively low and distorted tones. . . . To say that a telephone subscriber may produce the result in question by cupping his hand and speaking into it, but may not do so by using a device which leave his hand free to write or do whatever else he wishes, is neither just or reasonable. The intervenor's tariffs, under the Commission's decision, are in unwarranted interference with the telephone subscriber's right reasonably to use his telephone in ways which are privately beneficial without being publicly detrimental.[4]

Following the court decision, the FCC issued an order requiring AT&T to file new tariffs that canceled restrictive tariff provisions inconsistent with the court decision. AT&T filed new tariffs that narrowed the scope of the prohibition but continued to prohibit any device that involved direct electrical connection to the system, provided a recording device on the line, or connected the telephone with any other communications system. The Commission accepted the new tariffs without specifically ruling on whether they complied with the court-imposed requirements.

Soon after the revised tariff went into effect, Carter Electronics Corporation began marketing a device called a Carterfone that connected mobile radiotelephone systems to the telephone network. The Carterfone contained a cradle into which an ordinary telephone handset could be placed. The Carterfone transmitted voice signals from the mobile radio transmitter into the telephone handset and converted the voice signals received from the handset into radio signals for broadcast to the mobile radiotelephone without the need for a direct electrical connection between the two. Though the device violated the AT&T tariff because it provided a connection between telephone lines and other channels of communication, it at least arguably fit within the Hush-A-Phone court standard because it was merely receiving voice signals from the telephone set and transmitting voice signals back to the telephone set. In response to a Carter inquiry the Commission informed the company in 1960 that the Carterfone did not violate any Commission rules but that it appeared to violate the AT&T tariff. Carter continued to produce and market the device. AT&T asserted that the tariff prohibited the Carterfone and threatened to suspend telephone service to customers who used the Carterfone.

After further legal wrangling, including an antitrust suit by Carter and a court request that the FCC rule on the issue, the Commission concluded in 1968 that the Carterfone violated the tariff but that the tariff itself was illegal and violated the requirements of the court and the Commission in the Hush-A-Phone case. The Commission ruled that the tariff "has been unreasonable and unreasonably discriminatory since its inception" and ordered the companies to file new tariffs to allow all devices that did not cause actual harm.[5]

The Carterfone decision was a Commission implementation of the court-imposed Hush-A-Phone requirements rather than a Commission determination to relax regulation of customer equipment. However, it was the genesis of the transformation of the regulatory structure of the equipment market. Following the Carterfone decision, AT&T instituted new tariffs that allowed connection of customer-owned equipment to the network provided that an AT&T device known as a connecting arrangement was used. The connecting arrangement provided the network control signaling and provided circuitry to protect the network against malfunctions in the customer-provided equipment. The Commission again allowed the tariff to go into effect without specifically ruling on whether it complied with the requirements. Many parties complained that the connecting arrangement requirements improperly restricted consumer choice and were inconsistent with the Hush-A-Phone standard.

The expense of connecting arrangements prevented competition in residential telephones and small-scale business systems. But it did allow the beginning of competition for private branch exchanges (PBXs), the systems of telephones connected to a switch used by many businesses. Although the competitors' market share remained small, the introduction of competition revolutionized the PBX market. The PBX market had been characterized by long-lived equipment with relatively slow introduction of new products and features. The advent of competition together with the increasing use of computer technology in PBXs drastically shrunk the product cycle. AT&T reorganized its operations to increase the coordination between research and manufacturing arms and thus shorten the interval between innovation and actual product introduction.

The development of competition in one segment of the customer equipment market induced the Commission to institute a proceeding to consider direct connection of customer equipment without a telephone company protective device, thus opening a wider market to competition. Competition provided a lobbying group to present arguments in favor of greater competition. So long as the telephone company controlled all equipment connected to the network, there was little pressure on the Commission to open up parts of the market to competition. But once competition was allowed in some areas, competitors continually focused on the restrictions that defined the boundary between allowable and unallowable competition and presented arguments for moving the boundary. In 1972 the Commission began a formal investigation to explore the technical feasibility of direct connection of customer-supplied equipment without using telephone company connecting devices. In 1975 the Commission concluded that the protective devices were an unnecessary restriction on the customer's right to use the equipment and were an unjust and unreasonable discrimination among users and among suppliers of terminal equipment. The Commission prescribed that terminal equipment should be connected through standard plugs and jacks rather than direct wiring and that all terminal equipment (including that manufactured by the telephone companies) would be required to meet specified technical criteria to prevent harm to the network.[6]

Although direct connection rules removed regulatory barriers on the sale of terminal equipment, they raised another set of issues related to cross-subsidization and abuse of monopoly power. So long as the telephone network was a complete system, it was relatively unimportant exactly how costs were distributed among its parts. Consumers neither knew nor cared how much of their telephone bill went to pay for the telephone instrument itself and how much went to pay for other parts of the network. But in the new competitive situation, the competitors very much cared about the breakdown of costs. If, for example, a low price were placed on telephone instruments with the revenue to be recovered from a higher price being placed on other services, the monopoly control of the telephone instruments would be reestablished. One solution would have been to forbid AT&T to provide telephone instruments, but that solution appeared too drastic. A further complication came from the 1956 consent decree, which limited AT&T to regulated services. It was possible that by deregulating the terminal equipment market, the Commission could inadvertently exclude AT&T from that market altogether.

These issues came together in a more general inquiry concerned with the boundaries between telecommunications and computers. The technologies used in the two industries had converged to the point where they overlapped in many products. Computers or computer-like products were the basis for telephone switching machines.

Computers frequently communicated over telephone lines, making the telephone network a connecting link that performed the same function as cables directly linking computers. Computer terminals could be classified as either in the computer industry or in the communications industry or in both. The definition of industry boundaries was important because of regulatory restrictions on the communications but not the computer industry. To classify a product as part of the computer industry could imply prohibiting AT&T from that market because of its restriction to regulated communications. To classify a product as communications equipment could exclude IBM and other computer companies unless they went through the arduous process of submitting to FCC regulation.

After extensive controversy the Commission in 1980 passed a set of rules known as Computer II that attempted to solve both the regulatory problems of computer/communications boundaries and to resolve the issue of potential cross-subsidization in terminal equipment. AT&T was required to set up a separate unregulated subsidiary that would handle all terminal equipment, including telephone instruments and the disputed computer-related equipment. Regulation was limited to basic services.[7]

The 1980 Computer II rules completed the transition to full competition for telephone instruments and other types of terminal equipment begun by the Carterfone decision of 1968. In retrospect, the transition was a gradual "regulatory reform" in which the market was opened up in stages, beginning with allowing non-telephone companies to connect specialized equipment to the network and ending with the severing of terminal equipment from the regulated monopoly sector. The deregulation can be rationalized as a reasonable long-term plan in which the market was substituted for regulation because regulators recognized that terminal equipment did not have natural monopoly characteristics. However, an examination of the actual decisions indicates a very different basis for the regulatory changes. The original regulation of terminal equipment existed because the telephone companies defined terminal equipment as an integral part of the telephone network. The definition was accepted by the regulators without making an independent examination of the effects of accepting that definition of terminal equipment against treating it as a nonregulated adjunct to the network. The *Carterfone* decision was based on the legal precedent of the *Hush-A-Phone* case rather than an economic analysis of the issues at hand. Once competitors existed, the remaining decisions opening up the market flowed naturally from traditional fairness concerns.

During the transition the role of the Commission in the industry was increased. The Commission became the arbitrator between competitors and was forced to devise policies that prevented the dominant AT&T from using its power to exclude the new rivals. In contrast, the previous regulation of terminal equipment ensured that AT&T did not earn an excessive rate of return on its assets, including terminal equipment, without any particular concern over the methods of interconnection or the relative prices of terminal and other equipment.

LONG-DISTANCE COMPETITION

AT&T has never been given a legal monopoly on long-distance communication. AT&T's initial control of long-distance service arose as an adjunct to its control of local operating companies during the period of the original Bell patent (1876–1893). After the expiration of the patent, competitors set up local companies, but the Bell System remained the only company with a unified interconnected long-distance system. AT&T's own technological innovations and its patent cross-licensing agreements with other companies gave it continuing patent protection for long-distance technology. When the FCC was formed in 1934, AT&T still monopolized long-distance communications. AT&T's monopoly was accepted by the new Commission without an explicit ruling as to whether a monopoly was in the public interest.

The simultaneous development of television and microwave transmission technology in the years immediately following World War II provided a significant threat to AT&T's control of long-distance communications. The advent of television created extensive new demand for high-capacity trunk channels to transmit television programs among television stations. A television program could not be carried on ordinary wires because it required the communications capacity of approximately 1,000 telephone conversations. Television programs could be carried over a coaxial cable, developed by AT&T during the 1930s to carry a large number of telephone conversations simultaneously, or over a microwave relay system. The simultaneous availability of a significant new source of demand and a new technology that did not require rights of way provided the ability and the incentive for new firms to enter the long-distance telecommunications market.

Microwave radio systems were initially developed for the four to six GHz bands of electromagnetic radiation, over 3,000 times the frequency of AM radio. Microwave required a variety of advances in technology to allow the practical utilization of higher and higher radio frequencies. Although initial developments in microwave transmission occurred prior to World War II, extensive advances occurred during the war because of radar, an application of microwaves. At the close of the war microwave was known to be a viable technology for either television or multiple voice transmission, but further development was required to produce a commercial system. Because much of the work had been done for the government, microwave technology was relatively free of patent control. The equal footing of many different companies in microwave technology, the absence of patent protection, and the absence of right-of-way requirements eroded the barriers to entry for long-distance communication.

As a form of radio communication, microwave required frequency allocations from the FCC. Although the FCC freely granted experimental microwave licenses, it ruled in 1948 that permanent frequency assignments should be reserved for common carriers. Where common carrier capacity was unavailable for television transmission, broadcasters were allowed to set up their own temporary networks of microwave transmission facilities. However, the Commission also ruled in 1949 that although AT&T was required to interconnect its facilities with private broadcaster systems, it was not required to interconnect with any other common carrier. This presented a dilemma for potential microwave competitors. Only by applying for common carrier status could they obtain permanent rights to use the microwave spectrum. Yet, if they achieved common carrier status, AT&T had no obligation to interconnect with them, and they had to build a complete network on their own. The difficult regulatory hurdles together with AT&T's dominant position prevented new entry at that time.

The reason for the restrictive assignment in 1948 was that frequencies were limited and could best be utilized by common carriers. Although the effect was to give the field to AT&T, that was not the intent of the regulations. Frequency allocations were gradually relaxed as the availability of adequate facilities became clearer. Microwave systems for private use of railroads along their tracks and for television transmission to remote locations were established by companies other than AT&T. In 1956 the Commission began reviewing its initial microwave allocation decisions. Although microwave was extensively used by that time, technical advances had prevented the existing systems from pressing on the limits of frequency availability. Microwave manufacturers and potential private users advocated a more open policy of allocation and backed up their arguments with extensive engineering studies showing widespread availability of microwave frequencies. In 1959 the Commission issued a key decision that reversed the factual premise of the earlier restrictive decision and concluded instead that frequencies were adequate "to take care of the present and reasonably foreseeable future needs of both the common carriers and private users for point-to-point communications systems."[9] Consequently, the Commission reversed the previous policy that microwave should be restricted to common carriers and opened it up to any private user in a decision known as *Above 890* because it allocated frequencies above 890 Mhz for microwave.

At the time, economies of scale in microwave transmission were strong for a capacity of up to about 240 circuits, moderate between 240 and 1,000, and insignificant above 1,000 circuits. The economies of scale arose because each microwave transmission required a tower and radio equipment largely independent of capacity up to a maximum of about 1,000 circuits, but also required "multiplex" equipment to manage multiple voice conversations, which increased costs linearly with the number of circuits. In contrast, AT&T's pricing policy contained no volume discounts; the price for 100 circuits was 100 times the price for a single circuit. These characteristics made building a private system attractive for very large users who could utilize a substantial fraction of the system capacity, but unattractive for smaller users.

AT&T responded to the private microwave authorization with the Telpak tariff, a volume discounted price structure that gave an increasingly large discount for larger number of lines, ranging up to 85 percent for 240 lines. A set of 240 lines over 100 miles that would have been priced at $75,600 per month before the *Above 890* decision was reduced to $11,700 per month after the decision. Because the new microwave systems were to be built by individual users rather than companies seeking microwave business, there was no opposition to the Telpak tariffs from the companies planning to develop microwave systems. The users' goal was inexpensive bulk communications service, and if AT&T would provide it more cheaply than they could provide it for themselves, they were happy to continue as AT&T customers. Consequently, most of the potential users of the newly authorized private microwave systems willingly abandoned plans for their own systems, signed up for Telpak, and supported Telpak in subsequent hearings.

Although many users supported the Telpak volume discounts, AT&T competitor Western Union and equipment manufacturer Motorola opposed them, leading to extensive hearings on their lawfulness. The Telpak hearings became embroiled in a variety of other issues before the Commission, and hearings continued for sixteen years until the Commission ruled the discount was illegal in 1976. Meanwhile, the Telpak tariff served as an explicit discrimination between small- and large-volume customers. Large-volume customers could gain the advantages of either private microwave or the Telpak discounts, but prohibitions on the resale of Telpak circuits or circuits derived from private microwave systems prevented passing the cost advantages on to small-volume customers. This question of fairness played a key role in opening up wider competition in long-distance services.

In 1963 Microwave Communications Inc. (MCI) filed for common carrier status to offer communications service between St. Louis and Chicago over a microwave system. The proposed system was extremely small — a maximum capacity of 300 voice circuits on a single channel microwave with a total cost of $564,000. The MCI application was in effect a request for a shared private microwave system. The proposed system was no more extensive than many private systems, but MCI proposed to sell the capacity in small units rather than in bulk to a single user.

The MCI application provoked extensive controversy that was finally settled in 1969 by Commission approval of the application on a four to three vote. The question partially revolved around how much weight should be given to the particular application (which was too limited to make much difference either to customers or carriers) as opposed to viewing the MCI application as a determinant of general competitive policy. The majority opinion ruled in favor of allowing what was in effect a shared microwave system to bring some of the discount benefits to smaller volume customers. The minority viewed the application as a challenge to the established system of rate averaging and monopoly service. Although the approval of the MCI application was formally based on its limited scope, even the majority recognized the approval as a tacit move toward opening the telecommunications area to competition that could ultimately require changes in AT&T's rate structure. The Commission stated:

The averaging method is embodied neither in the Decalogue nor in the Constitution. Without danger to the republic, there may be a weighing of the possible public benefits or disadvantages resulting from authorizing competition in selected areas.

... In any event, whether MCI will be a real threat to the nationwide, averaged rate method is problematical, resting upon the say-so of the carriers.[9]

The 1969 MCI decision was the crucial "regulatory reform" decision for long-distance communication. The events begun by that decision led naturally to a full opening of the long-distance market to competition because of the difficulty of justifying distinctions between competitive and monopoly services. Yet the decision was made through traditional regulatory methods using traditional standards. The Commission, examining MCI's financial capability to perform the proposed services and the evidence of need for that service, concluded that the public interest would be served by authorizing the MCI applications for microwave stations. The decision was *not* the result of a broad-ranging investigation determining that competition was better than monopoly for private line services. Rather it was the application of the traditional public interest standard to MCI's request. AT&T's monopoly existed by default rather than by Commission design. Formally, the decision was not a change in regulatory policy but an application of existing policy that judged applications for microwave licenses by specified criteria. It was clear to all concerned that the decision created a significant change in the market structure and was likely to be a precedent for further changes. But the Commission did not have the data available to rule that general competition would be in the public interest. It could not predict the extent of new entry, the effect on prices, or other important variables that would be required to make an economic analysis of the overall effect of the movement toward competition. However, on the narrow grounds of authorizing construction applications for a small-scale system, the Commission could and did conclude that it was not required to evaluate the broader issues of competition because the system would be too small to affect significantly the existing carriers.

Following the 1969 decision authorizing the MCI entry, a large number of additional construction applications were filed by various parties to provide similar types of service. Rather than holding separate proceedings on each set of applications, the FCC initiated a broad policy inquiry regarding the desirability of specialized common carrier competition and invited comments from interested parties. The existing common carriers challenged the desirability of competition and the right of the Commission to authorize it, while potential new carriers, their equipment suppliers, and their potential customers all supported new entry. After receiving comments from over 200 parties, the Commission in 1971 announced a policy decision in favor of new competition in the "specialized communications field."[10] "Specialized communications" was not defined precisely, but was understood to mean primarily private line services and not ordinary long-distance service.

The *Specialized Common Carrier* decision brought new entrants into the market but also raised a number of new problems for the Commission. The first was interconnection. The private lines provided by the new carriers required connection with the local operating company to reach the final user. A useful analogy is the transportation market in which airlines provide service between airports but do not transport customers all the way from originating destination to terminating destination. MCI wanted to be in the "airline" business, not the "taxicab" business. However, because AT&T was an integrated company offering both local and long-distance services, it had an incentive to discriminate against MCI for local distribution in order to keep it out of the long-distance business. It was as if United Airlines was the only airline and also owned all the buses and taxicabs in a city. In that case a new airline would have to compete against the existing airline as well as gain rights to use the taxicabs or establish its own fleet.

AT&T had originally challenged the MCI application as useless because it would require use of local operating company facilities that AT&T would refuse to provide. In the *Specialized Common Carrier* decision, the Commission required interconnection but left the terms up to the carriers. This provoked many disputes over the rights of the new carriers to interconnection. At each stage of the dispute the Commission upheld a broad interpretation of the requirement to interconnect, leading to full interconnect rights by 1976.

A second issue was pricing. The AT&T prices were not explicitly based on cost for each service offered. Instead, they were broad averages designed to recover the total revenue requirement across all services. Just as the private microwave authorization provoked a pricing response with the Telpak tariff, so the new entry policy provoked pricing responses. AT&T cut prices on the high-density routes (which were the ones the new competitors were after) and raised prices on the low-density routes. AT&T cut prices for long-haul traffic and raised prices for short-haul traffic. Both changes were detrimental to the new carriers because the entrants carried primarily long-haul traffic on dense routes and sometimes ordered AT&T short-haul circuits to complete a circuit to a customer location for which they lacked facilities. Extensive litigation before the Commission and in the antitrust courts followed the price maneuvers. The Commission ruled that the price changes were improperly discriminatory, but the courts have been more favorable to the changes under the standards of the antitrust law.

The interconnection and pricing controversies caused the Commission and its staff to examine AT&T's claims more carefully and more skeptically than it had in the past. AT&T's predictions of total chaos in the industry as a result of competition did not come to pass. AT&T's public interest justifications for its actions were countered by MCI's arguments that the actions were those of a monopolist bent on thwarting Commission policy. AT&T's public attempts to stop the Commission's movement toward competition put AT&T and the

Commission in a more adversarial role rather than the close cooperation that had characterized their earlier relationship. The beginnings of competition consequently induced closer scrutiny of AT&T instead of less regulation. Questions of price structure had been largely left up to AT&T so long as the total level was within the allowed rate of return. After competition, price structure assumed a critical dimension because rearranging prices while maintaining the same total revenue could put a competitor out of business. Questions of interconnection and how that was done became regulatory concerns for the first time.

The *Specialized Common Carrier* decision specifically approved "specialized communications" without either explicitly limiting that term or explaining the relationship of specialized communications to switched long-distance service. Switched long-distance includes ordinary dial-up calls and the WATS volume discount service. It is distinguished from the much smaller private line market that was the focus of debate in the early MCI application in that private lines provide a continuous communication path between two points and are useful for connecting two branch offices of a single company, for instance. It was consequently unclear whether MCI and the other new carriers had authority to offer switched service.

Switched long-distance service presented a profitable opportunity to potential entrants because a large portion of AT&T toll revenue from switched long-distance services was returned to the local operating companies that originated and terminated the conversations. The companies, with approval of the Commission and state regulators, had established a complex system of sharing toll revenue between AT&T and local companies that allowed the local companies to support a substantial portion of their costs from their share of toll revenue. The cost-sharing system meant the toll prices were far above the cost of transmission between long-distance offices. If a new entrant could offer switched long-distance service by having a customer call its office as an ordinary local call, providing a separate long-distance network to the destination city and terminating the call with another ordinary local call to the final subscriber, it could bypass the cost-sharing system and its associated portion of the long-distance toll in order to undercut AT&T's price and still make substantial profits. In 1975 MCI began offering Execunet service, effectively a switched long-distance service although it was packaged as a special version of "shared private line service." MCI used the same facilities for switched service as for private line service and originated and terminated the calls with ordinary local calls between the customer's location and the MCI offices.

AT&T opposed the new service and the Commission initially upheld AT&T's position that the MCI Execunet service exceeded MCI's operating authority. MCI challenged the Commission decision in the appeals court and in 1977 won a crucial victory. The appeals court ruled that because the Commission had not precisely defined the boundaries of the specialized communications field when construction authorizations were granted, and because the Commission had not formally granted AT&T a monopoly over switched long-distance service, the Commission could not restrict the purpose for which the properly authorized facilities were used.[11] The decision meant that MCI was entitled to offer Execunet over existing facilities but not necessarily entitled to build new facilities to offer that type of service. Following the Execunet decision, AT&T announced that it would not provide local distribution facilities for Execunet service, justifying its refusal on the grounds that the previous FCC and court proceedings requiring connections applied only to private line services. The Commission upheld AT&T's contention that it had no obligation to provide local distribution facilities. MCI then returned to the appeals court and in 1978 obtained another reversal of the FCC position and an order requiring AT&T to provide facilities.[12] AT&T then agreed to provide the facilities but wanted to charge far more than the ordinary business rates. AT&T claimed that even though the facilities were functionally identical to ordinary business local telephone lines, they were really special facilities for interstate access and should be charged at a high rate to reflect the cost-sharing arrangements in AT&T's revenue-sharing formulas with local companies. The issue was temporarily settled by a compromise in which MCI paid an intermediate amount between the local business telephone rate and the cost-sharing implied rate, but the problem of pricing local telephone lines used for interstate access remains in contention. Although disputes have continued regarding the quality and price of local distribution facilities, the Execunet litigation clearly established the principle that competition in long-distance service would be allowed absent a specific Commission finding that it was not in the public interest.

The genesis of competition in switched services was the result of legal interpretations of established rules. The idea of monopoly switched services had been taken for granted by the Commission and not examined explicitly. The regulatory procedural requirements that normally favor the preservation of the status quo in this case were used to change the status quo. Because the Commission had not followed the procedure to grant a monopoly and had given MCI the right to own facilities, it could not after the fact deny MCI's right to use those facilities in previously unexpected ways without violating MCI's procedural rights. Yet, once MCI was in the market, it was far more difficult for the Commission to find that a monopoly was in the public interest. Following the Execunet litigation, the Commission instituted a formal proceeding to determine if competition for switched service was in the public interest and concluded that it was. There was little doubt of the outcome of that proceeding once competition in switched service had begun. The existence of competition put the burden of proof on AT&T to show why competitors should be eliminated, whereas prior to the actual beginning of competition the burden was on potential entrants to show why they should be allowed to enter. Because of the great uncertainty over what the effects of any particular regulatory action will be, it is difficult for any party to prove its position. Thus even though it had not planned to allow competition in switched services, once the court had required it to allow MCI into that market, the Commission could not rule that the public interest would be served by returning to monopoly in switched services.

THE ANTITRUST SUIT

In 1949 the Department of Justice filed a Sherman Act antitrust suit against AT&T seeking the divestiture of its manufacturing subsidiary Western Electric. That suit was partially based on the precedent of other public utility companies that earlier had been forced to eliminate ties between manufacturing equipment and the business of providing a regulated utility service. The reason for disapproving of such ties was that the manufacturing subsidiary was not subject to direct regulation, yet the prices paid to the manufacturing subsidiary for equipment determined the rate base on which allowable rates of return were calculated. Thus, if an integrated utility paid inflated prices to its manufacturing subsidiary, it could circumvent regulation.

The 1949 suit was settled by the 1956 consent decree in which AT&T agreed to confine itself to regulated activities and to freely license its patents in return for being allowed to retain its integrated structure. The 1956 agreement arguably could have been interpreted to confer antitrust immunity on AT&T in its regulated activities. However, the degree to which regulation provided antitrust immunity was a very murky point of law. The equipment controversies following the Carterfone case and the initial private line controversies induced companies that believed they had been wronged to seek redress through private antitrust suits. By 1974 thirty-five private antitrust suits had been filed against AT&T. That year the Justice Department filed a massive suit alleging that AT&T had monopolized the equipment market, the long-distance market, and the local telephone market. The Department sought divestiture of the company as relief.

The initial years of the suit were occupied with procedural litigation, particularly over the question of whether AT&T was subject to the antitrust laws at all. AT&T claimed that its actions had been taken in the context of pervasive regulation and could not be evaluated by normal antitrust standards. The Justice Department claimed that regulation was ineffective and largely irrelevant to the suit. AT&T lost the procedural battle, and after extensive preparations the trial began. At the end of the Justice Department's presentation, AT&T filed for a directed verdict. In a directed verdict the judge determines that the plaintiff has not presented enough evidence to constitute a violation and therefore rules in favor of the defendant without hearing the defendant's side of the case. The judge denied the directed verdict and announced that the Justice Department had presented convincing evidence of a violation that AT&T would have to rebut in order to prevail.

AT&T's setback caused it to begin intensive negotiations to settle the suit. The incentive to settle was strong because of the many pending and likely private suits. Normally, private plaintiffs must prove an antitrust violation as well as showing how the violation has damaged them. Proving an antitrust violation is a very complex undertaking, frequently involving vast numbers of documents and millions of dollars in legal fees. However, if a company has been found guilty of an antitrust violation by the government, then a private plaintiff can use that conviction as proof of violation and need only prove the amount of damages in order to collect three times the damages proved.

As a result of negotiations between AT&T and William Baxter, the Reagan administration's antitrust chief, a new consent decree was developed in which AT&T agreed to divest itself of the regional operating companies that provided local phone service. AT&T retained the long-distance business, Bell Laboratories, Western Electric, and the terminal equipment business but lost control of the local operating companies. The new decree freed AT&T from the 1956 decree's restriction to regulated service and allowed AT&T freedom to enter essentially any business it chose, but the divested operating companies were restricted to regulated local telephone service. The general theory behind the decree was that the components remaining with AT&T were potentially competitive and could eventually be deregulated, while the components being divested were likely to remain regulated monopolies. The divestiture took place on January 1, 1984.

The decree was an attempt to solve a fundamental regulatory problem: how to create a fair market in a competitive sector when that sector is highly complementary to a monopolized sector. The three basic components of a long-distance call are terminal equipment (the actual telephone instruments), local lines to connect the telephones with long-distance offices, and lines connecting long-distance offices. By the time of the antitrust suit, competition existed in terminal equipment and in long-distance lines, but not in the local lines. So long as all three components are necessary to complete a call, a monopolist of any one component has just as much power as the monopolist of all three components. An integrated firm such as AT&T before divestiture can reduce prices in the competitive sectors to whatever level is necessary to exclude competitors, while still making its allowed rate of return because of its control of the monopolized sector.

In proceedings before the Commission and in the antitrust courts competitors of AT&T claimed that AT&T's price cuts after competition were predatory moves designed to maintain its monopoly and that it was supported by profits from the products in which there was no competition. AT&T responded that the price cuts were efforts to bring prices more closely in line with costs, as is required in a competitive market. According to AT&T, the pre-competition pricing policy contained an intentional kind of rate averaging to subsidize high-cost services with profits from low-cost services. Because competitors entered the services with high-profit margins, it was consequently necessary to reduce the prices of competitive products and to raise the prices of noncompetitive ones to align prices with costs and avoid inefficient competition. The Commission attempted to deal with these problems through accounting allocations of cost to determine which prices were justified and which were not. The problem with this method is that a large proportion of telecommunications costs are related to personnel and plant used for many different services. Whether the price changes were justified depended on controversial accounting allocations. The Commission spent many years in a detailed examination of the proper accounting standards and finally adopted a cost allocation manual according to which some of the price cuts were illegal. But there was considerable dissatisfaction with the average cost standard used to reach that result. It was inconsistent with the marginal tests used for economic efficiency and could prohibit desirable price changes.

Related to the pricing problem was a general belief among economists and others that competition and regulation should not be mixed. If there are such substantial economies of scale that competition is not feasible, then a regulated monopoly structure is desirable. If competition is feasible, then regulation is unnecessary. Attempting to mix regulation and competition naturally leads the regulatory authority to serve as a handicapper among various competitors and can create a regulated cartel that has neither the production efficiencies of a monopolist nor the incentive and informational efficiencies of a competitive market.

The divestiture was an attempt to solve both the pricing problem and the problem of regulated competition by separating the ownership of the competitive from the monopoly sectors. Then there would be a regulated monopoly to provide efficient local exchange service, while the other sectors could be completely deregulated. Because AT&T would not have a protected monopoly market and the operating companies would not have competitors, there would be no incentives to subsidize predatory actions in the competitive sectors with profits from the monopoly sector.

The Commission did not initiate the divestiture, but it did support the divestiture in hearings before the trial judge regarding the desirability of accepting the negotiated settlement. However, the Commission's approval of the divestiture did not necessarily indicate its agreement with the economic analysis used to support the Justice Department case, nor did it indicate a decision to deregulate the activities in the "competitive" sector (terminal equipment and long-distance service). The Commission and the federal district court that handled the AT&T antitrust case are on an equal level of legal authority. Neither is subject to the other, and both may have their decisions appealed to the same appeals court. Consequently, the new consent decree introduced a second form of federal regulation on the industry, with some issues subject to rulings by both the antitrust trial judge (who administers the consent decree) and the Commission.

REGULATORY PROBLEMS AFTER DIVESTITURE

The divestiture successfully reduced AT&T's market power, but it has not solved the problem of pricing and of regulated competition. The Commission remains responsible for determining a variety of matters, each of which has major competitive implications. A favorable decision before the Commission can have more impact on the financial success of a company than a major technological innovation or a successful marketing program.

The most critical post-divestiture regulatory problem was the establishment of access charges. The Justice Department case viewed control of the local operating companies as the key component of AT&T's market power and therefore sought to ensure equal access to the originating and terminating facilities of local operating companies for long-distance competitors. The decree required that the cost-sharing settlements process for dividing toll revenue between AT&T and the operating companies be abolished and be replaced by a system of access charges in which the local companies charged fees for their part in completing long-distance calls. In addition, the local operating companies were required to offer the same technical connections to all long-distance companies as they offered to AT&T.

Two problems arose with this provision. First, the local switches were engineered automatically to switch long-distance calls to the AT&T toll office (which might simply be another part of the same building) and were not immediately able to offer the same technical quality to other companies. Although plans were made to convert most offices to "equal access" by the end of 1986, the Commission had to determine the appropriate access fees for nonequal access lines during the three-year transition as well as for offices that would not be converted because of technical problems. Because access fees consume over half of AT&T's toll revenue, the differential established between fees for different kinds of access has a critical competitive effect. If the same fee is charged for all kinds of access, the non-AT&T companies are disadvantaged because they receive inferior connections during the transition. If too large a differential is established, AT&T is disadvantaged because it pays the higher price for its superior connections. Thus the Commission was forced to make crucial competitive determinations through its tariff process. The Commission initially determined that the inferior access lines should be priced at a 35 percent discount to the AT&T lines, but after the competitors gained congressional support for their pleas that the differential was inadequate, the Commission raised the discount to 55 percent. All companies pay the same rate for lines that have been converted to equal access standards.

The second problem with the access provisions was that they threaten the monopoly control of the local exchange. The consent decree did not change the total amount of money the local companies were entitled to receive from the long-distance carriers, only the method of payment. Because the amounts were so large, they required very high rates for each originating and terminating minute if the total amount was simply converted into a price per minute. The implied rates were high enough to make it profitable for large companies to build their own facilities between the customer location and the long-distance carrier's office rather than using the access facilities of the local company or for the long-distance company to build special facilities to the premises of large customers. Long-distance business calling is highly concentrated: the top 1 percent of business locations accounts for approximately 50 percent of total switched calling minutes. Consequently, the long-distance companies need only build facilities for a small fraction of customers to greatly diminish the local companies' access revenue. Such facilities would not violate the local companies' franchise rights because they are a part of interstate service rather than local telephone service. The possibility of bypass means that the local companies do not have total monopoly power and face competition in some activities if their prices are too high.[13]

The transformation of cost-sharing payments into access charges and the associated possibility of the long-distance companies bypassing those charges indicated a need for reform in the pricing structure. As inflation increased local costs and technological progress reduced long-distance costs in the years prior to the divestiture, a greater share of local costs had been assigned to the long-distance pool. This was done at the request of the state regulators, who did not want to accept blame for local price increases while federal regulators took the credit for long-distance price declines. The cost shift helped stabilize both long-distance and local costs, but it created an increasing gap between prices and costs. So long as the system was dominated by the unified AT&T controlling both long-distance and local service, the cost shifting could be viewed as primarily an accounting transaction. But with the split of the system, each company gained incentives to minimize its own costs, and the ability to maintain the system of subsidies became doubtful. The Commission proposed to reform the pricing structure by bringing both long-distance and local prices closer to their true prices in an access charge plan scheduled to become effective with the divestiture in January 1984. However, prior to the effective date of the plan, massive opposition arose to the price restructuring. Under threat of congressional action to overrule the price changes, the Commission revamped the plan to make more modest changes and to maintain the basic structure of long-distance subsidizing local service.

Another post-divestiture regulatory issue is the extent of continued regulation of AT&T's long-distance services. Although competition exists in long-distance services, AT&T remains the dominant firm, and it is the only carrier on certain routes and for specialized services such as "800 service" (toll-free calling to a business). The non-AT&T long-distance carriers have been effectively deregulated through a policy known as forbearance, in which the Commission retains jurisdiction but chooses not to exercise control over the carriers. As part of the competitive battle, the non-AT&T carriers seek stringent regulation of AT&T in order to limit its competitive responses to them, while AT&T seeks freedom from regulation. The Commission is conducting an investigation as to how much regulation of AT&T should be retained, but in the meantime every routine regulatory action has important competitive effects.

A third major issue is drawing the appropriate boundary lines around the activities of the local operating companies as technological change increases their ability to perform new services in conjunction with basic telephone service. If the boundary lines are drawn tightly, the companies are prohibited from offering new services and cannot take advantage of technological opportunities to meet the needs of their customers. If the boundary lines are drawn loosely, the companies may use their monopoly power in basic telephone service to subsidize entry into competitive services, recreating the problems of mixed competition and monopoly that the divestiture was designed to solve.

The continuing regulatory issues are an indication that the basic issue of the extent of *economies of scale* and of *economies of scope* remains uncertain. Economies of scale are increases in the efficiency of production of one particular good as the quantity increases. Economies of scope are increases in the efficiency of production of multiple goods as they are produced jointly rather than individually. If it were true that local service exhibited economies of scale but not terminal equipment or long-distance, and if it were true that there were no economies of scope among local service, long-distance service, and terminal equipment, then the divestiture would have been an ideal solution to the competitive issues in telecommunications. Those propositions seem to have been the underlying assumptions of the consent decree, but whether they are true still remains uncertain even after the divestiture has taken place.

CONCLUSION

There has been no explicit regulatory reform in telecommunications. Regulation has evolved in response to court decisions and attempts to arbitrate among competitors. Although competition has greatly increased, the total impact of regulation on the companies has not decreased. As a monopoly, AT&T had wide latitude to run its business as it saw fit subject to an overall profit constraint and various ideas of fairness to customers. Now the profit constraint and fairness to customers concepts remain, but fairness to competitors has been added as a constraint. Any change in tariff structure that might be detrimental to competitors is given rigorous scrutiny. AT&T price reductions and offerings of innovative services have been delayed or denied because of their potential adverse impact on competitors. The divested Bell Operating Companies are subject to continuing state and federal regulation as well as to new regulations resulting from restrictions on their activities contained in the consent decree.

The complex interrelated nature of the telecommunications industry makes any simply "ideologically pure" solution to the regulatory problem unsatisfactory. The terminal equipment market is a part of the industry in which competition has clearly been beneficial. A single monopoly, no matter how innovative, is ill-suited to providing a wide variety of equipment to meet specialized needs. Since the opening of the terminal equipment market to competition, there has been an explosion of telephone styles and capabilities — novelty phones, cordless phones, phones with memory, sophisticated business phone systems, and so forth. But telephones are only useful when connected to telephone lines. And telephone lines continue to exhibit natural monopoly characteristics. Total deregulation of the local telephone companies would open up the possibility of massive price increases, especially to residential consumers, before competitive alternatives would become feasible. The simple solutions of a single regulated monopoly or total deregulation either lose the benefits of competition in sectors where it is feasible or leave consumers subject to unrestricted monopoly power. But any solution combining the two approaches must solve the difficult problem of drawing boundaries between regulated and unregulated activities and policing the relationships between the sectors.

NOTES

[1] American Telephone & Telegraph, *1910 Annual Report* (Boston: Alfred Mudge & Son, 1911), p. 33.

[2] T. N. Vail, "Some Truths and Some Conclusions," speech to Vermont State Grange, December 14, 1915, AT&T Historical File, New York.

[3] J. Warren Stehman, *The Financial History of the American Telephone and Telegraph Company* (Boston: Houghton Mifflin, 1925), p. 149.

[4] *Hush-A-Phone Corporation v. U.S. and FCC*, 238 F.2d 266 at 269 (1956).

[5] *In the Matter of Use of the Carterfone Device in Message Toll Telephone Service*, 13 F.C.C. 2d 420 (1968).

[6] *Interstate and Foreign Message Toll Telephone*, 56 F.C.C. 2d 593 (1975).

[7] *Second Computer Inquiry Final Decision* 77 F.C.C. 2d 384 (1979).

[8] *Allocation of Frequencies Above 890 Megacycles*, 27 F.C.C. 359 (1959).

[9] *Microwave Communications, Inc.*, 18 F.C.C. 2d 953 at 1008, 1009 (1969).

[10] *Specialized Common Carrier Services*, 29 F.C.C. 2d 870 (1971).

[11] *MCI Telecommunications Corp. v. F.C.C.*, 561 F.2d 365 (D.C. Cir., 1977).

[12] *MCI Telecommunications Corp. v. F.C.C.*, 580 F.2d 590 (D.C. Cir., 1978).

[13] For an examination of the bypass issues, see Gerald Brock, "Bypass of the Local Exchange: A Quantitative Assessment," Federal Communications Commision, Office of Plans and Policy Working Paper 12 (September 1984).

CASE 8

Reforming OSHA Regulation of Workplace Risks

W. Kip Viscusi
Northwestern University

INTRODUCTION

The Occupational Safety and Health Administration (OSHA) has perhaps been a more persistent target of criticism than all other federal regulatory agencies. Critics have not questioned the agency's fundamental objective. Promoting worker health and safety is a laudable and widely shared objective. Rather, OSHA is generally regarded as ineffective in promoting this objective and as imposing needless costs and restrictions on American business.

This branch of the U.S. Department of Labor began operation in 1971 after the Occupational Safety and Health Act of 1970 created it so as "to assure so far as possible every working man and woman in the nation safe and healthful working conditions."[1] Since ensuring a no-risk society is clearly an unattainable goal, the initial OSHA mandate established the infeasible as the agency's mission. Nevertheless, a regulatory agency focusing on worker safety issues could serve a constructive function.

The early operations of OSHA did not, however, even begin to fulfill the agency's initial promise. OSHA was the object of widespread ridicule for standards that prescribed acceptable toilet seat shapes, the placement of exit signs, the width of handrails, and the

---

This paper is based in part on the author's more detailed analysis of OSHA, *Risk by Choice: Regulating Health and Safety in the Workplace* (Cambridge, Mass.: Harvard University Press, 1983) and "The Structure and Enforcement of Job Safety Regulation," *Law and Contemporary Problems*, 47, 1 (1986).

Introduction

proper dimensions of OSHA-approved ladders. Many of the more frivolous standards were never among the most prominent concerns in the agency's enforcement effort. Nevertheless, they did epitomize the degree to which the federal government was attempting to influence the design and operation of the workplace — matters that previously had been left to managerial discretion.

In recent years the stories of OSHA's misguided regulatory efforts have been less prominent. One no longer reads amusing anecdotes such as that concerning the OSHA inspector who penalized a firm for allowing its employees to work on a bridge without the required orange life vests even though the riverbed was dry. The comparative inattention to OSHA's recent activities does not necessarily imply that the agency should receive a clean bill of health. There has been no widely publicized reform of the agency. Moreover, unlike transportation, natural gas, oil, and airlines, there have been no legislative changes or major administrative reforms. The decrease in OSHA's prominence may be because a continuation of past policies, however ill-conceived, is simply no longer newsworthy.

This paper focuses on a general assessment of the effort to promote worker health: why we have such policies, how the initial effort failed, whether there has been any improvement in this effort, and how these policies can be reformed. Although little more than a decade old, OSHA has been the subject of a variety of proposed reform efforts.[2] That OSHA has already become a chief target of proposed regulatory reforms suggests the kinds of fundamental changes needed in the agency's initial orientation.

The past two presidential administrations promised an overhaul of OSHA policies. The Carter administration sought to provide this risk regulation effort with greater legitimacy by eliminating some of the more frivolous standards and by enforcing the sounder portions of OSHA regulations more vigorously. Under the Reagan administration the attention shifted to decreasing OSHA's confrontational character so as to foster a cooperative business-government approach to promoting workplace safety.

Although these efforts have rectified many of the more ill-conceived aspects of OSHA's initial strategy, the need for reform continues. Regulation of workplace conditions is a legitimate role for the government, but as with other regulatory policies, a balance between competing objectives should be attained. In this case the principal trade-off is between the costs imposed by the regulation and the health and safety benefits they provide. Although the suggested reforms are often quite specific in character, many of the more promising reforms have a common element in that they represent attempts to achieve such a balance.

In addition, there may be more fundamental shortcomings whereby the government policy is failing to achieve as much safety improvement as is possible for the costs imposed. In more technical terms the difficulty may be that we are not on the frontier of efficient policies (that is, those policies that provide the greatest safety for any given cost), as opposed to simply making the wrong trade-off along such a frontier. Safety could be enhanced without any extra cost through more sensible policy design. Many of the most widely publicized standards initially promulgated by OSHA fall in the category of policies dominated by less costly and more effective alternatives. As in the case of other OSHA reforms, proper application of fundamental economic principles will illuminate the nature of the policy changes required.

HOW MARKETS CAN PROMOTE SAFETY

Before instituting a government regulation it is instructive to assess how the market functions. Basically, one should inquire whether there is any inadequacy in the way in which market forces operate. Although individual life and health are clearly valuable attributes, there are many other market outcomes that are also valued by consumers and workers but are not regulated by government. Because markets that operate well will allocate resources efficiently, there should be some perceived inadequacy in the way these forces function before interfering with their operation.

To ensure that market outcomes will be efficient, a number of stringent conditions must be met. For example, the outcome of any employment decision must affect the worker and employer only, not society at large, since these broader concerns will not be reflected in the job choice. A particularly pertinent requirement is that the job choice must be the outcome of a fully rational decision. Individuals must be cognizant of the risks they face and be able to make sound decisions under uncertainty. As discussed below, these assumptions are especially likely to be violated for many important classes of risks.

Even if there is a consensus that market outcomes are not optimal, it is essential to ascertain the extent of the market failure. It is important to understand if the operation of the market is fundamentally flawed or whether there is a narrower market failure, such as an informational shortcoming that can be remedied through an information transfer effort rather than direct control of workplace conditions.

Finally, the market mechanisms will be pertinent insofar as they establish the context in which the government regulation operates. Regulations do not dictate health and safety outcomes, since it is impossible for regulators to monitor and influence the health and safety attributes of all firms. Instead, these policies simply create incentives for firms and workers to take particular actions, such as installing new ventilation equipment. Whether regulations have any impact will hinge on the strength of the incentives created by the policy and the safety incentives the market generates for firms.

Compensating Wage Differential Theory

The fundamental economic approach to worker safety was sketched by Adam Smith over two centuries ago.[3] Smith observed that workers will demand a compensating wage differential for jobs that are perceived as being risky or otherwise unpleasant. The two critical assumptions are that workers must be aware of the risk (which often may not be the case) and that they would rather be healthy (which is not a controversial assumption). These differentials in turn will establish an incentive for firms to promote safety, since doing so will lower their wage bill. In particular, these wage costs are augmented by reduced turnover costs and workers' compensation premium levels, both of which also provide incentives for safety improvements by the firm. In effect, it is primarily the risk-dollar trade-offs of the workers themselves that will determine the safety decision by the firm.

Figure 1 illustrates how these forces will influence the level of safety provided. Suppose that the health outcome involved is reduction of job-related accidents and that improvements in safety have diminishing incremental value to workers, just as additional units of other types of "economic goods" have diminishing importance. The marginal value of the safety curve in Figure 1 consequently is a downward sloping curve, since the initial increments in safety have the greatest value. The firm can provide greater levels of safety, but doing so entails additional marginal (or incremental) costs that increase as the level of safety becomes increasingly great. Some initial safety improvements can be achieved inexpensively through, for example, modification of existing machines or work practices. The addition of exhaust fans is one such measure for airborne risks. More extensive improvements could require an overhaul of the firm's technology, which would be more expensive. This marginal-cost curve consequently is increasing rather than staying flat because safety equipment differs in its relative efficacy, and the firm will choose to install the most effective equipment per unit cost first.

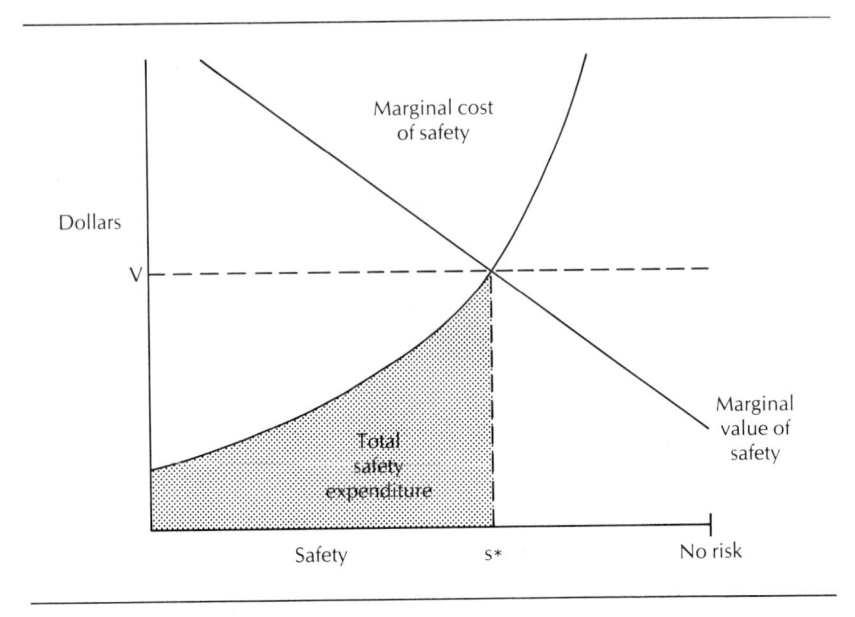

Figure 1. Determination of Market Levels of Safety

The price of safety set by worker preferences will determine where along this marginal-cost curve the firm will stop. The optimal level of safety from the standpoint of the market will be s^*. The shaded area under the marginal-cost curve will be the total safety-related expenditure by the firm. This level is short of the no-risk level of safety. At the level of safety provided, workers would have been willing to pay $\$V$ per expected accident to avoid such accidents. This additional safety is not provided because the cost to the firm for each extra accident avoided exceeds workers' valuation of the improvement: $\$V$ for any incremental increase in safety above s^*.

The level of health and safety selected will not be a no-risk level since promoting safety is costly. Almost all of our daily activities pose some risk because of the costs involved in reducing the hazards. Consumers, for example, routinely sacrifice greater crashworthiness whenever they select more compact automobiles in an effort to obtain greater fuel efficiency, since the typical small car is less crashworthy than the average full-sized car. Moreover, the order of magnitude of the risks is not too dissimilar to those that we encounter in other activities. The accident risk posed by one day of work in a coal mine (a relatively hazardous pursuit) is comparable in size to the risks of smoking 3.7 cigarettes, riding 27 miles by bicycle, eating 108 tablespoons of peanut butter, or traveling 405 miles by car.[4] Individuals trade off these and other risks against other valued attributes, such as the recreational value of cycling.

Risk Information

The first link in the compensating differential analysis is that workers must be aware of the risks they face. For example, if there is no perception of the risks, workers will demand no additional compensation to work on a hazardous job. The available evidence suggests that there is some general awareness of many of the risks workers face. Based on data from the University of Michigan Survey of Working Conditions, there is a strong correlation between the risk level in the industry and whether workers perceive their jobs as being dangerous in some respect.[5] This evidence is by no means conclusive, however, since the risk assessment question only ascertained whether workers were aware of the presence of some risk, not the degree of risk posed by the job.

A more refined test was developed by Charles O'Connor and the author in a survey of workers at four chemical plants.[6] In that study workers were asked to assess the risks of the job using a continuous scale that could be compared with published accident measures. Overall, workers believed that their jobs were almost twice as hazardous as the published accident statistics for the chemical industry suggest, which is expected in view of the degree to which health hazards, such as cancer, are not reflected in the accident data. Particularly noteworthy was that after the health hazards were excluded from consideration, the risk assessments equaled the accident rate for the chemical industry.[7]

These studies should be regarded as evidence of some reasonable perception of job risks by workers. It is unlikely that workers have completely accurate perceptions of the risks posed by their jobs. These risks are not fully known even by occupational health and safety experts.

The degree to which there will be errors in the risk assessment will not, however, be uniform across all classes of risk. As a rough generalization, one would expect safety risks (external hazards such as inadequate machine guards) to be better understood than health risks (internal risks such as excessive exposure to radiation). Safety hazards tend to be more readily visible and familiar risks, such as the chance of a worker in a sawmill losing a finger. In contrast, health hazards usually are less well understood. These risks often involve low probability events that may affect the individual decades after the exposure. These difficulties are enhanced in some instances by the absence of any clear-cut signals that a health risk is present. The odor and color of gases emitted in the workplace, for example, are not a reliable index of their potential carcinogenicity.

Compensating Differentials

In situations where workers are aware of the hazard, the riskier jobs should be expected to command a wage premium. The risk premium part of the analysis was never successfully tested until the 1970s because of the inherent difficulties in isolating the premium for risks. As John Stuart Mill observed, the most attractive jobs in society also tend to be the highest paid. This effect does not contradict the compensating differential analysis but is a consequence of the willingness to incur job risks to boost income declines as income status increases.[8] Compensating differentials do exist, but they do not outweigh the influence of other factors that drive individual income, such as worker education and job experience.

In some cases the levels of premiums for job risks are specified in labor market contracts. Because elephants are said to pose a risk to handlers whom they do not like, elephant handlers at the Philadelphia Zoo receive an additional $1,000 annually. Such explicit provisions are the exception. A more typical approach is to embed the wage level within the context of a complex job evaluation system. The firm scores the worker's job according to a variety of dimensions, such as working conditions and degree of responsibility, and it bases the worker's wage on the grade level corresponding to the overall job score.

The resulting risk premiums are then estimated by labor economists using statistical techniques that analyze the role played by different factors governing the worker's wage. The resulting wage premiums are substantial. Roughly $70 billion in wage premiums for risk is paid by the United States private sector each year,[9] above and beyond the amount that is paid in workers' compensation, which adds an additional $10 billion.

Not only is workers' compensation a much smaller part of the total risk compensation package, but it also is structured in a manner that is less effective in generating incentives for health and safety. Most firms covered by workers' compensation pay insurance premiums based on the performance of their industry group rather than on their own safety record. Higher accident rates at a firm consequently do not necessarily boost workers' compensation costs in these cases. The workers' compensation system also has been structured primarily to address accident risks, so that longer term health hazards are covered inadequately. This inadequacy stems not from an oversight in the design of workers' compensation but from the difficulty in monitoring the contribution of work experience to long-term health problems such as cancer.

An instructive measure of the rate of compensation is the amount paid per unit risk. In the case of fatalities the issue is the value of a statistical life. This value of life concept can be viewed in two equivalent ways. Consider for example 10,000 individuals, each of whom faces a risk of death of 1/10,000 — the average risk confronting a blue collar worker. Overall, there will be one expected death in this group. Suppose that they were willing to accept this risk for $200 apiece. Then the amount of money that the entire group will be compensated for the one expected death is the

$$\text{Value of life} = 10{,}000 \times \$200 = \$2 \text{ million}$$

Alternatively, one can view the value of life as being the value received per unit risk, or

$$\text{Value of life} = \frac{\$200}{1/10{,}000} = \$2 \text{ million}$$

The value of life will not be a natural constant, such as e or π. Rather one should expect different individuals to have different risk-dollar trade-offs just as they have different tastes in convertibles and television shows. This heterogeneity will be of consequence for market outcomes, because jobs in the economy are not assigned to workers on a random basis. Because of the element of choice involved, workers who place a relatively low value on life will tend to gravitate toward the higher risk jobs. They are willing to accept lower premiums per unit risk, other things being equal. The most affluent workers, who will be more likely to demand high unit levels of risk compensation, will tend to select jobs of lower risk.

These predictions are borne out in analyses of workers' implicit value of life. In a study of workers in high-risk jobs posing an annual death risk on the order of 1/1,000, Thaler and Rosen found that they received compensation associated with an implicit value of life of $600,000 (1983 prices).[10] Based on studies by Robert Smith and the author, workers in more moderate risk jobs, such as the average annual risk of 1/10,000 facing typical blue collar workers, receive compensation associated with an implicit value of life of about $3.5 million. Finally, the author's work on the heterogeneity of the value of life has yielded compensation levels as high as $7 to $10 million per life.[11]

Estimates at the high end of the value of life spectrum are probably less reliable, since the available risk data are not sufficiently refined to make fine distinctions among jobs posing low risks. Nevertheless, they are suggestive of the range of differences in individuals' value of life.

These figures represent what workers' risk-dollar trade-offs are, given their current information about the risk, not what they would be if they had full information about the risk. In addition, the calculations assume rational decision-making, whereas in practice workers may overreact to risks or they may neglect to take them into consideration. Although market behavior may not be ideal, the substantial magnitude of compensation per unit risks does suggest that there is substantial awareness of risks and their implications.

The value of life results are bolstered by analogous findings for nonfatal job injuries. These studies suggest that there is substantial compensation for job risks, when viewed both in terms of the total wage bill (6 percent of manufacturing workers' wages) and the rate of compensation per unit risk.

The level of compensation may vary by industry. One would expect that unions with a strong interest in health and safety issues would be particularly interested in securing workers hazard pay. Unions, such as that for petroleum and chemical workers, often have specialized expertise in the health and safety area and have the ability to bargain with greater expertise than workers could individually. My early research in this area suggested that unions were a substantial force in this area, but more recent work by Robert Smith and others suggests that the magnitude of the union effect on the wage-risk trade-off is sensitive to the particular set of survey data that is used.[12]

On-the-Job Experience and Worker Quit Rates

The presence of possibly inadequate worker knowledge concerning the risks remains a potential impediment to the full operation of the compensating differential mechanism. The result will not be that market mechanisms will work less effectively, although some decreased efficacy will undoubtedly occur. Rather there will also be new market forces that may be influential.

Consider a situation in which a worker starts a job without full knowledge of the potential risks.[13] After being assigned to the position he or she will be able to observe the nature of the job operations, the surrounding physical conditions, and the actions of co-workers. Similarly, during the period of work on the job the worker learns about some particular difficulties in carrying out the job tasks, and even more directly, he or she observes whether co-workers are (or have been) injured. The worker can then use these experiences to evaluate the risk potential of the job.

If the worker's risk perceptions become sufficiently unfavorable, given the wage paid, he or she can quit and move to another firm. Overall, job risks account for one-third of all manufacturing quit rates. Similarly, the periods of time that workers spend at hazardous firms before leaving are shorter than for safe firms. As a consequence, there will always tend to be more inexperienced workers in high-risk jobs, because the high turnover rates from these positions lead to frequent replacements.

The standard observation that younger and more inexperienced workers are more likely to be involved in accidents is not entirely attributable to greater riskiness of this demographic group. Rather the causality may be in the opposite direction, since new hires are more likely to be placed in the high-risk, high-turnover jobs. The firm will also have a strong incentive to avoid placing its most experienced workers in these positions, because it will lose the training investment if the worker is injured or quits.

All of the labor market responses by workers are simply variations of the compensating differential theme. If the job appears to be risky initially, the worker will require extra compensation to begin work on it. Similarly, once he or she acquires information about the risks that are present, the worker will reassess the job's attractiveness and remain with it only if the compensating differential is sufficient.

INADEQUACIES IN THE MARKET

If market operations were fully efficient, there would be no need for government regulation of health and safety. The decentralized operation of the market would be sufficient to ensure appropriate levels of the risk. Two broad classes of shortcomings limit the efficacy of market outcomes: (1) informational inadequacies and problems with individual decisions under uncertainty and (2) externalities.

Informational Problems and Irrationalities

For the compensating differential model to be fully applicable, workers must be cognizant of the risks they face and be able to make sound decisions based on this knowledge. The available evidence suggests that in many contexts workers have risk perceptions that appear plausible, but these studies in no way imply that workers are fully informed. There is a general consensus that many health risks in particular are not well understood.

With on-the-job experience, they undoubtedly will revise their perceptions of many of the risks they face. Once again, safety hazards are more likely to be treated in a reliable manner because they tend to be readily visible and to occur with much greater frequency than many health risks, which are low probability events. Thus the worker has fewer observable incidents of adverse health outcomes to use in forming his risk assessment. The long time lags involved in many health risks further impede efforts to learn about the implications of these risks through experience. A worker may get cancer two decades after job exposure to a carcinogen, but tracing the cause to the job usually is not feasible. As a rough generalization, there is probably reasonable, but not perfectly accurate perception of many safety risks and much less reliable assessment of the pertinent health risks.

Even with accurate perceptions of the risk, however, one cannot be confident that the decisions ultimately made by the workers will be ideal. Decisions under uncertainty are known to pose considerably more difficulties than decisions made in cases where the outcomes of alternative actions are known in advance.[14] These difficulties are likely to be particularly great in situations involving very low probability events that have severe outcomes after a substantial lag. The low probabilities and substantial lags make these decisions difficult to conceptualize. How averse, for example, is a worker to take a one in 20,000 risk of cancer twenty-five years from now? Because of the high stakes involved — possibly including the worker's life — the cost of mistaken choices will be high. Once again, it is likely that health hazards pose relatively greater demands on individual rationality than safety risks.

The final class of shortcomings in individual behavior relates to the degree workers can choose from a variety of alternative risk-wage combinations. For the relatively mobile, modern United States economy there seems to be substantial range of job options for almost all workers. Certainly, the classic textbook discussions of the one-company town no longer seem relevant and, even if true, would not have as great an impact in an era of interstate highways and substantial worker mobility. This mobility may be restricted during cyclical downturns when job opportunities are less plentiful, but since accidents move pro-cyclically, the net influence of adverse economic conditions is not clear cut.

Perhaps the most important constraint on individual mobility is related to the character of the employment relationship. Once on the job, individuals acquire skills specific to the particular firm as well as seniority rights and pension benefits that are typically not fully transferable. If workers had full knowledge of the risk before accepting the position, these impediments to mobility would not be consequential. The basic difficulty, however, is that workers may not have been fully cognizant of the implications of the position and will subsequently become trapped in an unattractive job situation. Available evidence for chemical workers suggests that the extent of serious job mismatches of this type is not high.

Externalities

An additional class of market inadequacies arises even if individual decisions are fully rational and ideal in all respects. Parties outside of the market transaction for the job may have a stake in the risky job insofar as there is a broader altruistic concern with individual health. This type of health-related altruism is probably of greater consequence than redistributional concerns in this context. Life and health are clearly quite special, as society has undertaken a variety of health-enhancing efforts, such as Medicare, to promote individual well-being.

The overall importance of these altruistic interests has not yet been ascertained, however. As we saw earlier, individuals' values of life are substantial, and it is not obvious that the external interests of society would boost these values substantially. Whether society's broader altruistic concerns are of great consequence in this area is an open empirical issue that merits further attention.

Fundamentally, however, there is the ethical issue of whether there exists in some instances an altruistic concern or simply an attempt by more affluent citizens to impose their own risk-dollar trade-offs on others. Until these questions can be resolved, the primary impetus for regulation of occupational hazards probably should be the shortcomings of worker decisions.

OSHA'S REGULATORY APPROACH

The general approach OSHA has taken to regulating job safety is dictated at least in part by the Occupational Safety and Health Act of 1970. This legislation authorizes OSHA to set standards and to do so in a manner that will ensure worker health and safety.[15] OSHA's enabling legislation did not, however, specify what these standards should be, what general character they should take, or how stringent they should be.

In addition, the legislation did not specify the nature of the enforcement of the standards. For example, OSHA could couple standards with a penalty for firms out of compliance, where the penalty is set at a level that could give firms some discretion as to whether compliance is desirable. For example, the penalty could be related to the health impacts on workers, and the firm could comply with the standard only if the health benefits exceeded the costs to firms. (The frequency of OSHA inspections could also influence the penalty.) In actuality, OSHA imposes an ever-escalating series of penalties on firms out of compliance; thus the standards can be viewed as rigid guidelines. Because of this binding character, the level and nature of the standards is of major consequence to firms regulated by OSHA.

Setting OSHA Standard Levels

One could characterize OSHA's general approach as that of adopting technology-based standards whose stringency is limited only by their affordability. Cost considerations enter only insofar as OSHA is concerned with shutting down affected firms. The strategy advocated by most economists is that the agency should pursue a more balanced approach that recognizes the necessity of taking into account both the costs and risk-reduction benefits in a comprehensive manner. Costs always should be a matter of concern, not simply when a firm may go out of business as a result of OSHA policies. Such a shift in emphasis need not always lead to more lenient regulations. Some very hazardous firms probably should go out of business if provision for efficient levels of safety and health will not permit them to earn a profit.

Much of the policy-oriented debate over the safety standards has concerned their stringency. Those advocating a more balanced approach note that the Occupational Safety and Health Act does not require a risk-free workplace, only one that promotes safety "as far as possible."[16] This and other qualifiers in the Act suggest that OSHA might have some leeway in being able to take costs into consideration. This view was bolstered somewhat by the U.S. Supreme Court's decision in the 1980 benzene case, in which it overturned the standard because OSHA had not shown that the reduction in risks would be "significant."[17] This significant risk criterion imposes a threshold benefit level, but it does not impose a requirement that OSHA balance benefits and costs.

Indeed, such benefit-cost tests were explicitly ruled out in the 1981 U.S. Supreme Court decision regarding the OSHA cotton dust standard.[18] The court upheld the OSHA cotton dust standard and interpreted the feasibility provisions of the Occupational Safety and Health Act as meaning "capable of being done." It is the technical possibility of compliance rather than benefit-cost trade-offs that should guide OSHA decisions.

In fact, however, in this instance OSHA had based its cotton dust standards on cost-effectiveness concerns, not simply affordability. Specifically, the standard is varied across different stages of processing because of difference in the severity of the risk in these areas and differences in the cost of reducing the risk.[19] Further reductions in the risk were clearly "capable of being done," and in fact many firms have already achieved cotton dust levels well below those specified in the standard.[20]

Clearly, technological feasibility cannot be divorced from cost considerations, since almost any risk can be reduced at sufficiently large costs. Drivers, for example, would face a lower risk of injury in an auto accident if everyone drove full-sized cars at speeds under thirty-five miles per hour. Such measures have not been undertaken because the safety benefits do not justify the increased travel time and loss in fuel efficiency. Likewise, OSHA varied the cotton dust standard because the severity of cotton dust exposures differs according to the stage of processing (since different types of fibers and dust are airborne at different stages) and because compliance costs differ.

Indeed, under the Reagan administration, OSHA now routinely calculates the costs and benefits of its proposed regulations.[21] The agency does not, however, explicitly compare these magnitudes when discussing the reasons for its policy recommendations. Inevitably, some comparisons of this type are made by OSHA, the Office of Management and Budget, and other players in the regulatory process. There would be greater likelihood of balanced policies if the Supreme Court reversed its narrow and unrealistic interpretation of OSHA's mandate or if Congress amended OSHA's legislation. In the absence of such a change, primary emphasis will continue to be placed on the level of risk reduction rather than the associated costs. Regulations sometimes may impose costs that appear to be well out of line with any reasonable values, such as almost $70 million per expected life saved by the OSHA arsenic standards.[22]

The Nature of OSHA Standards

The structure of OSHA's regulatory approach also has been overly restrictive, as the agency has adopted a narrow technology-based approach to safety regulation. Ideally, OSHA should permit firms to achieve any given level of safety in the least expensive manner possible, consistent with having well-defined regulations that are enforceable. Instead, OSHA has typically adopted uniform standards that attempt to prescribe the design of the workplace.

This orientation derives in part from the pattern set in OSHA's initial standard-setting activity.[23] Shortly after beginning operations, OSHA issued over 4,000 general industry standards for health and safety, the preponderance of which were safety related. These standards, which continue to constitute most of OSHA's safety policies, were derived from the national consensus standards of the American National Standards Institute, the National Fire Protection Association, and some existing federal standards for maritime safety. In doing so, OSHA converted a set of discretionary guidelines into a mandatory prescription for workplace design.

The upshot of this effort was to establish OSHA as a leading object of ridicule for its portable toilets for cowboys and other seemingly trivial standards. Perhaps more significant than these well-publicized OSHA horror stories was the *specification* character of the regulations. The OSHA handrail regulation specifies their required height (thirty to thirty-four inches), spacing of posts (not to exceed eight feet), thickness (at least two inches for hardwood and one and one-half inches for metal pipe), and clearance with respect to the wall or any other object (minimum of three inches).[24] Likewise, in its requirements for band guards for abrasive wheels, OSHA specifies the required thickness, the minimum diameter of rivets, and the maximum distance between the centers of rivets.[25]

In each case the specification standard approach may have imposed greater costs than equally effective alternatives. To provide guidelines for how such flexibility could be achieved, President Ford's Task Force on OSHA headed by Paul MacAvoy designed a model standard for machinery and machine guarding that indicated, for example, several alternative ways to guard a punchpress.[26] This flexibility also may enhance the safety that could be achieved through a performance-oriented approach. A performance-oriented approach would stress the need for firms to achieve a particular health and safety level through whatever means they chose rather than being required to install a particular type of technology. The present OSHA specification standards are so narrowly defined that they pertain to only 15 percent of all machines.[27] This model standard has not yet been adopted, but it provides an operational example of how OSHA could achieve greater flexibility in its regulatory approach without jeopardizing worker safety.

It is also noteworthy that the primary orientation of the standards remains in the safety area. Externally visible aspects of the workplace, such as handrail width, are given comprehensive and meticulous treatment. In contrast, only a small fraction of the carcinogens in the workplace have been addressed by OSHA standards. There are some health standards, such as those for radiation exposure, but for the most part the standards have been dominated by safety concerns.

In view of the earlier discussion of market inadequacies, this emphasis seems misplaced. Health risks rather than safety risks are handled least effectively by the market. The greatest potential gains from OSHA regulation are likely to come from addressing the dimly understood health risks that pose the most severe difficulties for worker decision-making.

Moreover, the structure of the health standards is also more likely to be conducive to more effective promotion of worker health. The health standards typically limit worker exposure rather than specifying particular technologies. For example, the cotton dust standard specifies permissible exposure limits to airborne concentrations of respirable cotton dust in different stages of processing, and it indicates the circumstances under which protective equipment must be worn. Respirators are needed during cleaning operations because of unusually high levels of cotton dust in that period. The standard does not specify how the lower levels of cotton dust are to be achieved, whether through use of exhaust fans, new machines for drawing and carding the cotton, or some other approach.

THE REFORM OF OSHA STANDARDS

The ideal economic reform of OSHA standards should consist of three components. First, there should be a shift in emphasis from safety to health. Second, there should be greater opportunities for firms to find less expensive techniques for promoting safety. Standards should consequently be more performance oriented when that is feasible. Finally, the level of the standards should be set in a more balanced fashion that attempts to recognize the health benefits to workers and the costs to firms.

Recent Regulatory Initiatives

Compared with its initial activity, OSHA's standard setting has been relatively modest in the past decade. During the Carter administration, much new regulation was stymied by the uncertainties caused by the court challenges of OSHA's legislative mandate in the cotton dust and benzene cases. The Reagan administration's emphasis has been on slowing the pace of new regulation, so that OSHA has been somewhat less active than in previous years. Nevertheless, OSHA has not been completely dormant in the standards area.

The dollar price tag of new OSHA regulations proposed from 1975–1980 is $94 to $492 billion.[28] This wide range results almost entirely from the 1978 OSHA carcinogen policy, which alone had a cost of $69 to $448 billion. This policy represented a generic approach to carcinogens; that is, it established a framework by which OSHA would set carcinogen standards, thus relieving OSHA of the task of going through the lengthy process of issuing a new regulation in each case. The overall emphasis was to regulate carcinogens with strong scientific support to a zero risk level and to set standards for other carcinogens on a case-by-case basis.

This policy does not take into account the strength of the carcinogen, the size of the affected population, or the costs of compliance. Although the prospect of a major initiative against health hazards would have been an important addition to OSHA's arsenal of safety-oriented standards, the carcinogen policy was not well designed. Under the Carter administration, OSHA never utilized this cancer policy for regulating carcinogens, and the Reagan administration rescinded the policy.

Changes in OSHA Standards

The chief legacy of the Carter administration in the area of regulatory reform was its overhaul of the safety standards. The primary emphasis was not on a general restructuring of the standards approach but on eliminating those portions of the standards that were most extraneous and ill-conceived. This emphasis was quite appropriate, in view of the importance of establishing the agency's credibility. The Assistant Secretary of Labor for Occupational Safety and

Health, Eula Bingham, eliminated or modified 928 OSHA regulations in all in October 1978.[29] In many cases these changes were only editorial and had no major substantive impact. Nevertheless, the net effect of the elimination of the "nitpicking" features of OSHA regulation was to reduce some of the harsher criticisms of the agency's regulatory approach. Because of the magnitude of OSHA's credibility problem, the importance of even cosmetic changes in the standards should not be underestimated.

The most important structural change in regulatory policy was OSHA's chemical labeling regulation, which was proposed at the end of the Carter administration.[30] By providing workers with information, this regulation represented an effort to utilize market forces to promote safety. The chief forms of information provision required were labels on the chemicals and a program for training workers in the handling of chemicals. This regulation addresses the primary source of market failure directly and, as a consequence, preserves the constructive aspects of the health-related decisions by firms and workers. In addition, the focus of the regulation is strongly oriented toward health hazards rather than safety risks.

Indeed, much of the impetus for this regulation came from the inability of direct regulatory controls to address the entire range of chemical hazards. Setting standards for all of the thousands of carcinogens in the workplace was viewed as infeasible.

In addition to addressing long-term health impacts and acute health effects (for example, skin rashes from chemical exposures), the regulation will also affect accidents from fires and explosions. These safety hazards also are likely to merit greater attention than more visible workplace characteristics, since the safety-related properties of chemicals will not be well understood in the absence of some information about the risk.

While providing an innovative approach to regulation, the chemical labeling standard is also a strongly performance-oriented regulation. Since different formats may be appropriate in different contexts, firms are permitted to design their own labeling system. This flexibility will, for example, permit the paint and coating industry to retain the labeling system that has been adopted on an industry-wide basis. This opportunity for discretion contrasts with the approach that OSHA took in its standard for radio frequency hazard warnings, which specify the sign's shape, the background color, the words and location of the warning, and the size and color of all letters.[31]

Whether the informational approach will be effective is not known. Much remains to be learned about the efficacy of such efforts and about workers' ability to process such information. The limited evidence available suggests that this strategy is promising, provided that the information represents new knowledge about the risks encountered rather than general exhortation to act safely.[32]

The chief new safety standard proposed by the Reagan administration is a set of extensive rules intended to decrease the risks associated with grain handling.[33] These hazards are often well publicized, since explosions in grain-handling facilities may lead to the deaths of dozens of workers.[34] Perhaps in part because of this publicity and the safety incentives created by the market and workers' compensation, there were no deaths from explosions in 1983.[35]

The 1984 OSHA proposal is intended to reduce this risk further by decreasing the dust levels in grain elevators, which in turn will reduce the risk of explosions. What is noteworthy about this standard is that firms are given several alternative options to decrease the dust: (1) to clean up the dust whenever it exceeds one-eighth inch; (2) to clean up the dust at least once per shift; or (3) to use pneumatic dust control equipment. This flexibility represents a major innovation in the design of OSHA safety standards. The regulation provides an opportunity for firms to select the most cost-effective option and will lead to lower compliance costs than would a uniform specification standard. OSHA's effort to utilize the advantage of a performance-oriented approach represents a significant, constructive contribution to OSHA policy development.

Overall, there has not been a dramatic change in the structure of OSHA safety standards since OSHA's initial standard-setting efforts. Some of the extraneous and more frivolous standards have been pruned; other standards have been updated to take into account technological changes; and a few new standards have been added.

Further reform in standards that have already been promulgated is expected to be minimal, since there is not a strong constituency for such changes. To the extent that more firms comply with the revisions of the OSHA standards, any impetus for relaxations or modifications of existing regulations will be diminished.

Some progress may be made with respect to future standards in the form of greater recognition of the costs of the regulations and the introduction of innovative approaches to regulation. Recent OSHA efforts, such as the chemical labeling standard and the grain-handling standard, represent significant advances in OSHA's regulatory approach. Further policies of this type should be encouraged. On balance, however, the level of activity in the standards area has not been great over the past decade, as OSHA has retained most of its original approach.

OSHA'S ENFORCEMENT STRATEGY

To design and enforce its standards, OSHA now has over 2,300 employees, ranking second behind the EPA among social regulation agencies.[36] This staff, in conjunction with the inspectors from states that choose to enforce OSHA regulations with state inspectors, come to the workplace, ascertain whether there are any violations, and penalize violators. The inspectors may return for a follow-up inspection, continuing to assess penalties until compliance is ensured.

Firms will choose to comply with OSHA standards if OSHA establishes effective financial incentives for doing so. The firm must consequently find it more attractive financially to make the safety improvements than to risk an adverse OSHA inspection. The penalties that result include fines levied by OSHA as well as possible adverse effects on the firm's reputation, which may in turn affect worker turnover or wages. To assess whether these safety incentives are strong, consider each link in the OSHA enforcement process.

Before OSHA can affect a firm's policies, it either must inspect the firm or create an effective threat of possible enforcement. OSHA undertakes four types of inspections: (1) inspections of imminent dangers, (2) inspections of fatalities and catastrophes, (3) investigations of worker complaints and referrals, and (4) programmed inspections.[37] This priority ranking has remained virtually unchanged over the past decade. Somewhat surprisingly, complaint inspections produce few violations per inspection, which suggests that disgruntled workers may be using the OSHA inspection threat as a means of harrassing the employer.[38] This pattern is unfortunate, since the role of workers and unions in promoting safety could potentially have been instrumental.

The three different eras of OSHA enforcement are reflected in the patterns shown in Table 1. The Nixon and Ford administrations established the general inspection approach, and there was little change in emphasis except for a gradual expansion in the enforcement effort. Under the Carter administration there was an attempt to eliminate some of the less productive aspects of the enforcement policy. The number of inspections and less important violations declined, and penalties for violations increased. The Reagan administration marked the start of a less confrontational approach and a more conscious inspection targeting. The biggest change was that the level of penalties assessed for OSHA violations plummeted.

Table 1. Characteristics of OSHA Enforcement

	Fiscal Year			
	1972	1973	1974	1975
Inspections (thousands)	28.9	47.6	78.1	80.9
Employees covered by inspections (millions)	—[a]	5.4	6.4	6.2
Proportion of health inspections	—[a]	0.05	0.06	0.07
Proportion of inspections with serious citations	—[a]	—[a]	0.04	0.04
Violations (thousands)	89.6	153.2	292.0	318.8
Proportion of serious violations	—[a]	—[a]	0.01	0.02
Penalties (millions of dollars)	2.1	4.2	7.0	8.2

Source: Based on calculations by the author using data from OSHA computer printouts.
[a]Data are not available or are not reliable.

Inspection Policies

The specific components of Table 1 reflect these shifts in emphasis. The total number of inspections rose steadily through fiscal year 1976, after which it dropped by one-third as a result of the Carter administration's attempt to reduce the less productive inspections. The present level of inspections of below 70,000 annually may seem substantial, but it covers very few workplaces. At this rate of inspection an enterprise would be inspected less than once every two centuries.

Since many firms are small businesses with few employees, a more accurate index of coverage is the inspection rate per worker. At present, almost three million employees are covered annually by OSHA inspections. This figure represents the number of workers at sites covered by inspections, not the number of workers whose particular job conditions were analyzed. Yet, even this generous estimate of OSHA coverage does not suggest a large-scale inspection effort, since a worker at a site covered by an OSHA inspection will see an inspector only once every thirty-four years. Moreover, there has been a substantial drop in the rate of coverage of employees.

The drop in employee coverage may also reflect a failure of OSHA to target large firms sufficiently. During its early operations, OSHA was the object of criticism for focusing on small firms where few workers could be protected as a result of OSHA inspections.[39] This misallocation of resources diminished somewhat, as OSHA be-

				Fiscal Year			
1976	1977	1978	1979	1980	1981	1982	1983
90.3	59.9	57.2	57.9	63.4	57.0	61.2	68.9
8.1	5.3	4.5	4.3	3.7	2.7	2.2	2.9
0.08	0.15	0.19	0.19	0.19	0.19	0.15	0.15
0.07	0.19	0.26	0.29	0.31	0.29	0.21	0.22
380.3	181.9	134.5	128.5	132.4	111.4	97.1	111.7
0.02	0.11	0.25	0.29	0.34	0.29	0.23	0.38
12.4	11.6	19.9	23.0	25.5	10.8	5.6	6.4

gan to cite an equal number of violations per hour of inspection time in small firms as in large firms.[40] Since more workers are affected per violation in large firms than small firms, this shift toward larger firms was still not sufficient. Under the Reagan administration the low level of employees covered by inspections suggests the need to continue boosting the coverage of large firms.

Two aspects of inspections that reflect desirable changes in emphasis pertain to the emphasis on health rather than safety and the emphasis on serious violations. Health violations merit relatively more attention, since there are greater inadequacies in the way these risks are treated. Safety risks are often well known to workers and generate compensating wage differentials, higher quit rates, and larger workers' compensation premiums — all of which establish incentives for firms to promote safety. In contrast, health hazards are less well understood and, because of difficulties in monitoring causality, are not covered as effectively by workers' compensation.

The role of health inspections doubled under the Carter administration, in part because the decline in overall inspections in fiscal year 1977 primarily represented a drop in safety inspections. The pattern through fiscal year 1981 is one of a gradual rise in the absolute number of health inspections. This increase was reversed under Reagan, not so much because of a conscious decision to abandon the health area but because of the shift toward construction inspections, which are primarily safety related.

Ideally, inspections also should identify serious violations rather than less consequential threats to worker safety. This emphasis on serious violations escalated considerably under the Carter administration, as almost one-third of all inspections began to generate serious violations. The frequency of serious violations under the Reagan administration is roughly the same as under the Carter administration.

Upon entering the workplace the OSHA inspector attempts to identify violations of OSHA standards for which he will assess penalties. In determining whether or not a firm is in compliance an OSHA inspector cannot consider costs of meeting the standard, only technical feasibility. More specifically, it is "the existence of general technical knowledge" that guides the compliance judgment.[42]

In fiscal year 1977, when OSHA eliminated less important inspections and citations for trivial violations, there was a dramatic drop in the number of OSHA violations. Thereafter there has been a gradual and steady decline in the number of violations, with an additional small downward shift under Reagan in fiscal year 1981–1983. At present, each inspection results in just under two violations of OSHA standards. A welcome change has been the emphasis upon violations for serious threats to worker health which, as the data in Table 1 suggest, now include over one-third of all standards violations.

OSHA Penalties

The ultimate determinant of the financial impact of an OSHA inspection is the amount of penalties that are assessed for noncompliance. Notwithstanding the widespread notoriety of the enforcement effort, these penalty levels have always been inconsequential. Annual penalties have always been below $26 million and are now down to $6 million.

One change in the penalty structure occurred in the reforms of fiscal year 1977 when, at the insistence of Congress, OSHA eliminated penalties for firms with fewer than ten nonserious violations.[43] The overall level of penalties, however, increased under the Carter administration to more than double its earlier level.

Under President Reagan OSHA has adopted a less confrontational approach in which penalties are well below their earlier levels. A particularly noteworthy change is that firms can obtain reductions in the assessed penalties by up to 30 percent if they make a serious effort to comply with the standards.[44]

The resulting financial incentives for safety are not great. Penalties now average $57 per violation, and total OSHA penalties are just over $6 million. In contrast, higher worker wages generated by job risks are $70 billion, and workers' compensation premiums are in excess of $10 billion.[45] OSHA enforcement efforts represent at best a modest addition to policies intended to promote workplace safety. These penalties are also dwarfed by the anticipated costs of compliance.

The level of the OSHA enforcement has declined by most measures of intensity, and this has been accompanied by a fundamental change in its character. Because of the reduction in penalties for firms that remedy OSHA violations, there is little threat from a random OSHA inspection. A firm need do little to promote safety, but simply await the OSHA inspector. The firm will avoid correcting safety problems that the inspector may not identify, and it will face few penalties if it makes the suggested changes. The elimination of the expected losses from inspections suggest that OSHA will have little impact on the great majority of firms that are not inspected, since inspections now have little deterrence value. Since the expected penalties have always been quite low, this loss may not be significant, however.

Enforcement Targeting

In addition to changes in the level of OSHA enforcement, there have also been shifts in the focus of the enforcement effort. Perhaps the most controversial recent change in OSHA enforcement policies was the introduction of records check inspections in October 1981. In these programmed safety inspections the OSHA inspector first examines the firm's lost workday accident rate for the past two years (three years for very small firms).[46] If this rate is below the most recently available national manufacturing lost workday rate, the firm is not formally inspected. For example, a firm inspected in 1986 would have available its 1984 and 1985 lost workday accident rates for comparison with the 1984 manufacturing rate, since there is a two-year lag in publishing the Bureau of Labor Statistics data. Records check inspections now constitute one-seventh of all OSHA inspections.

Ideally, OSHA should target riskier firms. Inspecting these outliers provides greater opportunities for safety gains. One might expect that OSHA would simply examine the injury reports submitted by the firm each year to the Bureau of Labor Statistics and use this information to target the inspections. In what appears to be a parochial dispute within the U.S. Department of Labor, the Bureau of Labor Statistics has refused to give OSHA access to the individual firm data on the grounds that doing so would undermine the confidentiality of the data, possibly tainting their quality. Since the Internal Revenue Service uses data submitted by taxpayers to enforce tax policies, and federal wage and price control efforts have elicited similar information to enforce these income policies, it would not be unprecedented to use such risk data for purposes of enforcement. The present practice of in effect gathering the data manually under the guise of a records check represents a highly inefficient means of acquiring pivotal information regarding accident rates.

Once the risk information has been acquired, it is clearly desirable to use the data to target OSHA inspections. The present procedure is an overly simplistic approach to doing so, however. Ideally, one would like to identify the risky outliers from the standpoint of what is achievable within a particular context, based on the costs of compliance for that industry. OSHA's procedure of targeting firms based on whether their record is better than the national manufacturing average does not incorporate this heterogeneity in the costs of promoting safety. A sawmill with an accident rate above the national manufacturing average may have a very safe technology for that industry, whereas a garment manufacturer with an injury rate just below the manufacturing average may be a high-risk outlier for that industry.

It is instructive to examine a performance measure of the efficacy of inspections to assess whether the increase in targeting has been beneficial. In the case of both safety and health inspections the citation rate per inspection has risen to levels that are only exceeded by the early OSHA years when trivial violations were often cited. Improved inspection targeting may have led to as much as a 50 percent increase in the citation rate per inspection.

The changing character of the OSHA enforcement effort is exemplified as well by the change in the mix of violations cited by OSHA inspectors. Although the OSHA standards have not changed dramatically over the past decade, the role of different violation categories has undergone many significant modifications. In OSHA's initial years violations for walking and working surfaces (for example, misplaced exit signs) constituted about one-fifth of all violations. Many of these violations were for less important risks, some of which were readily visible to workers as well. The roughly 50 percent drop in this category suggests that OSHA's resources have been redirected from a less profitable area.

Somewhat surprisingly, the other chief violations category — machinery and machine guarding — has exhibited an increase in violations: over one-third of all violations are in this group. Since the same standards have been enforced by OSHA for over a decade, the continued high violation rate appears to reflect a lack of compliance with OSHA standards. In contrast, there has been a dramatic improvement in electrical hazard violations.

The two categories that displayed the greatest relative increases are health related. The role of health and environmental control (for example, noise, ventilation, and radiation) has risen to 8 percent, and violations for toxic and hazardous substances (for example, asbestos and coke oven emissions) now include a similar amount. Although some of these increases are the result of an increase in the number of health standards, there has been a noteworthy upward shift in the role of health violations. OSHA enforcement policies remain primarily safety related, but health hazards no longer constitute a nontrivial portion of the enforcement effort.

THE IMPACT OF OSHA ENFORCEMENT ON WORKER SAFETY

Firms will choose to make the necessary investments in health and safety if the OSHA enforcement policy in conjunction with market incentives for safety makes it in the firm's financial self-interest to do so. More specifically, a firm will comply with an OSHA regulation if

$$\frac{\text{Expected costs}}{\text{of compliance}} = \frac{\text{Probability}}{\text{inspection}} \times \frac{\text{Expected No.}}{\text{of violations}} \times \frac{\text{Average}}{\text{penalty per}}$$
$$\text{per inspection} \quad \text{violation}$$

As discussed, the three links in establishing these incentives — inspections, violations, and penalties — are all relatively weak. A firm has less than one chance in 200 of being inspected in any given year. If inspected, it expects to be found guilty of less than two violations of the standards, and for each violation the average penalty is under $60. Overall, the financial cost per worker is only 57 cents. The cost of continued noncompliance is, of course, potentially greater. In contrast, market forces through compensating differentials in combination with workers' compensation premiums impose costs in excess of $800 per worker. Quite simply, OSHA's enforcement effort is too modest to create truly effective financial incentives for safety.

Even if these incentives were strong, not all risks could be eliminated. Many accidents stem from aspects of the work process other than the specific technological characteristics regulated by OSHA. That most workplace risks have not been readily amenable to the influence of OSHA regulations is in stark contrast to the optimistic projections of the framers of OSHA's legislative mandate, who anticipated a 50 percent drop in workplace risks.[47]

The chief contributing factor relates to worker actions. Although the estimates of the role of the worker in causing accidents vary, in part because of the difficulty in assigning accidents caused jointly by worker actions and technological deficiencies, it is clear that worker actions play a substantial role. OSHA found that over half of all fatal accidents on oil/gas well drilling rigs were caused by poor operating procedures,[48] and worker actions also have been found to be a major contributor to 63 percent of the National Safety Council's accident measure,[49] 45 percent of Wisconsin workers' compensation cases,[50] and the majority of accidents among deep sea divers in the North Sea.[51]

Recent studies reinforce the view that at best OSHA regulations could have a significant but not dramatic effect on workplace safety. One recent statistical analysis estimated that if there were full compliance with OSHA standards, workplace accidents would drop by just under 10 percent.[52] A recent detailed analysis of workplace accidents in California presented somewhat more optimistic conclusions. At most 50 percent of all fatal accidents were contributed to by violations of OSHA standards that potentially could have been detected by an OSHA inspector visiting the day before the accident.[53]

Injury Trends

Because of these limitations and the weakness of the OSHA enforcement effort, it is not surprising that OSHA has no substantial impact on workplace safety. Table 2 summarizes the injury rate trends for the 1972–1983 period for both the manufacturing industry and the entire private sector. The two risk measures are the overall workplace injury rate and the rate for cases that involved at least one lost workday. During the initial years of OSHA operations, firms tended to overreport injuries because they had to adapt to a new reporting system. Nevertheless, the overall trend is clearly downward in the case of overall injuries. Such a decline is not unexpected, since worker accident rates have been declining by about 2 percent annually over the past half century.[54]

The pattern exhibited by lost workday accident rates is more erratic. These more serious accidents increased throughout the 1970s, after which they have declined. Although some observers have pointed to the recent declines as evidence of OSHA's effectiveness, much of the decline is no doubt caused by cyclical factors. The years 1981–1982 were periods of escalating unemployment, as total civilian

Table 2. Injury Rate Trends, 1972–1981

	All Manufacturing		All Private Sector	
Year	Overall Injury Rate (Incidence Rates per 100 Full-Time Workers)	Lost Workday Injury Rate	Overall Injury Rate (Incidence Rates per 100 Full-Time Workers)	Lost Workday Rate
1972	15.6[a]	4.2[a]	10.9[a]	3.3
1973	15.3	4.5	11.0	3.4
1974	14.6	4.7	10.4	3.5
1975	13.0	4.5	9.1	3.3
1976	13.2	4.8	9.2	3.5
1977	13.1	5.1	9.3	3.8
1978	13.2	5.6	9.4	4.1
1979	13.3	5.9	9.5	4.3
1980	12.2	5.4	8.7	4.0
1981	11.5	5.1	8.3[b]	3.8
1982	10.2	4.4	7.7[b]	3.5
1983	9.7	4.2	7.5	3.4

Sources: Data for 1972–1981 from U.S. Department of Labor, Bureau of Labor Statistics, *Handbook of Labor Statistics,* Bulletin 2175, October 1983; data for 1982 from "Occupational Injuries and Illnesses 1982" microfiche, U.S. Department of Labor, 83-471, released November 4, 1983; and data for 1983 from U.S. Department of Labor, Bureau of Labor Statistics, press release, November 14, 1984.

[a] Data for agricultural production, all of mining except oil and gas extraction, and railroads were not included in 1972 estimates.

[b] Excludes firms with fewer than eleven employees.

unemployment rates climbed to 7.5 percent and then to 9.5 percent.[55] Since workplace accidents are less frequent during cyclical downturns, the recent declines may result in part from shifts in macroeconomic policy.

To distinguish the impact of OSHA from that of cyclical factors and other determinants of health and safety, one can undertake econometric studies that control for these influences. The general consensus of these studies is that there is no evidence of a substantial impact in the 1970s. The author analyzed the 1972–1975 period and failed to find any significant OSHA impact.[56] Smith found a drop in the lost workday rate at firms inspected in 1973, but not for firms inspected in 1974.[57] A replication of Smith's analysis by McCaffrey for the 1976–1978 period failed to yield any significant effects on manufacturing firms.[58] Similarly, Bartel and Thomas's analysis of the

1974–1978 experience did not reveal any significant OSHA impacts.[59] Mendeloff's analysis of the California workers' compensation records from 1947–1974 likewise produced mixed results, as some risk levels rose and others declined.[60] The strongest published evidence of OSHA's efficacy is by Cooke and Gautschi, who found a significant drop in lost workdays due to accidents in Maine manufacturing firms from 1970–1976.[61]

Preliminary estimates for the 1973–1982 period suggest that there may have been a modest decline in the rate of accidents as a result of OSHA enforcement.[62] Such an effect is suggestive of a possible increase in the efficacy of OSHA's activities. What was particularly striking is that the OSHA policy variable that seemed most instrumental was the rate of OSHA inspections rather than the penalty level. The degree of OSHA's presence in the workplace and the threat of penalties for continued noncompliance appear to be the fundamental determinants of OSHA's impact.

The possibility of a favorable impact of OSHA on workplace conditions is also borne out in a recent retrospective assessment of the OSHA cotton dust standard.[63] Although compliance with this 1978 standard was not required until 1984, by the end of 1982 the majority of the exposed workers were in work situations in compliance with OSHA standards. Firms' investments in cotton dust controls from 1978–1982 will lead to an annual reduction of about 6,000 cases of byssinosis (a lung disease) annually. The standard remains controversial, however, because it is a costly means for promoting worker health. For example, the cost per case year of total disability prevented will be $1.2 million.

In addition, there remain a number of advocates of the greater use of more performance-oriented alternatives to control cotton dust.[64] One possible policy alternative is to require the use of lightweight cotton dust masks for low to moderate cotton dust levels, which would produce the same benefits as engineering controls at negligible cost. Since byssinosis is a progressive disease that moves through a series of grades and is reversible in its early stages, disposable masks could be coupled with a worker rotation policy. Only for severe cotton dust levels would respirators or engineering controls be required. To date, protective equipment alternatives have not been treated as a viable policy option because of union opposition to such efforts.

The available empirical results for the overall OSHA impact and in the cotton dust case suggest that OSHA enforcement efforts may be beginning to enhance workplace safety. An improvement over the early OSHA experience should be expected, as the standards have been refined and there is more systematic targeting of the inspection effort. The overall impact remains relatively modest, however, as job risks continue to be largely dictated by forces other than government regulation.

AGENDA FOR POLICY REFORM

Since OSHA's performance continues to fall short of its potential, there remains a continued need for reform of its efforts. Even with these reforms, OSHA will not be the dominant force influencing worker safety. The role of the market in determining safety will continue to be instrumental. OSHA can augment the existing forces for safety, but even full compliance with all current OSHA regulations or those likely to be promulgated will not markedly reduce workplace risks. The no-risk society that some might envision as OSHA's ultimate goal is simply unattainable.

Nevertheless, constructive reform of OSHA could enable this agency to better foster the interests of workers and at the same time diminish the associated burden on society. A number of specific reforms have been advocated in the literature. Rather than review each of these proposals, the following focuses on changes for which there is likely to be a broad consensus about the nature of OSHA's inadequacy or the proposed remedy.

The first area where reform is needed is the area of emphasis. In over a decade of regulation OSHA policies have exhibited a slight shift toward health but have remained largely safety oriented. The emphasis of both the structure of new regulations and OSHA enforcement has continued to be predominantly in the safety area. This emphasis is misplaced, since market forces are best equipped to address safety risks through compensating differentials and related mechanisms. In addition, the incentives created by workers' compensation premiums already augment to some extent the market incentives for safety. Health hazards are handled less adequately by both the market and workers' compensation. Moreover, the coupling of substantial uncertainties with low probability events involving potentially catastrophic outcomes makes health risks a promising target for governmental regulation.

The second class of reforms is the need to ensure that we are "on the frontier" of efficient policies, that is, that we are achieving as much health and safety improvement as possible for the costs imposed. Much of the adverse reaction to OSHA's initial wave of regulations of toilet seat shapes and the like stemmed largely from the belief that the regulatory mechanisms had not been well chosen. Much more beneficial improvements in safety and health could have been achieved if OSHA had focused its efforts on issues of more consequence.

Some of the most extraneous features of OSHA policy have been pruned, but there is continued need to find ways to promote safety at less cost. The use of performance standards rather than narrowly defined specification standards could, for example, enable firms to select the cheapest means of achieving the health and safety objective. Such flexibility would reduce compliance costs and increase the incentive of firms to develop innovative technologies to foster health and safety. Moreover, if structured appropriately, as in the grain dust standard, a performance standard need not greatly increase firms' uncertainty regarding whether they are in compliance.

The final reform target is the need for striking a more explicit balance between the health improvements and the costs imposed on society. Labor market estimates of the value of life are now being used to provide guidance in terms of the appropriate trade-off. Such exercises remain controversial, but the need for making some kinds of trade-offs is apparent. It is unlikely that economic research will soon be able to pinpoint the compensatory value of a case of cancer, decreased lung function capacity, or a partial work disability. Nevertheless, if policymakers viewed regulatory alternatives in light of the cost per health benefit achieved, they would at least confront explicitly the nature of the trade-offs and ideally would pursue only those policies that they judged to be in society's best interest.

Although reforming OSHA's regulatory strategy remains a major item on any agenda of important regulatory reforms, it would be an oversimplification to say that OSHA has not improved its efforts over the past decade. The agency has introduced several promising new regulations, has eliminated some of the worst initial regulations, and has better targeted enforcement efforts than they once did.

The future OSHA policies no doubt will continue to exhibit the need for reflecting the three classes of reform elements suggested above, since they are at the heart of any regulatory strategy for workplace health and safety. As a result, complete regulatory reform will never be achieved with the same finality as economic regulation, where, for example, deregulation has transformed the airline industry into a more strictly competitive situation. The need in the health and safety area is for better regulation, not deregulation, and opportunities for improvement will always remain.

NOTES

¹Section 26 of the Occupational Safety and Health Act of 1970, 29 U.S.C. 651 (1976).

²The precursor to this volume included detailed analysis of the first decade of OSHA by Albert Nichols and Richard Zeckhauser, "OSHA after a Decade: A Time for Reason," in Leonard Weiss and Michael Klass (eds.), *Case Studies in Regulation: Revolution and Reform,* (Boston: Little, Brown & Company, 1981), pp. 202–234. Earlier critiques of OSHA's efforts include Walter Oi, "On Evaluating the Effectiveness of the OSHA Inspection Program," unpublished manuscript, University of Rochester, 1975; Robert S. Smith, *The Occupational Safety and Health Act: Its Goals and Achievements* (Washington, D.C.: American Enterprise Institute, 1976); John Mendeloff, *Regulating Safety: An Economic and Political Analysis of Occupational Safety and Health Policy* (Cambridge, Mass.: The MIT Press, 1979); and Lawrence Bacow, *Bargaining for Job Safety and Health* (Cambridge, Mass.: The MIT Press, 1980). My own proposals are detailed in W. Kip Viscusi, *Risk by Choice: Regulating Health and Safety in the Workplace* (Cambridge, Mass.: Harvard University Press, 1983).

³Adam Smith, *The Wealth of Nations* (New York: Modern Library, 1776, reprinted 1937).

⁴These calculations were made by the author using data from Richard Wilson, "Analyzing the Daily Risks of Life," *Technology Review,* 81, 4 (1979), 40–46.

⁵W. Kip Viscusi, *Employment Hazards: An Investigation of Market Performance* (Cambridge, Mass.: Harvard University Press, 1979).

⁶W. Kip Viscusi and Charles O'Connor, "Adaptive Responses to Chemical Labeling: Are Workers Bayesian Decision Makers?" *American Economic Review,* 74, 5 (1984), 942–956.

⁷The health risks were in effect excluded by informing one subsample of the workers that the chemicals with which they worked would be replaced by sodium bicarbonate (household baking soda).

⁸The theoretical and empirical basis for the role of wealth effects is provided in Viscusi, note 5.

⁹See Viscusi, note 2.

¹⁰See Richard Thaler and Sherwin Rosen, "The Value of Saving a Life: Evidence from the Labor Market," in N. Terleckyj (ed.), *Household Production and Consumption* (New York: Columbia University Press, 1976).

¹¹A 3.6 million estimate is the midpoint of the range in Viscusi, note 5. An earlier estimate of $3.4 million was obtained by Smith, note 2, using 1973 data. He also estimated a value of life figure of over $7 million using 1967 data. Lower estimates than these were obtained by Charles Brown, "Equalizing Differences in the Labor Market," *Quarterly Journal of Economics,* 94, 1 (1980), 113–134. Higher estimates were obtained by Craig Olson, "An Analysis of Wage Differentials Received by Workers on Dangerous Jobs," *Journal of Human Resources,* 16, 2 (1981), 167–185. For a discussion of heterogeneity in the value of life, see Viscusi, note 2. This analysis has been replicated success-

fully using more recent data by J. Paul Leigh, "Estimates of the Value of Accident Avoidance at the Job Depends on the Concavity of the Equalizing Differences Curve," *Quarterly Review of Economics and Business* (in press).

[12] See Viscusi, note 5; William Dickens, "Differences Between Risk Premiums in Union and Nonunion Wages and the Case for Occupational Safety Regulations," *American Economic Review*, 74 (1984); and Alan Dillingham and Robert S. Smith, "Union Effects on the Valuation of Fatal Risk," *IRRA Proceedings* (1984).

[13] The subsequent discussion of worker experience and quit behavior is based on Viscusi, note 5.

[14] For a diverse set of essays on the empirical aspects of decisions under uncertainty, see Daniel Kahneman, Paul Slovic, and Amos Tversky (eds.), *Judgment and Uncertainty: Heuristics and Biases* (Cambridge, Mass.: Cambridge University Press, 1982).

[15] Section 26 of U.S.C. 651 (1976).

[16] Section 3b, part 7 of 29 U.S.C. 651 (1976).

[17] *Industrial Union Department, AFL-CIO v. American Petroleum Institute*, 448 U.S. 607 (1980).

[18] *American Textile Manufacturers Institute v. Donovan*, 452 U.S. 490 (1981).

[19] See Viscusi, note 2, pp. 124–126.

[20] Centaur Associates, *Technical and Economic Analysis of Regulating Occupational Exposure to Cotton Dust*, report Prepared for the Occupational Safety and Health Administration, 1983, pp. 1–4.

[21] See, for example, the proposed rulemaking for grain-handling facilities, *Federal Register*, 49, 4 (January 6, 1984), 1004–1007.

[22] Viscusi, note 2, p. 124.

[23] For a more detailed discussion of the development of OSHA, see Zeckhauser and Nichols, note 2; Laurence Bacow, note 2; Robert S. Smith, note 2; John Mendeloff, note 2; and Viscusi, note 2.

[24] 29 CFR Part 1910.23.

[25] 29 CFR Part 1910.215.

[26] Paul MacAvoy (ed.), *OSHA Safety Regulation: Report of the Presidential Task Force* (Washington, D.C.: American Enterprise Institute, 1977).

[27] *Ibid*, preface.

[28] See Viscusi, note 2, p. 144.

[29] These changes are discussed in the unpublished briefing notes prepared for OSHA officials. See Viscusi, note 2, p. 11.

[30] *Federal Register*, 48, 228 (November 28, 1983), 43280.

[31] 29 CFR 1910.96.

[32] W. Kip Viscusi and Charles O'Connor, "Adaptive Responses to Chemical Labeling: Are Workers Bayesian Decision Makers?" *American Economic Review*, 74, 5 (1984), 942–956.

[33] *Federal Register*, 29, 4 (January 6, 1984), 996–1008.

[34] This prominence often is reflected in the academic literature as well. See the opening paragraph of Bacow, note 11, p. 3.

[35] Office of Management and Budget, Executive Office of the President, OSHA's Proposed Standards for Grain Handling Facilities, April, 1984, p. 17.

Because of the random nature of major explosions, however, one should not conclude that the risk has been eliminated.

[36] Occupational Safety and Health Administration, "History of Appropriations and Positions," internal OSHA report, 1984.

[37] OSHA, *Field Operations Manual* (January 27, 1984) II–3.

[38] U.S. Department of Labor, Assistant Secretary for Policy Evaluation, and Research, *Compliance with Standards, Abatement of Violations, and Effectiveness of OSHA Safety Inspections*, Technical Analysis Paper No. 62, 1980.

[39] Walter Oi, "On Evaluating the Effectiveness of the OSHA Inspection Program," working paper, University of Rochester, 1975.

[40] U.S. Department of Labor, note 38.

[41] *Ibid.*

[42] OSHA, *Industrial Hygiene Field Operations Manual*, 6 (1980), I–10, I–11.

[43] This change was mandated by a rider to the fiscal year 1977 OSHA appropriations bill.

[44] OSHA, note 42, pp. VI–10, VI–11.

[45] Viscusi, note 2.

[46] OSHA, *Field Operations Manual* (January 27, 1984) II–15, III–26.

[47] See Nichols and Zeckhauser, note 2, p. 202.

[48] OSHA, *Selected Occupational Fatalities Related to Oil/Gas Well Drilling Rigs as Found in Reports of OSHA Fatality/Catastrophe Investigations* (Washington, D.C.: U.S. Department of Labor, 1980).

[49] National Commission on State Workmen's Compensation Laws, *Compendium on Workmen's Compensation* (Washington, D.C.: U.S. Government Printing Office, 1973), pp. 287–288.

[50] Walter Oi, An Essay on Workmen's Compensation and Industrial Safety, in *Supplemental Studies for the National Commission on State Workmen's Compensation Laws* (Washington, D.C.: U.S. Government Printing Office, 1973).

[51] U.S. Council on Wage and Price Stability, *Comments on the Proposed OSHA Deep Sea Divers Standard* (1977).

[52] Ann Bartel and Lacy Thomas, "Direct and Indirect Effects of Regulation: A New Look at OSHA's Impact," working paper, Columbia University Graduate School of Business, 1983.

[53] John Mendeloff, The Role of OSHA Violations in Serious Workplace Accidents, *Journal of Occupational Medicine* (1984).

[54] See Viscusi, note 2, Chap. 2.

[55] Council of Economic Advisors, *Economic Report of the President* (Washington, D.C.: U.S. Government Printing Office, 1984), p. 255.

[56] W. Kip Viscusi, "The Impact of Occupational Safety and Health Regulation," *Bell Journal of Economics*, 10, 1 (1979), 117–140.

[57] Robert S. Smith, "The Impact of OSHA Inspections on Manufacturing Injury Rates," *Journal of Human Resources*, 14 (1979), 145–170.

[58] David McCaffrey, "An Assessment of OSHA's Recent Effects on Injury Rates," *Journal of Human Resources*, 18, 1 (1983), 131–146.

[59] Ann Bartel and Lacy Thomas, "Direct and Indirect Effects of OSHA Regulation," *Journal of Law and Economics* (1985).

[60] John Mendeloff, *Regulating Safety: An Economic and Political Analysis of Occupational Safety and Health Policy* (Cambridge, Mass.: The MIT Press, 1979).

[61] William Cooke and Frederick Gautschi, "OSHA, Plant Safety Programs, and Injury Reduction," *Industrial Relations,* 20, 3 (1981), 245–257.

[62] W. Kip Viscusi, "The Impact of Occupational Safety and Health Regulation, 1973–1982," working paper, Duke Center for Study of Business Regulation, 1985.

[63] W. Kip Viscusi, "Cotton Dust Regulation: An OSHA Success Story?" *Journal of Policy Analysis and Management,* 4, 3 (1985).

[64] *Ibid.* Also see John Morrall, "Cotton Dust: An Economist's View," in R. Crandall and L. Lave (eds.), *The Scientific Basis of Health and Safety Regulation* (Washington, D.C.: The Brookings Institution, 1981), pp. 93–108.

CASE 9

Uncommon Sense: The Program to Reform Pollution Control Policy

T. H. Tietenberg
Colby College

INTRODUCTION

As anyone who has tried it knows, regulatory reform is easier said than done. Reform concepts that appear so disarmingly simple in the abstract world of theory, turn out to be distressingly complex when applied. Regulations that, from a distance, seem so inherently unsupportable, upon closer inspection are discovered to have significant bases of support among various special interest groups. Since the status quo is often characterized by inertia, many promising ideas end up strewn along the wayside.

Hailed by Senator Pete Domenici (R-New Mexico) as "the one bright idea that has emerged in the 1980s," the emissions trading program initiated by the Environmental Protection Agency (EPA) is a particularly interesting example of a survivor. Prior to the inception of this program, all attempts to use policy instruments based upon economic incentives as a means of controlling pollution at the national level had been decisively rejected. The emissions trading program not only was able to overcome this traditionally powerful resistance within Congress (and even within some offices in EPA) to become a centerpiece in air pollution control policy, but it has now made limited inroads in water pollution control policy as well.

In this paper the impact of this particular reform on pollution control policy is assessed. The analysis begins with a brief review of the case for environmental regulation. This is followed by a description of the regulatory framework for stationary source air and water pollution prior to the reform and a history of the reform process as it has evolved. The final section evaluates the success and failures of this important regulatory innovation.

Markets, Property Rights, and the Environment

The manner in which producers and consumers use environmental resources depends on the property rights governing those resources. In economics "property rights" refer to a bundle of entitlements defining the owner's rights, privileges, and limitations for use of the resource. By examining such entitlements and how they are used, a better understanding can be gained of how environmental problems arise from government and market allocations.

The structure of property rights that could produce efficient allocations in a well-functioning market economy can be described in simple terms. An efficient property right structure has four main characteristics:

1. *Universality:* All resources should be privately owned and all entitlements should be completely specified.

2. *Exclusivity:* All benefits and costs accrued using the resources should accrue to the owner, either directly or indirectly by sale to others.

3. *Transferability:* All property rights should be transferable from one owner to another in a voluntary exchange.

4. *Enforceability:* Property rights should be secure from involuntary seizure or encroachment by others.

An owner of a resource with a well-defined right (one exhibiting these four characteristics) has a powerful incentive to use that resource efficiently because a decline in the value of that resource represents a personal loss. A farmer, for example, has an incentive to fertilize and irrigate his land because the resulting increased production raises his income level. Similarly, he has an incentive to rotate crops when that raises the productivity of his land.

The role of these attributes can be illustrated by showing the consequences that can result when they are not present. When resources are not private property, they become common property that can be exploited on a first come, first served basis. Common property resources (such as air and water) can become overexploited under conditions of scarcity. In the context of pollution control in particular, the air and water would be used excessively as repositories for the dumping of waste.

Exclusivity, transferability, and enforceability are all attributes that serve to stimulate investment in the resource and to preserve its value. With exclusivity, all investments are protected, since the fruits of those investments will accrue exclusively to the investor. Transferability guarantees that the resource is not excessively depreciated, because any such depreciation would lower the value received should the resouce be sold. It also ensures that the resource would be used in its highest valued application. Enforceability simply means that the property right is clearly defined and cannot be involuntarily taken away from the owner.

The Case for Regulation

The economic system does not always sustain efficient allocations, however, and environmental problems represent one important class of circumstances when it may not. Consider a concrete example. Suppose two firms are located by a river. Since the river is a common property resource, neither user has exclusive control over it. Thus both the universality and exclusivity conditions are violated.

Suppose the first firm produces steel, while the second, somewhat downstream, operates a resort hotel. Both use the river, though in different ways. The steel firm uses it as a receptacle for its waste, while the hotel uses it to attract customers seeking water recreation — swimming, sailing, and water skiing. If there two facilities are operated by different owners, an efficient use of the water is not likely to result. Because the steel plant does not bear the cost of reduced business at the resort resulting from waste being dumped into the river, it is not sensitive to that cost in its decision-making. As a result, it dumps too much waste into the river and an efficient allocation of the river is not attained.

This situation is referred to as an externality. An *externality* exists whenever the welfare of some agent, either a firm or household, depends directly not only on its activities but also on activities under the control of some other agent as well. In the example the increased waste in the river imposed an external cost on the resort, a cost the steel firm could not be counted upon to consider appropriately in deciding the amount of waste to dump.

The effects of this external cost on the steel industry can be seen in Figure 1 depicting the market for steel. Steel production inevitably involves producing pollution as well. The demand for steel is shown

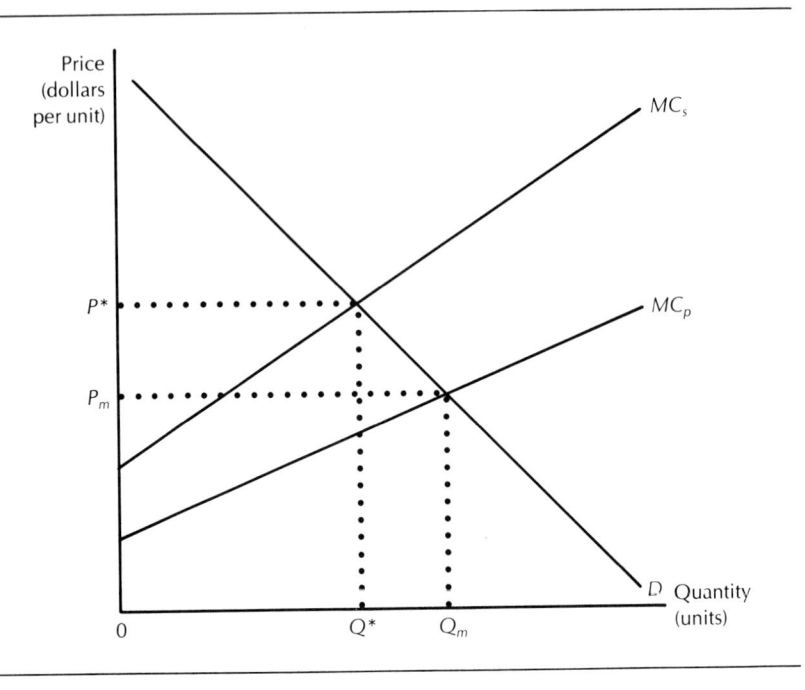

Figure 1. Market Allocation with Pollution

by the demand curve D, and the private marginal cost of producing the steel (exclusive of pollution control and damage) is depicted as MC_p.[1] Society, however, also considers the cost of pollution and the cost of controlling it. Adding these additional marginal costs to the private marginal cost yields the social marginal-cost curve MC_s.

If the steel industry faced no outside control on its emission levels, it would seek to produce Q_m. That choice, in a competitive setting, would maximize its profit. But that is clearly not efficient, since the steel industry is not considering all of the costs of its actions. In particular, it is ignoring the damage caused to the resort. From society's point of view, which attempts to maximize the joint profits of these two industries, the efficient output would be Q^* not Q_m.[2]

With the assistance of Figure 1, we can draw a number of conclusions about a market allocation of commodities that cause pollution in the absence of any outside influence:

1. The output of the commodity is too large.
2. Too much pollution is produced.
3. The prices of products responsible for pollution are too low.
4. There are no incentives to search for ways to yield less pollution per unit of output.
5. Recycling and reuse are discouraged, since the disposal alternative is so artificially cheap.

The effects of a market imperfection for one commodity end up affecting the demands for raw materials, labor, and so on. The ultimate effects are felt through the entire economy.

THE TRADITIONAL REGULATORY RESPONSE

One response to this market failure has been the establishment of an elaborate regulatory structure designed to limit the flow of pollutants into the nation's air and water. The approaches to controlling air and water pollutants have some significant differences.

Stationary Source Air Pollution Control Policy

The Clean Air Act currently tailors the regulatory structure to the types of pollutants being regulated.

Types of Pollutants. There are seven *criteria* pollutants. The characteristics shared by these pollutants are that they are relatively common substances, are found in almost all parts of the country, and are presumed to be dangerous only in high concentrations. The first six (sulfur dioxide, total suspended particulates, nitrogen dioxide, ozone, hydrocarbons, and carbon monoxide) were named in the Act itself, while the seventh, lead, was regulated as a result of a successful lawsuit brought by the Natural Resources Defense Council in 1975. *Hydrocarbons* (sometimes called *volatile organic compounds*) are included on the list primarily because their presence in the environment contributes to the creation of ozone, another of the pollutants. The central force of the Clean Air Act has been on criteria pollutants.

The class of *hazardous* pollutants contains a number of airborne substances that have been implicated in cancer, genetic damage, neurotoxicity, reproductive effects, and other serious health effects. Unlike the criteria pollutants, small doses of hazardous pollutants can produce serious damage. The Clean Air Act empowered the EPA to list and regulate any pollutants that fit this description. As of 1984, only seven pollutants had been listed.

- *Asbestos*, which has been associated with lung cancer and other respiratory diseases
- *Beryllium*, which can produce skin problems as well as chronic lesions in the lungs
- *Mercury*, which can attack the nervous system and the kidneys
- *Vinyl chloride*, which has been implicated in a rare form of liver cancer called angiosarcoma, brain cancer, and birth defects
- *Benzene*, which is known to cause leukemia and other diseases of the blood
- *Radionuclides*, which are radioactive nuclear species
- *Arsenic*, a familiar poison

As of 1984, regulations had been issued to control emissions for the first four only.

Whereas criteria pollutants exist virtually everywhere and affect large numbers of people, hazardous pollutants are found only in certain locations, typically with substantially lower numbers of the population exposed. Because they are toxic, however, they have the potential of being more harmful to those exposed than similar doses of the criteria pollutants.

Air Quality Standards. For each of the criteria pollutants, ambient air quality standards have been established by the EPA. These standards set legal ceilings on the allowable concentration of the pollutant in the outdoor air. These standards have to be met everywhere, though as a practical matter they are monitored at a large number of specific locations.

The *primary standard* is designed to protect human health. All criteria pollutants have a primary standard. The *secondary standard* is designed to protect other aspects of human welfare from those pollutants having separate effects. Currently, only sulfur oxides and particulates have separate secondary standards. Protection is afforded by the secondary standard for aesthetics (particularly visibility), physical objects (houses, monuments, and so on), and vegetation.

The ambient standards are required by statute to be determined without any consideration given to the costs of meeting them. They are supposed to be set at a level sufficient to protect even the most sensitive members of the population. These standards are periodically reviewed and, if the evidence warrants, they are revised.

State Implementation Plans. The EPA is responsible for defining the ambient standards, but the primary responsibility for ensuring that they are met falls on the state control agencies. They exercise this responsibility by developing and executing an acceptable state implementation plan (SIP), which must be approved by the EPA. This plan divides the state up into separate air quality control regions. (There are special procedures for handling regions that cross state borders, such as Metropolitan New York.)

The SIP spells out for each control region the procedures and timetables for meeting local ambient standards and for abatement of the effects of locally emitted pollutants on other states. The degree of control required depends on the severity of the pollution problem in each of the control regions.

By 1975 it had become apparent that, despite some major gains in air quality, many areas had not met (and would not meet) the ambient standards by the statutory deadlines. Therefore, in the 1977 Amendments to the Clean Air Act, Congress extended the deadline for attainment of all primary (health-related) ambient standards to 1982 with further extensions to 1987 possible for ozone and carbon monoxide. The Amendments also required the EPA to designate all areas not meeting the original deadlines as *nonattainment regions.*

The areas so designated were subjected to particularly stringent controls. After the 1977 Amendments were passed, all portions of state implementation plans applying to nonattainment regions had to be revised by the state control authorities to ensure compliance with the new deadlines. To prod the states into action, Congress gave the EPA the power to halt the construction of major new or modified pollution sources and to deny federal sewage and transportation grants for any state not submitting a plan showing precisely how and when attainment would be reached.

The statutes specifically required these plans to provide for the implementation of all "reasonably available control measures as expeditiously as practicable" on all existing sources. They also specified that "reasonable further progress" in meeting the standards be demonstrated on an annual basis. The former requirement mandates the specification of emission standards (legal limits on allowable emissions) for existing sources, while the latter requires annual reductions in emissions of sufficient magnitude to guarantee compliance by the deadline.

State implementation plans in nonattainment regions must also include a permit program for newly constructed large sources or large sources that have undergone some major modifications. Permits cannot be granted to these sources unless the state can demonstrate that emissions resulting from commencing or expanding operations would not jeopardize the region's progress toward attainment. The state can satisfy this requirement by controlling existing sources to a sufficiently high degree that progress toward attainment can be demonstrated even with the new sources in operation.

A second condition for the permit to be issued stipulates that all major new or modified sources in nonattainment areas must also control their own emissions to the *lowest achievable emission rate* (LAER). The LAER is defined as the lowest emission rate achieved by any similar state implementation plan whether or not any source is currently achieving that rate. This part of the law was designed to ensure that only the most stringent controls would be used by any source locating in a nonattainment area.

Regions with air quality at least as high as the standards by the original deadline were subject to another set of controls known collectively as the PSD policy. This policy derives its name from its objective, namely the *prevention of significant deterioration* of the air in cleaner regions. The origin of this policy is found in the preamble to the 1970 Clean Air Act, which stated as an objective: "to protect and enhance the quality of the nation's air."

In 1972 the EPA was successfully sued by the Sierra Club for promulgating regulations that did not ensure that this objective would be met. The system of ambient standards prevented the deterioration of the air beyond the standard, but air significantly cleaner than the standard would normally have deteriorated until it reached the standard. Following the court's decision, the EPA adopted a PSD program in 1974, and the 1977 Amendments to the Clean Air Act continued a modified version of that program. The PSD regulations specify the maximum allowable increases or increments in pollution concentration beyond some baseline.

New sources seeking to locate in PSD regions must secure permits. As a condition of securing their permits, these sources must install the *best available control technology* (BACT). The specific technologies that satisfy this requirement are determined by states on a case-by-case basis. Each new source permitted consumes a portion of the allowable increment. Once the increment has been completely consumed, no further deterioration of the air is allowed in that area even if the air is cleaner than required by the prevailing ambient standard. Thus, where the PSD increments are binding, for all practical purposes they define a tertiary standard varying in magnitude from region to region.

National Emission Standards. In addition to defining the ambient standards and requiring states to define BACT and LAER emission standards, the EPA, itself, has established national uniform emission standards for two categories of sources: (1) those emitting hazardous pollutants and (2) new sources of criteria pollutants or major modifications of existing sources.

For hazardous pollutants the EPA has assumed direct responsibility for defining the emissions standards rather than delegating it to the states. The standards governing new and modified sources of criteria pollutants are called the *new source performance standards* (NSPS), and they were designed to serve merely as a floor for BACT and LAER determinations by the states. Congess wanted to ensure that all sources would have to meet a minimum standard regardless of where it was located. This was seen as a way to prevent states from caving in as industry attempted to play one state off against another in its attempt to seek the lowest possible emission standards. Neither LAER nor BACT can be lower than the new source performance standards.

Intermittent Controls. The Clean Air Amendments of 1977 state unambiguously:

The degree of emission limitation required for control of any pollutant under an applicable implementation plan under this title shall not be affected in any manner by . . . any other dispersion technique. . . . for the purposes of this section, the term "dispersion technique" includes any intermittent or supplemental control of air pollutants, varying with atmospheric conditions.

Through this provision, the Act rules out tailoring the degree of control to the prevailing meteorological conditions. All strategies must achieve better air quality through constant emission reductions stringent enough to ensure compliance even in quite adverse conditions.

In summary, the pre-reform approach to stationary source air pollution control involved ambient standards, mandating acceptable upper limits on atmospheric pollution concentration, with emission standards imposed on individual discharge points as the means of achieving those targets. To conform to these standards the emission flows had to be sufficiently stringently controlled that the ambient standards would not be violated more than once a year, regardless of the prevailing conditions.

Federal Water Pollution Control Policy

There are two rather different sources of water pollution: point sources, where the specific source is identifiable (such as industrial or municipal polluters), and nonpoint sources, where the pollution is more diffuse and specific sources are more difficult to track down (such as urban runoff or agricultural erosion).

Federal policy for point-source water pollution control antedates federal air pollution control by a considerable period of time. The first hints of the current approach are found in the Amendments to the Water Pollution Control Act, which were passed in 1956. There were two especially important provisions of this act: (1) federal financial support for the construction of waste-treatment plants and (2) direct federal regulation of waste discharges. Legislative concern over nonpoint sources is more recent and relies much more heavily on the states to play the major role.

Point Sources. An air of frustration regarding pollution control pervaded Washington in the 1970s, leading to the enactment of a very tough water control law in 1972. The tone of the act is established immediately in the preamble, which calls for the achievement of two goals: (1) "that the discharge of pollutants into the navigable waters be eliminated by 1985" and (2) "that wherever attainable, an interim goal of water quality which provides for the protection and propagation of fish, shellfish, and wildlife and provides for recreation in and on the water can be achieved by July 1, 1983." The stringency of these goals represented a major departure from past policy.

This Act also introduced new procedures for implementing the law. Permits were required of all dischargers. These permits, issued by the EPA (at least until the states met certain conditions) were to be granted only when the dischargers met certain technology-based effluent standards. These effluent standards were uniformly imposed and hence could not depend upon local water conditions.

According to the 1972 Amendments, the effluent standards were to be implemented in two stages. By 1977 industrial dischargers, as a condition of their permit, were required to meet effluent limitations based on the "best practicable control technology currently available" (BPT). In setting national standards the EPA was required to consider the total costs of these technologies and their relation to the benefits received, but not to consider the conditions of the individual source or the particular waters into which it discharged. In addition, all publicly owned treatment plants were to have achieved secondary treatment, a specific level of effluent control, by 1977. By 1983 industrial dischargers were required to meet effluent limitations based on the presumably more stringent "best available technology economically achievable" (BAT), while publicly owned treatment plants were required to meet effluent limitations that depended upon the "best practicable waste treatment technology."

The program of subsidizing municipal waste-treatment plants, begun in 1956, was continued in a slightly modified form by the 1972 Act. Whereas the 1965 Act allowed the federal government to subsidize up to 55 percent of the cost of construction of waste-treatment plants, the 1972 Act raised the ceiling to 75 percent. In 1981, however, the federal share was once again reduced to 55 percent.

The 1977 Amendments continued this regulatory approach, but with some major modifications. This legislation made a more careful distinction between conventional and toxic pollutants, with more stringent requirements placed on the latter, and it extended virtually all of the deadlines in the 1972 Act.

For conventional pollutants a new treatment standard was created to replace the BAT standards. The effluent limitations for those pollutants were to be based on the "best conventional technology," and the deadline for these standards was set at July 1, 1984. In setting these standards the EPA was required to consider whether the costs of adding the pollution control equipment were reasonable as compared to the improvement in water quality. For unconventional pollutants and toxics (any pollutant not specifically included on the list of conventional pollutants), the BAT requirement was retained, but the deadline was shifted to 1984.

Other deadlines were also extended. The date for municipalities to meet the secondary treatment deadline moved from 1977 to 1983. Industrial compliance with the BPT standards was delayed until 1983 whenever a contemplated innovative system had the potential for application throughout the industry.

The final modification made by the 1977 Amendments involved the introduction of pretreatment standards for waste being sent to a publicly owned treatment system. These standards were designed to prevent any discharges that could inhibit the treatment process and to prevent the introduction of toxic pollutants that would not be treated by the waste-treatment facility. Existing facilities were required to meet the standards three years after the date they were published, while facilities constructed later would be required to meet the pretreatment regulations upon commencement of operations.

Nonpoint Sources. In contrast to the control of point sources, the EPA was given no specific authority to regulate nonpoint sources. Though initially point sources were much more important sources of pollution, after they were cleaned up, nonpoint sources increased in importance. This type of pollution was seen by Congress as a state responsibility.

Section 208 of the Act authorized federal grants for state-initiated planning that would provide implementable plans for areawide waste-treatment management. Section 208 further specified that this areawide plan must identify significant nonpoint sources of pollution as well as procedures and methods for controlling them.

As of 1981 ten states had passed and five others had proposed programs under which the state would share with farmers the cost of controlling nonpoint pollution. In Illinois, for example, the General Assembly enacted a $500,000 program to encourage farmers to use farming techniques that would stem soil erosion. This program would pay farmers from $3 to $25 per acre, depending upon the methods chosen.

Drinking Water. The 1972 policy focused on achieving water quality sufficiently high for fishing and swimming. Because that quality is not high enough for drinking water, the Safe Drinking Water Act of 1974 issued more stringent standards for community water systems. These set maximum allowable concentration levels for bacteria, turbidity (muddiness), and chemical-radiological contaminants. There are currently standards for some twenty chemicals or organisms. The regulations also required monitoring for the covered contaminants. One final noteworthy provision attempted to protect groundwater drinking supplies by controlling subsurface fluids injection (injection of liquid wastes into deep wells).

THE NATURE OF THE REFORM

Identifying the Regulatory Problem

There are two principal participants in the process to regulate the amount of pollution in the nation's air and water. While the regulatory authority has the statutory responsibility for meeting pollution targets, the human sources of the pollutant (such as industries and municipalities) must ultimately take the actions that will reduce pollution sufficiently to meet the target.

The main responsibilities of the regulator are to decide how to allocate the control responsibility among the various sources, to design the regulations implementing the decision, and to enforce the resulting regulations. This is a challenging responsibility, since the number of sources is extremely large. There are, for example, an estimated 27,000 major stationary sources of air pollution in the United States, with each source usually containing many discharge points.

As discussed, the regulatory authority has traditionally gone about its job by establishing separate emission standards for each point of discharge from major sources of the pollutant. For ease of reference this means of distributing the control responsibility among points of discharge shall henceforth be called the *command-and-control approach*. Since each source will typically contain several pollutant discharge points, each with its own unique emission standard, the amount of information the control authority would need is staggering if it were to assign this responsibility so as to minimize the cost of producing the desired amount concentration. (This least-cost assignment of the control responsibility shall henceforth be known as the cost-effective allocation.) Typically the amount of information available to it when the allocations are made falls far short of what is needed for this task.

In some ways the managers of plants emitting pollution are in exactly the opposite position. Because each plant manager typically would know the unique array of possible control techniques most suited to his or her operation, as well as the associated costs and reliability of these techniques, the quality of information at this level of decision-making is very good. Plant managers generally will have a very good feel for which control technologies would produce the most cost-effective emission reduction at their plant.

Unfortunately, however, profit-maximizing plant managers lack the incentive to act on this information in a manner consistent with cost-effective emission reduction. Since any unilateral increase in cost incurred by individual plants faced with competition either from existing or potential rivals could weaken their competitive position, plants would seek to minimize their own costs using any means at their disposal. Possible means include overstating costs to the control authority or to the legislature in hopes of being allocated a weak standard and seeking an exemption from the courts on grounds of affordability or technological unfeasibility.

The fundamental problem with the command-and-control approach is a mismatch between capabilities and responsibilities. Those with the responsibility for allocating the control responsibility, the control authorities, have too little information available to them to allocate it cost effectively. Those with the best information on the cost-effective choices, the plant managers, have no incentive either to voluntarily accept their cost-effective responsibility or to transmit unbiased cost information to the control authority so it can make a cost-effective assignment. Plant managers have an incentive to accept as little control responsibility as possible in order to maintain or strengthen their competitive positions.

The Role of Emissions Trading

In this policy environment it is not surprising that the command-and-control allocation is not, and by itself could not become, cost effective. What may be surprising in light of the complexity of the task is that cost effectiveness is not an unreasonable objective for economic incentive approaches such as emissions trading.

The emissions trading program has attempted to inject more flexibility into this approach by allowing sources a wider range of choice in how to meet their assigned control responsibilities. The general thrust of the program is to allow sources to seek alternative means of reducing emissions as long as the substitute means produce equivalent or better effects on air quality. Because of their interest in keeping costs as low as possible, sources will tend to search for the lowest cost means. In general they use excess emission reductions at cheaper-to-control discharge points to offset equivalent increases at other, more difficult to control discharge points.

Because creating excess reductions can yield monetary rewards for the firm (either by selling them or using them to alleviate the need to undertake more expensive reductions elsewhere in the plant), emissions trading provides an incentive to seek and exploit opportunities for creating excess reductions. By stimulating a demand for new, cheaper control possibilities, the program encourages innovation in pollution control techniques. Whereas under the command-and-control system the only allowable technologies were those discovered by the EPA; with emissions trading, every source has an incentive to search for new approaches. This program encourages technological progress in controlling pollution.

Finally, the program was seen as a means of encouraging compliance with the standards. Because it offered greater flexibility in how the sources could meet their legal responsibilities, the program made it easier to achieve compliance with the law. Financially troubled industries (such as steel) could use their financially precarious positions to postpone compliance with the expensive command-and-control standards. By providing a lower cost means of complying, emissions trading made compliance easier for those industries and reduced the benefits of fighting the standards in court.

In one sense this was a radical reform. Whereas traditionally the pollution control authorities retained the exclusive authority to mandate the amount of emissions allowed at each discharge point, under the emissions trading program the responsibility for picking the mix of discharge point reductions used to achieve the stipulated overall emission reduction was transferred to the managers of the pollution sources. Environmentalists feared, and no doubt some industrialists hoped, the program would open a large number of loopholes, leaving a legacy of reduced compliance.

This reform package did not command an immediate constituency and building one was not easy. Even industrial sources, the most natural constituents in light of the flexibility offered by the program, were far from unanimous in their enthusiasm. To some extent they feared that this flexibility entailed greater risk. For example, when an EPA-recommended technology failed to live up to standards, the source could claim it had lived up to its responsibilities; but when the control mix was up to the source, it would lose this defense.

Though this was a voluntary program, requiring full cooperation of state control agencies, state cooperation was not inevitable. State authorities feared that the new programs would be more difficult to administer and saw it as a threatening departure from their comfortable, customary way of doing business.

The emissions trading program is in fact an amalgam of four separate policies developed at different times to meet different needs and brought together under the emissions trading rubric for the first time in 1982. The thread that holds these programs together is the emission reduction credit. Any source reducing its emissions more than required by law at any discharge point can apply to have this excess reduction certified as an emission reduction credit. Once certified, this credit becomes available for sale or use as a means of meeting the assigned control responsibilities for that source (at other discharge points) or for other sources. The conditions under which these credits can be created, stored, transferred, and used, as defined by the bubble, offset, banking, and netting policies, are described below.

Defining the Promise

Because any change in policy has its own set of costs, it is difficult to overcome the inertia of the status quo. New grounds for legal challenge are exposed. Bureaucratic staffs trained in one set of procedures must learn new ones. The comfort of familiarity is lost to both regulators and sources.

To overcome this inertia successful reforms must offer large benefits relative to these transition costs. By being a complement to, not a replacement for, the traditional approach, the EPA emissions trading program held down the transition costs. At the same time it offered the potential for achieving the desired environmental outcome at a lower cost of compliance.

The actual savings achieved by the emissions trading program are determined both by the potential cost savings, measured as the deviation of the cost of the traditional command-and-control allocation from the lowest possible cost of achieving the same pollution target, and by the degree to which the costs resulting from the actual emissions trading program can be shown to approximate the least-cost solution. While in theory the emission trading program can be shown to result in the least-cost allocation (because of the previously discussed incentives for sources to seek and exploit the lowest cost means of controlling pollution), in practice this equivalence is more problematic.

The magnitude of the potential cost savings in any particular emissions trading market depends on many local circumstances, such as prevailing meteorology or hydrology, the locational configuration of sources, and how sensitive incremental costs are to the amount controlled by each type of source. Several simulation models have now been constructed that integrate these factors for specific pollutants. These models are capable of deriving the least-cost means of controlling pollution *among the already identified control technologies*. To the extent that lower cost technologies are available that the analyst may not know about, these simulations will overstate the cost of the lowest cost means. These simulations therefore fail to capture one powerful source of cost reduction that emissions trading would provide.

The air pollution results are presented in Table 1. Since for a variety of reasons the estimated cost cannot be directly compared across studies, the potential cost savings are presented as a ratio of command-and-control costs to the lowest cost of meeting the same air quality objective. A ratio equal to 1.0 implies that the command-and-control allocation would be fully cost effective (implying zero potential cost savings from an emission trading program), while a ratio greater than 1.0 implies positive potential cost savings. When 1.0 is subtracted from this ratio and the remainder multiplied by 100, the result can be interpreted as the percentage increase in cost that results from using the traditional command-and-control approach rather than the lowest cost allocation. The higher this number, the greater are the potential cost savings from any policy that is able to approach the least-cost allocation.

With the one exception of the Hahn and Noll study, these studies indicate the potential for large (and frequently very large) cost savings[3]; the command-and-control policy was strikingly cost ineffective. Because of this cost ineffectiveness, the potential for achieving air quality goals at lower cost using a more flexible approach loomed large. This potential for complying with the law at a lower cost was not lost on industrial sources as pressure for reform began to mount.[4]

Large potential savings also seem to be possible for water pollution. The estimates of these savings are presented in Table 2. The cost savings are clearly there for water as well as for air, but the magnitude for the average pollutant and geographic area is smaller for water pollution than for air pollution. The largest ratio for water pollution is 3.13, compared with 22.0 for air pollution. Indeed, if the Los Angeles sulfate and Lower Delaware Valley sulfur oxide studies are excluded, the *smallest* percentage cost savings for air pollution exceeds the *largest* percentage cost savings for water pollution.

THE EVOLUTION OF THE REFORM PROGRAM

The Original Bubble Policy

The program got off to an inauspicious start. Following a period of some five years of industry pressure, the EPA published its first version of the bubble policy in December 1975 (Table 3). Prior to this policy, all new portions of polluting facilities had been forced to meet a stringent, nationally uniform set of emission standards known as the new source performance standards (NSPS) regardless of whether the facilities were newly constructed or were modified or expanded operations of existing facilities. The *original* bubble policy proposed by the EPA (as distinguished from the subsequent bubble policy to be discussed below) sought to excuse the operator of an existing plant from meeting the NSPS requirement as long as any increase in pollution caused by an expansion or modification of the plant would be offset with a compensating decrease in the same pollutant from other units within the plant as a whole.

The courts took a dim view of this particular application of the emissions trading concept. Concluding that EPA had exceeded its statutory authority by incorporating the bubble policy in this way, in *ASARCO Inc. v. EPA* the court voided these particular regulations without precluding the use of emissions trading principles in other contexts. The bubble had burst, but only for a while.

Table 1. Empirical Studies of Air Pollution Control

Study and Year	Pollutants Covered	Geographic Area	CAC Benchmark	Ratio of CAC Cost to Least Cost
Atkinson and Lewis (1974)	Particulates	St. Louis Metro. Area	SIP regulations	6.0[a]
Roach et al. (1981)	Sulfur dioxide	Four corners in Utah, Colorado, Arizona and New Mexico	SIP regulations	4.25
Hahn and Noll (1982)	Sulfates	Los Angeles	California emission standards	1.07
Krupnick (1983)	Nitrogen dioxide	Baltimore	Proposed RACT regulations	5.96[b]
Seskin et al. (1983)	Nitrogen dioxide	Chicago	Proposed RACT regulations	14.4[b]
McGartland (1984)	Particulates	Baltimore	SIP regulations	4.18
Spofford (1984)	Sulfur dioxide	Lower Delaware Valley	Uniform percentage reduction	1.78
	Particulates	Lower Delaware Valley	Uniform percentage reduction	22.0
Harrison (1983)	Airport noise	United States	Mandatory retrofit	1.72[c]
Maloney and Yandle (1984)	Hydrocarbons	All domestic DuPont plants	Uniform percentage reduction	4.15[d]

| Palmer et al. (1980) | Chlorofluorocarbon emissions from nonaerosol applications | United States | Proposed emission standards | 1.96 |

Sources: Scott E. Atkinson and Donald H. Lewis, "A Cost-Effectiveness Analysis of Alternative Air Quality Control Strategies," *Journal of Environmental Economics and Management* 1, 3 (November, 1974), 247; Fred Roach, Charles Kolstad, Allen V. Kneese, Richard Tobin, and Michael Williams, "Alternative Air Quality Policy Options in the Four Corners Region," *The Southwest Review*, 1, 2 (Summer 1981) Table 3, pp. 44–45; Robert W. Hahn and Roger G. Noll, "Designing a Market for Tradeable Emission Permits," in Wesley A. Magat (ed.), *Reform of Environmental Regulation* (Cambridge, Mass., Ballinger Publishing Co., 1982), Tables 7–5 and 7–6, pp. 132–133; Alan J. Krupnick, "Costs of Alternative Policies for the Control of NO_2 in the Baltimore Region," unpublished Resources for the Future Working Economic Strategies for Controlling Air Pollution, *Journal of Environmental Economics and Management*, 10, 2 (June 1983), Tables 1 and 2, pp. 17, 120; Albert Mark McGartland, "Marketable Permit Systems for Air Pollution Control: An Empirical Study," Ph.D. dissertation, University of Maryland, 1984, Table 4.2, p. 67a; Walter O. Spofford, Jr., "Efficiency Properties of Alternative Source Control Policies for Meeting Ambient Air Quality Standards: An Empirical Application to the Lower Delaware Valley," unpublished Resources for the Future Discussion Paper D-118, February 1984, Table 13, p. 77; David Harrison, Jr., "Case Study 1: The Regulation of Aircraft Noise," in Thomas C. Schelling (ed.), *Incentives for Environmental Protection* (Cambridge, Mass.: The MIT Press, 1983), Tables 3.6 and 3.16, pp. 81, 96; Michael T. Maloney and Bruce Yandle, "Estimation of the Cost of Air Pollution Control Regulation," *Journal of Environmental Economics and Management*, 11, 3 (September 1984), Table IV, p. 256; and Adele R. Palmer, William E. Mooz, Timothy H. Quinn, and Kathleen A. Wolf, *Economic Implications of Regulating Chlorofluorocarbon Emissions from Nonaerosol Applications*, Report No. R-2524-EPA prepared for the U.S. Environmental Protection Agency by the Rand Corporation June 1980, Table 4.7, p. 225.

CAC = command and control, the traditional regulatory approach, SIP = state implementation plan, RACT = reasonably available control technologies, a set of standards imposed on existing sources in nonattainment areas.

[a]Based on a 40 g/m³ at worst receptor.

[b]Based on a short-term, one-hour average of 250 g/m³.

[c]Because it is a benefit-cost study instead of a cost-effectiveness study, the Harrison comparison of the command-and-control approach with the least-cost allocation involves different benefit levels. Specifically, the benefit levels associated with the least-cost allocation are only 82 percent of those associated with the command-and-control allocation. To produce cost estimates based on more comparable benefits, as a first approximation the least-cost allocation was divided by 0.82 and the resulting number was compared with the command-and-control cost.

[d]Based on 85 percent reduction of emissions from all sources.

Table 2. Empirical Studies of Water Pollution Control

Study and Year	Pollutants Covered	Geographic Area	CAC Benchmark	DO Target (mg/l)	Ratio of CAC Cost to Least Cost
Johnson (1967)	Biochemical oxygen demand	Delaware Estuary — eighty-six-mile reach	Equal proportional treatment	2.0 3.0 4.0	3.13 1.62 1.43
O'Neil (1980)	Biochemical oxygen demand	Twenty-mile segment of Lower Fox River in Wisconsin	Equal proportional treatment	2.0 4.0 6.2 7.9	2.29 1.71 1.45 1.38
Eheart et al. (1983)	Biochemical oxygen demand	Willamette River in Oregon	Equal proportional treatment	4.8 7.5	1.12 1.19
		Delaware Estuary in Pennsylvania, Delaware, and New Jersey	Equal proportional treatment	3.0 3.6	3.00 2.92
		Upper Hudson River in New York	Equal proportional treatment	5.1 5.9	1.54 1.62
		Mohawk River in New York	Equal proportional treatment	6.8	1.22

Sources: Edwin L. Johnson, "A Study in the Economics of Water Quality Management," *Water Resources Research*, 3, 1 (second quarter 1967), Table 1, p. 297; William B. O'Neil, "Pollution Permits and Markets for Water Quality," Ph.D. dissertation, University of Wisconsin–Madison, 1980, Table 3.4, p. 65; and J. Wayland Eheart, E. Downey Brill, Jr., and Randolph M. Lyon, "Transferable Discharge Permits for Control of BOD: An Overview," in Erhard F. Jceres and Martin H. David (eds.), *Buying a Better Environment: Cost-Effective Regulations Through Permit Trading*, (Madison, Wis.: University of Wisconsin Press, 1983), Table 1, p. 177.

CAC = command and control, the traditional regulatory approach; DO = dissolved oxygen: higher DO targets indicate higher water quality.

Table 3. Evolution of the Emissions Trading Program: Major Milestones, 1975–1984

Date and Citation	Title	Significance
December 16, 1975 40 FR 58416	Standards of performance for new stationary sources	First use of bubble concept; would excuse modified plants from NSPS so long as total emissions do not increase
December 21, 1976 41 FR 55254	Emissions offset interpretive ruling	Initiated offset policy
August 7, 1977 91 Stat. 712	Amendments to Clean Air Act	Statutory recognition of offset policy
January 27, 1978 578 F.2d 319	ASARCO Inc. v. EPA	Struck down 1975 NSPS bubble
January 16, 1979 44 FR 3274	Emission offset interpretive ruling (revised)	Revised offset policy to conform with 1977 Amendments; allowed banking
January 18, 1979 44 FR 3740	Recommendations for alternative emission reduction options within state implementation plans	Proposed rules establishing bubble policy
December 11, 1979 44 FR 71780	Recommendations for alternative emission reduction options within state implementation plans	Final bubble rules
August 7, 1980 45 FR 52676	Requirements for preparation, adoption, and submittal of implementation plans and approval and promulgation of implementation plans	Separate netting rules established for PSD and nonattainment areas
April 6, 1981 45 FR 20551	Approval and promulgation of state implementation plans: New Jersey	Approved New Jersey's generic VOC bubble; encouraged other states to develop generic rules
October 14, 1981 46 FR 50766	Requirements for preparation, adoption, and submittal of implementation plans and approval and promulgation of implementation plans	Netting rules changed to provide for uniform treatment of sources in attainment and non-attainment areas
April 7, 1982 47 FR 15076	Emissions trading policy statement: general principle for creation, banking, and use of emission reduction credits	Integrated bubble, offset, banking, and netting into a single emission trading program
June 25, 1984 52 LW 4845	Chevron U.S.A. v. Natural Resources Defense Council, Inc.	Upheld use of netting rules for nonattainment as well as PSD regions

Source: T. H. Tietenberg, *Emissions Trading: An Exercise in Reforming Pollution Policy* (Washington, D.C.: Resources for the Future, Inc., 1985), Table 2, p. 10.

The Offset Policy

A second attempt to introduce emissions trading was more successful. By 1976 it had become clear that a number of regions would fail to attain the ambient air quality standards by the deadlines mandated in the Clean Air Act, and the EPA was faced with the unpleasant prospect of prohibiting any new sources from entering these regions. As an alternative to prohibition, the EPA established the offset policy. Under this policy new sources were allowed to enter these regions providing they met strict emission standards and they acquired sufficient offsetting reductions from other facilities in the region that total regional emissions would be lower after their entry than before. In essence this program provided a way to improve air quality by reducing emissions at existing sources, but it did so by forcing new sources to find the offsetting reductions and to finance them.

With the advent of the offset policy, emissions trading had established a precarious foothold in air pollution policy, but a high price was paid. The bias against new sources that characterized the command-and-control policy has persisted (albeit to a lesser degree) in the emissions trading program. Not only are new or expanding sources required to offset any remaining emission increases (after the installation of required controls) with acquired emission reduction credits, but new sources must typically meet the prescribed emission standards by installing the control equipment necessary to meet the mandated reductions at each discharge point. By contrast, existing sources are not required to acquire credits to offset their remaining emissions, and they can use emission reduction credits to meet their statutory responsibilities (rather than producing the mandated emission reduction at every discharge point). This bias in the regulations has the effect of delaying the replacement of older heavier polluting facilities with newer, less polluting facilities.

When writing the 1977 Amendments to the Clean Air Act, Congress included a specific section providing legislative authorization for the offset program. To this day the offset program remains the only component of the program specifically authorized by statute; the other components are purely bureaucratic creations, resting solely on general principles articulated in the act.

Emissions Banking

The next component of the emissions trading program, banking, was added in 1979 as EPA issued new regulations designed to bring the interim offset program into conformance with the 1977 Amendments. Emissions banking allows sources creating emission reduction credits to store those credits for subsequent sale or use. Prior to these regulations the banking of emission reduction credits had been disallowed on the grounds that it was incompatible with the EPA's statutory responsibility to ensure that nonattainment areas met the ambient standards as rapidly as possible. Confiscation and retirement of emission reduction credits not immediately used was seen as one rapid means of improving air quality. Since the 1977 Amendments and their associated implementing regulations provided specific procedures compatible with emission banking for attaining the ambient standards by the new statutory deadlines, these objections were overcome.

This was potentially an important boost to the program, since without banking, the incentives for controlling emissions beyond the minimum legal requirements are diminished substantially. Without banking, excess control would be valuable to the creating source only if another source needed an offsetting reduction precisely at the time it was created. One can easily imagine what would happen in more traditional markets, such as furniture, if the product were confiscated by the state whenever a buyer could not be found soon after the product was finished. Less furniture would soon be available. The same principle holds for emission reduction credits. The source has absolutely no incentive to undertake additional control voluntarily unless it retains an exclusive and transferable property right over the emission reduction credit until it can be used or sold.

Successful banking programs do exist, as illustrated by the bank established in Louisville, Kentucky. By May 1984 this bank had some fifteen deposits of emission reduction credits for total suspended particulates, sulfur dioxide, volatile organic compounds, nitrogen dioxide, and carbon monoxide. This particular banking program has clearly been successful in stimulating excess reductions.

Unfortunately, this bank remains a rather isolated example. Emissions banking has taken less of a hold than might have been expected. As of May 1984, the EPA had approved only two statewide banking rules (Oregon and Rhode Island) and had proposed to approve one other (Kentucky). Although another eleven states or localities had adopted some type of banking rule, only two of the thirty-five bubble transactions consummated by the end of 1983 involved banked credits. Not so coincidentally both of these transactions involved credits deposited in the Louisville bank.

The Revised Bubble Policy

Whereas the establishment of the offset program had been pretty much a response to a specific, passionately felt political need to remove the prohibition on growth in nonattainment areas, during the late 1970s interest grew in expanding the application of the emissions trading concept. Since the first attempt at a bubble policy in 1975 had been overruled by the courts, the EPA had to proceed cautiously. In view of the need to build a constituency while protecting its flanks from judicial attack, the EPA initially proposed heavily circumscribed programs intended to assuage fears and to move slowly. By taking this approach the EPA sought to ensure that the first trades would demonstrate clear, unambiguous benefits and set a useful precedent. At the same time the number of possible trades would be intentionally limited, giving states time to plan for and become comfortable with the program before any flood of applications overwhelmed them.

The reincarnated bubble policy, promulgated in 1979, took the form of allowing stable, existing sources some flexibility in fulfilling their assigned control responsibilities. Whereas the original bubble policy had sought to limit the applicability of the regulations, this new policy focused on making compliance easier. According to the 1977 Amendments, existing sources in nonattainment areas were required to meet emission standards based upon "reasonably available control technologies" (RACT). Instead of forcing each source to produce the stipulated emission reductions at each and every discharge point (as would be required by strict adherence to the RACT standards), the new bubble policy allowed each source to choose its own mix of emission reductions as long as the air quality effects were equivalent to those resulting from the RACT standards.

The relatively slow pace of trading following these initiatives convinced the EPA that these substantive reforms would have to be accompanied by procedural reforms if the program was to live up to its potential. Originally the bubble policy could only be used if the approving state included the intended trade in a formal revision to its state implementation plan (SIP). Because the SIP approval process is the primary means by which the EPA exercises its responsibility for assuring state compliance with the Clean Air Act, SIP revisions are bureaucratically cumbersome. When the Reagan administration took office, for example, a backlog of some 643 proposed changes in SIPs were awaiting EPA approval.[5] Because any SIP revision has to fulfill a large number of procedural requirements, state control authorities are reluctant to file revisions except when absolutely necessary. Requiring bubble trades to be approved through SIP revisions was a surefire way to limit state control authority interest in the program.

In 1981 the EPA significantly lowered this procedural burden by approving a generic rule for a volatile organic compound (VOC) bubble drawn up by New Jersey. Other states were invited to follow suit. Though initially the invitation included only this one pollutant, it was subsequently extended to include other pollutants as well. By approving the generic rules states intended to use to govern possible trades, the EPA eliminated the need for states to obtain SIP revision approval for each bubble trade. As long as subsequent trades conformed to these rules, no SIP revision was necessary.

This was a major change because it allowed state control authorities to see the bubble policy as something other than a procedural nightmare. As of December 1983, some forty-nine generic bubble applications were under various stages of development or approval as states began to take advantage of this new flexibility.[6] Since with generic rules the policy could be applied with much greater rapidity and much less red tape, by April 1984 the number of bubbles approved under the New Jersey generic rule exceeded those SIP revision bubbles approved directly by EPA for the nation as a whole during a comparable period.[7]

Emergence of the Baseline and Multiplant Problems

As the program began to expand, new problems began to surface. The first of these concerns the definition of the trading baseline. Since only those reductions which are surplus (defined as emission reductions greater than the baseline) can be traded, the baseline definition can have a major effect on the level and consequences of trading activity.

Because the emissions trading program was superimposed on an existing air pollution control program based on emission standards, those previously defined standards became the baseline. Though this choice of baselines facilitated the transition into emissions trading, it created some rather severe administrative problems.

Traditionally, emission standards were defined for categories of sources (rather than individual sources), with the levels of control chosen to ensure that even the most difficult-to-control source within the category could comply. For the other sources within the category actual emissions frequently turned out to be considerably lower than allowable emissions.[8]

To maintain consistency with the SIPs in those nonattainment areas basing their demonstrations of attainment by the deadlines on allowable emissions, the EPA adopted an allowable emissions baseline.[9] As a consequence, whenever its actual emissions were lower than its allowable emissions, a source could have the difference certified as an emission reduction credit. This credit could either be used by the source as one means of meeting another emission standard or sold to another source.

As a practical matter this has meant that a few trades have resulted in emissions increases.[10] Though the vast majority of trades have either reduced emissions below levels required in the absence of emissions trading or held them at the same level, it is true that the proponents of this program can no longer claim that trades always reduce compliance cost without degrading the environment. The purity of that portion of the concept was sacrificed in the implementation process, one part of the price of survival.

This baseline issue was not the only example where practical considerations intruded in a significant way upon the purity of the theoretical concept of emissions trading. Both the bubble and offset policies allow emission reduction credit trades among spatially separated facilities in the same airshed in order to maximize the set of trading opportunities.[11] The difficulty in implementing this facet of the policy lies in assuring that interfacility trades do not jeopardize attainment.

Although ton-for-ton trades between spatially separated sources would leave emissions constant, they would not generally leave air quality constant. The air quality would improve near the site of the emissions decrease and deteriorate near the site of the emissions increase. When the deterioration takes place near a monitor recording pollutant levels close to the ambient standard (so that the increase could trigger a violation), the problem is particularly serious.

Although in principle detrimental air quality changes can be anticipated with the use of dispersion models, in practice these models are expensive to construct. To avoid unnecessary expense the EPA attempted to tailor the stringency of the modeling requirements to the need for them by establishing three levels of modeling requirements. Full-dispersion modeling is required only when simpler models indicate that any air quality deterioration would be "significant." No modeling is required in the first level, while the second level allows the use of much cheaper screening models.[12]

Despite the EPA's efforts, this part of the market is not living up to expectations. Of the thirty-four SIP revision bubbles, only four have involved spatially separated facilities; two of these four have involved facilities under the same ownership.[13] These numbers fall far short of what reasonably could have been expected on the basis of the simulation studies reported above.

No doubt some of the discrepancy results from the transactions cost for interfirm transfers being higher than for intrafirm transfers, a factor not considered by the simulations. But that cannot be the whole story (or even a major part of it) given how common interfirm transfers are for other kinds of commodities. The lack of an effective emissions banking system, coupled with air quality modeling requirements that are unrealistically burdensome, must bear a major part of the responsibility.

The burdensome modeling requirements have two sources — the

first a matter of philosophy, the second involving more practical administrative considerations. Those regulators implementing the regulations seem to reject out-of-hand one basic type of trade that is an important part of any truly cost-effective strategy — a trade in which improvements in air quality in an area violating the ambient standards are offset by some deterioration of the air in an area in the same airshed where the air quality exceeds the standards. The current approach triggers expensive, third-level modeling whenever significant deterioration occurs, regardless of the size or location of any offsetting improvements. This approach is inconsistent with cost effectiveness, which allows such trades as long as they cause no violation of an ambient standard or make a current violation worse.

The administrative aspect arises in determining how any required third-level modeling is to be financed. Currently, any source required to supply third-level modeling must pay all the costs of constructing and using the appropriate dispersion model. This method of assigning the financial responsibility for developing the models is most unfortunate. Once constructed, these models could be used by a large number of sources for several purposes at a relatively low marginal cost. Only the fixed cost of construction and running these models the first time is very high. Because the first user bears that large fixed cost under the current system, no source has an incentive to be the first user. As a result, trades requiring third-level modeling are discouraged. Not one of the bubble trades consummated prior to the end of 1983 involved third-level modeling.[14]

Shifting the Focus to Regulatory Relief

The design and fate of the "netting" program, the final component of the emissions trading package, provides an interesting example of what happens when the irresistible force associated with a bureaucracy committed to regulatory flexibility runs into the immovable object represented by rigid statutes. Both the bubble and offset policies had offered more flexible ways to comply with the statutes, but not all areas of pollution policy allowed this flexibility. In particular, the statutory language seemed to permit very little opportunity for emissions trading in complying with the new source review process in either nonattainment or PSD areas; emission reduction credits could apparently not be used to meet the applicable emission standards. The only recourse was to use emissions trading as a part of the determination of whether the new source review process was applicable to that source; it could be used as a means of regulatory relief rather than regulatory reform.

Netting allows modifying or expanding sources to escape the burden of new source review requirements so long as any net increase (counting the emission reduction credits) in plantwide emissions is insignificant. Prior to the inception of the netting program, the test of whether a source was subject to the new source review process was applied by calculating the expected increases in emissions occurring after modernization or expansion (without considering any compensating decreases). When these increases passed predetermined thresholds, the source was subject to review. Netting allows emission reduction credits earned elsewhere in the plant to offset the increases expected from the expanded or modernized portion of the plant for the purposes of establishing whether the threshold has been exceeded. By "netting out" of review the facility may be exempted from the need to acquire preconstruction permits as well as from meeting the associated requirements such as modeling or monitoring the air quality impact of the new source, procuring offsets and meeting emissions standards more stringent than the NSPS. The source is not exempted from meeting the NSPS, the characteristic that differentiates this program from the ill-fated original bubble policy. By forcing these sources to adopt NSPS even when exempted from new source review, EPA attempted to satisfy the concerns raised earlier by the court about its previous effort to use emissions trading as a form of regulatory relief.

While this program could have immediately exempted a large number of modified sources from review, it was successfully challenged in the lower court by the Natural Resources Defense Council.[15] Ruling that exempting modified sources from review in nonattainment areas was inconsistent with the statutory intent to reach attainment as expeditiously as possible, the appeals court voided the netting rules as they apply to sources in nonattainment areas. By constantly referring to netting as the bubble policy, the court cast a cloud over the application of the bubble policy in nonattainment areas as well as over the application of netting. On appeal to the U.S. Supreme Court, this ruling was reversed,[16] but not before a lengthy period had passed during which the use of netting and the bubble policy in nonattainment areas lay dormant as states awaited the outcome of judicial review.

Extending the Concept to Water Pollution Control

With the advent of the bubble, offset, and netting policies, emissions trading had become the centerpiece of the regulatory reform and relief movement in air pollution control. Though no comparable scale of activity exists for reforming water pollution control policy, action has been initiated by the State of Wisconsin.

The Lower Fox River flows from Lake Winnebago to Green Bay, Wisconsin. Lining the banks of a key twenty-two mile segment of this river are ten pulp and paper mills and four municipalities that discharge effluent into the river. During the summer the desired dissolved oxygen targets are not reached at two critical sag points, even when the industrial polluters are in compliance with BPT standards and municipal polluters are providing secondary treatment.

The Wisconsin Department of Natural Resources was forced to meet the ambient standards in the face of industrial resistance. To assist in choosing a policy strategy, they funded a simulation model of the river to compare traditional regulatory rules with a marketable permit system.[17]

This model revealed significant differences among dischargers, a precondition if the emissions trading approach was to save a significant amount of money. Transfer coefficients varied by a factor of three, and under traditional abatement rules, marginal abatement costs differed by a factor of four. The study concluded that the control cost would be some 40 percent higher if the department were to rely on traditional abatement rules and denied the opportunity for emissions trading. The potential annual savings realized from a permit approach were estimated at $6.7 million.

In March of 1981 the department approved regulations allowing dischargers on the Lower Fox River to transfer permits by approved contracts. By 1982 the first trade had already taken place. To date this initial movement toward applying the concept to water pollution control has not been taken up by other states.

AN APPRAISAL

Accomplishments

There is little doubt that this program has improved upon the command-and-control policy that preceded it. The EPA has estimated that some 2,500 offset transactions have taken place since the inception of the program.[16] These transactions have facilitated the modernization and expansion of existing plants as well as the construction of new ones in areas of the country not meeting ambient air quality standards.

By the end of 1983 the EPA had approved thirty-five bubbles as

SIP revisions and proposed to approve eighty-seven more. In addition, fourteen bubbles had been approved under state generic rules.[19] Each of these trades represents an affirmation of the basic premise of emissions trading—allowing sources to trade emission reduction credits reduces the cost of complying with the law. Compared with the costs associated with the command-and-control approach, the total estimated savings resulting from all approved or proposed bubbles was over $700 million. Over $10 million is being saved every year in reduced operating costs.

In theory one of the substantial anticipated subsidiary benefits of this lower compliance cost is an increase in the ease with which sources can be brought into compliance. By lowering compliance cost, emissions trading makes remission reductions easier to secure without placing sources in economic jeopardy. Control authorities are less likely to back down from their responsibility to seek attainment when the impact on jobs is smaller. Not only would sources find that litigation is less attractive, since the savings from delay or an overturned standard would be smaller than when compliance costs are high, but courts would be less likely to look favorably on a claim for a reduced burden when the costs are not unreasonable. The expectation of enhanced compliance is certainly reasonable.

Unfortunately, the data are not sufficiently reliable to permit a definitive judgment on whether this expectation has been fulfilled. Reports by the General Accounting Office indicate that the available compliance data are generally unreliable.[20] Many sources reported in compliance are, in fact, not. Add to this unreliability the fact that the vigor with which compliance actions have been enforced has not been constant over the program's history, and the uselessness of the data for supporting any systematic test of changes in the speed of compliance is apparent.

Fortunately, some limited evidence is available from those bubbles approved through the SIP revision process. The first piece of evidence concerns two trades that have been responsible for a demonstration of attainment in areas where no such demonstration had been previously possible.[21] In both cases allowing cheaper particulate controls to be substituted for the mandated emission reductions resulted in both lower costs and larger total emission reductions. Since the larger emission reductions were located in areas violating the standards, a demonstration of attainment became feasible once those reductions were taken into account.

In addition to being the vehicle by which some nonattainment areas have been able to demonstrate attainment, the bubble policy has also served in many cases as the means by which individual sources demonstrate compliance with their control responsibilities.[22] In most cases, by switching to cheaper means of control, sources were able to achieve the required reductions at lower cost, allowing them to come into compliance.[23]

Although lower compliance cost does not automatically mean more rapid compliance, counterexamples seem to be infrequent and unique. For example, the Uniroyal Plastic Products bubble[24] approval contains a provision extending Uniroyal's deadline for compliance, but the extension was specifically granted for the purpose of allowing Uniroyal to substitute an innovative (and presumably superior) process involving waterborne coatings and inks for more additional control processes involving carbon adsorption or incineration.

One of the hopes held out for emissions trading was that by making excess emission reductions valuable, it would stimulate the introduction of new, innovative means of controlling pollution. As Table 4 reveals, the majority of emission reduction credits have been created on the basis of such noninnovative techniques as fuel substitution and changes in the degree of control of already controlled discharge points. There were, however, four innovative bubbles, all involving a conversion of a solvent-based process (high in VOCs) to a solvent-free process.[25] The policy was the impetus for this switch.

The Price of Survival

Although on balance it substantially improved upon the policy that preceded it, the emissions trading program has fallen short of fulfilling the expectations of the theoretical and empirical economics literature. Paradoxically the very attributes that enabled it to gain a per-

Table 4. Sources of Emission Reduction Credits for Approved SIP Revision Bubbles through 1983

Fuel substitution	10
Shutdowns	2
Leased credits	2
Controlling fugitive sources	3
Innovations	4
Changing the degree of control mix	14
	35

Source: Author classification based on the information in the *Federal Register* proposals and approvals.

manent place in United States enivironmental policy are responsible for its failure to be fully cost effective.

The enduring role that the EPA's emissions trading program is currently playing is directly attributable to the fact that it was preceded by a very cost-ineffective regulatory policy. Not only did this create a demand for approaches that offered to reduce cost, it also provided a ready-made baseline for the trades, making the transition to emissions trading rather smooth. Had the command-and-control policy been more cost effective, it is doubtful that the emissions trading policy could have gained the foothold it has.

Although the ability to overlay this program on an existing, but cost-ineffective policy was a key to its political success, it has also diminished the effectiveness of the program in several specific ways:

- In response to command-and-control regulation, a great deal of capital equipment had already been installed prior to the inception of the emissions trading program. Since much of this installed durable capital was cost ineffective and unable to benefit from the emissions trading program, this has reduced the cost savings achievable by the program below that possible if the program had started with a clean slate.

- A particularly unfortunate side effect of overlaying emissions trading on a preexisting command-and-control allocation arises when some sources comply rather rapidly and others prove more recalcitrant. Because the emissions trading option appeared late in the game, sources that had chosen to comply immediately with the command-and-control regulations were precluded from using the emissions trading program to their greatest advantage, while those who were able to fend off early, expensive standards could, with the advent of emissions trading, reach compliance at a substantially lower cost. In this way the introduction of an emissions trading program rewarded slow compliance, which strikes many potential supporters as patently unfair.

- One of the most appealing aspects of this approach is that costs can be reduced with no sacrifice in air quality. Unfortunately, in its somewhat overzealous attempt to encourage the use of this concept, the EPA has allowed some trades that permit some degree of air quality deterioration.[26]

- The notion that firms might have a property right in surplus emission reductions was not a part of the command-and-control system and has been hard for some control authorities to swallow. In some jurisdictions, confiscation of certified credits is a distinct possibility, destroying much of the incentive to create additional emission reductions.

- Because trades involving spatially separated facilities played no role in the command-and-control approach, the current system has been slow in facilitating these trades. The barriers include a philosophical opposition to one of the basic principles of cost effectiveness — trades improving air quality at receptors with pollution levels exceeding the standards should be encouraged, even if some deterioration of air quality in portions of the airshed cleaner than required by the standards results — and a system of financing the construction and use of dispersion models that creates an inefficient bias against their use.

- The failure to consider adequately the timing of emissions, a serious shortcoming of the previous regulatory approach, has persisted under the reform. Meeting the short-term ambient standards cost effectively means controlling the timing as well as the quantity of emissions. The high costs associated with using a continuous control strategy to pursue a short-term standard have tended to discourage the establishment of new short-term standards, have opened the door to variances, and have delayed attainment. The Clean Air Act prohibition against periodic contol eliminates any special incentives for sources to adopt flexible control technologies, those which can reduce emissions further as needed at reasonable cost. These malaligned incentives create a bias in the types of control adopted toward those with high fixed and low variable costs, a condition that makes post-installation additional control very difficult.

These flaws must be kept in perspective. In no way should they overshadow the very positive accomplishments of this program. Although the emissions trading program loses its utopian luster upon closer inspection, it has nonetheless made a lasting contribution to environmental policy. It is comforting to close by noting that occasionally in regulatory reform there is some overlap between the realm of the possible and the realm of the desirable.

NOTES

[1] The marginal-cost curve shows the functional relationship between the level of output and the cost of producing the last unit of that output.

[2] One possible outside influence would be if the resort should sue the steel industry for damages. If successful, this suit would force the steel industry to consider the damage it was causing the resort because it would have to pay it.

[3] Hahn and Noll attribute their lower estimates to three sources: (1) the degree of control in their area of study was very stringent, so all sources were close to controlling as much as was technically possible, (2) the conscious attempt by the California Control Authority to levy cost-effective emission standards, coupled with their unusual ability to do so, and (3) a bias in their cost data that would tend to underestimate the potential cost savings. See Robert W. Hahn and Roger G. Noll, "Designing a Market for Tradeable Emission Permits," in Wesley A. Magat (ed.), *Reform of Environmental Regulation* (Cambridge, Mass.: Ballinger Publishing Co., 1982), pp. 125–126, 131.

⁴Some of this early history is described in the court decision in *ASARCO Inc. v. Environmental Protection Agency,* 578 F.2d 319 (1978) at 323, and Michael H. Levine, "Getting There: Implementing the Bubble Policy," in Eugene Bardach and Robert A. Kagan (ed.), *Social Regulation: Strategies for Reform* (San Francisco, Calif.: ICS Press, 1982).

⁵See Robert W. Crandall and Paul R. Portney, "The Environmental Protection Agency in the Reagan Administration," in Paul R. Portney (ed.), *Natural Resources and the Environment: The Reagan Approach* (Washington, D.C.: Urban Institute Press, 1984), p. 48.

⁶Office of Standards and Regulations, *Annual Report* (Washington, D.C.: U.S. Environmental Protection Agency, 1983), p. 2.

⁷Telephone conversation with Michael Levine, Director of the Regulatory Reforms Staff, EPA, April 3, 1984.

⁸The cement industry provides a concrete example (no pun intended). The NSPS for Portland cement plant kilns was set at 0.15 kg/mg of dry feed. Initial compliance test results for 29 kilns subject to the standard averaged 0.073 kg/mg (less than half the allowable emissions). These lower emission levels resulted not from any additional control effort, but rather from the adoption of the technologies that formed the basis for the standards yielding a lower emission level because of their individual circumstances.

⁹For those states using actual emissions as the basis for their demonstration of attainment by the deadlines, an actual emissions baseline was required. Se 47 FR 15077 (April 7, 1982).

¹⁰Two of the thirty-four SIP revision bubbles approved prior to the end of 1984 either have resulted, or are expected to result, in increased emissions. See the Coors bubble, 46 FR 17549 (March 19, 1981), and the Owens-Corning bubble, 46 FR 53408 (October 29, 1981).

¹¹Empirical research on the emissions trading concept has shown that the potential cost savings from implementing the program are quite sensitive to the geographic trading boundaries. If trading were restricted to proximate facilities, the cost savings would be substantially lower than if unrestricted trading is permitted within the airshed. See Scott E. Atkinson and T. H. Tietenberg, "The Empirical Properties of Two Classes of Designs for Transferable Discharge Permit Markets," *Journal of Environmental Economics and Management,* 9, 2 (June 1982), 119.

¹²Generally no modeling is required for trades of VOC or No_x, since for these emissions the resulting concentrations are presumed to be insensitive to the location of the sources within the airshed. For the other pollutants no modeling is required when there is no net increase in baseline emissions, the relevant emission sources are in the same vicinity, and no increase in emissions occurs at the source with the lower effective plume height. Only limited modeling involving the specific sources in the trade is needed for trades not satisfying the level-one criteria as long as there is no increase in baseline emissions and if emissions after the trade would not cause a "significant" air quality impact at the receptor of maximum predicted impact. Separate significance thresholds are established for each pollutant. Trades failing these two sets of criteria must submit full dispersion modeling results as a condition for approval. See 47 FR 15076 (April 7, 1982) at 15082.

[13] The two bubbles involving multiplant trades under common ownership involved Narragansett Electric, 46 FR 5980 (January 21, 1981), and U.S. Steel, 48 FR 6980 (February 17, 1983). The remaining bubbles involved trades between General Electric and International Harvester, 47 FR 1291 (January 12, 1982), and Borden Chemical and B. F. Goodrich, 47 FR 20125 (May 11, 1982).

[14] For a series of detailed recommendations on how these problems could realistically be overcome in the context of the current program, see Thomas H. Tietenberg, *Emissions Trading: An Exercise in Reforming Pollution Policy* (Washington, D.C.: Resources for the Future, Inc., 1984), Chap. 9.

[15] *Natural Resources Defense Council, Inc. vs. Gorsuch*, 685 F.2d 718 (1982).

[16] *Chevron, U.S.A. v. Natural Resources Defense Council, Inc.*, 52 LW 4845 (1984).

[17] William B. O'Neil, *Pollution Permits and Markets for Water Quality*, unpublished Ph.D. dissertation, University of Wisconsin–Madison, 1980.

[18] Office of Standards and Regulations, *Annual Report* (Washington, D.C.: U.S. Environmental Protection Agency, 1983), p. 4.

[19] *Ibid*, p. 2.

[20] U.S. General Accounting Office, *Improvements Needed in Controlling Air Pollution Sources*, Report CED-78-165, 1979, p. i.

[21] See the approved bubbles for Armco, 46 FR 19468 (March 31, 1981), and Shenango, 46 FR 62849 (December 29, 1981).

[22] For examples of sources brought into compliance by the bubble policy, see the approved bubbles for Union Carbide, 47 FR 21533 (May 19, 1982); Progressive Foundry, 47 FR 15583 (April 12, 1982); and 3M, 46 FR 46130 (September 17, 1981).

[23] In one case compliance was achieved at the expense of an increase in actual emissions. This bubble was approved because it lowered allowable emissions in an air quality region where the attainment demonstration was based on allowable emissions. See Coors (Colorado), 46 FR 17549 (March 19, 1981).

[24] Uniroyal Plastic Products (Ohio), 48 FR 30628 (July 5, 1983).

[25] The innovative bubbles include McDonnell Douglas, 46 FR 20172 (April 3, 1981); 3M, 46 FR 41778 (August 18, 1981); Fasson-Avery International, 46 FR 61653 (December 18, 1981); and U.S. Steel, 48 FR 54347 (December 2, 1983).

[26] See the references in note 10.

Index

Access charges
  to cable channels, regulation of, 101
  establishing, for telephone industry, 229–230
Accident rate, lost workday, 260
Accounts, automatic transfer by computer, 194
Adams, Brock, 19
Agencies, regulatory, major, jurisdictions and budgets of, 4–6(t)
Air pollution
  control policy, stationary source, 273–278
  studies of, 284, 286–287(t)
Air quality standards, 274
Aircraft, size of, comprising fleets of trunk and local carriers, 50
Airline Deregulation Act (ADA), 45
  effects of, 47–51
Airline industry
  changing, 40–77
  regulation of, 6–7, 9
Airport(s)
  access, 68–89
  scheduling committee mechanism, 69
  underutilized, use of by new carriers, 57
Alexis, M., 10, 21
Allocation
  of cost, accounting, 228
  cost-effective, 281
  market, with pollution, 272(f)
American Airlines, "Supersaver" fares of, 44–45
American Conservative Union, 19

American National Standards Institute, 248
American Trucking Association, opposition of, to deregulation, 18
Antileapfrogging rule for cable system, 86
Antitrust suit against AT&T, 226–229
Antitrust violations, Supreme Court decision of, 105–106
ASARCO Inc. v. EPA, 285
AT&T, 95
  dissolution of, 210–233
Average cost standard, 228

Bailey, E. E., 9–10
Bank(s)
  failures, 176(t), 184–186
    in Depression, 175
  number and size of, 199
  size distribution of, 171(t)
Bank Holding Company Act and Amendments of 1970, 179, 183, 189
Banking
  deregulation, consequences of, 194–199
  emissions, 290–291
  regulation of, 2–3
    under Reagan, 10
Banking Acts, 174, 175, 177
Bankruptcy(ies)
  in airline industry, 48
  deregulation and increase in, 34
  of Penn Central, 18
Baxter, William, 227

305

Index

Besen, Stanley, 101
Bingham, Eula, 251
Branch banking, 174, 185, 186–188, 197
Braniff Airline, bankruptcy of, 48
Broadcasting, regulation of, by FCC, 7–8
Brokerage services in commercial bank affiliates, 197
Bubble policy, 285, 291–293, 298–299(t)
Burch, Dean, 83
Business telephone calls, long-distance, 230–231
Byssinosis, 262

Cable, coaxial, development of, 218
Cable Communications Policy Act of 1984, 99–103
Cable Network News, 94
Cable system, physical design of, 79(t)
Cable television regulation, 78–104
Canada, banking in, 186
Carrier(s), air
　load factors of, 61–62
　new, 48, 58(t)
　　strategies of, 56–57
　property, entry and number of, 31(t)
　routes of, in past, 52
　single, 52–54
　size of aircraft comprising fleets of, 50
Carter administration
　cable deregulation under, 84–85
　deregulation of depository institutions under, 196
　oil deregulation under, 114
　oil prices under, 10
　OSHA under, 235
　　inspection, 253, 255, 256
　　penalties, 256
　regulatory initiatives under, 250–251
　trucking deregulation under, 19
Carterfone, 214–215
Carter-Kennedy bill, 20

Channels
　access to, leased, in cable system, 97–98, 101–103
　programming, 87
　educational, on cable system, 101
　pay-TV, 80
　VHF and UHF, 81
Charter service of airlines, 44
Chemical labeling regulation, OSHA, 251
Christian, Betty Jo, 18
City of Boulder Supreme Court decision, 97
Civil Aeronautics Board, 9–10, 41–44
Clapp, Charles, L., 18
Clean Air Act, 240, 273–275, 290
Clean Air Amendments of 1977, 277
Command-and-control approach to regulation, 281, 282
Commercial banks
　compared to thrifts, 192
　insured, concentration ratios for, 189(t)
　and investment banking, separation of, 177, 183–184, 190
　profitability of, 193(f)
Compensating differentials, 240–242
　wage theory, 237–239
Compensation, average, and real freight rates, indexes of, 32(t)
Competition
　in airline industry, 64–66
　　fare moderation due to, 51
　in banking
　　as cause of failure, 184
　　nonprice, 185
　　protection of local institutions from, 186–189
　　via entry into field, 186–188
　in cable systems, encouraging, 99–100
　among railroads
　　early, 14
　　with motor carriers, 16
　in telecommunications, increasing, 11–12, 212
　　equipment, 213–218

Index

long-distance, 218–226
protection from, 211
Computer II FCC rules, 217
Computers
  automatic transfer accounts by, 194
  reservation systems with, airline, 66
  and telecommunications, boundaries between, 216
Congress, "affordable" housing as goal of, 184
Connally Hot Oil Act of 1935, 111–112
Consumer Federation of America, 19
Consumer Product Safety Commission, 13
Consumption, natural gas, 144–145(t)
Continental Airline, bankruptcy of, 48
Continental Illinois National Bank, failure of, 199
Contracts
  carriage in natural gas pipelines, 163
  government, for carriage of mail, 41
  low-bid, for air service to small communities, 67
  in natural gas markets, 155–164
Controls, price, of crude oil, 109–111
  welfare costs of, 125(f)
Copyright Act of 1976, 88
  General Revision of, 90
Copyright liability of cable system, 88–90
Copyright Royalty Tribunal, 90
Corber, Robert, 18
Cost(s)
  accounting allocation of, 228
  labor
    in airline industry, reducing, 65
    in trucking industry, 32
    under regulation, 55–56
  marginal, of oil, and price regulation, 121(t)

welfare, of crude oil price controls
  domestic, 125(f)
  imports, 123(f)
  measuring, 119–126
Cost-effective allocation, 281
Cost-sharing system of AT&T and local operating companies, 224
Cotton dust standard, OSHA, 262
Crude Oil Windfall Profit Tax Act, 114–115, 118

Depletion allowance for oil producers, 112
Deposit(s)
  insurance, 177, 184–185, 201
  interest rate ceilings on, 192
  large, deregulation of, 194
Deregulation
  of banking and its consequences, 194–199
  of cable TV
    future of, 193
    since 1980, 92–99
  of natural gas and contracts problem, 158–160
  of oil industry, 114–115
    energy policy after, 127–132
  rail and trucking, 14–39
Direct broadcast satellite (DBS), 95
Discharge point reduction for pollution, 283
Discount fares, airline, 43–44, 62–64
Dispersion models, construction of, 294–295
Distant signals
  FCC regulation of cable system using, 88–90
  importation of, by cable system, 82–83
Distribution, oil, 107
Domenici, Pete, 269
Domestic Passenger Fare Investigation (DPFI), 44
  fare formula, airline fares as percentage of, 61(t)
Douglas Amendment, 179, 182
Drinking water, 280

Economic efficiency
　in natural gas market, 147–151
　oil price controls and, 115–118
Economic regulations, 2
　of banks, 169
Economies of scale
　in banking, 187–188
　in rail industry, 15
　in telecommunications, 228, 232
Efficiency, economic (*see* Economic efficiency)
Efficiency loss in natural gas market, 149(f)
Embargo, oil, 129
Emergency Petroleum Allocation Act, 112
Emission reduction credit, 283, 299(t)
Emission standards, national, 277, 293–295
Emissions banking, 290–291
Emissions trading program, 269, 281–283, 298–299
Employee coverage by OSHA inspection, drop in, 254–255
Employee productivity, airline, 60(t)
Energy, total, percentage produced by type, 138(t)
Energy Information Administration, 160–161
Energy policies
　international coordination of, 130–131
　after oil price deregulation, 127–132
Energy Policy and Conservation Act, 114
Enforcement of OSHA standards, 252–259
Entitlements
　and crude oil prices, 118(f)
　old oil, 113
　subsidy
　　deadweight loss from, 126(t)
　　wealth transfers abroad due to, 127(t)
　welfare costs of, 122(t)
Entry into banking, 177, 182–183, 186–188

Entry of banks into new fields, prevention of, 189–190
Environment, property rights, and market, 270–271
Environmental Protection Agency (EPA), 12, 269–303
Environmental regulations, 2
Essential Air Service Program, 45, 67
Exceptions and Appeals Relief system, 114
Exclusivity rights of local television stations, 86
Execunet service of MCI, 224–225

Fares, air
　ceilings, 47
　discount, importance of, 43–44, 62–64
　formula, DPFI, airline fares as percentage of, 61(t)
　moderation in, due to competition, 51
　relationship of among markets, 61–62
　"Supersaver," of American Airlines, 44–45
Fatalities in scheduled passenger service, 71(t)
Federal Aviation Administration (FAA), 68
Federal Communications Commission (FCC), 11–12
　regulation of broadcasting by, 7–8
　rulings of, on AT&T, 212–233
Federal Credit Union Act of 1934, 178
Federal Deposit Insurance Corporation (FDIC), 177
Federal Energy Regulatory Commission (FERC), 151
Federal Home Loan Bank, 3
Federal Home Loan Bank Act of 1932, 178
Federal Home Loan Bank Board (FHLBB), 178, 195
Federal legislation affecting regulation of banks, 172–173
Federal Power Commission (FPC), 140

Federal regulation of savings and loans associations, 178
Federal Reserve Act, 174
Federal Reserve System, 174, 177, 196
Federal Savings and Loan Insurance Corporation, 178
Federal water pollution control policy, 278–280
Ferris, Charles, 84
Fines, OSHA, 259
First Amendment protection of cable operators, 98
Food and Drug Administration, 13
Forbearance, policy of, 231
Force majeure clause, 162
Ford administration
 cable regulation under, 84
 oil deregulation under, 114
 OSHA inspection under, 253
 trucking deregulation under, 18
 Task Force on OSHA, 248
Franchising authority for cable system, 97
 denial of renewal by, 102
Franchising standards for cable system, 85
Freight rates
 real, indexes of, and average compensation, 32(t)
 trucking, 31
Freight transportation, surface, 10

Garn–St Germain Depository Institution Act of 1982, 196–197
Gas (*see* Natural gas)
Gaskins, D., 10, 21
General Accounting Office, 298
Glass-Steagall Act, 177, 182, 183, 189, 190
Government
 contracts for carriage of mail, 41
 information on oil market available to, 109
 intervention in oil industry, 115–127
Grain handling standards, OSHA, 252

Great Depression, 175
Groundwater, protection of, 280

Hazards, health
 efficiency of market in handling, 263
 and safety, 239–240
 and worker decisions, 244
Health hazards (*see* Hazards)
Health regulations, 2
Health violations of OSHA standards, 255
Holding companies, bank, 178–179
Home mortgage loans, limitation of thrifts to, 180–181
House Communications Subcommittee Staff Report, 84
Housing
 "affordable," as goal of Congress, 184
 market, effect of interest rate ceilings on, 192–193
 and thrift institutions, 191–193
Hub-and-spoke route networks, growth of, 51–55
Hush-A-Phone, 213–214
Hydrocarbons, 273

Imports, oil
 restriction, 112
 welfare costs of price controls of, 123(f)
Income redistribution in natural gas market, 146–147
Inflation, effect of crude oil prices on, 110
Injury trends, 260–263
Inspections, OSHA, 253–256
Insurance
 deposit, 177
  problems of, 201
 and effect of disruption on oil market, 109
Interest Rate Control Act of 1966, 179–180
Interest rates
 in banking in 1970s, 181–182

Interest rates *(cont.)*
  ceilings, 184, 188–189
  on deposits, 192
  on loans, 198–199
    mortgage, 191–192
    problems caused by, to thrift institutions, 179–181
Internal Revenue Service, 257–258
International Banking Act of 1978, 180
International coordination of energy policies, 130–131
International Energy Agency (IEA), 130
Interstate Commerce Act, 15–16
Interstate Commerce Commission (ICC), 10, 16, 41, 212
  and trucking deregulation, 19–36
Interstate natural gas markets, shortage, 142–146
Interstate wellhead market, 146(f)
Intrastate carriers, expansion of, 48
Investment and commercial banking, separation of, 177, 183–184, 190

Jet service
  interstate, scheduled, new entrant airlines to, 58(t)
  for small communities, 54–55
Job evaluation system, 240
Johnson, Leland, 101
Johnson, Nicholas, 84
Johnson administration, trucking regulation under, 18
Jurisdictions and budgets of major regulatory agencies, 4–6(t)
Justice, Department of, actions of, against AT&T, 226–229

Kahn, A. E., 9
Kennedy, Edward, hearings held by, on trucking rates, 19
Kennedy, John, trucking deregulation under, 18
Kennedy-Carter bill, 20

Labor, Department of, 234, 357
Labor agreements, renegotiation of, in airline industry, 59–60
Labor costs
  in airline industry, reducing, 65
  in trucking industry, 32
  under regulation, 55–56
Labor market estimates of value of life, 264
Labor Statistics, Bureau of, 257
Leased channel access, mandatory, on cable system, 87, 97–98, 101–103
Lending, regulation of, 180
Liability, copyright, of cable system, 88–90
Licenses, operating, for trucking, value of, 29–30
Load factors of air carriers, 61–62
Loans
  home
    and interest rate, 191–192
    limitation of thrifts to, 180–181
    interest rates on, 198–199
  tying of, by bank, to other services, 189
Localism, policy of, of FCC, 81, 86
Long-distance telephone competition, 212, 218–216, 230

MacAvoy, Paul, 84, 248
Mail, carriage of, government contracts for, 41
Mandatory leased access on cable system, 101–103
Mandatory Oil Import Program (MOIP), 112
Market
  allocation with pollution, 272(f)
  equilibrium with oil price controls, 116(f)
  failure and economic efficiency in oil production, 106–109
  inadequacies in, to promote worker safety, 243–245
  labor, estimates of value of life, 264

Index

levels of safety, determination of, 238(f)
promotion of safety by, 236–243
property rights, and environment, 270–271
role of, in determining safety, 263
Massachusetts, NOW accounts in, 194
McFadden Act, 174, 182
Microwave Communications, Inc. (MCI), 221–226
Microwave relay systems, 83
Microwave transmission technology, development of, 218–220
Mobile radiotelephone systems, 214
Mobility, worker, 245
Money market mutual funds (MMMF), 185–186, 194
Monopoly
  domestic, oil industry as, 106–107
  local telephone, 95–96, 230
  natural
    of railroads, 15
    telephone industry as, 210
  power in natural gas industry, 150
Monopsony
  in natural gas industry, 150
  in oil market, 109
Mortgage loans
  home, limitation of thrifts to, 180–181
  and interest rate, 191–192
  variable rate, 195
Motor Carrier Acts, 16, 17, 26, 35(t)
Motor carriers (see Trucking)
Motorola, 220
Movies, premium, on cable TV, 93
Multi-channel Multipoint Distribution Service (MMDS), 93
Municipal waste-treatment plants, 279
Mutual funds (see Money market mutual funds)
Mutual savings banks, NOW accounts by, 194

National Association of Manufacturers, 21
National Bank Act of 1864, 172
National banks, limitations on branching by, 174
National Credit Union Administration, 178
National Currency Act of 1863, 172
National emission standards, 277
National Fire Protection Association, 248
National Highway Traffic Safety Administration, 13
National Housing Act of 1934, 178
National Petroleum Council, 129
National Recovery Act, 16
National Safety Council, 260
National security issue and oil market, 109
Natural gas
  price limits on, 8, 152–154(t)
  regulator transition in, 137–168
Natural Gas Act of 1938, 140
Natural Gas Policy Act of 1978, 137–139
Natural Gas Power Authority (NGPA), 151–155
Natural monopoly (see Monopoly, natural)
Natural Resources Defense Council, 273, 296
Netting policy, 296
Nixon administration, OSHA inspections under, 253
Nonattainment regions, air pollution, 275
Nonpoint source water pollution, 280
Nonstop air service, change in number of carriers providing, 50
NOW accounts, 194

Occupational Safety and Health Act of 1970, 240
Occupational Safety and Health Administration (OSHA), 12, 234–268
Office of Comptroller of Currency, 172

Office of Telecommunications Policy, 83
Oil cost, marginal, and price regulation, 121(t)
Oil import restriction, 112, 123(f)
Oil industry, public intervention in, background, 111–115
Oil market, world, United States as price taker in, 119–121
Oil prices
  controls and economic efficiency, 8, 109–110, 115–118(f)
  measuring welfare costs of, 119–126
  under Carter administration, 10
  world
    effect of, on airline industry, 47
    and U.S. policies, 124(f)
Oklahoma, oil restriction by, 106
O'Neal, Daniel, 18
Operating companies, local
  and AT&T, cost-sharing system of, 224
  loss of control of, by AT&T, 227
  monopoly of, 230
Organization for Economic Cooperation and Development (OECD), 125
Organization of Petroleum Exporting Countries (OPEC), 108, 139
Origination of cable system, 86
Ownership of cable system, 87
Ozone, 273

Passengers, air
  domestic service, shares of, 49(t)
  preferences in service, 54
  scheduled, fatalities in, 71(t)
  time sensitivity of, 62
Penalties, OSHA, 256–257
Penn Central, bankruptcy of, 18
People Express, 57
  performance of markets entered by, 59(t)
Permits for waste discharge, 278
Petroleum (*see also* Oil)

industry, United States companies in, 107(t)
regulation and public policy, 105–136
Phillips Petroleum Company v. Wisconsin et al., 140–141
Piggyback traffic, regulation of, 23–24
Pipeline-producer contractual agreements, 155–158
Pipelines, natural gas, contract carriage in, 163
Point source water pollution, 278–279
Poles, telephone, use of, by cable system, 95–96
Policy intervention in oil production, 106–111
Pollutants, types of, 273–274
Pollution
  control policy, reform of, 269–303
  market allocation with, 272(f)
Preferred Communications Incorporated (PCI), 98
Price
  gas
    ceilings, 8, 152–154(t)
    weighted average, intrastate and jurisdictional, 143(t)
  oil, controls, 8
    crude, 109–110, 111, 118(f), 119–126
    and economic efficiency, 115–118
    effect of, on airline industry, 47
    regulation and marginal cost, 121(t)
    under Carter administration, 10
    and United States policies, 124(f)
  taker, United States as, in world oil market, 119
  wellhead
    average, gas supply, and consumption, 144–145(t)
    regulation, Supreme Court decision on, 141
Pricing
  incremental, of natural gas, 151

Index

in long-distance competition, 223
policies in deregulated airline industry, 61–64
of telephone service, 231
Private branch exchanges (PBX), 215
Produce, exemptions of, from regulation, 23
Producer-pipeline contractual agreements, 155–158
Production, oil, 107
Profit margins, operating, of airlines, 46(t)
Profit-sharing in airline industry, 59
Profits, railroad industry, 26
Programming, leased channel, of cable sytem, 87
Property carriers, entry and number of, 31(t)
Property rights, markets, and environment, 270–271
PSA, expansion of, 56–57
Public intervention in oil industry, background, 111–115
Public policy and petroleum regulation, 105–136
Public utility commission, first modern, 3

Quality, air, standards, 274
Quit rates, worker, and on-the-job experience, 242–243

Radio regulations, history of, 81
Radiotelephone, mobile, systems, 214
Rail carloadings of various types of traffic, index of, 23(t)
Railroad industry, 14–39
  deregulation, 14–39
  regulation, 6–7
Railroad Revitalization and Regulatory Reform Act, 18
Ratemaking, natural gas, 142
Rates
  freight
    real, indexes of, and average compensation, 32(t)

rail, 21, 31–32
trucking
  changes in, 27–28
  control of, 17
  freight, 31
  hearings on, held by Edward Kennedy, 19
Reagan administration
  AT&T antitrust suit under, 227
  banking regulation under, 10
  new natural gas market arrangements under, 163–164
  OSHA under, 235, 247
    inspection, 253, 255, 256
    penalties under, 256
  regulatory initiatives under, 250–252
  regulatory reform under, 1
Recessions, effect of, on trucking industry, 34–35
Records check inspections, 257
Redistribution, income, in natural gas market, 146–147
Refining, oil, 107
Reform movement, regulatory, 1–13
  of pollution, nature of, 280–285
  railroad, 21–27
  trucking, 26–37
Regulation Q, 177
  effect of, on interest rates, 181
Regulatory agencies, major, jurisdictions and budgets of, 4–6(t)
Regulatory reform movement, 1–13
Reservation systems, computer, airline, 66
Resources, as common property, 270–271
Restriction, oil import, 112
Revenue, average, of motor carriers, 33
Risk (see also Hazards)
  health and safety, 249
  information, 239–240
  perception of, by workers, 244
  in workplace, 234–268
Roosevelt, Franklin, 175
Route authority for airlines, 42–43
  changes in, 45
  regulation, end of, 47–48

Route networks of airlines, hub-and-spoke, growth of, 51–55
Runs on banks, effect of deposit insurance against, 184–185

Safe Drinking Water Act of 1974, 280
Safety
  hazards (*see* Hazards)
  market levels of, determination of, 238(f)
  promotion of, by market system, 236–243
  record, air industry, 70
  regulations, 2
  role of market in determining, 263
  worker
    economic approach to, 237
    OSHA enforcement of, impact of, 259–263
Satellite Master Antenna Television (SMATV), 95
Satellite services and growth of cable TV, 94
Saving and loan associations
  federal regulation of, 178
  profitability of, 193(f)
Scheduling committee mechanism, airport, 69
Securities, corporate, underwriting of, 183–184, 190
Service
  customers, in banking, effect of competition on, 187
  quality of, after Motor Carrier Act of 1980, 35(t)
Shenefield, John, 19
Sherman Act, 226
  prohibitions of, of monopoly, 188
Shippers, trucking, opinion of, of deregulation, 27
Shortage, natural gas, in interstate markets, 142–146
Sierra Club, 276
Signals for cable system, 85–86
Single-carrier service, 52–54
Small Refiner Bias Program, 113–114
Smith, Adam, 237

Southwest Airline
  expansion of, 56–57
  performance of markets entered by, 59(t)
Specialized Common Carrier policy, 222–223, 224
Spoke-and-hub route networks, growth of, 51–55
Spot markets for natural gas, 165
Stagflation, 110
Staggers Rail Act, 22
Standard Oil, early development of, 105–106
Standards
  emission, baseline for, 293–295
  OSHA
    cotton dust, 262
    nature of, 248–249
    performance, 264
    reform of, 249–252
    setting, 246–248
  pretreatment of waste, 279
State chartering of banking, 182
  branching regulations, 174
State implementation of air quality standards, 275–277
State implementation plan (SIP), 275
  and emission trading, 292–293
State pollution control agencies, cooperation of, 283
State regulation of depository institution, 171–172
Stationary source air pollution control policy, 273–278
Stations, TV, political power of, 91
Stock market
  crash of 1929, 175
  regulation of, changes in, 9
Stockpiles, public oil, 128–131
  using, 130–131
Storer Communications, swap of cable system with Times Mirror, 103
Subsidy(ies)
  to early railroad industry, 14
  entitlements
    deadweight loss from, 126(t)
    wealth transfers abroad due to, 127(t)

Index

welfare costs of, 122(t)
service to small communities, 66–68
Supersaver fares, American Airlines, 63
Superstations, 94
Supply, natural gas, price, and consumption, 144–145(t)
Supply-side distortions in oil production, 117
Supreme Court decision
  on antitrust violations, 105–106
  City of Boulder, 97
  on benzene case, 247
  on bubble policy, 296
  on cotton dust case, 247
  on interstate pipelines, 139–140
  on interstate trucking, 16
  on wellhead price regulation, 141
Surface freight transportation, regulation of, changes in, 10
Switched long-distance services, 224–226

Take-or-pay clause in natural gas contracts, 156–157, 161(t)
  by NGPA section, 162(t)
Tariff
  AT&T, 214–215
  oil (import), 128
Taxes
  favorable, for oil producers, 112
  windfall profits, 10
Teamsters, opposition of, to deregulation, 18
Technology and growth and airline industry, 42
Telecommunications, regulatory change in, 210–233
Telephone versus cable, 95–96
Telephone companies, independent, 210–211
Telephone industry, 11–12 (*see also* Telecommunications)
Telephone instruments, 212
  competition, 213–218
Telephone monopoly, local, 95–96
Television
  cable, regulation, 78–104

  development of, 218–219
Telpak tariff of AT&T, 220–221
Texas, oil restriction by, 106
Thrift institutions, 179–181, 191–193
TOFC (*see* Piggyback traffic)
Time sensitivity of air passengers, 62
Times Mirror, swap of cable system with Storer Communications, 103
Trantum, Thomas, 21
Travel agents, reliance on, 65–66
Trucking deregulation, 14–39
Trunk airlines
  routes of, in past, 52
  size of aircraft comprising fleets of, 50
Two-way interactive services, 95

UHF commercial stations, 94(t)
Unions, 242
Uniroyal Plastic Products, bubble policy at, 299
Unit banking, 174, 185
United States
  companies in petroleum industry, 107(t)
  depository institutions in, 170(t)
  policies and world oil prices, 124(f)
  as price taker in world oil market, 119–121
Usury ceilings, 190–191
  on interest rates, 180–191
  state, 196

Vail, Theodore, 211
Vertical integration
  in natural gas industry, 163
  in oil industry, 107–108
VHF channels, 80
Videocassette recorders (VCR), effect of, 92–93
Volatile organic compounds, 273
Vulnerability in oil market, 109

Wage differential, compensating, theory, 237–239
Wage structures, two-tiered, in airline industry, 59

Waste-treatment plants, municipal, 279
Water, drinking, 280
Water pollution, 278–280, 285, 288(t), 296–297
Water Pollution Control Act, 278
Welfare costs
 of entitlements subsidy, 122(t)
 of oil price controls
  crude, measuring, 119–126
  domestic, 125(f)
  imports, 123(f)
Wellhead market structure, 150
 interstate, 146(f)
Wellhead price, 141, 144–145(t)

Western Electric, 226
Western Union, 220
Whitehead, Clay T., 83
Windfall profits taxes, 10
Workday, lost, accident rate, 260
Worker
 compensation of, 240–241
 decisions, irrationalities in, 244–245
 quit rates and on-the-job experience, 242–243
 safety, 234, 237, 259–263
 value of life to, 241–242
Workplace, risk in, 234–268